Critical acclaim for

WE BELIEVED

A LIFETIME OF AUBURN FOOTBALL

VOLUME 1: 1975–1998

"This book is (double fire). Unbelievably well done.
If you are an SEC fan, you need to grab this ASAP."
—*Jake Crain, host of The JBoy Show*
and son of legendary AU linebacker Kurt Crain

"Van and John are the Sullivan-to-Beasley of Auburn football
analysis. Or Slack-to-Wright. Maybe Nix-to-Sanders. The point is,
when you open the book, expect a touchdown."
—*Jeremy Henderson, publisher of the War Eagle Reader*

"Reading *WE BELIEVED* is like settling in to a long, glorious tailgate
outside Jordan-Hare and tuning in your favorite highlights
with a happy group of fellow Auburn obsessives.
All you need now is a drink and some Guthrie's."
—*Will Collier, co-author of The Uncivil War:*
Alabama vs Auburn, 1981-1994

Also by Van Allen Plexico and John Ringer:

Decades of Dominance: Auburn Football in the Modern Era

Season of Our Dreams: The 2010 Auburn Tigers

More Auburn Football, from White Rocket Books:

Lorendo, by Ken Ringer

Edited by Van Allen Plexico:

Assembled! Five Decades of Earth's Mightiest

Assembled! 2: Earth's Mightiest Heroes and Their Foes

"I believe in Auburn, and love it."

WE BELIEVED
A LIFETIME OF AUBURN FOOTBALL

VOLUME 1: 1975–1998

VAN ALLEN PLEXICO
& JOHN RINGER

HOSTS OF THE AU WISHBONE
AUBURN FOOTBALL PODCAST

WHITE ROCKET BOOKS

WE BELIEVED: A LIFETIME OF AUBURN FOOTBALL
VOLUME 1: 1975-1998

Copyright 2021 by Van Allen Plexico and John Ringer

Interior illustrations by Jarrod Alberich

Cover design by Van Allen Plexico for White Rocket Books

Portions of this book originally appeared as audio clips on podcasts produced for the AU Wishbone Podcast: www.AUWishbone.com

A White Rocket Book
www.whiterocketbooks.com

ISBN-13:   9798536996751

This book is set in Times and Calibri.

First printing: August 2021

0 9 8 7 6 5 4 3 2 1

– THE AU WISHBONE FAMILY –

Van and John extend their eternal thanks and appreciation to these fine members of the Auburn Family and the AU Wishbone Family (as of July 2021) whose support helps to make our podcasts and other projects (such as this book) a reality. *War Eagle!*

Carl Von Drunker
Chris and Clinton Stewart
Christopher Burleson
Patrick Hays
Samuel Salvatore
Jeremiah Shuman
Allison Rich
Bart Lindsey
Bradley Blackmon
Chris Usher
Gary Grant (aka
AU_Fan@KSC)
Logan Chilton
Michael Kirshner
Phil Amthor
Richard Stephens
Steve Trawick
Susan Trawick
Trombone tiger
William Cardin (Willy)
Anne Khandjian
Au falling up
Remembering Al Beckum
Ben Bloodworth
Robert J. Politte
Clay Henson
Dan Thompson
Daniel Odom
David Evers
David Hegler
Emmanuel Seyman

Eric Morgan
George Gaston
Jacob & Robin Fleming
John Otsuki
Kathryn England
Kevin Smith
Mickey Bee aka Mike
Bradley
Preston Settle
Reynolds Wolf
Rich Reimer
Rusty Owens
Spanky
Steve Harlan
Timothy
WDERICHIE Butler
We got to get better
  at celebratin'
Wes Atkinson
William Morgan
Wilson Beard
Winston Boddie
Blake Herrin
Boris the Tiger
Cato the Barner
Chris the Hilton
Colby Butler
Danny Flack
Daris Benton
David Simpson
Dyebama

Earl Ricks
Erik Mayhan
Hu Anderson
Josh Teal
Kevin Kennoy
Kevin Mahan
Kristjan Thorvaldsson
Lane Middleton
Melissa Blackstone
Mike Findley
OwlGoRhythm
Papa Todd
Patrick Williams
Randall Walker
Rob Morgan
Ross
Russell Milling
Sarah Hines
Sasquatch
Shane Bailey
Shannon Butson
Snowdog
Steven Huston
Tim Pittman
Tony Perry
'76 Tiger
   (OK, it's Bob Sammons)
Alex Nguyen
Auburn Elvis
Ben Amos
Ben Rigas

Brandon Smith
Charles Mauney
Chris Comeaux
Colonel Dad
Daniel Barnett
Darren Pyle
David Smilie
Donnie Reynolds
James Taylor
Jason Alberich
John Stubbs
John Zavatchen
Joseph A. Miller
Joseph Iliff
Josh Corbett
Justin Bean
Kathy Bright
Kenneth Brent Raines
Mark Squire
Matthew Flowers
Mick Vijakkhana
Paul Bankson
Public Land Owner
Robert Drane
Russel Suther
Ruth & Darrin Sutherland
Stephen Thompson
Trevor Johnson
Brant Rumble
Chris

Plus our one-time & anonymous donors!

To join their illustrious ranks, go to **www.auwishbone.com** and click on the big orange button that says "Become a Patron!"

We thank you all—and *War Patron Eagle!*

6

– CONTENTS –

To my parents, Joyce and Ken Ringer, who took me to games and taught me to cheer for Auburn, win or lose.

—John

This one is for Dr. Joseph Lee Plexico, Sr. (1902-1987), who sent a son and a grandson to Auburn; and for Joseph Lee Plexico, Jr. (1933-2021), who didn't get to see this book, but did get included in it.

—Van

The authors would also like to dedicate this book to the memory of Coach Patrick Fain Dye (1939-2020)

A note on transcriptions:

This book *is not* and is not *intended* to be a transcription of the podcast mini-series of the same name, produced by the AU Wishbone. The conversations in those podcasts merely served as a starting point for this far more in-depth discussion of Auburn Football and the Auburn Family during the years covered.

In addition to the very large amount of new and original material, the conversations in those episodes have been substantially altered to work better in written form. Every effort has been made to preserve the original *intent* of the hosts and guests. Any gross misquotations or distortions of a speaker's meaning and intent are inadvertent and entirely accidental in nature.

A note on sources:

The authors gratefully acknowledge their debt to numerous reporters, analysts, and broadcasters whose historical coverage of Auburn football over many years contributed to this book.

This book contains a great many quotes from a great many sources, across many years. Where bylines were available today, the speaker as well as the source that reported the quote (newspaper; book; video; etc.) are cited along with the quote. Where only the media outlet is cited, there was no byline included in the original material being quoted. (This was often true of some of the forty-year-old articles in the *NY Times* and *Sports Illustrated* online archives.) Where only the name of the speaker is given, the quote came from an open press conference or similar event and was reported by multiple media outlets. Every effort has been made by the authors to fully credit sources when those sources can be known.

The authors also express their gratitude to all who took part in the initial recording sessions for the podcast series, and to those who contributed material afterward for this book.

– INTRODUCTION –

The history of modern Auburn football has always been a key ingredient in almost everything John and I have done with the AU Wishbone, either in print or on our podcast. It's just that, prior to 2018, we'd never actually sat down and tried to comprehensively document it all, in the proper order and in depth.

Then we came up with the idea for the "We Believed" mini-series of podcasts.

Originally, we planned the ten episodes as a sort of "walk down memory lane," allowing us to relive some of our greatest memories (as well as some of the not-so-great moments) as members of the Auburn Family. A bonus would be that we could record interviews for it with luminaries like former AU Athletic Director David Housel and former player Cole Cubelic, now with WJOX and the SEC Network, as well as Jerry Hinnen (of CBS, the *Joe Cribbs Car Wash*, and the *War Eagle Reader*) and many others. Of course, we *had* to secure the services of Reynolds Wolf, star meteorologist of the Weather Channel and one of the greatest Auburn men you will ever know, as our "show voice" and for additional commentary. Their reminisces, we knew, would only add in a very positive way to the mix. We didn't want the audio mini-series to be simply more hours of the two of us yakking about Auburn. We needed other perspectives—and we got them.

What resulted was the podcast mini-series you can hear on various podcast apps and at the AUWishbone.com site. We're proud of it.

But we wanted to do more with it. We wanted to expand upon it; to go beyond the limitations of what we'd said in a few recorded conversations late in the evenings here and there. To add in-depth game descriptions, statistics and analysis. To bring in more voices and more perspectives. To make it bigger and better.

In short, we wanted to expand it all into a *book*.

Into *this* book.

So here we are: presenting to you the reader our third book about Auburn Football. The first one, *Season of Our Dreams*, covered the 2010 season and our real-time reactions to what was happening around that incredible team and its improbable run to the national title. Our second one, *Decades of Dominance*, offered up various chunks of material that together, we felt, constituted an argument for the greatness of Auburn's football program since 1981.

This book goes beyond what either of those did. This book attempts to lay out the entire history of the program—its coaches and players; its games and championships; its highest highs and lowest lows; its moments of transition and moments of transcendence, from the end of Shug Jordan's era in 1975 through the end of the Terry Bowden era in 1998—and share with you *our memories of* and *our reactions to* those events. The prevailing question throughout this narrative is, "What was it like to be an Auburn person when ___ happened?" Along the way, we also try to address how those events *changed* us, and made us into the people we are today.

Once we got to working on the book in earnest, during the COVID lockdown of mid-2020, we quickly realized we had way more material than would fit in just one book. It didn't take long for us to understand we'd have to split the timeline in half, with the Pat Dye and Terry Bowden years covered in one volume, and everything after that in another.

The second volume, which will follow in due course, will pick up with the arrival of Tommy Tuberville at the end of 1998 and then conclude at some undefined point in "the Future of Auburn Football." It will take the same approach, as we explore what it was like to be a member of the Auburn Family for *those* years and *those* events.

You may think you know everything John and I have to say about Auburn. Then again, you might be surprised. And this time, we're not alone, because there are lots of other viewpoints being included and considered.

In the pages ahead, John and I will break down all the big games and defining moments of those years of Auburn history, yes—but first, in Chapter One, you'll hear from various members of the Auburn Family—including members of our *own* families—as we try to discover exactly what it means to be an Auburn person, with all that that entails. Those folks are diverse in their backgrounds but united in that one simple premise laid out in the Auburn Creed: They believe in Auburn, and love it.

This is *We Believed.*

—Van Allen Plexico
Southern Illinois, Summer 2020-Summer 2021

· 1 ·

SIXTY MINUTES
Shug Jordan to Doug Barfield
to Pat Dye, 1975-1981

"Third and fourteen at the 38 late in the game... screen over to McIntyre, broken up incomplete. They smelled that out real good, covered it extremely well. That essentially was the end of the game. Alabama got one more possession and moved down to the 1 yard line.

"And there's the meeting at midfield between Coaches Jordan and Bryant as Coach Jordan ends his coaching career at Auburn University. Final score in the final game, Alabama 28, Auburn nothing."
—Radio broadcast of the 1975 Iron Bowl

With the conclusion of the 1975 Iron Bowl, a long and storied era of Auburn football came to an end. More specifically, a former University of Georgia basketball coach retired. Normally, the retirement of a former UGA hoops coach wouldn't seem to be of much interest to Auburn people. But that coach just happened to be

Ralph "Shug" Jordan, who left his hoops coaching career at UGA behind to become Auburn's head football coach in 1951.

Shug's twenty-five-year reign on the Plains brought with it 176 wins (against 83 losses and 6 ties), an SEC title, a Heisman Trophy for quarterback Pat Sullivan and, most notably, the 1957 AP National Championship. His penultimate season, the 1974 campaign, saw the Tigers finish 10-2, with a final AP Poll ranking of sixth in the country. The 1975 season, however, took a disastrous turn very early on, with the team's first win not coming until an October 11 trip to Kentucky. That team finished with a record of 3-6-2 (prior to Mississippi State's later forfeit of one of those ties) and, along with the aging coach's declining health, brought his storied career to an end.

Mike McClendon is a longtime Auburn football fan and observer, whose knowledge and expertise with regard to the Tigers extends a few years farther back than that of John or Van. They asked him for his thoughts on the middle and later Jordan years. What happened to Auburn in the Sixties? From 1957-1958, Auburn had gone 19-0-1, finishing no. 1 and no. 4 in the AP poll. Then, from 1959-1969, Auburn's record was 66-40-2. While this does include a no. 5-ranked team in 1963, the majority of those teams finished unranked.

Shug did turn things around for a bit in the early Seventies. But— why were the Tigers so mediocre in the Sixties?

Mike McClendon

Bryant changed everything when he came to Alabama. He owned recruiting, and the talent dried up at Auburn.

Shug had a great recruiting class in 1961. He signed Jimmy Sidle, Tucker Fredrickson and a bunch of other great players. Sidle was the starting QB in 1962, and in 1963 he was an All-American. (Mailon Kent, though, was the star of the Alabama game in 1963 where Auburn won 10-8.) In 1963 Sidle finished 2nd in rushing in the country as a quarterback. Sidle was set to be the top QB in football in 1964 and Auburn was a preseason pick to win the national championship by a lot of places. Unfortunately, he tore his rotator-cuff in the season opener. He couldn't throw a pass at all after that. He was eventually moved to running back. The team was never the same without that run/pass option threat that Sidle brought to the game.

The thing in the late Fifties to remember is this: Not only did we lose to Alabama, but from 1959 through 1962 we did not score. Alabama won those four games by a total score of 85-0. We played decent games in 1959 and 1960, losing 10-0 and 3-0, but the talent was already going away. Then, from 1964 through 1968, we managed just two TD's. It was a combination of talent (they had it and we didn't) and better coaching. The 1965 team (5-5-1) and the 1966 team (6-4) would probably have gotten the head coach fired today. Those were bad football teams.

Bryant changed the way football was played in the SEC. Whether you liked him or not, he brought a very different mentality to the game. His teams were extremely physical. If you think they have a recruiting machine today, it is nothing like what Bryant had throughout the Sixties and Seventies at Alabama. It was down and dirty, and I mean *very* dirty. The NCAA was afraid of him, though, and there was no way they were ever going to go after Alabama with Bryant in charge. Bryant owned the state and pretty much college football.

One other note: Bryant is responsible for perhaps the dirtiest play in the history of college football. It's certainly one of, if not *the* worst I've ever seen on a football field. Alabama was playing Georgia Tech. Late in the game with Tech leading, GT punted. The Alabama safety called for a fair catch and caught the ball. After the catch, Darwin Holt, a senior linebacker for Alabama, veered off and hit a Tech player, Chick Granning, who was running in the open field and thought the play was over. He hit him under his facemask with his elbow, fracturing pretty much every bone in his face. The play was already over. The hit was totally uncalled for and completely unnecessary. Bryant never acknowledged the late hit or the infraction and refused to suspend Holt. If there is an example of the way Bryant coached and the way he taught his players to play, this is it. Holt remains somewhat a legend in Alabama athletics, partially because of this. He should have been kicked off the team.

Bryant got lazy in the late Sixties. He wasn't recruiting as well and, to be honest, they weren't a well-coached team. That led to us winning three of four from 1969-1972. I think our improvement in those years was as much due to Bryant as it was to Shug.

All that changed in 1970. Bryant decided to take it all back. They were signing every kid in Alabama and from all over who Bryant thought might play at Alabama, and just as importantly, signing the players that he didn't want playing somewhere else. You have to remember that you didn't have the strict recruiting restrictions you have today.

Then Shug retired and we got Barfield, which is a whole other story. That led to the nine consecutive Iron Bowl losses, and a lot of those were bad—worse than the scores.

To get a real appreciation for Auburn football you have to understand Alabama football. The two are interrelated in more ways than you might realize. To understand Auburn football in the Sixties and Seventies you have to understand Bryant. He changed the way football was played. It took us almost two decades to catch up.

The years that immediately followed Shug's retirement brought little in the way of promise for future success on the Plains.

Doug Barfield, Shug's offensive coordinator in his final seasons, was elevated to head coach in 1976. The results were disappointing. Even with some of the most talented running backs in Auburn history at his disposal—Joe Cribbs, James Brooks and William Andrews, to name the three most prominent—the Tigers only managed a record of 29-25-1 over the ensuing five seasons. Five straight losses to Alabama only made things worse. At the end of the 1980 season, Barfield was let go.

With the end of Doug Barfield's tenure, Auburn football and its fans and supporters found themselves at a crossroads. The glory days of the 1950s through the early 1970s seemed far in the rear-view mirror by December of 1980. Coach Jordan had passed away after a battle with leukemia in July of that year. Archrival Alabama had asserted itself as the dominant program in the country, winning multiple national championships during the Seventies under the sport's most successful coach of the era, Paul "Bear" Bryant, and eventually extending its win streak over the Tigers to nine straight games. Auburn at the end of 1980 seemed perpetually trapped in the bottom half of the SEC, forever subordinate to its cross-state rival

18

and with little obvious hope for the situation to improve. Dark days indeed.

Yet hope springs eternal, and nowhere more so than in the hearts of college football fans. Auburn was patient, combing the coaching ranks for a suitable replacement, and eventually Tigers fans would be rewarded. Little did we guess what lay only months in our future: Pat Dye, Bo Jackson, and a return to glory.

In those depressing days of 1980, however, with Doug Barfield on his way out and Pat Dye still the head coach at Wyoming, an Auburn fan could be forgiven for being tempted to utterly despair— to just give up on the whole thing and walk away.

Of course, we didn't do that. We never do. We love Auburn too much to ever turn our backs on the Loveliest Village. And we love football as the means of proving ourselves, our worthiness, our way of life itself, against our most bitter rivals.

Which begs the question we address first here: Why *do* we care? Why does it all matter? Why do we love not just our team and our university but the sport itself so very much?

Even when things are at their worst for Auburn, why are we unquestionably in it for life? Why, exactly, do *we believe*?

It was with those questions at the forefront of our thoughts that we started out our journey into the hearts and minds of the Auburn Family.

Van Allen Plexico

John, you and I are about the same age. We grew up as Auburn fans pretty much from birth. There was never any chance of us changing. There was never a time when you stopped and said, "Okay, what college football program am I going to be for?" I mean, it was already written into your programming code at the base level, into your brain's operating system, from the beginning, right?

John Ringer

Yeah, there wasn't a lot of variance from that.

Van Allen Plexico

Yeah, it wasn't really optional.

Here's my deal: I grew up in Sylacauga, about forty-five minutes south of Birmingham on 280, the same highway that runs down to Auburn. That meant I was living in Ground Zero, right between the poles. That just makes it all that much more intense. The football team at my high school, Sylacauga, wore red, and the coaches and the teachers had all gone to the University of Alabama, and they would all leave town every Friday afternoon to spend the weekend at Alabama games in Birmingham or Tuscaloosa. Our marching band was called the "Half-Million-Dollar Band" and we played in "Legion Stadium." This should give you a sense of what Sylacauga is like. Auburn fans were in the minority and Alabama was riding high that whole decade—the Seventies—and we had to hear about it constantly. You had to truly love Auburn to be willing to put up with that daily torture. And yet we all did.

What's my first memory of knowing I was an Auburn person? I was already predisposed to go down that orange and blue path, because my dad graduated from there around 1960 and my granddad who raised me was a huge Auburn football fan throughout my entire childhood. That meant it was all around me at home, as a positive countervailing influence to what I was getting at school and from most of my friends. But, beyond even that, there was a singular moment that it crystallized for me. It involved a jacket.

I can vividly remember being in kindergarten and somebody—maybe it was my older brother—gave me a hand-me-down navy-blue nylon jacket. It was slick, almost a raincoat, a plastic nylon navy-blue jacket. And the only thing on it—because this was like the early Seventies and the technology wasn't there yet for the fancy accoutrements we have today—the only thing on it was the word "AUBURN" in simple, orange block letters on the lapel. Today they wouldn't even sell something like that. People would think it was too boring. Nobody would buy it. Today it would have to have the AU logo or tiger eyes, and there'd be orange stripes and all that kind of stuff. But this was just a plain blue jacket that said "Auburn" on the lapel. And yet this was one of my most cherished belongings. I clung to it and loved it. I held on to it. It gave me a sense of identity in that environment even before I realized that was what was happening. For a matter of weeks or months I just wore it and didn't think that much about it beyond that.

Flash-forward to Halloween of that year. That was the moment the whole "Auburn" aspect of it truly clicked in my head. I was standing in line for a haunted house in Sylacauga with my sister and some other people. I remember looking down at my jacket and thinking, "You know, I love this jacket." Followed by, "So does that mean I'm an Auburn fan? I guess it does." And I sort of nodded to myself, and that was the last time I ever thought about that question. Well, until maybe 2003. But we'll get to that later. I'm just kidding.

Before further exploring what it was like to grow up as an Auburn person in Georgia or Alabama, another question needed to be addressed: "Why do we even care? Why does football matter to us? Why does it get our hearts pumping so fast and so hard on a Saturday afternoon? Why does it become the thing that dominates our conversations for months at a time, if not the entire year? Why does football matter so much—particularly to Auburn folks?"

To find answers and insights into that profound question, we start with Jeremy Henderson, creator of *the War Eagle Reader*, a website for which John and Van have written many articles in the past.

Jeremy Henderson

I mean, everything about football is just this martial metaphor. Even with all the language that you use, and being this heroic effort just to move the ball ten yards. There's this heroic aspect of it, of taking land, of moving in one purpose toward a goal. I'm currently very much deep in research on the earliest days of football and when it really became a national craze, and there was just something about it that Americans seemed to take to. Maybe it was because of the physicality of it and the science of it, compared to everything that was out there at the time—and I'm talking like in the 1890s—and it just seemed to really strike a chord. Especially on campuses, because it was so much more of a spectacle to watch (compared to other sports of the day), from the pace of it to the violence to the team aspect of it. And so the answer to your

21

question is, I have no idea. [Laughter.] I don't know. I don't know what it is, but it gives me chills. So I just go with it.

We all do, Jeremy, we just go with it. And how do you see it, Jerry Hinnen, formerly of CBS Sports and the "Joe Cribbs Car Wash" Auburn blog, and legendary contributor to *the War Eagle Reader*? Why do Auburn people care so much about football?

Jerry Hinnen
This is our drama fix. We need some kind of excitement. We need to have something harmless where we can invest ourselves and still get the sugar rush of the great things happening, of the bad things happening, of not knowing what things are going to happen. And we don't get that in our day-to-day life. We wake up, we go to work, go to school. But really thrilling, "I have no idea what's going to happen" sort of things, those things don't happen very often. And sports gives us that little sort of injection, we get our fix through sports. But sports has that extra added dimension of being real life. Like these are actual people. These are not actors. These are not reality show contestants. And that's sports.

Okay, that makes sense. Sports are like a drug, and Auburn football is our drug of choice. But maybe there's something on a more emotional level as well.
Here's Delvin Williams, a part of our White Rocket podcasting family and an Auburn alum:

Delvin Williams
Why do we love Auburn so much? It's hard to say and it's easy to say. It's hard to say because if someone asks you why you love cookies you could look at them and simply say, "Duh, cookies!" And that's enough of an explanation because you're saying everyone should know cookies are awesome just because! But that doesn't *really* explain why, right?
Then you think of all the good times you've had with cookies. The years spent smelling them and the friends you've eaten them with. No one really ever has a bad time with cookies. Well, with Auburn, it's good times *and* bad. It's the

laughs and the crying and all the friends you've done both with. It's knowing you left Auburn a little bit better than you came, and you're grateful for it...

...and somehow every time you come back to Auburn for a football game and you're instantly reminded of some or all of those experiences. Auburn loves its football and by extension football becomes a distillation of whatever original fruit you pulled from the first time you were there. Does that extended metaphor make sense? Maybe, maybe not. Does it make sense there are any Auburn fans after 2012? Definitely not.

But trust me, if you went to school at Auburn, you get it. You want the good times and the bad. The bad times you forget. The cookies? Oh man. You never forget the cookies.

Most Auburn fans can get quite passionate about their love of Auburn and its football program; some take that passion to nigh-legendary levels. Perhaps you've encountered our very own "Auburn Elvis" at a game, or seen him on television. We asked him for his views on the question at hand:

Auburn Elvis

I think I love Auburn now for different reasons than when I was a kid. My family became Auburn fans because my uncle was a gifted athlete and went to Auburn on a partial track scholarship. He and my dad have always been very close, so my parents became Auburn fans because of my uncle.

Growing up, Auburn fandom had a uniqueness to it. I'd say about two-thirds of the kids (around me) were Alabama fans, and so I liked that we Auburn fans were underdogs, but not obscenely outnumbered. Plus, I grew up during the halcyon days of Bo Jackson, Charles Barkley, and Pat Dye, so they certainly made being an Auburn fan something you could be proud of.

But while it was sports that made me love Auburn growing up, I think the way I function creatively as an adult has led me to gravitate towards Auburn, even more than I did as a young man. Coming up with crazy ideas (like inventing a costumed persona) and working on silly projects is a big part of my personal identity, and I think there's a legitimate "Auburn

Spirit" that attracts people with "can-do" attitudes like mine. I'll admit the Auburn Creed might seem kind of corny, but I think it does a great job expressing the balance between idealism and practicality that typifies Auburn people. And while I obviously can't say no other place has that balance, I can say Auburn *does* have it, and that's why I love Auburn.

But bringing the topic back around to football, I think football is obviously the marquee sport in this country, and with Auburn being such a significant force in it, it's rewarding to support Auburn football. We Auburn fans joke about the toll Auburn fandom takes on us (and there's a lot of truth to that), but I don't think we'd make these many emotional sacrifices if we didn't believe we were somehow rewarded for them. Also, I've had conversations with Auburn folks like ADs Jay Jacobs and Allan Green, and I think they honestly value Auburn fans and the effort we put into supporting Auburn. So that mutual appreciation, from me as a fan of how great Auburn football can be, and also from Auburn football for the degree to which we care about what they're doing, keeps me invested in Auburn year-after-year.

The Weather Channel's Reynolds Wolf is very famously a big fan of the Tigers. Why does he love Auburn so much?

Reynolds Wolf

My gosh, it's, I don't know, it's a religious experience. The changes that you have going on: that first blast of cool air in the fall, you see the leaves change, and there's something about it. It's kind of like a demarcation point in our soul.

Why do we love it so much? That's a great question. That's *the* question. I can tell you what it means to *me*. There's a weird thing when it comes to Auburn football. It's like being in a time machine. When I'm in Auburn, and I park the car up behind Toomer's Corner and I make the walk down towards the stadium—and usually it happens every year when I'm right near Haley Center—I hear the drumline. And there's that rush of cooler air that you have just as the approach of October comes calling. And all of a sudden, I feel like I'm a twelve-year-old kid again. It's this transformative thing. It's a time machine. It takes me back to a time when mom and dad were alive. They were healthy, didn't have a care in the world. And the most important thing in the world was Vincent "Bo" Jackson catching a ball on a toss sweep and running downhill and… there's nothing like it. It makes you young again.

I can tell you that when I'm in Jordan-Hare Stadium and I get a press pass, and right before the game—you've got a window of, say, five minutes or so before the game starts, before they send you back up to the booth—and you see the band spill out onto the field and you hear the fight song and you feel the goosebumps. They're unavoidable. And instantly you feel like it's 1982 and you're twelve years old. It's a fountain of youth.

A fountain of youth. Something to bring us together. And something to separate us from our rivals—our opponents—dare I say, our *enemies*? Maybe not enemies *all* the time. But certainly, when families are being torn apart, marriages dissolved, and, you know, *trees being poisoned.* Those who are not familiar with life as a fan of an SEC program might not understand.

So what's it like to live part or even all of your life in that kind of an environment, where there's you and your team, and there's the other guy and his team, and you have to live and work with those people almost every day?

Van Allen Plexico

What was it like growing up in Georgia as an Auburn fan and having not only Alabama fans all over the place, but also having *Georgia* and its fan base right there in your face? Because I lived for eleven years just outside Atlanta, and I know you have them in your face all the time, over there.

John Ringer

I don't think there were nearly as many Alabama fans in Atlanta back then as there are now. I grew up in Tucker, which is on the northeast side of Atlanta, kind of near where Interstates 285 and 85 come together. And the high school I went to isn't even a high school anymore. I went to Henderson High, and now it's a middle school. Tucker was our rival High

School, and Auburn has recruited a number of good players from Tucker including some current recruits.

I grew up there in the Seventies and Eighties. In 1980 Georgia won the national title, and there were more Georgia fans coming out of the woodwork than you could believe. It was like they were suddenly *everywhere*. We had some neighbors who were diehard Georgia fans and they were really, really crazy for a while after that. I also knew a number of Georgia Tech fans. I had some family that went to Georgia Tech, and my grandfather and uncle and some cousins on the other side went to Georgia Tech. So I had some feelings for Georgia Tech and I had some neighbors and friends who were Georgia Tech fans. But really that was it. I mean, occasionally you'd meet somebody who cheered for some other team— Clemson or Florida or Tennessee—but the people I knew were mostly Georgia, Georgia Tech or Auburn fans.

Alabama fans have spread like a plague across the land in the last six or seven years and, I mean, even where I live now, in central Virginia, there are Alabama fans all over the place. And I often want to stop them and ask them, "Have you ever actually set foot on the campus or do you just put stickers on your car?"

My parents both went to Auburn as students and afterward they had season tickets. We went to a lot of Auburn events; football games and other events. Some of my earliest memories are getting in the car on Saturday and going there and tailgating with them and their friends and going to the game. In the earliest days that I can remember, before Pat Dye even, there was an area behind the concession stands under the stadium where it was dirt and you could get back there and just hang out with other little kids if you didn't feel like watching the game. Because, back then, sometimes those games were fun and sometimes they weren't. I have a lot of fond memories of that as a young child, going to the tailgates and throwing a football around or playing in the grass or whatever, usually near Sewell Hall because we always tailgated in that area.

You're right about the fandom. There were mostly Georgia fans in our area back then, and we had to deal with them. We didn't have a lot of success against them until Pat Dye came along, and it was tough to deal with them early on.

There's no wrong way to have become an Auburn person. However you go about getting there is fine. If you went to the school, that's great. If you graduated from the school, that's great. If you married into it, that's great. If you just decided the uniforms look cool, that's great. It all works. We'll take all comers. We're not picky, you know. We're one big happy family and we welcome everybody. All you have to do is just support Auburn.

Reynolds Wolf has an interesting story about how *he* became a member of the family:

Reynolds Wolf

I became an Auburn fan back around 1978 or so. The reason why I became an Auburn fan is because my family owned horses, and I had a horse that was dying.

I came home from school, got off the school bus, and my mom was hysterical because one of the horses was dying. The vet looked at me, looked at Mom, and it wasn't good. Dad came home from work and said, "Okay, we've got two options. Either we can put the horse to sleep, or we can put this horse on a trailer, and we can send it to Auburn, Alabama. There's an equine center there, and maybe they can pull a miracle and save this animal's life." And at the age of eight, I became an Auburn fan because of a dying horse.

We may take different paths, but we all come to the same place. We come to believe in Auburn and love it. And that's what matters: *We believe.* Though, heaven knows, when it comes to football, it hasn't always been easy.

Like John's dad, Van's dad attended Auburn in the late Fifties. He was there as a freshman for the 1957 National Championship. His senior class graduated as the first class to graduate from "Auburn University" rather than "API" (Alabama Polytechnic Institute). And he tells it this way:

Ralph "Shug" Jordan, by Jarrod Alberich

Lee Plexico

I remember when Shug Jordan was the coach and they had a get-together in the stadium. I think they had won part of a national championship that year. That was the only thing I went to. I can remember leaving Auburn and hearing the crowd over in the stadium, hollering. I never even bought a ticket (to a game). My interest in Auburn football didn't start until way after I graduated.

Van Allen Plexico

So yeah, it took my dad a little while to come around. But by the time I was a kid, he was getting on board, and my granddad that raised me was always a huge fan.

I didn't always understand in my earliest years why we rooted so hard for this team that seemed to lose so often, especially compared to our rivals, who just won all the time and constantly rubbed that in our faces. Why did we choose this life? Could it have been any different?

Yes, it was pretty hard back in those years, because that was the dreaded *Barfield era.*

Reynolds Wolf

In 1978, it was the world of Doug Barfield. If you're an Auburn fan, the world is not good. It isn't. And being a kid growing up in Birmingham, Alabama and going to Valley Elementary School? I bet it was maybe 90-10 weighted towards Alabama fans in the school.

You just expected punishment every fall when you got to November. The question was not, "Is Alabama going to win?" The question was, "Does Auburn have a prayer of looking presentable? Could they put a decent product on the field? Could they look like they had some kind of a pulse?" More often than not, the inevitable happened. The Tide would win, and it was awful as an Auburn fan.

Mike McClendon

Doug Barfield is an interesting case. He was not a bad coach. In my opinion he was a victim of incredibly bad luck

29

and circumstance. In the 1970s, Barfield was up against a machine that made it almost impossible for him to succeed. Then he made some mistakes that could not be overcome.

1. *Recruiting*: By the early Seventies Alabama football and Bear Bryant were dominating this state. No one in this state or in the NCAA did anything unless Bryant approved. Even though Jordan managed to produce a few very good teams, by the time 1972 was done, Auburn was quickly falling behind. It was difficult to recruit because Bryant was signing every kid who could play or who he thought might play somewhere else. Jordan was having trouble finding enough athletes to stay competitive.

In the 1970s you did not have scholarship limits like you do today. The first real limits on scholarships came in 1973 and limited each school to 105 football scholarships. (That was reduced to 95 in 1978 and to 85 in 1992, where it is today.) Plus, there weren't limits on the number of kids you could sign each year. As long as you stayed under 105 you could sign as many as you wanted. At Alabama, Bryant was signing everyone in the state who he thought could play at Alabama plus everyone he thought might play against him somewhere else. He would just trim the roster down each year to make room for however many kids he wanted to sign.

It didn't mean that Auburn and other schools did not get talented players. It meant that you never got the numbers you needed to be really competitive. You were always having to play from behind.

To be honest, Bryant got lazy in the late Sixties, and Jordan's best recruiting years came between 1968 and 1971. After losing two in a row to Auburn in 1969 and 1970, that changed. Bryant took over, and things deteriorated for Auburn. By 1975, when Jordan announced his retirement, the talent level at Auburn had already declined and Barfield inherited a bad situation. You could call it rebuilding, but that would be understating it. Plus, he was going to have to do it in the face of a recruiting machine at Alabama that made it an almost impossible task.

2. *NCAA Sanctions*: With all the recruiting problems going on, Auburn got hit with NCAA sanctions in 1979 and 1980.

Both cases involved paying players and other recruiting violations. The 1979 case carried a two-year postseason ban along with a TV ban. Then Auburn was hit with additional sanctions in 1980 for a similar incident involving a booster. This destroyed whatever recruiting momentum Barfield had built and set Auburn back even further than where he started.

NCAA issues don't start when the NCAA announces the findings and hands down punishment. The problems start a year or two earlier when the NCAA sends out the preliminary letter of inquiry and tells you they are investigating. That is when your opponents start telling recruits how bad it's going to be and convincing them they shouldn't consider you at all. In this particular case, the violations occurred in 1976-1977 and the impact of the investigation started in 1977-1978. By the time the punishment was announced in 1979, recruiting was already damaged.

The bottom line was that, going into 1980, you had a team that did not have the talent to compete, and recruiting was in trouble. Basically, Auburn was set up for failure, and it was going to take a long time to work out of the problems.

Barfield was not fired specifically because of the NCAA issues, but they did hurt him. The 1980 case in particular came back on Barfield, even though he took prompt action when he learned about the situation. I don't think these caused Auburn to fire Barfield, but when it came time to fire him, they were definitely contributing factors in the decisions.

3. *Alabama*: At Auburn and at Alabama, you are expected to beat the other team. You may not have to win every game, but you are expected to win your share, and you simply cannot go long stretches without winning that game at all. Shug Jordan managed to do that twice—two long losing streaks to Alabama, 1959-1962 and 1964-1968—but he was an exception. Jordan had lost three in a row when he retired, and in Barfield's five years at Auburn, he never managed a win.

When Alabama beat us in 1979 by dominating the fourth quarter, I think most people had come to believe Barfield was never going to be competitive with Bryant and Alabama. He was not competitive on the field, and he was not competitive off the field.

4. *Defense and hard-nosed football*: Barfield was an offensive coach. He was Jordan's offensive coordinator before Jordan hand-picked him to take over in 1976. He suffered from the same problem that a lot of offensive coaches who get promoted have: He was never able to produce a defense that complemented the offense. Barfield produced some good offensive teams, but defense was always a problem.

P. W. (Bear) Underwood, the defensive coordinator under Barfield, catches a lot of blame for those poor teams. He deserves some of that, but the truth is that he never had great talent to work with. He had good talent but not great talent. He produced good, but not great defensive teams. Even in 1979, when Auburn went 8-3, the defense averaged giving up over 21 points per game.

As an aside, Underwood did, however, manage to produce one of the best and least-talked-about defensive players to ever play at Auburn, Freddie Smith. Smith holds the all-time record for tackles, 528. No. 2 on the list is Gregg Carr with 453, and that's 75 fewer, which is a huge number in this case. Smith holds the no. 1 and no. 4 positions on Auburn's single-season tackles list. Most likely those records will never be broken. "Fast Freddie" was a true sideline-to-sideline linebacker. On Auburn's list of top ten single-game tackling performances, he holds five of the slots. To put this in perspective, Jeremiah Dinson was the leading tackler on the 2019 team with 57 tackles. Freddie Smith averaged 132 a year for four years.

The other problem is somewhat philosophical. In the 1970s, Alabama under Bryant was the poster team for hard-nosed, physical football. They ran the wishbone and they played hard-nosed, physical defense. Auburn ran the Houston-Veer, which was also a triple option offense, but we relied more on the option part than on the knock- you- off- the- line-of- scrimmage physical football. Also, we were not that same kind of monster physical defense like Alabama. We had a very different type of philosophy of football than Alabama. That was partially due to personnel and partially due to the way Barfield coached.

When you compared what was going on at Auburn to Alabama, there was not much to compare. We were a finesse team and we did not fare well against good physical teams. We didn't match up well with Alabama. Even in 1979, when we had a chance to win the game in the fourth quarter, Alabama just took over and beat us physically when it mattered. I think a lot of Auburn people compared the two teams and wanted a different approach.

Van's dad offers a more...*visceral* reaction to the Barfield era:

Lee Plexico

I think when we changed coaches, after Shug retired and we hired his assistant, it was so terrible... *Barfield.* I didn't even like to go into the same stadium with him. Honestly, he was terrible. After we changed coaches again, and Pat Dye came in, he just rejuvenated the whole thing. I sort of got interested then, and pretty soon I got to be a real fan. And I've been a real fan ever since, I guess.

But that deal with Barfield, they liked to have shut down the whole school.

While they were on the subject of Doug Barfield, Van couldn't help but ask his dad one other question, and I don't think many of you are going to like his answer.

Van Allen Plexico

What did you think about the orange jerseys Barfield had the team wear several times during his five-year tenure? Did you approve or disapprove of them?

Lee Plexico

I approved of that.

A longtime Auburn fan actually *approved* of the orange jerseys? He may not have understood what a controversial topic he was stepping into there.

What exactly was the deal with those alternate tops, which have come to be reviled by so many among the Auburn faithful? We turned to Clint Richardson, keeper of the Auburn Uniform Database, to address the infamous orange jerseys:

Clint Richardson

When Doug Barfield took over the head coaching position vacated by the retiring Shug Jordan, he immediately changed bits and pieces of the Auburn football aesthetic.

In 1976, Barfield's first season, the Tigers wore their first and only set of award decals on the back of the helmet. The "weagle" decal features a stocky eagle silhouette rather similar to the logo of the United States Postal Service.

For the 1977 season, Auburn began to wear orange belts, changing from the white belts used for many years prior.

The following season, Barfield dug a bit deeper, surprising the team with orange jerseys for the marquee matchup against the Georgia Bulldogs. Georgia entered Jordan-Hare Stadium ranked no. 8 in the country. Auburn had struggled during the season, carrying a 6-3 record into this game. The Tigers had missed a bowl game for three straight seasons and were on the outside looking in for their first bowl bid under the new head coach.

After warming up pre-game in the traditional navy tops, the Tigers returned to the locker room to find the new orange jerseys hanging in the lockers. The players, and eventually the crowd, were shocked. Auburn went on to play one their best games of the season but ended up with a 22-22 tie. One newspaper described the game as "Auburn Wins, Bulldogs Lose – 22-22."

The orange jerseys would be broken out three more times during Barfield's tenure. Despite the popular "bad luck" superstition, Auburn wore the jerseys to a 2-1-1 record under Barfield. The Tigers never played poorly in the alternate tops. The two victories came against Mississippi State in 1979 and Southern Miss in 1980, the latter of which resulted in a 31-0 shutout. The lone loss was against Herschel Walker's top-ranked Georgia team in 1980, but it was still a rather tight game, finishing 31-21 Georgia.

So, even in orange jerseys, we of the Auburn Family love our football program and its storied, roller-coaster history. But—what is it about Auburn in particular, that draws us to it so much?

Reynolds Wolf

It's not really the idea of football. It's the experience. It's much more than just the football. It's much more than just, "Is Auburn going to beat Arkansas? Are they going to topple Tennessee? Are they going to beat the Tide?" It's greater than that.

Jerry Hinnen

Auburn really is a community. Now, lots of colleges and universities form communities; that's part of the essential nature of attending a university in this country. But Auburn, I do think, is a tighter community, particularly for a university of its size. It really is through and through a college town, start to finish. If you go to Auburn, you are in Auburn, that's why you're there. It really is the hub of everything. It's not the only one in the country, but it is very different from a lot of other college experiences. And then what Auburn football does on top of that is it keeps that community sort of reconnected. I went to Birmingham Southern for undergrad; I went to Auburn for grad school; but I grew up in Dadeville, which is about thirty minutes, forty minutes from Auburn. The son of Auburn parents, plenty of Auburn family members. At Birmingham Southern I made lots of friends. But I don't feel that same connection with the Birmingham Southern community on an annual basis in the fall, the way you necessarily do with Auburn. It's every Saturday, we've got 80,000 people in the stadium. We've got everybody watching at home, we're talking on Twitter, we're talking on Facebook, we're going out to the grocery stores and stopping in the aisles to chat about what happened. It connects us as an Auburn community in a way that I'm not sure anything else does.

It really does connect us. But while Van was talking with his dad, he had one more question along the same lines for him. Because Lee and Annette Plexico still lived in Sylacauga, Alabama, right there in Ground Zero between Auburn and Birmingham.

Van Allen Plexico
What has it meant to live in this area on a daily basis? To be an Auburn person, as opposed to an Alabama person? What's the life experience like?

Lee Plexico
You're an underdog. Yeah. You're an underdog. That's about it.

Annette Plexico
It's H-E-L-L. [Laughter]

While Van's stepmother summed it up pretty succinctly, using one word that she spelled out, his dad used another word: "underdog." And he's not the only person to use that word.

Jeremy Henderson
My grandparents lived in Auburn when I was a student, and they still live in Auburn. My dad grew up here, my parents met here and everybody went to college here. When I was growing up, coming down to Auburn was synonymous with going to great-grandma's, so it was always this magical place to me. And so, for me, being an Auburn fan or an Auburn person really just stems so much from that. Sometimes I'm almost envious of the experience that other people have here. They're looking to go to a college, you know; just somewhere to go to college. They come, they fall in love with the place, but then they have to go. To me it wasn't like that, because I still live here. And I've essentially, save for a year in Texas, lived here since I came to school.

There's that whole phenomenon of what makes Auburn *Auburn*, and why it's so strange and unique. The relationship between the town and the university and how it's just so completely intertwined. I think more so with Auburn than with any other team, any other fan base and school I could think of in the country, really.

In a certain sense, the Auburn spirit is inextricably tied to the spirit of the underdog. And, I mean, everybody wants to be or root for the underdog. To me, that's one of the reasons why

36

it's so great to be an Auburn fan: because, especially when talking about our archenemy, they really don't have any underdog comeback stories. At least, not in our rivalry; not any that immediately come to mind. Heaven forbid they would ever consider themselves underdogs.

Reynolds Wolf

When it comes down to Alabama and Auburn and it comes to football, it's easy in this life to become an Alabama fan. The easiest thing in the world is to back success. It's simple to be a Patriots fan; to be a Yankees fan; to be a fan of the Alabama Crimson Tide. But to be an Auburn fan, it takes something a little bit different. Wins and losses matter, but there has to be something else that draws you.

Does that mean it takes something a little extra little special to be an Auburn person?

Van Allen Plexico

My family always were Auburn fans, at least on my dad's side, but we were certainly in the minority. I remember coming up through elementary school and middle school and up into high school, we Auburn fans—we Auburn Family—man, we stuck together, because there were just so many more Alabama fans, and they loved—they *reveled* in—sticking it to you. Every November or December it was time to once again have to deal with it. And it was so bad for so long. The first year we won the Iron Bowl, that I was old enough to be aware of it, was my freshman year of high school, in 1982. So, from kindergarten through eighth grade, Alabama won every year. And that's tough on a little kid. It's really tough.

The thing is, though, there's never a temptation to change sides. I think it's very interesting that, as an Auburn person, you don't get that sense of "Oh, my team isn't winning, so I'm just going to go cheer for somebody else now." You stick with them, even if you keep losing. If you can lose to your hated arch rival—whose fans are taunting you in school every day by the dozens—every single year, for nine straight years, well then, you can pretty much stand up to anything. Even though all you know as a child is losing to them. Kindergarten through eighth grade! I was too young to remember Punt Bama Punt (in 1972), which was the last Iron Bowl win for Auburn before that nine-game losing streak.

That says a lot about the resilience of Auburn fans, and I guess college football fans in general, that we don't change sides. We're not fair-weather fans. Well, most of us, maybe. There are some out there, obviously, and we were just mentioning some of them but, I mean, is that particular to Auburn? Or is that a lot of teams? It certainly doesn't seem to be true of Alabama—their fans roll in and roll out like the tide, depending entirely on if they're winning or losing.

John Ringer
My opinion is that some of the people who consider themselves Alabama fans only do so because they win, not because they've actually ever seen the school or care about the school. They just like to associate themselves with a program that wins all the time. And that doesn't require any great sacrifice or character.

I think part of being an Auburn fan is that there are a lot of really good people who are Auburn people. I think it makes for a really good environment when Auburn people get together at games and other events. I really like that. But also, I think you're right: There was never a moment when we were going to change our minds and not be Auburn fans anymore. That's not how it works.

You just keep your head up and keep going and trust that things will get better. And that's how it is.

Van Allen Plexico
It's just part of what comes with being an Auburn person: You realize that we're in the SEC, it's tough—it was tough back then; it's tough now—and you just deal with it.

John Ringer
But part of that comes down to a "sometimes the winning doesn't feel as good as losing feels bad" kind of thing.

Van Allen Plexico

"Losing hurts more than winning feels good," is what Lewis Grizzard famously said. I thought that was a very, very important statement that he made. And so ever since I first heard it, years and years and decades ago, I've always tried to make sure that I fully appreciate and enjoy our wins, and never take them for granted. Because I want them to feel at least as good as the losing hurts. I feel like psychologically we have some control over that. Something hurts you, in part, because you *let* it hurt. But something feels good because you stop and let it feel good. You take the time to enjoy and appreciate it and savor it. And if you just say, "Okay, we won; I totally expected that," and you yawn and move on, you're not taking time to smell the roses and appreciate what you've got. You're taking it for granted. So, yeah, every time Auburn wins a game, unless it's just the most blow-out-est of blowouts against totally overmatched programs, I try to be happy for a little while. I try to revel in it and enjoy it a little bit. Because I know how bad I would feel if it were Georgia or Alabama and we lost. So I think to myself, "I want to enjoy this just as much as I would be miserable if we'd lost."

John Ringer

Yes. Because if your expectation is that you're going to win everything, you're going to be unhappy quite often.

Van Allen Plexico

Yeah, exactly. And who wants that? If you tie yourself to Alabama and the bare minimum you will accept without disappointment is going undefeated every year and going to the playoffs and winning there every year, then you could go 13-1 and that's a disappointing season to you, and you're bitter all offseason. Who wants that? You know, I've said this before—I would rather be an Auburn person and have the 2010 National Championship than be an Alabama person today with any three of their titles, because, I promise you, they did not enjoy any of those three titles nearly as much as I enjoyed 2010, just because of everything that went into it.

Reynolds Wolf

I remember Pat Dye talking about the type of player that he would recruit. He said that the Auburn recruit had something a little bit different about them, and the ones they would sign had something that was a little bit deeper than just the wins and losses. They fell in love with the experience of being at Auburn. They looked at Auburn as a home. They looked at Auburn as the center of the universe. They really did, and it stays with them.

It's easy for me to say it as an Auburn fan, but I don't think Alabama fans or Georgia fans have much of the same. When I was in high school, I remember my sister dated this guy who was a huge Alabama fan. He had no connection to the University of Alabama; had no connection to Tuscaloosa; had never been to the Capstone to see a game. And I remember asking him, "Why are you an Alabama fan?" And he said, "I'm a Bama fan because Alabama is the state in which I live." As a seventeen-year-old I thought that was hilarious, but as a guy who's forty-eight it makes a damn good bit of sense. It really does. It's common sense to be an Alabama fan. But to be an Auburn fan, it's a little bit deeper, I think it's a bit more nuanced. We don't have the same success and we've not had the same history that they've had. And I think that we look at the wins and losses with much more gratitude. It's a very big difference between the fan bases. Like I said, it's easy to be an Alabama fan. An Auburn fan? It takes a lot of patience. It really does.

Van, as you've said before, time and time again, when you're an Auburn fan, this is what you get. These things happen. You have these great expectations, but it's never automatic. It's never easy to be an Auburn fan. But the thing is, *I'll take it*, though. I'll take and accept it as an Auburn fan, I will. I'll take the losses. I'll take the wins when they come. And it's great because when you do have the winning times, it carries more weight, it does matter. It resonates.

At Alabama I am convinced that, when they win a title, after a year passes, they throw it out like yesterday's newspaper; like yesterday's coffee grounds. But at Auburn we will always have 2004. We will always have 1983. Even years we don't win titles, like those years, they mean something to us. We hold onto them; they keep us warm during the cold months. I mean, think about 2013! That was my favorite team of all time.

It stays with you, as an Auburn fan. And I think that with Alabama winning is so easy, it doesn't matter as much.

Van Allen Plexico
Reynolds makes a good point. I mean, if 2010 had happened after we had just won the national championship in 2009, I would not have enjoyed it as much as I enjoyed it coming so many years after 1957. You know what I mean?

John Ringer
Yeah, amen to that.

Van Allen Plexico
Or 1983. Or everything that happened in 1993, or 1988, or 2004.

Here's Jarrod Alberich. He's the "Yardsale Artist" and Art Director for White Rocket Entertainment, and also one of the network's podcast co-hosts. He has an interesting story to share with us, of how he came to be an Auburn person.

Jarrod Alberich
I was the son of a military man. My dad was in the Army. We moved around a lot. I'm originally from South Bend, Indiana, so I grew up a Notre Dame fan. Then I went to high school here in Alabama. When the time came to go to college, I put in for all the military scholarships, and got accepted by Air Force ROTC. They actually accepted me to go to Tennessee. So I was headed to Tennessee. My then-girlfriend got accepted to Auburn and she said, "Hey, come up with me to E-Day." They have E-Day at Auburn every year where high school students can come check out Engineering at Auburn. I went up there. I talked to the ROTC folks at Auburn and said "I've got a scholarship to Tennessee" and they said, "Well, would you come to Auburn?" And I said, "Sure," because I

wanted to be with my girlfriend. And I don't know how that works in the world of government paperwork, but I never signed anything. I never did any paperwork. When I got home from that trip, I had a voicemail that said, "This is Colonel Butler and I will be seeing you in the fall, and you will be coming here for your ROTC and your college." I thought, "Cool." And that worked out well because I ended up marrying that girl. We've got two kids now.

And that's how I became an Auburn fan. I said, "Okay, I guess I'm going to Auburn." It just absolutely was the fickle finger of fate.

Van Allen Plexico

So how aware were you of Auburn football before you were living in Alabama? And then, over the course of time, how did it become more and more something you were aware of?

Jarrod Alberich

Yeah, that's another layer to the story. I had an awareness of it because, being an army brat, we had lived here in Alabama, down at Fort Rucker, and my mom had some friends that were big Auburn people and were always giving me Auburn gifts. I remember getting an orange and blue Auburn digital watch and a Bo Jackson t-shirt, and I always thought Bo Jackson was cool, so I got a little influence. And this is when I was in about second or third grade. But then again, I sort of stuck with Notre Dame. I was just coming into awareness of Auburn football.

I went to high school here in Alabama, which meant I was around it, but it didn't really penetrate me and it wasn't a part of me. Even when I went to Auburn, it was just sort of a college decision. Football didn't have its hooks into me yet. In fact, I considered football—believe it or not; I know this is considered heresy, but—I considered football an inconvenience. I was like, "Oh my gosh, it's a football day. So now it'll be a pain in the butt to drive from one place to another," and that kind of thing.

My entire four years of going to Auburn, I went to two football games. And I did that because ROTC worked a food booth for one game and I went volunteer at the food booth. And we also worked the President's box. We basically were glorified hat check/coat check people at the President's box. We opened the door. We welcomed people, we hung up their coats, things like that. I did two games, one at the food booth and one working in the President's box, and at that point I really didn't care much about Auburn football. I graduated, moved away, started my Air Force career, stationed at Pope Air Force Base, North Carolina. And I just started missing Auburn, just missing Auburn in general. Football was the way I could reconnect: to start watching Auburn play football.

I started watching Auburn football in 2000. I attended Auburn from 1995 to 1999, but I actually started watching it and caring about the football team in 2000. And from there on, it just got its hooks into me.

Van Allen Plexico

Well, as we discovered earlier, apparently you still went to more games as a student than my dad did. And he was there when we won the first national championship.

Jarrod Alberich

[Laughter.] Okay, so I don't feel as bad.

I think Auburn football matters because it seems to be that one thing that just binds us all together. It binds us, penetrates us, runs through us like "the Force." But no, in a sense, it kind of *is*. It is almost like "the Force" of the Auburn Family. It's kind of weird how it landed on football. I guess football being a predominantly popular American sport probably led to that, but I could see it in any alternate dimension being any other sporting event or something else like that. Something that just brings everyone together.

You've got a stadium full of 87,000 people, and it's just the beacon of home. That's where you go to have your highest of highs, your lowest of lows. It's emotionally wrapped up into it. That's where you meet your friends. That's where you go for the cookout, especially in the fall with the weather in the great State of Alabama, finally breaking and becoming halfway decent, so you can actually get together. We don't get together for summer sports. But I would say, yeah, it really could be any sport in any timeline, but I think because football is so popular, the most popular sport there, it just becomes that home base where we all go to meet and experience the highs and experience unfortunate lows from time to time. But mostly you get to spend time with your friends. Isn't that really the ultimate high?

Van Allen Plexico

And what does it add to things, that you have another university with another team, right across the state, who have seemingly chosen football as their form of ultimate expression—of their worthiness? Is there a little bit of us trying to compete on what they see as *their* playing field, and say, "It's not just yours?" Is having a big rival part of that?

Jarrod Alberich

What is this other team you're talking about? I'm not sure I know. [Laughter.]

Sure, that plays into it. I would say it's been my experience that the football identity has mattered even more to that fan base. But I think you're right, I think it's partly because our rivals are so focused on it. That's sort of our natural line of communication.

Reynolds Wolf

I started in television about twenty-five years ago, so that puts it around 1993 or 1994, and I was in Anniston, Alabama. I left my job in Alabama to go to San Luis Obispo, California. And let's see, my gosh, this was the day after Christmas in 1993. Back in 1993 the Internet was in San Francisco. I went from one side of the country to the other, and when I left Alabama, I was essentially leaving Auburn football. I was moving to a place where I had no money. I couldn't afford cable TV and I was on the West Coast, so I tuned in to anything. I was watching Pac 10 football. I lost all of that connection to Auburn. It was like having part of my soul amputated.

44

But I can tell you, being in a place without Auburn football, and driving down to Los Angeles one day and walking through Hollywood and seeing someone walk up the street wearing an Auburn t-shirt, I almost burst into tears. It was like seeing someone from your home planet and you've been living on Mars. It was the greatest, most comforting thing in the whole world. And there was this great connection. It made me appreciate, made me realize just how special this being part of and loving Auburn happens to be.

Jeremy Henderson

I was in a punk band in Auburn back then, and they didn't like that I was singing about Auburn football, but that's what I was singing about. I was like, "I'm the singer, so screw it. I'm singing about what I want to sing about." So I was singing about the 1969 Iron Bowl; the 1972 Iron Bowl; I was singing about "eleven and oh, eleven and oh!" It was such a huge deal.

I felt then, and I still do, to a certain extent, that I'm on some sort of mission almost to celebrate Auburn football. I guess that's just weird. I mean, I'm not entirely *proud* of it; it's almost like a disease. But here it is. I'm living the best life I can with it.

I totally wonder, is it like this for other fan bases, for other people? Even for other Auburn fans? Do people at Vanderbilt feel this way? Do people at Kentucky feel this way? Does UCLA? I mean, can you imagine somebody at UCLA feeling this way about their football team? No, I can't.

Jerry Hinnen

You've got Tim Cook. And it's awesome that an Auburn grad is in charge of the first trillion-dollar business in the world. But at the same time, we don't get that same connection through those kinds of successes. For example, our aerospace engineering program is so great. It's fantastic. But we're not going to stop in the grocery store aisles to talk to each other about it. I think that's why Auburn football matters: It's this connective tissue. It's necessary every fall that we get those bonds strengthened; that we have the connective tissue reforged, so to speak. And when you tie in not just the people we went to Auburn with, but our families, our friends, the larger community out from there, it's a sort of thing that, once you're connected to it, it's not likely I think that you're ever *not* going to be connected to it.

It seems we are connected to one another across the Auburn Family by many different means, but perhaps the one common currency that binds almost all of us together is football. Even those who don't enjoy the sport itself can still indulge in the pageantry and hoopla surrounding it; in the way it allows for an outward expression of tribal identity. (Wearing orange and blue clothes and accessories; painting our faces; waving shakers; yelling strange phrases that probably seem alien to outsiders; writing entire books like this one about it all.)

Perhaps, as Jarrod said, it's because football has always been the most popular sport, certainly in our part of the country. Perhaps, as Jerry suggested, it's the forge in which we strengthen our links to one another on an annual basis. And perhaps, as Van mentioned, there's that other school, right across the state, holding football up as their ultimate test of worthiness and success.

That being the case—do all Auburn people dislike Alabama equally? Do we despise them *enough*? How do we define "enough?" Are there different levels of animosity within the rivalry? If so, why?

Such questions probably seem nonsensical to someone not steeped in the culture of the Auburn Family and the great rivalry with the Crimson Tide. To Auburn people, though, it's an interesting proposition: What factors shape our feelings toward Alabama? How do those factors vary from person to person?

Van Allen Plexico

John, were you able to appropriately despise the University of Alabama? Growing up in Georgia and being that far removed from them, compared to me. I'm not saying my experience was better or worse than yours. I just know that I had Alabama fans in my face all the time. What was it like for you, not being in the middle of it as much?

John Ringer

It was definitely different. This predates playing the Iron Bowl in our home stadium. My parents had season tickets for Auburn, but we didn't go to Legion Field, so we didn't go to Alabama games when I was a kid. I did come into contact with Alabama fans; we knew some; but I'm sure it wasn't a tenth of the level of stuff that you got. And I got stuff at school from other people when Alabama won. But it was more because they knew I was an Auburn fan and looked at it as a chance to give me crud or whatever. And some of them weren't diehard Alabama fans, they just wanted a chance to mess with me.

It's fascinating to consider that people who would not have identified themselves at all as Alabama fans were so taken by the Iron Bowl rivalry that they would go out of their way to give grief to an Auburn fan when the Tigers would lose to the Tide. Even outside the two fan bases, the rivalry is that strong, that well-known and that powerful.

Van Allen Plexico

Can I just say, I've never understood that thing where someone must think, "I'm a fan of Team A and you're a fan of Team B; I know that you and Team C hate each other; so when Team C beats you, I'm going to use Team C's battle cry and taunt you with it." What is that?

John Ringer

That's some people who need more to do in their lives.

Van Allen Plexico

It's like the Oregon fans in Arizona, at the 2010 BCS National Championship game, that yelled "R*** T***" at us. I was bewildered. "That's not your battle cry! Quack at us or something, don't pick some other random team and use their thing at us." It's just bizarre.

John Ringer

I've never understood that. I never have.

Van Allen Plexico

I would never go up to a Florida fan and do the tomahawk chop at him. Why would I? It just makes no sense. It's not our thing. I would never go up to a Tennessee fan and wave an encyclopedia at him, like I was a Vanderbilt fan.

I don't understand these things, John.

Jeremy Henderson

The "Seventies"—that was just like a dirty word for me, growing up. That decade of Auburn football was like the wilderness or something, that you didn't talk about. Nobody wanted to talk about it. It was like a wilderness that our fathers wandered through, searching for food and water from the Lord, but he had abandoned us. This is the way I grew up thinking of that time period.

As I've gotten older and I've gone back and I've researched and studied, I kind of *love* the Seventies now, for a variety of reasons. But in the early Seventies, I mean, we were pretty dang good. The 1974 team was actually a really, really good team and totally should have beaten Bama and would have, and pretty much got robbed. [Auburn had a long touchdown— potentially the game-winning score—called back by the referees due to an "illegal touching" penalty, in which receiver Thom Gossom was pushed out of bounds, if he went out of bounds at all, by an Alabama defender, prior to catching the pass and scoring. This incident directly led to the "illegal touching" rule being changed by the NCAA to exclude players who are pushed out of bounds.]

Florida was the only other team that beat us that year, and we wound up stopping Texas in the Gator Bowl, so that's always going to be good. And then Barfield had a decent year or two and I think came close to turning the corner with the program. I've interviewed him a time or two and it's interesting to hear his thoughts. Having to be "the man *after* the man." Nobody wants to be that guy. It just didn't work out for him for a variety of reasons. But yeah, it was hard for somebody growing up in the Eighties and that decade being my first experience with Auburn football. In my mind, Auburn only lost once in a blue moon. Trying to imagine what it was like for my dad, it just... it didn't make any sense.

Van Allen Plexico

Do you remember your first trip to see a football game in Auburn?

John Ringer

I honestly don't. I'm sure I went before I can remember it. But I know I was at games in the early Seventies.

Van Allen Plexico

I never really had the opportunity to go. My parents didn't go often, and nobody I hung out with went.

The first game I attended might have been Mississippi State in 1977. That seems right. I know it was when Barfield was coaching. I think it was that year because I remember going into the Auburn University Bookstore in Haley Center—where you and I would both later work! —and they had the big *Star Wars Treasury Edition* comic book on the magazine rack. I bought it and it was one of my treasured belongings for many years, not just because of Star Wars but because I got it at Auburn. I put Auburn stickers all over the front of that Star Wars comic book.

I remember going the next year and I think we lost again. That one might have been against Georgia Tech. I'm not sure which year it was, but I know our team wore orange jerseys for at least one of those games. That was strange enough for a little kid like me to see back then, because I'd seen Auburn play on television a few times (not many, though, because only the biggest games each week were televised, and Auburn only played in a very few of those in the Seventies). Looking back now, though, it seems even stranger. From our current vantage point, it's hard to imagine we ever wore orange. Back then, I don't remember a whole lot of uproar over it. Nothing like you'd hear now. Today there would be a bunch of fans wanting to fire Barfield just for putting the team in orange jerseys!

In any case, I didn't go to a game in Auburn again until 1985, the year before I started classes there. It was the Mississippi State game, it was the only time I got to see Bo Jackson play in person, and it was his senior year—the year he won the Heisman Trophy. I remember very well that the score was 21-9 Auburn, and I remember our seats were in one end zone; probably the North Stands. And the reason I know all this is because, in the first half, Bo scored three touchdowns, and all of them were at the other end of the field from us. We barely saw them. Then, in the second half, Auburn didn't score, and Mississippi State kicked three field goals—and the teams had switched ends at halftime, so those field goals also all happened at the other end from us. All thirty points scored in the game were scored as far away from us as possible, and we barely saw any of it. That's just how it goes sometimes.

Prior to becoming a student, I wasn't physically *in* Auburn very much at all, and they weren't on television all that much. But I sure listened to Jim Fyffe on the radio a lot.

Were you able to hear Jim's radio calls back then?

John Ringer

Yeah, the Auburn Network (back then it was the Auburn Football Network) was in Atlanta. We could listen. Today it's probably mind-bending to think that, back then, Auburn was probably on TV like three times a season, if we were lucky. That meant you had to listen to our other games on the radio. We did some of that. At some point in the Eighties, we got a VCR and we would record the games, too. [By then, with the advent of ESPN, the dramatic rise in the number of college football games being televised and the rise in Auburn's football prestige, the Tigers were on television much more often.] Eventually we had a bunch of VHS tapes with Auburn games on them.

My parents had season tickets and we all went to games in the Seventies and Eighties, until I was a student. I was a freshman in the fall of 1987, and I went to every home game when I was a student. We won three SEC titles while we were students.

Van Allen Plexico

Yeah, we were there at the right time, for sure. You and I went to the games together, along with our friends and girlfriends, in 1989 and 1990. When I went back and finished my Master's degree there, Auburn went on that 20-game winning streak under Terry Bowden, so I got to enjoy that, too, as a sort of second helping. I felt greedy getting to experience that second stint of being in the student section, but I did enjoy it.

Let's go back and talk a little bit about what it was like in those earliest days, when very few Auburn games were televised. Can you believe the 1984 Florida State game in Tallahassee was only on the radio? It's hard to fathom the idea that Auburn vs Florida State was not even considered a game worth broadcasting on TV by anyone. And that happened as recently as 1984.

John Ringer

Florida State was a women's college for a long time. They don't have a football history going back a hundred years, like most programs do. They're very *nouveau* in that category. But you're right—the idea that Auburn and FSU could play this big game and there was no TV at all—no chance to see any of it—is crazy.

Van Allen Plexico

I have a video tape of it that was produced years later by the Auburn Network, and it's also probably on YouTube, like everything else at this point. It was made from the closed-circuit video inside the stadium. It has the Jim Fyffe and Charlie Trotman radio play-by-play as the audio.

That was such a masterful performance by Jim. I can recall lying on the bed with a notebook and pen, listening to that radio broadcast and tracking the teams on paper. The game was a shootout, and Jim had so many great turns of phrase and moments of excitement in it, for all the listeners to go nuts about.

"Auburn trailing by five, Washington looking, throwing. This one is complete inside the twenty and out of bounds at the Florida State 14-yard line.

"Washington hits tight end Jeff Parks. Driven out of bounds by Mike Hayes. And another Tiger first down. Can it come down to this? Can you stand *a finish like this? What an exciting finish to this football game.*

"He's got a block on the outside... Brent turns the corner to the ten, broke a tackle to the five, goes out of bounds at the 5- yard line. With 1:13 to play, 41-36, the Tigers trail Florida State.

"Two tight ends for Washington. He's gonna pitch the ball to Fullwood. Tries to get outside—he dives for the pylon—He's in! He's in! He's in! TOUCHDOWN AUBURN! Touchdown Fullwood from four yards away. And the Tigers! The Tigers have done it. They have marched literally the length of the field and gone ahead, 42-41!"
—Jim Fyffe, Auburn radio broadcast at Florida State, 1984

Van Allen Plexico

That was absolutely an amazing, masterful job. Some of his greatest work was on that one game at Tallahassee where Auburn got the ball back, trailing by like six with about a minute to go, and he said, "Here they go, their backs to the wall, their feet to the fire," because they were up against their own goal line and had to go ninety-nine yards for the touchdown, with only a few seconds to go. It was just amazing how Jim could paint a picture with words like that.

Let's look back at that time. What memories do you have of the Doug Barfield era as it leads us up to Pat Dye? I mean, you might even remember Shug. I don't remember Shug much at all. He was sort of trailing off in health in his last couple of years, as far as I can remember. And I know the team wasn't doing that great. His last year we went 4-6-1 and, in fact, we would have been 3-6-2 if not for Mississippi State later having to forfeit a game that we tied with them. Three wins in his final year is pretty depressing.

John Ringer

I do not have any direct memories of that time, no.

Van Allen Plexico

Right. I barely do.

Barfield took over as head coach starting in 1976. We had five years of the Doug Barfield era. His first year was 4-7, not exactly promising. Then in 1977, 6-5-1, and in 1978, 6-4-1. So he was not off to a roaring start. It seemed like he could put together a pretty good offense, but the defense just seemed very weak back then, and we would lose a game to a Wake Forest-type team by a score of 45-41 or something of that nature, you know?

John Ringer

Yes. Yes. It was a time of option football. There was very little passing back then. Our defense wasn't very good, on a routine basis. We gave up a lot of points, and we'd score some points. You're right, we moved the ball and scored points. We had some talented players, at least on offense.

"Their quarterback wears number six, Charlie Trotman. He's not very big but he's a great quarterback in a lot of ways because they run the option well. He's a good leader and very solid performer—a good passer, 52% on the passing side of it—and he's just an excellent young player.

"Here he finds number 82, Byron Franklin, one wide receiver along with number 45, Rusty Bird, the speed merchants Trotman will look to if the Auburn running game bogs down. I don't think there's anybody in the country that has the receivers that have the speed that Auburn does.

"Certainly one of the most underrated backs as far as we are concerned in all the country would be this fella, number 21, James Brooks. He may not be a household name outside of Alabama right now, but that may change in a month or so. Certainly will. Last year he was the Freshman of the Year in the Southeastern Conference. He's third in all-purpose running in the country right now, at 205 yards (per game). He's very powerful. ...James Brooks is only a sophomore and a fellow who might wind up in the top 10 in overall rushing before the year is out.

"Joe Cribbs, his running mate, number 20, has been injured so far this season and hasn't seen much action, but... last year he was the number three rusher in the Southeastern Conference. And of course, he's about ninety percent strong and he's back and they're glad to have him. They've got a tremendous backfield with Cribbs healthy and Brooks healthy.

"And another man who should be healthy today who has been hurt... normally is the blocking back, but ...you can see what he can do if he finds any daylight whatsoever. William Andrews. So Auburn seems to have enough offensive punch."

—*Al Michaels, TV audio commentary from the late Seventies*

John Ringer

We had an offense at one point with James Brooks, Joe Cribbs and William Andrews, who all went on to be starting NFL running backs. For a while all were the historical leading rushers for their NFL teams. Brooks for the Bengals and Cribbs for the Bills and William Andrews for the Falcons. Andrews was a fullback at Auburn, but became the main running back for the Falcons in the early Eighties. It's amazing to think that we had three NFL running backs on the team.

During Doug Barfield's five-year run as head coach on the Plains, the SEC featured ten teams and no divisions. Auburn rarely played LSU or Ole Miss during that era. In addition to Alabama, Georgia and Mississippi State, the Tigers' main annual opponents included Tennessee, Florida, and non-conference foe Georgia Tech, a team Auburn had played yearly for decades, going back to their original time as members of the conference.

From 1976-1980, Barfield's record against those six teams was a combined 11-18-1. The only one of them he had a winning record against was Tennessee, at 3-2. He actually managed a .500 record against Georgia, at 2-2-1, in one of their better periods that included their national championship year of 1980. Against all the others, his Auburn teams went 2-3, except of course for Alabama, against whom his teams went 0-5.

1979

Van Allen Plexico

The only Barfield year that really was good, win-loss-wise, was 1979. And when I say really good, I mean 8-3. Of course, we lost to Alabama; that was one of their national championship years. That was probably their most definitive national championship year in that era. It wasn't split like in 1973 or 1978. In 1979 we were 8-3 and, relatively speaking, it was a huge success. We had a great rushing attack. That was one of the years we wore orange in a game or two. We tied eighth-ranked Georgia in 1978 in orange jerseys.

Auburn traveled to Athens on November 17, 1979, to meet a Bulldog team on the verge of winning a share of the SEC championship and going to the Sugar Bowl. Oddly enough, while only 5-4 overall, Georgia's four losses had come to non-conference opponents. Against fellow SEC members, they were undefeated.

The game was tight early on, but one key sequence seemed to indicate how the day would go for both teams. Midway through the first quarter, with the score still 0-0, Auburn had to punt from deep in their own territory, meaning UGA would likely begin their drive with good field position. The Bulldogs were called for holding on the play, however, giving Auburn a first down near midfield.

Again the Dogs held, but this time Auburn was able to punt from a much more advantageous area of the field. Skip Johnson's effort traveled 46 yards before a host of Tiger kick-coverage men downed the ball on the Georgia 2.

On the very next play, Georgia's Buck Belue took the snap, faked a handoff to his running back, and was instantly gobbled up in his own end zone by Auburn's Frank Warren, scoring a safety for the Tigers. Belue lay on the ground after the play, had to be carried off the field and was rushed to a nearby hospital, suffering from a dislocated ankle.

"I think he tried to pivot, his cleats caught in the ground and I hit him. I didn't know he was hurting when the play was over, though."
—*Frank Warren, Auburn defensive lineman*

Following the safety, Georgia was required by rule to free-kick the ball back to Auburn. The Tigers marched right back down the field in 10 plays, scoring the first touchdown of the game on a 1-yard plunge by Joe Cribbs. At that point, remarkably, Auburn had run eighteen plays while the Bulldogs had run one.

Georgia managed a couple of scores and actually led at the half, 10-9. They would only manage 3 more points the rest of the way, though.

When the third quarter began, Auburn's amazing running back duo, Joe Cribbs and James Brooks, took over. Cribbs scored on his second 1-yard touchdown run of the day, while Brooks exploded for scores coming from 67 and 44 yards away.

"Brooks and Cribbs made history Saturday, becoming the first two backs on one Southeastern Conference team to surpass the 1,000-yard mark. Brooks has 1,153 and Cribbs 1,027."
—*Roy Thomas, Montgomery Advertiser*

Against Georgia that day, the Tigers rushed for 392 yards, pushing their season total to 3,151, a school record for a season at that time.

The loss to Auburn not only bounced Georgia out of the SEC championship and the Sugar Bowl, it also dropped them to 5-5, meaning that even after they defeated Georgia Tech the following weekend, they still wouldn't go to a bowl game. From the Sugar to nothing, in one afternoon of football combat with the Auburn Tigers—the only SEC team to defeat them that season.

The game had repercussions not just in Auburn and Athens, but also in Tuscaloosa. By knocking Georgia out of the Sugar Bowl, Auburn actually did *Alabama* a disservice, as well. Bear Bryant was on the record as hoping Georgia would get the bid to New Orleans so his undefeated Tide could perhaps play a higher-ranked opponent in the Orange or Cotton Bowl, giving his team a clearer shot at the national championship. With Georgia out of the running for the

Sugar, Alabama would automatically get that bowl berth with a win in the Iron Bowl. If they lost to Auburn, and given the odd bowl game structure of the late Seventies, the Tide might actually miss out on a bowl game entirely.

"It's not up to me anymore. They (bowl officials) don't invite me. I guess if we win the next game (Auburn) we go to the Sugar Bowl. If we lose, we stay home. It's not up to me but, if we can't beat Auburn, I'd just as soon stay home and plow."
—Paul "Bear" Bryant, Alabama head coach

Of course, Alabama did go on to win the 1979 Iron Bowl, so the Bear did not have to stay home and plow. Auburn stayed home because probation prevented them from playing in a bowl game that season.

1980

Van Allen Plexico

In 1980, with expectations higher, we finished 5-6, with no wins in the SEC, a loss at home to top-ranked and eventual national champion Georgia, and blowout losses to Tennessee and Alabama. At the end of 1980 Doug Barfield was 0-5 against the Crimson Tide, albeit to very good Alabama teams. At that point he was 29-25-1 overall (he gained two wins thanks to Miss State having to forfeit two entire seasons). Auburn had had enough, and handed him his walking papers. He ended up, eventually, I think, as the Opelika High coach.

I'll never forget what Lewis Grizzard said about him. He wrote a column simply called "Doug Barfield," where he talked about how unfair and unreasonable bad ol', mean ol' Auburn was being, to fire poor Doug Barfield after 1980. With a record of 29-25-1. All I can figure is, that 1978 tie with UGA notwithstanding, Grizzard, the big Georgia fan that he was, wanted Barfield to be Auburn's coach for as long as possible.

John Ringer

It was a different era. The fans were more patient. It wasn't all a huge, money-making business yet. College coaches, unless they were terrible, or were doing something terrible, were supposed to be "institutions," and to be there at a college for twenty years, and that was the expectation.

Van Allen Plexico

So, in a way, Barfield was the first time Auburn began our tradition of having the reputation for having a "quick trigger finger" with firing coaches. It's funny that we get accused of that when you realize Alabama has had many more coaches than we have in that time. And yet you never hear anybody say Alabama has that "quick trigger finger." But we had Shug for a quarter of a century. Then, after Barfield, we had Pat Dye for twelve years. We had Terry Bowden through the mid-nineties. We still don't all agree over how that ended. We had Tuberville for another decade. And then Chizik, and then Gus, until the end of 2020. And that's it. That's it, going all the way back to 1976.

So, I mean, I just can't quite see how we have this reputation of having the "quick trigger finger" when we've had a handful of coaches going all the way back to the mid-Seventies.

John Ringer

It's perception, for the most part. But it's also caused by, like, if we don't outright fire them, we may not always be *happy* with them.

Van Allen Plexico

Yeah, we do a lot of waving the gun around, whether we pull the trigger or not, I guess. Maybe that's what they're thinking about. We're not that quick with the trigger but we do like to wave the gun around.

John Ringer

A good analogy.

As far as the Barfield era goes, I remember Auburn fans were there at the games, but I don't think there was a lot of confidence. I think everybody had a good time, but it wasn't really as enjoyable as it could have been, because we wanted to beat our rivals, and we were not accomplishing that, most of the time. There wasn't a lot of hope.

Van Allen Plexico

There was a thing that used to be called "the Auburn mindset." It involved understanding our limitations and tempering them to the realities of playing in the SEC and having Alabama as our main in-state rival. Shug used to talk about it.

I feel like my Auburn mindset back then was, "Man, I sure am tired of Alabama winning all the time." But we didn't feel back then like beating them even semi-regularly was a realistic goal. They were winning national championships under the Bear, and we couldn't even always beat Georgia Tech or Miss State. It just didn't seem realistic that we could compete with them every season on an even basis.

I remember thinking, "Gosh, I hope we at least have a winning season this year. And it would be awesome if we could beat Alabama. Maybe this is the year. Maybe *this* is the year we'll beat Alabama." Hope springs eternal, and every November, you'd be thinking, "Well, maybe this is the one. Maybe this is the one." But it never was, year after year.

And then I remember thinking, "Maybe we'll go to a bowl game." Because we hadn't been in a while. We could have gone to one in 1979, except that we were on probation. And let me just tell you, if you get on probation after consecutive seasons of 4-6-1 and 4-7 and 6-5 and 6-4-1, well, whatever shady thing you did to get on probation, maybe you needed to do *more* of it, not less. Because clearly it didn't work. [Laughter.]

John Ringer

It was not the Hugh Freeze full-implementation strategy. No.

Van Allen Plexico

I'm just trying to figure out why NCAA investigators even *looked* at Auburn in 1975-78. What investigator in his right mind looked at that team and said, "I need to investigate *those* guys. Clearly, there's something shady going on." I mean, wouldn't most investigators look at those seasons and say, "Oh, those boys are obviously toeing the line. They're honest to a fault, down there. Four-and-seven? There's nothing shady going on there." Wow. I mean, the NCAA probably would look at that 1976-77 team and call up Barfield and say, "You know, Coach, if you *need* to cheat a little bit, we could look the other way. We could look the other way this one time." I mean, come on, man. This is embarrassing. We got on probation while *losing*! I always say, if you've just got to cheat, at least *win*, right? At least get something out of it. Even if they take it away later, you still had that feeling. But the feeling they took away from us with that probation was the feeling of *four-and-seven*, John.

Gaaah.

Mike McClendon

Barfield's final year, 1980, reminds me in a lot of ways of Terry Bowden's last year in 1998. After finishing 8-3 in 1979 a lot of people thought we had turned the corner. There was a lot of optimism about where we were headed. We had a lot of the same thing in 1998. Terry had built up a lot of optimism and raised the expectations to a very high level.

In actuality, the optimism was not based on reality. We had lost key players from the 1979 team, and the talent level overall was down due to the recruiting problems. Again, the similarity to 1998 is striking.

We opened the year with good wins against TCU and Duke. Then Tennessee came to Auburn and handed us one of the worst losses in Auburn history, winning 42-0. It wasn't just that we lost, it was that we were completely outclassed in every way. Leaving that game, it was clear that we had serious problems, and that they weren't going to be fixed any time soon. Tennessee beat us because they had significantly better players all over the field. They were better prepared and better coached.

"We were beaten (by Tennessee) in every way known to Man."
—Doug Barfield, Auburn head coach

"It was very embarrassing. I'm still trying to figure out what happened, myself. Really, I thought I was dreaming. 42-0. If somebody finds out what happened, I wish they'd tell me. I just think we need some more leadership.
"I think our main problem is we just weren't tackling hard enough. I don't guess we were mentally prepared for the game."
—Frank Warren, Auburn defensive tackle

"In all the years I've been playing football, this is the first time I've ever been beaten like this."
—James Brooks, Auburn running back

Mike McClendon

When you have very high expectations, you simply cannot fall flat. You have to produce something. The Auburn team in 1980 was just not able to do that. No coach at Auburn, except maybe one in his first year, can survive an 0-fer season.

To summarize all of this, I think there were a variety of things that brought Barfield down. I'm not sure anyone could have done significantly better. (Meanwhile, the crap that was going on at Alabama made the things the NCAA nailed us for look like amateur hour.) In 1980 when you stopped to look at where we were and where we were headed, it was clear that we had to make a change. We had to change the entire program if we were going to be competitive. This whole finesse thing was never going to work, and we had to find someone who could change that completely. You had to find someone who understood the crap that was coming out of Tuscaloosa and who knew how to play the game on the same level. There was no choice but to move on from Barfield.

With an overall record of 29-25-1, Doug Barfield was gone, and Auburn needed a new head coach.

And even as Barfield was being let go, the University of Georgia was preparing to defeat Notre Dame in the Sugar Bowl and claim the national championship. Their head coach at the time just happened to be a former Auburn quarterback. Consequently, there was a certain buzz on the Plains.

Van Allen Plexico
You probably remember this better than I do, because I was just seeing it on Birmingham local TV. You were actually over in Georgia. Who were they talking about getting?

John Ringer
Vince Dooley. Oh, man. He was an Auburn alum and he was winning the national title. Yeah, I think if they had not won the national title at Georgia and with Herschel Walker as just a freshman on that team, I think we might have hired him.

Van Allen Plexico
I think so. But I think there was just no way he could leave Georgia after 1980. And with Herschel still there? That'd be insane. That's like if Pat Dye had left Auburn after 1982 to go to Florida, and left Bo Jackson and Lionel James and that defense they had built. But, on the other hand, hadn't Johnny Majors just left Pitt after a national championship to go to Tennessee?

John Ringer
Yes, pretty soon after.

Van Allen Plexico
So there was a precedent for it. I think it was Herschel being there, as much as it was the national championship, because Johnny Majors had just done it after the 1976 season. Auburn people were looking at what Majors had done and saying, "Hey, if he would leave a national championship-

winning team and program to come to his alma mater, then maybe Vince would do the same thing."

We tried to get him. Ultimately, though, he remained in Athens. Georgia was poised for a few more very good years, and it's tough to walk away after you have built something like that.

Mike McClendon

The search for a new coach started long before the 1980 season was done and Barfield was fired. There were high expectations going into the 1980 season, and none of them were realistic. After Tennessee wiped the field with Auburn, Barfield was done. You had to play the rest of the season, but it was over. The Board of Trustees and especially Fob James, who was the governor, were ready to move on.

Vince Dooley had accepted the job and actually signed a contract before he backed out. The real problem was that the whole thing with Dooley was done under the table for the most part during the season. Fob James, who was governor at the time and Dooley's college roommate, had worked all this out. It all fell apart once the season was done, Barfield was fired and they began to seriously try to hire someone.

Another thing to remember is that Auburn really did not have the money to hire a big-name coach. Bobby Lowder paid half of Pat Dye's original salary through a personal services contract. In 1980, Auburn football was really in dire shape in a lot of ways.

Phillip Marshall, formerly of the *Montgomery Advertiser* and now of 24/7 Sports, has told Bobby Lowder's version of the story of Dooley's near-hire. Lowder said that Fob James had indeed grown tired of Barfield's act by 1980 and decided to pursue his old roommate as Auburn's next coach. Lowder was prepared to pay Dooley $50,000 himself, with another $100,000 coming from Auburn. Dooley agreed in principle, but changed his mind when he returned to Athens and found out Georgia was about to name him the new athletic director.

At that point, according to Lowder, James told him, "I'm through. Go hire who you want."

Mike McClendon

Bobby Bowden wanted the job. This was before Bowden became a household name at Florida State. He had been at FSU for four years and had them rolling. Plus, Bowden had a lot of ties throughout the state of Alabama. Bowden wanted to coach in the state of Alabama and he tried to get both the Auburn and Alabama jobs at different points in time.

Bowden would have been an interesting hire. He was a great coach and an equally great recruiter. It would have been interesting to see how he would have fared against Bryant and the machine at Alabama.

The guy who absolutely wanted the AU job was Jackie Sherrill, who at the time was the head coach at Pittsburgh. Sherrill pretty much begged Lowder for the job and was ready to accept on the spot. Sherrill has taken over the Pitt program from Johnny Majors and had been very successful. He was probably the highest profile coach in the running. Sherrill was another coach from the Bryant and Alabama system.

Sherrill stayed at Pitt through 1981 and was very successful there. He then took the Texas A&M job and was there for seven years. He won the old Southwestern Conference three times. He then went to Mississippi State where he stayed for thirteen years. Sherrill took State to their one and only SEC West championship. He left them in a very bad situation including problems with the NCAA; big problems.

Auburn interviewed a bunch of guys for the job in 1980. Part of the reason Pat Dye got the job was that the Alabama folks, including Bryant, were so adamantly *opposed* to him coming to Auburn. Bryant pretty much promised Dye the head coaching job at Alabama if he would wait a couple years.

Van Allen Plexico

With Barfield out and Dooley a no-go, we looked around for the next-best candidate. What did you think when that new name emerged? Do you remember thinking anything about it? I mean, I have vague memories.

John Ringer
I wasn't exactly doing flight tracking back then.

Van Allen Plexico
You weren't looking at the tail number on the airplane?

John Ringer
We're joking about it, but they probably didn't even do planes back then. They just drove around and met in some coffee shop.

Van Allen Plexico
Well, it was a coffee shop somewhere between Auburn and Wyoming, I guess.

John Ringer
That's it. So, no, I didn't have any feeling in particular when I heard we had hired the Wyoming coach. I was like, "Well, I hope he's better than what we just had." That was kind of my feeling.

Interestingly enough, Shug Jordan had actually recruited Pat Dye to play for Auburn, back in the Fifties. He was friends with Dye's father, and one day in 1957 Shug was sitting on the elder Dye's porch, chatting with him for a while. Finally, as he was about to leave, Shug asked if he could speak with the younger Dye, who was a high school senior and a coveted recruit. Pat came out and said hello, and Shug told him he'd love to have Pat at Auburn and would welcome him onto the team—but he also understood the young man was probably going to follow his older brothers to Athens, and there wouldn't be any bad feelings. At the end of their brief conversation, Shug told Pat, "I want you to know there will always be a place for you at Auburn."

How prophetic those words would prove to be.

"And I am confident that with the support of the Auburn people, alumni, the former players, the student body, the faculty, administration, that we will be able to bring this great football tradition back to what it once was."

—*Pat Dye, introductory press conference, 1980*

Van Allen Plexico

The first thing we really heard about Pat Dye, he'd been the coach at East Carolina and then, for a couple of years, he was at Wyoming.

Wyoming gave Pat Dye an ultimatum. He would have to sign a new contract with the school, or they would consider him gone and start looking for a new coach. Dye refused to sign the contract, so Wyoming moved on. Dye was unemployed when Auburn hired him.

"I think Pat Dye would have come (to Auburn) for nothing. The subject of money didn't even come up until he'd taken the job. He said 'what are you going to pay me?' We told him I'd pay him $50,000 and his university salary would be $50,000. He said 'sounds good to me' and that was it."
—*Bobby Lowder, interview with Phillip Marshall, 2020*

Van Allen Plexico

We later learned he hadn't gotten along well with the ECU administration, and had jumped at the first chance to leave, seeing Wyoming as the opportunity for a new adventure, as well as an escape hatch from a bad situation in Greenville.

My reaction was, "The *Wyoming* coach? Well, that doesn't sound good." But then you find out, "Oh, he's one of Bear's boys." As an Auburn fan, I was initially turned off by the very idea that he was associated with Bryant. "Well, I don't think I approve of this 'Bear' connection." As someone who wanted the best football coach we could get, though, I had to grudgingly admit that maybe hiring one of Bear's disciples wasn't the worst idea ever—as long as he would be loyal to Auburn and not to Alabama. Clearly the Bear could coach, even if we despised him. If Dye learned something from him there, that was good.

The second thing we learned about him was, he had been a Georgia Bulldog, an offensive lineman, of all things.

It all added up to a kind of pedigree. It wasn't a *head coaching* pedigree, necessarily. His head coaching resume was pretty thin, really. But he had the right kind of background.

He was an old country boy from Georgia. He was an All-American player in Athens. And the story came out that he'd been in the Army and, right when he got out of the Army, he called up Bear Bryant and asked for a job, and Bear said, "Be in my office first thing tomorrow morning." So Dye showed up in his Army uniform— I think it was his dress uniform, because that was all he owned—at Bryant's office, at something like five o'clock in the morning. And of course Bear was already there, saying, "What took you so long? You're late." Bryant always prided himself on working ridiculously long hours, and he expected his assistants to do the same. I always used to wonder what Bryant would've made of Steve Spurrier, who, in his heyday, dressed and acted like he was always in a hurry to wrap up the football activities and get to his tee time at the country club.

Dye got that assistant job at Alabama and worked his way up from there. There are always these fun stories about how coaches started out their careers, just doing anything. You remember, Tommy Tuberville lived in a trailer and was frying catfish in a fish restaurant or something.

Pat Dye had left a fairly decent situation as head coach at East Carolina after the 1979 season because he wasn't getting along well with the university president. He spent a year at Wyoming and has said he enjoyed life out there, but it had to be like an alien planet to him and, clearly, he had designs on getting back to the Southeast. Despite warnings from the Bear not to do it, he came in for an interview for the Auburn job.

John Ringer

They asked him how long it would take him to beat Alabama, and he said, "sixty minutes."

Van Allen Plexico

Yep. It actually took him 120 minutes. But that's quibbling, right? Because we lost the first time, in 1981, but we did give them a tough game.

John Ringer

The spirit of the answer was right. Absolutely. The spirit of the answer was not, "I need a five-year plan." It was, "Let me get on the field with them and I will beat them."

Van Allen Plexico

Yeah. What he was saying was, "You have to play football for all sixty minutes." So, rather than saying, "It's going to take me this many years to build a program up to that level," he was saying, "If my guys will play to the best of their abilities for sixty minutes of football, we can beat them," and that was true.

It didn't hurt having the greatest athlete in history as a freshman running back that second year, either.

1981

Van Allen Plexico

That first season with Coach Dye, we finished 5-6. And I remember my granddad saying, "Well, he had the same record as the guy we just fired." Granddaddy wasn't that patient. But we did win a couple of SEC games, and the ones we lost were competitive. We did lose another one of those stupid Wake Forest games. In fact, the Wake Forest game on September 19, that we lost by three, was the first regular-season night game we ever played at home. Unfortunately, the Demon Deacons knocked our lights out with their short passing game, 24-21.

"When the pass opened up underneath, we took advantage of it. I'm not a genius, but I know when it's working, we should keep on doing it."
—Al Groh, Wake Forest head coach

"Some of the things we did wrong tonight I cannot fault the players for. It is the coaches. We have to get them lined up right."

—Pat Dye

Van Allen Plexico

The next week we went up to Neyland Stadium to play Tennessee, and that was a team we had struggled with the last few years. In front of 92,612 people, Auburn came within three points of knocking off the Vols. It was an absolute heartbreaker. Pat Dye spoke in the locker room afterward and delivered those lines that have become so well-known among Auburn people. The players were down and disappointed and some of them were crying, and that's when he gave that speech that really got them motivated going forward from there.

"There's gonna be a lot of days when you lay your guts on the line and you come away empty handed. There ain't a damn thing you can do about it but go back and lay them on the line again. And again and again.

"Every coach, every manager, is glad to be associated with you.

"You will keep fighting like you did today, you keep playing like that, we will build a foundation that we can live on a long, long time, at Auburn."

—Pat Dye, in the locker room after the 1981 loss at Tennessee

John Ringer

You've got to put it on the line. Yeah, you've got to do it again and again and again.

Van Allen Plexico

And you're not always going to win, but that's all right. You just get up and you do it again. That's right. And it was really motivating, very inspirational.

The next week we went to Lincoln, Nebraska, and played the Cornhuskers, who was a year away from being the alleged "team of the century," and we lost 17-3, and that's not bad. In fact, the story was the Nebraska fans, who appreciate teams who give them a good fight, applauded the Auburn players when they left the field.

Pat Dye, by Jarrod Alberich

70

Against Nebraska, Auburn actually led, 3-0, at the half. Unfortunately, the Tigers turned the ball over seven times in a downpour, gifting the Huskers with touchdown drives of 7 and 9 yards.

Van Allen Plexico

This was before Bo, too. There was no Bo Jackson on this team. This was just a scrappy bunch in their first year under Pat Dye. Only his fourth game as our head coach. We went and lost by three at Tennessee and lost by fourteen at Lincoln, Nebraska. And you could tell something was changing. The tide was turning a little bit, so to speak.

Auburn under Pat Dye had changed offensive approaches. Gone was Doug Barfield's "Power-I." In its place, Dye and his assistants installed the wishbone.

The wishbone resulted from the contributions of a number of coaches over the years, but its "father" has always been considered to be Emory Bellard, the offensive coordinator for Darrell Royal at Texas in the 1960s and 1970s. Oklahoma used the formation to great success under Barry Switzer, setting rushing records that still stand, and Bear Bryant installed a version of it at Alabama.

The wishbone is a triple-option rushing attack, meaning the quarterback has three rushing options on a given play, in addition to passing the ball. One option is to give the ball to the fullback, who is standing a short distance behind him at the start of the play, and who then dives into the middle of the line of scrimmage. When defenses react to this by attacking the middle of the line, the quarterback can go to the second option, which is to keep the ball himself and look for a hole to the right or left of center to dive through. The third option is for the quarterback to pitch the ball to one of the two halfbacks, the traditional "running backs" of the formation. The halfbacks stand just behind and to either side of the fullback, thus completing the "Y"-shaped "wishbone" formation. The halfback who catches the ball sweeps to either side of the formation and looks to cut up field, while the other halfback can serve as a lead blocker.

One major benefit of the wishbone attack is that it tends to overpower one portion of the defense with a larger number of blockers ahead of the ball carrier. It is therefore a formation favored by smaller teams—for example, the service academies such as Army, Navy and Air Force—who often require a numbers advantage to compensate for their players' relative smaller size.

Alabama under Bear Bryant used the wishbone to great success in the Seventies, and Bear's former assistant, Pat Dye, turned to it as soon as he took over at Auburn.

Van Allen Plexico

We'd gone to the wishbone under Pat Dye. What did you think about that? We'd been using all kinds of offensive sets and formations under Barfield. Dye came in and put in the wishbone when it was still kind of the cutting-edge thing.

John Ringer

Oh yeah, that was exciting. I mean, it was different from what we'd been doing, and from what most teams were doing. And it was fun.

Football wasn't the same back then. Drives were much longer and slower, because there weren't many explosive, chunk-kind of plays. It was more running than passing, by far, but the wishbone seemed to generate big plays on offense, and keep the other team off balance, and it allowed you to keep the ball away from them. It was great, and we had good players for it. It was fun to watch the quarterback making quick decisions and it was fun to watch the running backs in it. I enjoyed the wishbone. We started putting it in immediately under Pat Dye and I thought it was really entertaining to watch.

Van Allen Plexico

Particularly when we found the quarterback that could run it so smoothly, in the person of Randy Campbell in 1982. In 1981 we were still feeling around for a quarterback. Ken Hobby played a good bit, and Joe Sullivan. We actually had six quarterbacks on the roster that year and five of them threw at least one pass. Ironically, the only one that didn't attempt a pass would be the starting quarterback the next fall: Randy Campbell. The *Inside the Auburn Tigers* magazine in the summer of 1982 had a cover image of a quarterback with no face, and the headline read, "Question at Quarterback." That wouldn't be the case for much longer, though!

We had several there in the mid-Seventies through the early Eighties that were mostly *running* quarterbacks, or at least that's how they were used. Phil Gargis; Charlie Trotman. The Sullivan-to-Beasley air attack days seemed to be well and truly behind us at that point.

After that relatively close loss at Nebraska, Auburn welcomed LSU to Jordan-Hare and beat them, 19-7, in what was really the first big win for Coach Dye. It was only his second win at Auburn. It didn't hurt that it was the same day that Southern Mississippi shocked Bear Bryant's Alabama by tying them, 13-13.

Even more shocking was the fact that it represented Auburn's first win over LSU since 1942! It was only the sixth time the two Tigers teams had played one another since that year, but LSU had won all of the previous five.

Auburn's quarterbacking corps had been shaken up by injuries, promotions and demotions prior to the LSU game. Even so, they gained 257 yards rushing on 72 attempts, while completing only four passes the entire game.

"Auburn used four quarterbacks (in the LSU game)—John Murphy, Joe Sullivan (who had the flu), Randy Campbell and Clayton Beauford, in that order. Regular starting quarterback Charles Thomas was moved to halfback and backup Ken Hobby was out with a sprained ankle."
—Darryal Ray, Montgomery Advertiser

"Our defensive football team has been getting better each week. They are playing well together and having fun. I've got to be proud of the players, the coaches and the whole organization for coming back from three straight heartbreakers that we should have won."
—Pat Dye

The next week, Auburn went to play Georgia Tech at Grant Field. The Yellowjackets had upset Alabama, 24-21, in the first week of the season.

Auburn was not impressed. The Tigers beat the Rambling Wreck, in what appeared to be a laugher, 31-7, but the game was actually much closer than the score would indicate.

Early in the fourth quarter, Auburn led by a score of 17-7, but Tech was attempting a field goal that could have narrowed the gap to one score, at 17-10. Instead, AU defensive back David King blocked the kick and linebacker Chris Martin returned it 77 yards for a touchdown. Instead of being within seven points, Bill Curry's Yellowjackets were suddenly down 24-7. The Tigers would go on to add one more insurance score before the game was over.

"Even if it had not been run back for a touchdown, it would have been the turning point. It gave the game a different complexion. If we kicked the ball, it was a chip shot, the score is 17-10. Instead, they run it back for a score and the momentum is in their favor."
—*Bill Curry, Georgia Tech head coach*

John Ringer
The wins over LSU and Georgia Tech gave us the sense that we were turning things around. There was some momentum building.

Van Allen Plexico
Yeah, it was very similar to Tommy Tuberville's first year where we went 5-6 under him in 1999, but you could feel that things were changing. There was a different sense to it all.

Pat Dye and his players would talk about "wolf sign." He would say there's "wolf sign" all around after a practice. Everything's all bloody and torn up. Some of our best players in 1981 said that the toughest practices they ever had in college or pro football were during that first year in 1981 under Pat Dye. Our big defensive lineman, Edmund Nelson, later said he wanted a t-shirt that said, "I survived the 1981 Auburn spring practice." "Pat Dye tried to kill us," he basically said later. Coach Dye drove off some guys. But the ones that stayed... It's like the famous story of Bear Bryant at Texas A&M with the "Junction Boys." The ones that stayed had been through the fire together.

Pat Dye would talk about wolf sign, like blood and fur and bits of skin lying around on the ground and it looks like everything's torn up. And that's what his early practices supposedly looked like: blood and fur lying around and things having been torn up.

I think Pat Dye pretty much conveyed the sense that things were changing and changing pretty rapidly, and certainly the next season would be a different year for Auburn football.

Meanwhile, after a narrow, 21-17 loss to a top ten-ranked Mississippi State team, we beat Florida at home, which is always awesome. And we did it on Halloween; we seemed to play Florida on Halloween a lot back then.

The game was another nail-biter, though.

Auburn led the Gators late in the fourth quarter, 14-12, and was running out the clock when quarterback Ken Hobby fumbled. Florida recovered on the Auburn 31. Three plays later, Brian Clark came out to attempt a field goal that would give the Gators the lead in the game's waning moments, and probably the victory. Clark had made four field goals already. This time, however, the kick sailed wide left.

"I knew we could hold them. I didn't know (Florida's kicker, Brian) Clark was going to miss that field goal. He'd been kicking since warmups and that was the first one he missed."
—Pat Dye

The defense had come through again, stopping the Gators in their tracks and forcing them to try for the kick.

"We have a lot of fun out there on defense. We enjoy playing, going out there and going after the quarterback and passing some licks. Like I said, we got a little tired in the fourth quarter, but we sucked it up. We had a good time."
—Donnie Humphrey, Auburn defensive lineman, who sacked Florida's quarterback three times

Van Allen Plexico

After beating Florida, we went on to lose by eleven to a great, fourth-ranked Georgia team. Turnovers killed any chance we had of pulling the upset.

The Tigers again played well on defense against Georgia, and again were the victims of turnovers and mistakes by their own offense.

"For the season, Auburn has fumbled 48 times to its opponents' 20 and lost 22 to its opponents' 12. That is not the prescribed path to victory."
—Phillip Marshall, Montgomery Advertiser

After taking a 7-3 lead, and on the way to rushing for an amazing 282 yards against the Bulldogs' vaunted defense, Auburn turned the ball over three times. Georgia quarterback Buck Belue responded by throwing for two touchdowns, putting UGA ahead for good in the second quarter. Herschel Walker added a rushing touchdown in the third to put the game on ice. Auburn's fourth quarter touchdown served only cosmetic purposes.

Walker rushed 37 times for 165 yards in the game, but was held to a long of only 19 yards. Auburn meanwhile had *eight* different players rush for double-digit yards, led by backs George Peoples and Lionel James. It simply wasn't enough.

"Georgia hasn't played anybody that can run the ball. We're not great, but we can run it a lot better than anybody they've played."
—Pat Dye

Van Allen Plexico

Georgia moved up to second in the polls after beating us. Alabama came up to take that no. 4 spot they'd been in. So we ended up playing the no. 4 team in the country two games in a row.

It looked like the loss to Georgia had ruined our chances at a bowl game. What we had left was a shot at ruining Alabama's season and the Bear's big celebration.

The 1981 Iron Bowl was big for a number of reasons, mostly involved Alabama. For a while, though, it looked like Auburn might trump all those storylines by pulling of a stunning upset.

Auburn missed numerous opportunities to build a lead over the shell-shocked Tide early. The Tigers held the Tide to three-and-out on their first possession, and then Auburn return man Chuck Clanton returned the punt back to the Tide 13-yard line. The Tigers could do nothing on offense, however, and Al Del Greco missed his field goal attempt. Later, with Alabama leading 7-0, Tiger QB Ken Hobby threw an interception at the Alabama 1 yard line. On the next Tigers possession, Del Greco missed another field goal, this one from the 26.

Fullback George Peoples finally leveled the score by racing for a 63-yard touchdown with 3:47 to go before halftime. Just after that, the Tigers recovered an Alabama fumble at the Tide 10—but they squandered yet another scoring opportunity. They were held to a field goal attempt but, this time, Del Greco never even got the opportunity to kick; holder Joe Sullivan fumbled the snap and Alabama recovered to end the threat. The two teams went into the break tied 7-7, but Alabama knew they had been extremely fortunate to survive the Auburn onslaught and to not be trailing by multiple scores.

In the third quarter, Alabama scored a quick touchdown to go ahead, 14-7. They then forced Auburn to punt, but Joey Jones fumbled the return and Auburn recovered on the Tide's 2 yard line. Lionel James took it around right end for the score, and the game was tied again, 14-14, midway through the third.

On Auburn's next punt, Jones fumbled again. This time Auburn was held to a Del Greco field goal, but it put the Tigers ahead, 17-14, two minutes into the fourth quarter. The Tigers led Alabama in the final frame, and Tide fans were suffering heart failure all across Legion Field.

That was when Alabama found its offense and put the game away. They scored on a Walter Lewis pass with 10:07 remaining, then on a 32-yard run by Linnie Patrick with 7:07 to go.

Auburn made a final effort to catch up, but Hobby was intercepted by Alabama at their own 7 yard line, after which the Tide ran out the clock.

"We were lucky to come out victorious. We knew they (Auburn) were tough and expected that type of game. We expect great things from them in the future."
—Joey Jones, Alabama wide receiver

The final minutes notwithstanding, the Tigers' defense played a marvelous game. Auburn actually outgained Alabama, 311 yards to 279, and ran 87 plays to Alabama's 64. Auburn's fullback, George Peoples, was the game's leading rusher, with 155 yards on 26 carries.

"In the third quarter, I didn't know what to think. I didn't know what we were going to have to do to win... We have better personnel than Auburn but they were very well-prepared. Pat Dye has done a great, great job. I told (assistant athletic director) Charley Thornton to vote for him for Coach of the Year."
—Paul "Bear" Bryant, Alabama head coach

"I hope we didn't disappoint anybody. I'd like to congratulate Coach Bryant and the Alabama football team on their accomplishment here today.
"I'm proud of our players and our coaches. We had a good enough plan to win."
—Pat Dye

Pat Dye's words at his interview had proven correct: It would take 60 minutes to beat Alabama, and on this day in 1981, the Tigers had played only about 50. But they were getting much closer than before, and the time was coming.

John Ringer

Another significant thing about that Iron Bowl was, it was Bear Bryant's 315th win. Amos Alonzo Stagg had won 314 games in his coaching career, which was the record up until then.

Van Allen Plexico

The Bear became the winningest Division I coach in history for a while. When word started getting out at the beginning of the season that he would probably be setting the record by winning his 315th game that season, I looked at the schedule and noted with relief that it would probably happen a couple of games before the Iron Bowl. Remember—back then, it was generally safe to assume Alabama would win all or most of them every year.

In 1981, however, that wasn't the case. They lost to Georgia Tech in week 2, and I thought, "Oh, gosh—there's not much leeway now! If they lose one more game, the Iron Bowl will be for his big record-setting win. And I most definitely did not want that to be the case. Just knowing how much more motivation Alabama would have to win against us, and how much more their fans would rub it in if we were the ones to lose that big game. So I was hoping for Alabama to either go undefeated the rest of the way, or else lose a few more!

Then they got tied by Southern Miss on October 10, and that meant that if they won the rest of the way, the Iron Bowl potentially would be the 315 game. I was miserable at the thought! And, of course, they won the rest of the way. To me, it always seemed inevitable that it would play out that way. It was Bear's coronation, he was the king of all college football, and beating us in the Iron Bowl to achieve that was just the cherry on top for them.

We didn't go to a bowl, so that game marked the end of Pat Dye's first year. As Auburn fans, we weren't thrilled with 5-6, but you had to feel like things were getting better, right?

John Ringer

Absolutely. Things were moving in the right direction.

Van Allen Plexico

So, you and I, at this point at the beginning of the Eighties, we were still in our hometowns, in grade school. But even then, we probably knew that one of these days we would be down there on the Plains, as part of that student section. I don't know if we could have ever guessed that by the time we got there, Auburn would be winning, and winning a lot—beating Alabama four years in a row, 1986-89. Playing Alabama *in* Auburn for the first time ever. Winning three SEC championships in a row.

John Ringer
Nope.

Van Allen Plexico
You can see why Pat Dye became so beloved so quickly.

Now that we've spelled out what it was like to be an Auburn fan *before* Pat Dye, and how it changed when he arrived, we're ready to look at what it was like in his early years on the Plains, when things were getting better and better. We had Bo. We had Lionel James and Brent Fullwood. We had a defense that was world-class. After so many years of having a sieve for a defense, we suddenly and completely flipped that. For many years afterward, Auburn having a rock-solid and reliable defense was the one thing you could depend on. Pat Dye is the one that made Auburn and "defense" synonymous for so very long. And it made all the difference.

Any final thoughts as far as up through 1981, and what it was like as an Auburn fan, and what it felt like going forward from there?

John Ringer
There was untapped potential. It was hard to see it at the time, with a 5-6 record, but you could sense it coming. There were not a lot of huge wins early on, and it wasn't a great season at the start, but the losses were close and the team looked a lot tougher than before. We enjoyed what the team had become in only one season, and we looked forward to brighter days ahead.

"There's no question we made a lot of progress with our program. Nobody likes to lose, but our players have accepted our way and I think they believe in our way. I'd rather have that than have a couple more wins and face problems down the road."
—Pat Dye, after the 1981 Iron Bowl

Oh, indeed things were changing on the Plains, and changing much more rapidly than many would have guessed. The defense was getting stronger. A quarterback able to operate the wishbone to near-perfection was trapped at sixth on the depth chart for the moment—but not for much longer. And a certain young running back with the given name of "Vincent" would soon be departing McAdory High for the Loveliest Village on the Plain, and he would change everything.

No, it would not be long at all before we would be hearing those famous words, courtesy of Jim Fyffe:

"Give to Bo—up and over! And in! Touchdown! Touchdown Auburn!"

1975:

4-6-1 overall; 2-4 SEC

9/13	Memphis St	L	20-31
9/20	at Baylor	T	10-10
9/27	at (16) Tennessee	L	17-21
10/4	Virginia Tech	L	16-23
10/11	at Kentucky	W	15-9
10/18	at Georgia Tech	W	31-27
10/25	at Florida State	W	17-14
11/1	(11) Florida	L	14-31
11/8	Miss State	W	21-21*
11/15	at (20) Georgia	L	13-28
11/29	(4) Alabama (Bham)	L	0-28

*MSU later forfeited this game.

1976:

4-7 overall; 3-3 SEC

9/11	at Arizona	L	19-31
9/18	Baylor	L	14-15
9/25	Tennessee (Bham)	W	38-28
10/2	at (16) Ole Miss	W	10-0
10/9	Memphis St	L	27-28
10/16	Georgia Tech	L	10-28
10/23	Florida State	W	31-19
10/30	at (12) Florida	L	19-24
11/6	Miss St (Jackson)	W	19-28*
11/13	(7) Georgia	L	0-28
11/27	at (18) Alabama (Bham)	L	7-38

*MSU later forfeited this game.

1977:

6-5 overall; 5-1 SEC

9/10	Arizona	W	21-10
9/17	Southern Miss	L	13-24
9/24	at Tennessee	W	14-12
10/1	Ole Miss	W	21-15
10/8	NC State	L	15-17
10/15	at Georgia Tech	L	21-38
10/22	at Florida St	L	3-24
10/29	(18) Florida	W	29-14
11/5	Miss State	W	13-27*
11/12	at Georgia	W	33-14
11/26	(2) Alabama (Bham)	L	21-48

*MSU later forfeited this game.

1978:

6-4-1 overall; 3-2-1 SEC

9/16	at Kansas St	W	45-32
9/23	at Virginia Tech	W	18-7
9/30	Tennessee (Bham)	W	29-10
10/7	Miami FL	L	15-17
10/14	at Vanderbilt	W	49-7
10/21	Georgia Tech	L	10-24
10/28	Wake Forest	W	21-7
11/4	at Florida	L	7-31
11/11	at Miss State	W	6-0
11/18	(8) Georgia	T	22-22
12/2	at (2) Alabama (Bham)	L	16-34

1979:

8-3 overall; 4-2 SEC

9/15	Kansas St	W	26-18
9/22	Southern Miss	W	31-9
9/29	at Tennessee	L	17-35
10/6	(14) NC State	W	44-31
10/13	Vanderbilt	W	52-35
10/20	at Georgia Tech	W	38-14
10/27	at (18) Wake Forest	L	38-42
11/3	Florida	W	19-13
11/10	at Miss State	W	14-3
11/17	at Georgia	W	33-13
12/1	(1) Alabama (Bham)	L	18-25

Final AP Ranking: 16

1980:

5-6 overall; 0-6 SEC

9/13	at TCU	W	10-7
9/20	Duke	W	35-28
9/27	Tennessee	L	0-42
10/4	Richmond	W	55-16
10/11	at LSU	L	17-21
10/18	Georgia Tech	W	17-14
10/25	Miss State (Jackson)	L	7-21
11/1	at Florida	L	10-21
11/8	Southern Miss	W	31-0
11/15	(1) Georgia	L	21-31
11/29	at (9) Alabama (Bham)	L	18-34

1981:

5-6 overall; 2-4 SEC

9/5	TCU	W	24-16
9/19	Wake Forest	L	21-24
9/26	at Tennessee	L	7-10
10/3	at Nebraska	L	3-17
10/10	LSU	W	19-7
10/17	at Georgia Tech	W	31-7
10/24	Miss State	L	17-21
10/31	Florida	W	14-12
11/7	N Texas	W	20-0
11/14	at Georgia	L	13-24
11/28	Alabama (Bham)	L	17-28

-2-

SUGAR SWEET
Pat Dye, 1982-1983

"Fourth and goal to go for Auburn and I see the Auburn players are asking for quiet.

"Nobody split, give the ball to Bo. Up and over—and in, I believe! Touchdown! Touchdown Auburn!"

"Well, that was pure second effort by Bo Jackson. Everyone knew what was coming. He got hit behind the line but got in."
—Jim Fyffe and Pat Sullivan on the radio broadcast of the 1982 Iron Bowl

There had been no question things had to change at Auburn, and change in a big way, at the end of Doug Barfield's five-year run as head coach. The question was, what changes had to be made—what changes were advisable, and which ones were possible—and who would actually be able to pull them off?

Mike McClendon
Most Auburn people do not like being compared to Alabama, and Alabama fans certainly don't like to draw any

comparisons to Auburn. However, the two schools are interrelated in just about every way possible. You can't understand Auburn football unless you have a good understanding of Alabama football and Bear Bryant specifically. Bryant's impact on football in the state of Alabama is tremendous. That is not just about what happened in Tuscaloosa. It impacted Auburn and changed Auburn as much as it changed Alabama. Bryant was the leader. His approach to football, while not entirely new, was different. From the time he stepped on the practice field in Tuscaloosa, everyone else was playing catch up. From his second year at Alabama in 1959 until 1963, Auburn not only did not beat Alabama, they did not *score* on them. In that period Alabama beat Auburn by a combined score of 85-0. Between 1958 and 1968, Auburn managed to score 10 or more points 4 times, and Auburn managed over 14 points only once, in 1968.

Bryant gave everyone the blueprint for a successful football team. He did it at Kentucky, replicated it at Texas A&M and then brought it to Alabama. It wasn't difficult to understand. Bryant played hard-nosed, win-at-all-costs, physical football. His teams played defense, *physical* defense. They didn't just beat their opponents; they wore them out in the process. Alabama invented that fourth quarter hand-in-the-air salute because when it came to the fourth quarter, they were the best team on the field.

When Doug Barfield left Auburn in December 1980, Auburn had a lot of problems. Auburn was still under NCAA sanctions. The team had very little real SEC-caliber talent returning. Recruiting was in a sad state, and that is being kind. Support for the program was at its lowest point since before Shug Jordan took over in the early 1950s. The athletic department was having trouble selling season tickets. You didn't have to buy a priority to get season tickets. They were begging people to take them in August and September. The Auburn radio network was paying affiliates to carry the games. It was bad.

Everyone knew that a major change was needed. It wasn't just implementing a new offense or new schemes. If Auburn was going to be competitive in football, Auburn needed to press the reset button and start over. Alabama was the model for the restart. (A lot of Auburn people will not want to hear that, but it is true.) The model for a winning football program was a physical, hard-nosed team, the kind of team that was whipping us annually in Birmingham in November. The problem, of course, was that you were starting from a deficit, and recruiting the talent to accomplish that was difficult (*very* difficult). Auburn was going to have to *build* those teams, at least initially, and they were going to have to do it by developing the players they had and were able to get.

Pat Dye was about as opposite from Doug Barfield as was possible. Dye was an All-American offensive lineman at Georgia under Wally Butts. He coached linebackers for Bear Bryant at Alabama. He knew about physical football from his time playing at Georgia. He understood Bryant's philosophy of football, and more importantly he understood what was required to play the kind of football Auburn needed. Dye was not simply a coaching change. He was a *culture* change. From the moment he was introduced as the head coach and the moment he took over, everything was different.

The 1981 season showed us all the potential of what Auburn football could be.

Though the Tigers hadn't been able to lure Vince Dooley away from Georgia, some wondered if perhaps this up-and-coming former Bulldog from that same state, by way of Alabama, East Carolina and Wyoming would actually turn out to be the perfect fit for the Loveliest Village.

Perhaps, many of us thought, all this new coach needed was a little time and patience. That, and maybe a few more top-level players, to lift our team's talent level up to near that of our competition. After all, Dye's first team had come oh-so-close in most of its six losses, with just the talent the team already had on hand.

Mike McClendon

There have been a lot of great football teams at Auburn. In my almost seventy years of going to Auburn games and watching Auburn play, my favorite team is Pat Dye's first team in 1981. That team finished 5-6. There wasn't a lot of talent on that team. (There were players on that roster who would turn out to be very good players at Auburn. I do not mean to imply that the team had nothing to work with, because that was not true. There just wasn't an *abundance*.)

Dye didn't have the time or the means to really recruit after he was hired in 1980. He was playing with the players who were left by Doug Barfield, and it was not much. Still, that team played with more heart and effort than any Auburn team I have ever seen. They lost to Tennessee in Knoxville, 10-7. They lost to Georgia in Athens, 24-13, in a game where they had a chance to win in the fourth quarter. They gave a great Nebraska team in Lincoln all they could handle before falling, 17-3. That team left everything on the field in every game. Even today, I am convinced that if we could get Auburn teams to play with a fraction of the heart and effort that the 1981 team had, we would be unstoppable.

Pat Dye brought physical, hard-nosed, smash-mouth football back to Auburn University. Auburn might lose, but when the game was over the opponent was going to limp off the field just glad it was over. Also, they marked their calendars for the next time to remember what was coming. Pat Dye brought a different attitude, a different work ethic and, more than anything else, *confidence*. That was the biggest change.

Again—let me apologize for this, but—what Pat Dye brought to Auburn was Alabama football. It was the same philosophy and methodology that he had learned under Bryant and that had built the program at Alabama. It was all about conditioning, preparation and physical play. There was no finesse in it. It was right at you, in your face. "We're going to run the wishbone. You know what's coming but you're not going to be able to stop it. We're going to win the line of scrimmage on both sides of the ball because we will play harder and be more physical. We're going to line up and whip you one-on-one and eleven-on-eleven." As I said earlier, Bryant gave everyone the blueprint. It wasn't complicated, but it wasn't easy to implement.

Dye brought a new mentality to Auburn. That mentality extended to every aspect of the program, and nowhere was it more evident than in recruiting. For most of the 1970s the University of Alabama had dominated recruiting in the state of Alabama. They signed almost every high school player of any consequence. It wasn't that we didn't try to recruit those kids. It was more of a fatalistic view: We just expected that if Alabama wanted them, we weren't going to get them at Auburn. It was assumed in most cases that top high school players would go to Tuscaloosa to play for The Bear. Now, to be honest, we signed some, but not enough. That was just the way life was.

Dye challenged that immediately. Everyone knew that to be truly competitive you had to have the top athletes. We just had not been successful at bringing them in for almost a decade. The first real recruiting class at Auburn under Dye in 1982 included players like Tim Jesse, Pat Washington, Alan Evans, Rob Shuler, Steve Wallace, Donnie Humphrey, Ron Middleton, Gerald Robinson, Gerald Williams, and of course Bo Jackson. In order to level the playing field, you had to recruit, and Dye and his staff did that. They weren't afraid to go after the top players. More importantly, they expected to sign them, and they did. Not all of them, of course, but more than enough. Pat Dye flipped the recruiting field quickly. After a couple of classes, Auburn never lined up again under Dye with a huge talent deficit. For most of his tenure at Auburn we always had the talent necessary to win.

After the 1980 season the support for Auburn football was bad. Barfield had one pretty good year in 1979, but it had been six years since we had fielded a very good football team. We had not been to a bowl game since 1974. (We were on probation during the 8-3 year and ineligible.) At the same time, across the state, in addition to beating us every year, Alabama had won a couple of AP National Championships and were regularly at the top of the national polls. My point here is that Auburn had a serious problem with fan support. It wasn't that it was at a low point, which it was, it was that there was this overall feeling of inferiority. Having lived through that, buying season tickets every year, and attending every home football game during that period, I can attest that we had a serious problem. In truth, we *felt* inferior because we *were*.

When Dye was hired there was some degree of skepticism. He had been one of Bryant's top assistants, and he had strong ties to Alabama. He had been successful at East Carolina and Wyoming, but no one really knew what to expect. In addition to the actual football team, I think he was faced with this huge public relations problem. Not only did he have to fix the football team, but he had to fix the Auburn fan base. I think it is true that winning will overcome a lot, but the odds of Dye producing a winning program in short order were slim.

What the 1981 team did was to give everyone a big dose of hope. Even when they lost, you went away thinking they had given their all. I think that is really all the fans can hope for, a team that is prepared and plays the best they possibly can. That's what we saw in the fall of 1981. While he did not totally fix the PR problem in 1981, he certainly changed it.

For all the promise evident in the team's performances, though, 1981 ended up as yet another losing season.

Auburn fans had little idea what to expect, going into 1982. Clearly, Coach Dye was moving the program in the right direction. But how quickly, if at all, could he get it to where the fans all wanted to be? Would he be able to bring in the talent necessary to win? To finally beat Alabama? Maybe even to compete for championships? Most Auburn fans felt generally good about the program—for the first time in years—but they really had no idea what the future held.

The 1982 season was therefore at its start a year of hope, potential and promise—but also a year of mysteries. As the games played out, it became a year of excitement, of growing confidence, and of victories. The future opened up before us like a glorious sunrise.

Pat Dye was the leader with the vision. The other parts were about to fall into place around him.

Reynolds Wolf

Doug Barfield was a great man. There's no question about it. Offensive coordinator, if memory serves, with Shug. So he had the pedigree, he had the DNA, but the results just weren't there. And although I think the players fought hard, there was something lacking.

Patrick Fain Dye took care of that. And the thing about Patrick Fain Dye is, when Bear Bryant drifted away from Alabama football, the person in the Southeastern Conference who was the most Bear Bryant-esque was Patrick Fain Dye. Which I'm sure actually caused the rivalry to just explode. That was one of many factors.

Pat Dye had a swagger about him. I know it's a trite expression, but Pat Dye would walk into a stadium like a gunslinger. Fearless, edgy, insurmountable, unstoppable. He was the dude and he had that South Georgia accent. He had a voice that was like molasses. Incredible. He was my John Wayne when I was a kid. He was. He approached the game with a fearlessness. And I mean, look at the guy. He had been at East Carolina for a short time; he had been in Wyoming for a 6-5 season and then he erupted on the Plains. He came to the Plains like Everest in Kansas. And what a mark he made.

Auburn Elvis

I was always an Auburn fan, but I didn't start really paying attention to Auburn football until Pat Dye arrived. I was in grade school, so I didn't really comprehend just how dominant Bama had been for the past decade, but I do remember my parents' attitudes changed a lot once Dye became the coach. For instance, we didn't attend football games (my dad *hates* gameday traffic), but my folks were so excited after Auburn won the 1982 Iron Bowl that they made our family Christmas vacation into a trip to Orlando to see Auburn's victory over Boston College. So even though I didn't appreciate how bad things were before Dye, I could tell from how differently my folks acted about Auburn football that something important was happening.

Jeremy Henderson

I mean, to me, Pat Dye was God, basically, growing up. Having a coach like that. And when Terry Bowden was fired or resigned or whatever happened in 1998, I didn't know all the details behind it, but I remember my dad called me to let me know. And I was like, "Oh, that's awful," because for me that 1993 season was just this gift from God, and Bowden was obviously God's messenger. How could anybody—I mean, he was our coach! And Pat Dye had taught me, you didn't question a coach. For me, somebody growing up under Pat Dye, it would have been like a soldier questioning a general. It was just so weird to me to think that somebody wouldn't want our coach to be there. Which sounds crazy now, given all the drama and all the history and everything. But, at that time, I was actually as an adult completely baffled at the idea that somebody wouldn't be a hundred percent behind our coach. And that's because of Pat Dye, because that's what I grew up with.

Pat Dye had left the coaching job at Auburn, but that was because of some outside force. It was his health, or a scandal, or just evil forces that had taken Pat Dye from us. The idea that somehow Auburn people would want our coach to be gone? It just blew my mind. And that was all coming from this childlike faith I had in Pat Dye. That was what a coach was to me.

Pat Dye won football games, and Pat Dye was a badass, and Pat Dye coughed, and Pat Dye said it like it was, and it was so great. I mean, I felt like we were in the best hands in the business. Bar none. There was nothing beyond him. Growing up in that era, we just didn't—in my mind—we didn't lose.

"I think everybody who came in with my class, we came to Auburn because we wanted to go to Auburn, but I don't think we were thinking about conference championships or national championships. And when Coach Dye came in, he instilled that. And now it's something we really believe in."
—Gregg Carr, Auburn All-American linebacker

"You're talking about a little small country town where there's 18,000 students and all they got is each other. And it's a setting where there's a lot of warmth, and a close relationship between the student body and the players and each other, and the town and the community, it's just one big happy family."
—Pat Dye

Auburn had brought in Pat Dye from Wyoming. One of Bear's boys from back at Alabama in the old days, and a big-time player at Georgia before that.

Looking back, he seems a natural to have succeeded either Bryant at Alabama or Dooley at Georgia. Neither of those things happened, though. Instead, he found a home for himself among the Auburn Family, and he embraced it even as it embraced him.

He seemed to like the place. He definitely saw the potential in it; potential that had largely remained untapped during the previous regime. Most of all, he seemed to be a perfect fit: a rural Georgia guy at a rural Alabama university, both yearning to accomplish more in football than they had up until then, and to do so consistently. Both the coach and the university had seen what was possible, right across the state. Both carried with them the confidence that it could be done on the Plains as well—that Auburn could be a winner on the field. A *big* winner.

Coach Dye had posted a 5-6 record with what he had to work with that first season. The six losses were to Wake Forest, at Tennessee, at Nebraska (a team building up toward being a juggernaut), Mississippi State, Georgia in Athens and Alabama in Birmingham. But the wins were against TCU, LSU, Georgia Tech, Florida and North Texas. The Tennessee loss was close; the Nebraska loss was relatively close; the Wake Forest loss was close. All the losses were pretty darn close. Auburn even led Alabama 17-14 late in the second half, before the Tide used their depth to pull away at the end.

Yes, most of the pieces were in place. Randy Campbell would become the unlikely field general. A solid and rapidly improving defense, a sound kicking game, and a strong offensive line would all contribute greatly.

What the Tigers needed was a breakout star; an offensive weapon that could give them a chance against almost any opponent.

Pat Dye found that weapon, and brought him to the Plains: Vincent "Bo" Jackson. Perhaps you've heard of him.

Van Allen Plexico

Do you remember the end of the 1981 season and knowing we had a freshman named Bo Jackson coming in? How much do you remember actually knowing or thinking about what 1982 could be? How soon did you know it was going to be a pretty darn good year and things were going in the right direction?

John Ringer

I don't know. I was too young to have those kinds of preseason expectations. I'm sure I bought the *Sports Illustrated* college football preview and read it before the 1982 season, but I don't think I had nearly the same level of perception about how good we were and how good we were going to be. When you described the season before that, though, it makes me think of the Jimmy Johnson description of the four stages of a program, where you lose big, then you lose close, then win close, then win big. By then we had moved to losing close, yes—to good teams. Now we were ready to move to winning close against good teams. And that's kind of a segue from 1981 to 1982. I'm sure my parents did have a perception of what Bo Jackson could turn out to be. I knew that people were more optimistic and felt better about where the team was headed than they had in the years before that.

Van Allen Plexico

Well, let's pause for a second to talk about *how* we knew what we knew back then, because (in terms of information getting out to the public) that was a very different world, right?

John Ringer

It was the Dark Ages, in terms of the availability of sports information.

Van Allen Plexico

Yeah, probably eighty percent of what we knew came from the *Birmingham News* and the *Montgomery Advertiser*. Is that fair to say?

John Ringer

I never saw either one of those papers ever during that time. We got the *Atlanta Journal-Constitution*—

Van Allen Plexico
I'm so sorry.

John Ringer
—and back then there wasn't a good bit of college football information available. It was pre-Internet. Auburn was on TV like four times a year. We went to the home games, and I went to most of them with my family. But we listened to the radio broadcasts when we had an away game. I would buy a program from some guy on the side of the road and read it. But no, there was no internet, there were no podcasts, there were very few sources of information about the program.

Van Allen Plexico
No message boards, no Facebook groups, no Twitter, none of that.

Back then, I was living in Sylacauga, and my granddad got the *Birmingham News* every day. The Sunday *Birmingham News* would come, and it would have a big Sports section, especially on a Sunday after an Auburn game. The default was the Alabama game would be at the top of the page and Auburn would be second, below the fold. Maybe if the Auburn game was bigger, there was a chance they might put us at the top of the page. If Alabama had played Louisiana-Monroe or whoever and we had played Florida State—and won—we'd probably be at the top. Sometimes they'd vertically split the page down the middle, Auburn on one side and Alabama on the other, which was interesting. Just a few times they did that, like when we played Florida State in 1985 and Alabama had played Tennessee. But there was never any doubt which team was favored by that newspaper.

The other sources of information you had, like, say, *Inside the Auburn Tigers* magazine—I remember seeing Mark Murphy's by-lines on articles there in 1982 and 1983. He's been around a long time and he's really dedicated his life to reporting on Auburn sports, and that's amazing. You also had your network of people around the state. Again, I don't know about Atlanta. I assume you had your own network over there that your dad and your mom were probably tight with. But there was that network of Auburn people around Alabama for sure. In every business, people that would travel around and share and swap information that was photocopied and spread around. I remember seeing all kinds of Auburn football information that would come through that pipeline. My stepmother worked at a lumber company, and she would get football information from the traveling salespeople that would come by. A lot of them were former Auburn or Alabama players, and now they were sales representatives for big companies. So there was this whole informal network out there—it was like the Internet before the Internet—of people that just traveled around and shared information on the programs.

That was pretty much what we had. We knew a little bit about what was coming. We knew we had a new player named Bo Jackson. I don't think we need to go into the whole background story of Bo Jackson. I think most people know the deal: He was a fairly well-regarded running back at McAdory in Birmingham. Before he arrived on the Plains, he was not expected to be the second coming of Herschel Walker or anything.

How would you describe the way Bo was regarded before he came to Auburn?

John Ringer

I think he was a high-profile recruit, but not one of the top ten recruits in the country back then. It really was the Dark Ages of recruiting services and reporting. People knew he was a good player but there was no Scout, no 24/7, those kinds of services, ranking the recruits. There was an informal network of people; my dad was part of the informal network for Auburn for high school players in that area, where he would go to watch games and then pass the word on about good players. There wasn't instant game film with these players. Bo was highly regarded, but nobody knew how good he would be and how good he could become when moving from high school to college.

Vincent "Bo" Jackson, by Jarrod Alberich

"In the state of Alabama back then, as a young kid, the only football talked about was the University of Alabama.

"Coach Bryant called. He sent a gentleman to recruit me, and the first time I met him we sat and talked... and he said, 'Bo, we'd love to have you in Tuscaloosa, but personally I don't think you'll get a chance to play until the end of your sophomore or beginning of your junior season.' And I just looked at him with a look on my face like, 'You gotta be out of your damn mind if you think I'm gonna go somewhere and sit on somebody's bench for two years until I can play,' not knowing at the time that they were recruiting me to be a linebacker.

"The next week, Coach Dye and one of his assistants came up to visit me. And he said, 'If you tell me that you're going to commit to Auburn, I will make sure that I give you every opportunity on the planet to be the starting running back at the beginning of next season.' And I looked at him and I said, 'Coach, I'm coming to Auburn.' That's all I needed to hear. If the other gentleman had said that a week earlier, I would have gone to the University of Alabama."

—*Bo Jackson*

Mike McClendon

When Bo was signed by Auburn, he wasn't even considered to be the top athlete in the state of Alabama. He was also pretty far down the list of running backs in the country that year. By today's standards he would have been listed as a 4-star at best.

The Bo Jackson story is still one of the more interesting recruiting stories of all time. Back then recruiting was not the business it is today. It was in the days before there were recruiting services, camps and all the other stuff that goes on in ranking high school players. This predates even the magazines and the recruiting specialists like Forrest Davis. Mostly the rankings were based on physical attributes, high school performance and reports from college coaches attending games and practices. You did not have all the metrics that you have today.

McAdory High School was a small school that didn't attract a lot of attention. They didn't have great football teams or great anything else for that matter. So Bo really did not get the attention he probably deserved in high school. When Auburn baseball coach Hal Baird went to McAdory to visit their baseball coach, he mistook Bo for an employee because he was so big.

If you've watched the ESPN show on Bo, he talks about being recruited. Bear Bryant called him and sent an assistant to his house. The assistant told him he would be a linebacker at Alabama, and if he worked hard, he might get to play by his junior year. That tells you what they really knew about him and how much they had actually scouted him.

Marcus Dupree, from Philadelphia, Mississippi, was the top-rated running back and overall top-rated player in the country. Alan Evans, who also signed with Auburn, was a Parade All-American and the top back in the state of Alabama. Bo wasn't even on the lists. I remember reading one of those pre-season publications in the summer 1982; they were talking about recruiting, and one of the writers said that, quietly and without a lot of fanfare, Auburn had signed probably the best athlete in the country in Bo Jackson. They talked about McAdory finishing third in the state track meet, which by itself was no big deal—except that Bo was the only person from McAdory to qualify for the state meet. Basically, Bo Jackson finished third in the entire state, *by himself*, and would probably have done even better, except that he was only allowed to compete in so many events.

Today, with all the hoopla that surrounds recruiting, it is virtually impossible for any player to go as far under the radar as Bo did. You still have players who develop late and turn out to be much better than their rating, but it is much rarer today than it was even ten years ago.

Reynolds Wolf

Vincent "Bo" Jackson. The thing about Bo Jackson was every time I remember watching him, you didn't want to leave. You didn't want to go to the bathroom. You didn't want to take a sip of your drink. You didn't want to do anything that would distract your attention from the field because the odds were, you were going to see something happen on the field that you might never see again, and you certainly had never seen before. And the thing about Bo, especially when Pat Dye went to the wishbone formation and you had Pat Washington (at quarterback) on the toss sweep, sending it out to Bo... It was like watching a Saturn V rocket explode up the sidelines, unstoppable and obliterating anything and everything in his path.

"My freshman year, at that time, Auburn was unsuccessful at beating Alabama the last 9 years. The coach that came up to recruit me from Alabama, he said, 'Mr. Jackson, Auburn hasn't beaten Alabama since 1972.' This was in 1982. And then he looked me in the eye and said, 'They never will.' That motivated me a lot."
—Bo Jackson

Van Allen Plexico

We still had Lionel James left on the roster, out of all the great running backs from the late Seventies. The rest were all gone by this point to the NFL, or to the USFL, at some point in there. We had Lionel and we needed a quarterback. Pat Dye looked around and tried out a few people and ended up picking the one who was way down the depth chart the year before: scrawny little Randy Campbell from Hartselle, Alabama.

Campbell was never going to be a pro-style quarterback. He was never going to be a run-and-shoot quarterback or anything like that. But one thing Randy Campbell could do was make good decisions on the option. He was also very good at ball security. He was a good and reliable field leader and he could make good decisions and he didn't turn the ball over, and that's what Pat Dye wanted out of a quarterback, now that we were running the wishbone, the triple-option wishbone. In that offense, the quarterback's primary job was to get the ball to Bo Jackson and Lionel James. You just needed somebody that would make good decisions about when to do that. Which was almost every play.

John Ringer
As the quarterback in that offense, every play you keep it is a failure.

Van Allen Plexico
Exactly. Randy was not too bad at doing little quarterback sneaks for a couple yards for a touchdown or a first down, though. He could do that. He had a couple of games where he actually gained good yardage by himself, when the other team would find ways to take away the pitch to the halfbacks. But you always worried he was going to get killed because he seemed so scrawny.

We had Lionel James; we had Randy Campbell; now here came the true freshman, Bo Jackson. The defense was getting a lot tougher. Dye had really hardened that defense up in 1981. Remember, we said before that the main liability of those great offensive Auburn teams in the late Seventies and 1980 was they could score forty points a game but they gave up forty-five. Dye addressed that immediately. He was really going to build up our defense. He started bringing in those big defensive linemen and bringing in some fast defensive backs. You know, Kevin Porter types, eventually; Carlo Cheatham, Alvin Briggs; guys like that. Big men on the defensive line like Donnie Humphrey and Doug Smith early on, and later Tracy Rocker. Those were all guys that would hit you—just punch you in the mouth and run you over. With those kinds of players, in Pat Dye's system, the defense was getting nasty.

Of course, this was also when Coach Joe Whitt started making us into Linebacker U, too. I know that Alabama considered itself Linebacker U in the Eighties. Honestly, Auburn was not far behind Alabama. Alabama had maybe two or three bigger names by the time the decade was over, but I would argue that Auburn's linebackers top to bottom were every bit as good as Alabama's during the Eighties.

John Ringer
A hundred percent. I mean, the defense got really, really good during this time. Better coaches, better players, better schemes. Also, we were running the wishbone as our offense,

so we were limiting possessions for the other team. We were taking advantage of being able to put pressure on the other team, and make them somewhat desperate when they had the ball, to make something happen. We had Bo Jackson operating out of a wishbone offense, so we had scoring opportunities. It was really, really exciting to see the *defense* become a force, too.

Van Allen Plexico

It's a good point about the offense. You can see why Dye went to the wishbone because it did several important things. It kept the defense off the field for long periods of time, if you could make first downs on offense. Other than when Bo was turning a toss sweep into an eighty-yard run, it was not an offense that was going to go out there for three plays and then sit down again. If it got off the field in a hurry it was because they punted or because of a big play. Otherwise, it would stay out there and stay out there. It would usually eat up the clock and take a long time to score, unless they were in a hurry.

And they really only threw the ball when they had to. Pat Dye famously said—I'm sure he was quoting somebody, but— he famously said, "When you throw the football three things can happen, and two of them are bad." Presumably those would be an incomplete pass or an interception. So he didn't like to throw the ball very much. He liked to run. And one of the things that running the wishbone did was give the defense plenty of rest and let them stay fresh. Of course, Dye also was big about rotating the players on the defensive line in and out, keeping them fresh. The television commentators were always talking about how we were just constantly shuffling defensive linemen in and out almost every play, so they would always be fresh.

The other thing the wishbone did was give a team where the offensive line was still growing and trying to come into its own a better chance against top competition. One of the things the option attack does is let you replace power at the point of attack with numbers. So if your guy isn't as big or as good as their guy at the point of attack, now you had two guys against their one guy. That's the idea. A lot of times the triple option is about how you're trying to move players around, so that you outnumber the defense at the point of attack. Of course, it's also why, within a few years, the wishbone really stopped working as a top-flight philosophy: because defenses got so fast that you couldn't really outnumber them at the point of attack for very long anymore. They'd get defensive players to the ball carrier very quickly, as soon as they figured out what was going on. That meant teams that had for a long time depended on option attacks had to start moving toward more NFL pro-style offenses, where they passed the ball more. The West Coast offense, the Run and Shoot, the Spread, the Air Raid. Miami was one of the teams that led the way on that, throwing the ball effectively and winning championships doing it, and then later Steve Spurrier brought his version, the Fun and Gun, to the SEC and did very well with it.

But yes, the wishbone was really interesting during this time, very fun to watch, and it helped Auburn to be successful, given the personnel we had on offense and on defense.

John Ringer

We also had really good special teams. By 1985, our punter, Lewis Colbert, was All-SEC. And Al Del Greco as the kicker. The greatest golfer in NFL history. I remember his kicks in the Sugar Bowl.

Van Allen Plexico

There have been several seasons over the years that, when you first glanced at it, it didn't look like Auburn had top-level personnel. But then you break it down, position by position, and realize we had maybe an All-SEC player at running back; an All-American at defensive end; a big overachiever at linebacker; a super-reliable kicker. And suddenly you realize that while we didn't have a ton of depth in some years, you find a top-level player starting at almost every position. Guys that went on to successful careers in the NFL. So that's kind of an Auburn trademark, that we wouldn't necessarily have the depth of a Miami back in the day, or Alabama nowadays, but we'd have that one really great player at almost every position on the field that could really make a difference, as long as they didn't get hurt.

1982

Van Allen Plexico
Let's look at the 1982 season. The first thing that jumps out to me is that we played the first six games at home.

John Ringer
That's true, and the other thing that's weird, looking back from our vantage point now, is the non-conference games. We only played six SEC opponents, out of eleven. We played five non-conference games. The non-conference opponents in 1982 were Wake Forest, Southern Miss, Nebraska, Georgia Tech, and Rutgers.

Van Allen Plexico
Isn't that a strange combination? We take for granted now that Auburn plays eight conference games instead of six, and we even talk sometimes about playing nine. Back then there was no SEC championship game, so you played your eleven games, and a bowl game if you were pretty good. And you were playing in a ten-team conference, which meant there were three teams you were not playing every year. It did rotate around a little bit. You had some teams you played every year, and some you didn't. For example, Auburn played Tennessee, Miss State, Florida, Georgia and Alabama every year in the SEC, and Georgia Tech every year, out of conference.

John Ringer
We hardly ever played LSU, Kentucky, Ole Miss or Vanderbilt in those days. The only way it could have been harder for Auburn is if we had played LSU every year instead of Miss State.

Auburn started off the 1982 season by gaining revenge on Wake Forest, 28-10. The Tigers jumped out to a 14-0 lead on a team that had beaten them the previous year, and never looked back.

"Their offense controlled the ball more than it did last year. I'd say it's a much-improved offense from last year—at least in this game it was. Another big difference was that they didn't turn the ball over. Last year that was a big part."
—Gary Schofield, Wake Forest quarterback

The fierce Auburn defense limited the Demon Deacons to just 16 yards rushing in the game, on 32 attempts.

"Their defense was real sharp. Their defensive secondary looked excellent. Mark Dorminey and Bob Harris are some kind of players. There's a big difference from last year to this year. Last year in the second half, their defense had a letdown, but tonight they were really up for us."
—Tim Ryan, Wake Forest wide receiver

"Auburn executed better than last year. They will definitely be a factor in the SEC this year. Auburn played appreciably better this year."
—Al Groh, Wake Forest head coach

Bo Jackson, making his first college football appearance ever, was the game's leading rusher. He carried 10 times for 123 yards and two touchdowns, in a game where twelve different players carried the ball for Auburn. Lionel James added 118 yards on 10 carries, with a long touchdown run of 67 yards, that started off the scoring on the fourth play of the game.

"You don't have to be very smart to look at what we lined up with at running back tonight and see there is a big difference from last year."
—Pat Dye

In week two, Auburn edged Southern Miss, 21-19, in a game that came very close to spelling disaster for the Tigers.

Auburn led the Golden Eagles 21-3 in the third quarter, after Randy Campbell hit receiver Mike Edwards for two long touchdowns and Bo Jackson tacked on a 5-yard scoring run. At that point, the game appeared to be in the bag.

Reggie Collier, the USM quarterback, had other ideas. He'd amassed over 500 yards of total offense in the first two games of the season, and in the fourth quarter he led USM down the field, whereupon running back Sam DeJarnette punched in two touchdowns to bring the Golden Eagles to within 2 points, at 21-19.

Southern Miss then stopped Auburn, got the ball back, and moved to the Tigers' 32 yard line. Collier threw a pass to fullback Clemon Terrell for 5 yards to the 27, with the clock showing 13 seconds remaining. The Golden Eagles tried to reset and snap the ball, but the clock expired before they could get off another play or attempt the field goal—something the visiting coaches and players were very unhappy about.

"We had 13 seconds left when he caught the pass and we still can't get a play off. We were ready to snap the ball and the officials just stood there looking around. We didn't even get a chance."
—Reggie Collier, USM quarterback

"If you say your prayers, something good will happen to you. I was praying on the sideline. Could y'all tell it? I told the Good Lord, 'If You're ever going to help us, help us now.'"
—Pat Dye

Auburn's star defensive lineman, Donnie Humphrey, was injured during the game when Steve Carmody, the USM center and the son of the head coach, threw a "cut" block into his legs. After the game, Humphrey—on crutches—visited the Golden Eagles' locker room.

"Carmody apologized to Humphrey, saying, 'I didn't mean to cut you,' and left quietly after learning his adversary would miss the rest of the season."
—Mike Perrin, Montgomery Advertiser

Bo Jackson was the leading rusher with 99 yards on 13 carries, with one touchdown.

"Their no. 34 (Jackson) makes them a completely different team from last year. The only player I can compare him to is Herschel Walker when he was a freshman. He runs low to the ground, gives you a stutter step and he's gone."
—Jim Carmody, USM head coach

The third week of the 1982 season saw Auburn, still not ranked in the Top 20 AP Poll, take down Tennessee, gaining some redemption for the bitter disappointment of the previous year.

The Vols scored on a long pass but otherwise were held in check. Auburn managed a single touchdown in the first half, as well, but Al Del Greco missed the extra point. He added a field goal—his first of the season—just before the half, putting the Tigers up, 9-7.

Going into the fourth quarter, the game was still tight, at 17-14, Auburn. That was when Randy Campbell pitched the ball to Lionel James—who then threw a long pass downfield. The ball looked to be picked off by the awaiting Joe Cozart of Tennessee, but Bo Jackson ran around in front of him, caught the ball, and took it for a 43-yard gain to the Tennessee 29. Eight plays later, James scored from the 2, and the Tigers were able to hold on from there for the win.

Auburn held the Vols to only 94 yards rushing for the game. Tennessee's two scores came on long passes of 38 and 78 yards to star receiver, Olympic sprinter and future Chicago Bear, Willie Gault.

"Auburn is really physical up front. The defensive secondary is all right, but it's not the best I've faced. Auburn has a good team overall. I think they'll do well this season. They have really improved from last year."
—Willie Gault, Tennessee wide receiver

"You couldn't tell it by the way we played, but we went into the game a badly crippled football team, particularly on defense. There

was something wrong with just about everybody on our defense, but they played through it."
—Pat Dye

On October 2, the no. 8 Nebraska Cornhuskers came to Jordan-Hare. They remembered their narrow escape in Lincoln the previous season, and they played like it.

Auburn hung with the Huskers early on. After Nebraska scored on a 15-yard run by fullback Doug Wilkening, Auburn came right back and Bo Jackson took it in from 4 yards away to tie the game at 7-7.

Nebraska scored a second touchdown on a 58-yard pass from Turner Gill to Todd Brown. The play came on a 3rd and 22 on the Huskers' side of the field, temporarily deflating the Auburn defenders and putting the team in red ahead, 14-7. Neither side scored again before halftime, and it looked like Nebraska was in for the same kind of scare they'd gotten from Auburn the year before.

Instead, the Cornhuskers came out on fire in the second half, and a depleted Auburn squad could barely slow them down. Nebraska added a third touchdown in the third quarter to go up, 21-7, and then exploded for three more late scores to turn the game into a rout, 41-7.

The Cornhuskers amassed 404 yards of total offense and 31 first downs against the Auburn defense. Future Heisman Trophy winner Mike Rozier gained 88 yards on 24 carries. Most of Nebraska's big plays came on third downs; they converted time and again, just as the Tigers' defense looked ready to stop them.

"I'm embarrassed, hell yes I'm embarrassed. I didn't believe they could run on us like they did. Hell, I still don't believe it."
—Doug Smith, Auburn defensive tackle

The Tigers had hoped before the game that the southeastern heat would work in their favor in the fourth quarter, wearing down the boys from the Midwest. Instead, it seemed to impact the Tigers.

"The heat factor worked in reverse because we had a lot of injuries. We didn't have enough people left to keep them fresh."
—Frank Orgel, Auburn defensive coordinator

Lionel James, the Tigers' leading rusher for the afternoon, left the field with a bruised shoulder late in the first half, and gained only 3 yards in the second half. He finished with just 66 yards. Bo Jackson, the SEC's leading rusher at this point in the season, gained 18 yards on only 5 carries.

"The game was still 50-50 at the half. The defense played so much better the second half. That was the difference."
—Tom Osborne, Nebraska head coach

"You saw what took place. It was just a good, old-fashioned whipping that we won't be forgetting for a long time to come."
—Pat Dye

The next week, Al Del Greco kicked six field goals to polish off Kentucky, 18-3. The game set a record for most field goals in an SEC game, a mark not equaled until Daniel Carlson in 2016 kicked six for Auburn against LSU.

"To be honest, I am very excited to win the football game. It's not easy to get ready to play after a game like last week. I didn't see any lack of effort from our team today. I was proud of our defense, that they kept Kentucky out of the end zone."
—Pat Dye

Freshman Quarterback Pat Washington was pressed into service with 12 seconds to go in the game. He'd been expecting to redshirt the season, but injuries across the board were forcing the Auburn coaches to spread the playing time around. We would be seeing much more of him later in his Auburn career.

"We'd like to be in a position where we had so many players, we didn't have to play freshmen. But we don't have that luxury. Coach Dye has said if they're good enough to play, then play 'em!"
—Frank Orgel, Auburn defensive coordinator

Freshman running back Alan Evans, a high school All-America recruit and future father of Alabama linebacker Rashaan Evans, also got his first playing time of his career. He carried the ball 6 times for 22 yards.

"It's really been all my fault. I came into practice out of shape and wasn't ready to do things college players have to do. I wasn't ready mentally. I'm glad the coaches waited on me and didn't stick me in early."
—Alan Evans, Auburn running back

"We've got those young backs in there. If I could give them a pill to make them mature overnight I would. They've got to get that experience on the field."
—Pat Dye

On October 16, the Tigers shut out Georgia Tech, 24-0.

"Auburn's defense was the entire story. (They) were better than I thought. They've shut down everyone they've played except for Nebraska."
—Bill Curry, Georgia Tech head coach

Tech rushed 33 times for only 62 yards, and completed 14 of 35 passes for just 91 yards, with three interceptions.

Bo Jackson didn't dress for the game, due to a thigh bruise suffered in practice that week.

The Tigers hadn't scored a touchdown in seven quarters, dating back to the first quarter of the Nebraska game. They took care of that situation quickly, scoring three against the Yellowjackets.

Lionel James led the way with 15 carries for 75 yards, while backup Tim Jessie added another 74 yards on 9 carries. But even with their efforts, the Tigers netted only 149 yards on the ground, to go with 135 through the air, via Randy Campbell's 7-of-13 passing. Lionel James provided a boost with 123 yards in kick returns.

The offense was experiencing some growing pains—not to mention injury pains—but the defense was picking up the slack. Over the course of two games after the Nebraska debacle, Auburn's defense had given up a total of just 3 points.

Up until that point in the season, the Tigers had played every game within the friendly confines of Jordan-Hare Stadium. On October 23, they finally left town, traveling to Starkville to face Mississippi State.

The Tigers and Bulldogs traded scores back-and-forth through two quarters. Auburn led, 14-10, at the half. The Bulldog touchdown came on a blazing, 87-yard run by their quarterback, John Bond.

Bond started off the third quarter by adding to the Bulldogs' total with a 61-yard touchdown pass. Suddenly the home team was in the lead, 17-14. Auburn, meanwhile, failed to score throughout the third quarter. The visiting Tigers appeared to be on the ropes.

Then Bo Jackson entered the game.

He hadn't played the week before, against Georgia Tech. He hadn't practiced all week. He hadn't played a down in the first half that day. And he gained only 59 yards on 8 carries against the Bulldogs. But his mere presence seemed to make a huge difference for the Tigers.

"Just Bo's presence changes things. When he came into the game, it just seemed like everyone gave more effort. It gave everyone more confidence."
—Randy Campbell, Auburn quarterback

After Bo entered the game—and scored a short touchdown to put Auburn back ahead—Lionel James became energized himself. He ripped off a 32-yard touchdown and raced 29 yards to set up another one.

"Sure it makes a difference (when Bo enters the game). A real big difference. The defense always reacts in a way that opens up everything else."
—Lionel James, Auburn running back

The Auburn coaches had wanted to hold him out for one more game and get him ready to face Florida the following week. That plan went out the window when the maroon Bulldogs took the lead in the second half.

"I was very antsy on the sidelines. I said to myself that when I went in there, I had to go full-speed. I didn't really know how fast I'd be able to go on (my leg). It's okay now. Once I got in the game, it just felt normal.

"It was just another game that we won. We have to get ready for the next one."
—Bo Jackson, Auburn running back

Bo was on the field for four Auburn possessions in the second half. The Tigers scored touchdowns on three of them, all in the fourth quarter, finishing off the Bulldogs for good.

"He made three or four runs that really gave us a spark. I knew he hadn't taken a snap in practice all week, but I also know he is a great athlete. A great athlete can get by like that when some others might not."
—Pat Dye

"Bo said all along he was going to play. Friday afternoon, it looked like he could hardly walk. Coach Dye just walked up and said Bo was going in. I sure wasn't going to argue."
—Jack Crowe, Auburn offensive coordinator

Coming out of the Mississippi State game, the Tigers felt as confident in their team as they'd felt all season. The injury bug, though, continued to nip at them—and at a very inopportune moment, as huge games were rapidly approaching against Florida, Georgia and Alabama—the fabled trio of annual, late-season opponents Pat Dye would later nickname "Amen Corner."

"You can be confident and still not be good enough. There was no way to know what was going to happen.

"I think our football team is getting better every week. I just wish we could get healthy."
—Pat Dye

Van Allen Plexico

Talk about getting off to a strong start; we were actually 6-1 after the first seven games of the 1982 season.

We had some offense, too. I remember Bo Jackson coming in and playing in the Southern Miss game, and making quite a splash. Listening to Jim Fyffe's play-by-play on the radio for that game, Bo didn't stand out to me any more than the other running backs, but clearly there was something going on if you were actually able to watch, because afterward, on the post-game show, he was all they could talk about.

Speaking of our paltry few sources of information back then, there was another besides the *Inside the Auburn Tigers* and the newspapers and the radio that we didn't mention. And that was the weekly call-in show the coaches would do. Those were much bigger back then than they are now, because that was one of your very few sources of information.

John Ringer

Another one was the coach's review show on TV.

Van Allen Plexico

"The Auburn Football Review." Yeah. Brought to you by South Central Bell.

Those were big because, as you said, our games were only broadcast on TV a couple of times a year. You watched the Auburn Football Review with Phil Snow and whoever the coach was, because in some cases that was the only time you got to see any highlights from a game. Even some of our biggest games didn't make it onto TV, and sometimes it was a big surprise when one of them did.

John Ringer

This is before ESPN and SportsCenter and cable TV came along. So even if you were at the stadium, if you happened to get up to get a Coke or go to the restroom or something, you might miss a Bo Jackson eighty-yard run. There were no highlights available everywhere to watch later. But if you watched the coach's show, they would definitely show it.

Van Allen Plexico

They'd have the Auburn and the Alabama shows on Sunday afternoon, and then maybe show them again at other times in other markets. We would get them on Channel 12 out of Montgomery, and I think maybe Channel 6 out of Birmingham would show them as well.

I guess the film was still wet when they were showing them, because they'd put the footage together overnight or early Sunday morning, record the coach and the TV host talking about it early Sunday morning, and then they would show it at noon or one or two o'clock on Sunday afternoon. I remember the Auburn show was a half hour, but the Bear Bryant Show was an hour long. So you got an hour of "Bourbon, bourbon, Coca Cola, Frito-Lay, bourbon, grumble-grumble, talked to the mamas and the papas, bourbon, smoke a cigarette."

In the later years, when Pat Dye would be on the show with Phil Snow, Dye would cough his way through the whole thing, bless his heart. He had a physical problem that was getting worse, involving his blood—which they later corrected. But in the time period we're talking about, he was still young and healthy, and it was always interesting to hear his comments about the games and the players.

John Ringer

Yeah, the Football Review shows were really important because Auburn did not appear on TV during the 1982 season until October 30 against Florida.

"Auburn-Florida game could be televised."
—Montgomery Advertiser headline, the Sunday before the game

Van Allen Plexico

Right. We were 6-1 and ranked 19th in the country, and going down to Florida Field to play at Florida. Miraculously, ABC decided to air that game. This was before Jefferson-Pilot. This was before ESPN. Before the CBS contract, all of that. So there weren't that many options for being on TV.

The 1982 Auburn-Florida game was played a day short of a year after the previous year's game, in which Florida had missed a 40-yard field goal that would've given them the win in Auburn. This time, they didn't miss.

The Gators led the game early, 10-0. Auburn managed to pull the margin closer before halftime, as a Randy Campbell touchdown pass to Mike Edwards made it 10-7 at the break.

In the third quarter, Bo Jackson took a 7-yard run into the end zone and gave Auburn its first lead, at 14-10. After that, the game became a field goal fiesta.

Florida's Jim Gainey kicked it through from 32 yards away to make the score 14-13, Auburn. Al Del Greco responded early in the fourth quarter with a 23-yard kick to push the Tigers further ahead, 17-13. Gainey came right back with a 31-yard field goal, narrowing the lead to 1 point again, at 17-16, after Auburn's defense held great Gator backs Lorenzo Hampton and John L. Williams out of the end zone and forced the Florida offense backwards.

Time was quickly ebbing away, so the Gators attempted an onside kick. Lionel James dived on the ball and claimed afterward that he recovered it at the bottom of a pile, but the referees awarded it to Florida.

"Mike Shanahan, our offensive coordinator, made that onside kick call. It was a great call and a courageous decision. It was a borderline thing. It could have turned out good or bad. Fortunately for Florida, it turned out good."
—Charley Pell, Florida head coach

"I thought I had it, but the referees called it the other way. It took a high bounce and I caught it. I came up with it and I thought I had it the whole time. It was just a matter of mutual possession, and I guess the referees saw it their (Florida's) way. When I got up, I was surprised. That's all I can say. I never talk back to the referees."
—Lionel James, Auburn running back

Gainey came out and kicked his fourth and final field goal just before time expired, giving the Gators the win—along with, as they saw it, righteous revenge for what had happened to them the year before in Auburn.

"This one (kick) is the best one in my entire life—ever."
—Jim Gainey, Florida kicker

The Florida defense held Bo Jackson to just 23 yards on 10 carries, with one touchdown, while Lionel James gained 34 yards on 6 attempts. Quarterback Randy Campbell led all Auburn rushers with 54 yards on 11 carries.

"It turned out just as we thought it would, coming down to one or two plays, if we could come back and play the kind of defense we are capable of doing, and that was just about the way it turned out—one or two plays.
"That was just a good old-fashioned Southeastern knock-down, drag-out. Auburn is always an excellent football team. They have excellent coaching, excellent plays. I want to commend Auburn for having a great team."
—Charley Pell, Florida head coach

"I don't have any excuses why we weren't ready to play in the first half. Our team hasn't acted like that all year long. We came back in the second half and really played well, but it took a lot of encouragement at halftime to get them in the right frame of mind."
—Pat Dye

Van Allen Plexico

We lost at Florida, and that was an interesting game because Florida was mad that we had beaten them the year before, when they missed a late field goal. So they came out and kicked a field goal late in this game to edge us, 19-17.

It was one of a series of very close, frustrating losses at Florida over the years. The 1986 game down there always jumps out as well—and we'll talk about it in depth later on, obviously. But we went into that game undefeated, potentially on our way to the SEC title. Kerwin Bell was their quarterback and he had a leg injury and was hobbling around the entire game, and at the end he was somehow able to bring them back and then run in a two-point conversion, right through our entire defense. I've always joked he was able to roll his wheelchair over the goal line without anyone being able to stop him. And those two points gave them the win and gave us our first loss. He went on to play for the Orlando Thunder in the WLAF, and I hated that team because of Bell.

A 30-7 beat-down of Rutgers got the Tigers back into the win column on November 6. The week after that, the no. 1-ranked Georgia Bulldogs, still featuring Herschel Walker, came to town.

Van Allen Plexico

This was the 1982 Georgia team that would go on to play in the national championship game. Georgia was ranked no. 1; they were undefeated and were on their way to losing the Sugar Bowl to Penn State. That would be their third attempt in a row at a national championship with Herschel Walker, and it was Herschel's last year of the three. After this season he turned pro and went to play for Donald Trump and the New Jersey Generals.

This is the game where you had Bo Jackson and Herschel Walker on a college football field together for the only time, and 74,900 people can say that they saw it firsthand. The rest of us couldn't, because it wasn't even on TV. Can you believe that?

John Ringer

Georgia was the no. 1 team in the country. It was Bo Jackson vs Herschel Walker. And it was not on TV.

Van Allen Plexico

Yeah. At the time, we were like, "Well, of course it wasn't." But it's hard to imagine now.

Auburn led 7-3 early on the strength of a Randy Campbell touchdown—Campbell actually had more carries in the game than any of the Auburn running backs—but Herschel Walker scored a touchdown on a run of 47 yards to put Georgia ahead, 10-7.

119

Auburn re-took the lead, 14-13, on the second play of the fourth quarter when Lionel James exploded for an 87-yard touchdown run. At the time, it was the second-longest run in Auburn history.

"Their quarterback, Campbell, is a winner. As for Lionel James, I've already said what a fan I am of him. I didn't know Lionel could run that fast. I was just waiting for us to catch him. He looked like James Brooks did when they came over to Athens. What year does he graduate?"
—Vince Dooley, Georgia head coach

Georgia came right back with an 80-yard drive that saw Walker go in from the 3-yard line to put the Bulldogs back ahead, 19-14. The 2-point conversion attempt failed.

Auburn got the ball back, trailing by five, with 8:42 remaining in the game; plenty of time to do what needed to be done. They methodically moved the ball down the field, eating up yards and draining the clock, until they reached Georgia's 14 with 3:21 remaining. At that point, momentum shifted back in the favor of the Bulldogs.

A penalty, a sack, a loss of 2 yards by Bo Jackson; as time drained from the clock, the Tigers were moving in the wrong direction, away from the Georgia end zone.

Randy Campbell's final pass attempt fell incomplete. Top-ranked Georgia had held on and survived, but they knew they'd been in a fight.

"I thought it took a championship effort on our part to win today. We came back each time they scored and that's championship effort."
—Vince Dooley, Georgia head coach

"We knew we could score. We just blew it. That's what makes it so hard to take. We blew it. We dominated the whole second half on the line. We were in control up fornt and I just knew we were going to score. I knew it."
—Pat Arrington, Auburn offensive tackle

Van Allen Plexico

We can't complete that final pass, and we lose, 19-14, and it's another one of those heartbreakers like the Tennessee game the year before. We played them so close, though, and Georgia knows in their hearts—all the knowledgeable Georgia fans know in their hearts—that if you get Auburn when you're having a big season, at a key moment in the season, you better look out, because our worst teams have given their teams nightmares in their best years. That continues to apply, because think about what we did to them when they were no. 1 in 2017. So Georgia is very used to getting their brains beaten in by us at unlikely times, and having their greatest seasons ruined by us; it's not anything new.

So at that point we are 7-3 and we've got Alabama coming up in Legion Field. And we haven't beaten them in nine years.

"If it hadn't been for that effort on that drive against Georgia, a drive that failed, I don't believe we could have had the confidence to make the last winning drive two weeks later against Alabama in Birmingham."
—*Pat Dye, In the Arena*

"You're damned right we'll be ready (for Alabama). I can guarantee you that. We'll be ready to fight just like we were today. We didn't win it, but this game proves we are able to play with the best. I won't be here to be a part of it, but I dare say in four or five years Auburn is going to be no. 1."
—*Pat Arrington, Auburn offensive tackle, after the UGA game*

John Ringer

This was the game that would end up being Bear Bryant's last regular season game ever, and his last Iron Bowl. His one and only attempt against Bo Jackson. Because of that, it was televised by ABC.

Van Allen Plexico

How much do you remember about the whole rigmarole around that game?

John Ringer

I remember thinking that, for the first time in forever, it felt like we had a chance.

We'd gotten our brains beaten in for nine years in a row, but this year going into that game, and during the game, it felt like it was more of an even matchup, and we had a real chance to win.

Van Allen Plexico

Yeah, that's exactly how I felt.

I remember having a conversation about it with a classmate who was an Alabama fan. It was my freshman year of high school. I've told you before, ever since kindergarten, Auburn had lost the Iron Bowl every year I was in school. And I remember saying to him, "I think this is the year we win," and I remember him smiling in sort of a condescending way and saying that we were improving and were on the way to being competitive with them, but that we weren't good enough yet to beat the Bear and Bama. He thought it would take us at least one more year to get to that level.

There must have been some talk of Bryant retiring. I think a lot of people felt like it was coming, sooner or later, obviously, because he was getting up there in years. It also didn't help that the team's won-loss record was sliding a bit after the heights of 1978-79, and by losing this game to Auburn, he lost three games in a row for the first time ever as coach at Alabama. But I don't remember anyone I talked with saying it was going to happen that year. My recollection is that it was a surprise, announced in between the Iron Bowl and their bowl game. ABC may have thought the same thing—sensed that this might be his last Iron Bowl—and figured it was worthy of putting on TV. They had televised the one the previous year, the game where he got his 315th win, and advertised it as a big historical moment.

But, in any case, the Alabama people I knew acknowledged that Pat Dye was good. They would grudgingly admit that they admired him as a head coach and maybe even liked him a little bit. Some of them wanted him to come in and replace Bryant

122

after he retired. But, in my experience, most of them didn't think 1982 was the year the Bear was retiring or that this was the year we'd finally beat them.

John Ringer
What do you remember of that game?

Van Allen Plexico
I remember Walter Lewis being their quarterback, along with Ken Coley. They would swap back and forth between Coley and Lewis. Coley was more of an option runner, and Lewis was more of a passer. Lewis was a mobile passer in a day when that was still a very new thing; he could run around the backfield and find an open receiver. Coley would take the snap, fake a handoff and do a quarterback sneak or dive up the middle for about three yards, like a Tim Tebow or Cam Newton. I remember Frank Broyles doing the color commentary alongside Keith Jackson on the game, and Broyles kept referring to Walter Lewis as the "running quarterback," which I think was misleading, because he was more the scrambling passer, while Coley literally was a "running quarterback."

Bear was switching back and forth between them all season. In fact, going in at halftime, a young reporter for ABC asked Bryant why he was switching back and forth between the two, and he just about bit her head off. He snapped at her, "I'm trying to win the ballgame. Everything I do, I'm trying to win the ballgame." And she just sort of melted. I always wondered if there was more to it than that, but we'll never know.

Walter Lewis ended up playing quarterback for most of this game and he had a pretty good game. But we got a couple of key turnovers. We intercepted him a couple of times.

One of our defensive backs, Tim Drinkard, caught a ball in midair that had gotten knocked loose from the running back, and he almost scored with it. The Alabama back went into the pile and the ball just popped straight up. Drinkard took the ball out of the air and ran back the other way for 62 yards, but got caught from behind by Walter Lewis himself at the 14-yard line. Drinkard wasn't particularly fast—and I'm talking about a defensive back. Yes, the game has changed a good bit since 1982.

Tim Drinkard's return set Auburn up at the Alabama 14, and on third and ten, Lionel James took a draw and slipped almost untouched through the entire Alabama defense and into the end zone, to tie the game at 7-7. That kept the Tigers in the game at a moment when it looked like Alabama would pull out to a double-digit lead in the first half; very similar to the way the 1993 game against Florida unfolded in the first quarter.

Auburn actually had the lead at the half, 14-13. Auburn fans had seen this movie before, though. In so many of those previous nine losses, the Tigers had been competitive up until the third quarter, and then the Tide would pull away late. But not this time.

In the third quarter, Alabama drove 67 yards for a touchdown, but misfired on the two-point conversion. The score was now 19-14 Alabama—the same score Auburn had faced against Georgia in the fourth quarter of the previous game.

A short time later, Alabama marched 93 yards to the Auburn 1-yard line, but Bear Bryant settled for a short Peter Kim field goal rather than going for it on fourth down. The kick put the Tide on top, 22-14. How different things might have been if the Bear had gone for the touchdown.

Bo Jackson chose that moment to make his presence known. He ripped off a 53-yard run to the Alabama 12. The Tide defense held, and Al Del Greco kicked a 23-yard field goal with 9:06 left, to close the gap to 22-17.

The Tigers' defense held and forced a punt, and Auburn got the ball back at its own 34-yard line with 7:06 to go.

Randy Campbell hit Mike Edwards for a crucial third down conversion pass, giving Auburn a first down at the Alabama 30. Two plays later, the Tide's great defensive back, Jeremiah Castille, intercepted a Campbell pass, but the referees ruled Castille had interfered with the receiver. The penalty gave Auburn a first down on the Alabama 9 with less than three minutes remaining.

Bo caught a screen pass and took it to the Alabama 1-yard line, but now it was fourth down, with the Tide still leading, 22-17. Auburn's coaches had no doubts about what to do next. They had Campbell give the ball to Jackson.

Van Allen Plexico

On fourth down, at the Alabama goal line, we all witnessed one of the most famous moments in Auburn football history.

John Ringer

Bo Over the Top.

At this point in the game, you knew Bo Jackson was the man. The key was, "What's he going to do? Is he going to go left? Will he go right?" Instead, you got the middle. Campbell handed the ball to him and Bo took it over the top and stretched out into the end zone and scored the touchdown for Auburn to win, 23-22.

The game wasn't over with Bo's amazing play, though. Auburn's defense stopped Alabama and got the ball back again, and the Tigers methodically drove down to the Alabama red zone, just trying to run the clock out and put the game away. The one thing they couldn't afford was a turnover. So of course Bo Jackson fumbled and the ball was recovered by Alabama. It happened on the exact same play Bo had scored the touchdown on a couple of minutes earlier. Not only that, it happened right after Keith Jackson named Bo the MVP for Auburn.

Alabama's offense came back on the field with a little over a minute to go, and Walter Lewis was completing every pass he threw. It all seemed so predictable for Auburn people. So much a matter of fate and destiny. Or maybe just a curse.

Van Allen Plexico

You just knew they'd find a way to stab us in the heart, after those nine years of seeing Alabama always pull it out at the end. After Bo fumbled and Alabama went back out there with one more chance, it was absolute terror, because we all just knew they would drive right down the field and kick a field goal or score a touchdown and win. In fact, the way things had gone the previous couple of years, I was sure they would somehow score two touchdowns in the final minute, and make it look like they totally kicked our brains in again, because that's what usually would happen. We would be leading in the fourth quarter by maybe one point, and they'd score two quick touchdowns at the end to make it look like they had killed us. That happened over and over in the late Seventies and early Eighties.

So yeah, Alabama got the ball back and I remember Dye yelling and screaming, "Rush three," because remember what defensive formation we used through most of the Eighties. We used the 3-4. We had a nose guard and two defensive ends along with two inside linebackers and two outside linebackers. And that was a formation that Dye brought to Auburn with Frank Orgell and Wayne Hall, that we used through most of the decade. So Dye was yelling, "Rush three, drop eight," and we had eight men in pass coverage. And even rushing only three, we still managed to sack and intercept Walter Lewis and run the clock out and win.

"On fourth down and six, plenty of time to throw, Lewis now throwing over the middle. It is intercepted! It is intercepted! Bob Harris intercepted it at the thirty yard line! An Auburn interception, taking it away from the intended receiver Turner. And Auburn has the football with a minute and forty-five seconds to go, and a one-point lead over the Alabama Crimson Tide.

"A sea of orange and blue celebrants are tearing down the goalposts in this monumental victory, ladies and gentlemen, as the Auburn Tigers have defeated the Alabama Crimson Tide by the score 23-22. Sullivan, did you think we could do it? I didn't think we could do it. We have done it!"
—*Jim Fyffe, radio call of the 1982 Iron Bowl*

"1982 would have to be one of Auburn's sweetest wins over Alabama, ever. It was the game that broke the drought."
—*David Housel*

"That team gave the Auburn fans hope again. People say 'Bo Over the Top' or that game laid the foundations for what was to come after that, all of the years. It showed that we can compete on the other side's level."
—*Bo Jackson*

"I had never seen a fanbase let loose more than this. It was like the Berlin Wall coming down. (Auburn people) had been freed from the rule of Bear Bryant."
—Paul Finebaum

Mike McClendon

After the promise of 1981, it took another year to completely fix the problems Auburn had (coming out of the Barfield era). I purchased season tickets with my college roommate, who I had been friends with since the first grade. We both graduated in 1969, and after my stint in the US Air Force, we made the trek on Saturday mornings to Auburn for every home football game. We never missed one. On November 27, 1982, we went to the game at Legion Field together with our wives. We sat in the North end zone just to the right of the goal posts, above the entrance to the Auburn locker room. It was a great game, and I still have a video of the TV broadcast with Frank Broyles and Keith Jackson. When Bo Jackson went over the top and scored to put us ahead and we subsequently won the game, it wasn't just winning a football game. It was like this enormous sigh of relief from Auburn fans all over the state and country went up. There are very few moments like that in Auburn sports history. That day, that game, changed Auburn fans. If we suffered a self-image problem before, it was gone. I watched one of the posts from the North end zone goal post leave Legion Field heading down Graymont Avenue in the early evening. That was thirty-eight years ago, and I remember it like it was yesterday. There was no more image problem after that. The inferiority complex was erased.

Van Allen Plexico

Pat Dye was crying a little bit after the game because of course he loved the Bear. Bryant had believed in him when he was first starting out, and had given him his career, basically; given him an opportunity. I think we all understood that when Dye went out and hugged Bryant in the middle of the field after the game. Dye later said there was no coach he less wanted to beat than Bryant. I recall the headline in the *Birmingham News* the next day was, "Auburn Ends a Nine-Year Wait," but the secondary headline was over a photo of Dye hugging Bryant, with a tear in his eye, and it said, "Pat Dye and a Tear for the Bear."

I know a lot Auburn fans want to be cynical about all that. I totally understand it, and that's fine—it's Alabama, so be as cynical as you want. But just know, from Pat Dye's perspective, Bear Bryant was a guy that he tremendously respected, who had given him his chance to start his career and gotten him going. I mean, if you're Pat Dye, you had to respect him. Love him or hate him, he was a legend. But regardless of that, we got the last laugh.

So the Auburn fans tore the goalposts down. And this I was in favor of, because any dismantling that happens at Legion Field, especially when we do it, is a good thing.

John Ringer
So why do you have those feelings about Legion field? Let's talk about that. It was the location of this game and many other games in the series.

Van Allen Plexico
On Graymont Avenue. The "iron girders on Graymont."

Up through the early 1980s, Jordan-Hare Stadium was still smaller than Legion Field, and similar in size to Bryant-Denny in Tuscaloosa. Jordan-Hare had expanded a few times, but hadn't quite caught up to Legion Field yet. Auburn had always been seen as not having a big enough stadium for the big teams on the schedule to agree to come to Auburn to play. There also weren't enough accommodations in general. Today that seems unbelievable, but back in as recently as the late 1980s, it was thought that Auburn didn't have enough hotels, hotel rooms, restaurants or restrooms available. If 30,000 more people, in addition to the Auburn fans, were going to come into town for a sporting event, where were they supposed to use the bathroom? That was a serious question back then. Up through the 1970s Auburn had a couple of gas stations and a restaurant or two, a small hotel or two, and that was about it.

Other programs would hold Auburn's lack of public facilities out as a reason to not play games in Auburn. Tuscaloosa, however, didn't have much better. Bryant-Denny Stadium was not super-big; not as big as Legion Field. Because of that, both Alabama and Auburn played most of their really big games in Legion Field in Birmingham for many years. Alabama would play a Rutgers or a Duke in Tuscaloosa, but they'd play Penn State or Notre Dame in Birmingham, with its 75,000-seat capacity. For many years, an agreement was in place that the Iron Bowl would be played there, as well, with the crowd divided 50-50 and the teams alternating which was considered the "home" team in a given year.

Auburn started moving its bigger games to Auburn well before the 1980s. Tennessee and Georgia Tech resisted for a while, but finally they gave in. Eventually the lone holdout, the only team Auburn regularly scheduled that absolutely would not come to Jordan-Hare to play, was Alabama. It started to seem less and less about accommodations and more and more about the Tide having a little advantage and not wanting to lose it.

Van Allen Plexico

It's so funny how it was Alabama's home stadium for all their big games, and yet magically when Auburn played them there, it was supposedly a "neutral site."

John Ringer

It was a neutral site where the ushers all wore Alabama hats.

Van Allen Plexico

Yeah. And eventually they put up a statue of Bear Bryant outside.

John Ringer

Alabama played four games a year there, while we only went there for the Iron Bowl, but it was "neutral."

Van Allen Plexico

The only thing that was neutral about it was they would divide the tickets down the middle. Half the stadium was supposed to be for Auburn and half for Alabama. But even that was an advantage for the Tide. During that stretch of losses, Alabama usually had the better team, so they didn't much care if half the stadium was filled with Auburn fans—not that it ever was. But in our home years, when an overwhelming home-field advantage might have made the difference and given us a critical boost, Alabama still had half the seats.

In reality, of course, the seats were never evenly divided. Pat Dye understood all of this. He knew he needed to get our home games moved out of Legion Field and down to Auburn, so he started a process of expanding our facilities, expanding Jordan-Hare, expanding all the other infrastructure—not just the stadium, you have to have a hotel and conference center. You need hotel rooms, restrooms. You have to be able to accommodate that many people, that much traffic coming in.

John Ringer
Legion Field didn't have much of that, either, though. You had to park in people's yards and driveways.

Van Plexico
People would stand out in the street, waving towels, and they'd rent you their yard for like five bucks. And you just had to hope your car was still there after the game was over. I can think of several times—not just for Iron Bowls—that I went up to Birmingham to some event in Legion field. I'd leave my car in somebody's yard and just hope that everything went okay. I have some interesting stories from those days. After a soccer game there in the Nineties, I watched as a group of South American soccer fans literally lifted up a minivan and slid it across the grass so they could get their vehicle out of a yard.

John Ringer
And also, when it was the Iron Bowl, you might have a situation where you came out of the stadium and walked back to your car and were surrounded by Alabama fans, even though you were the home team and it was supposed to be divided fifty-fifty. And it's getting dark in downtown Birmingham and you don't know what's going to happen.

Van Allen Plexico

Yeah, that's true. It's one thing to be walking out of an on-campus stadium past the dorms where drunk frat guys are yelling at you. It's another thing to be walking out of Legion Field late at night. It was just not a good environment; nobody really liked it except the city of Birmingham.

The stadium was never in very good shape. A bunch of the light bulbs in the scoreboard were always burned out. I remember the *Birmingham News* columnists would constantly say stuff like, "For God's sake—Notre Dame's coming to play Alabama—can we can we put some new light bulbs in?" And they never would. They always had burned-out light bulbs, so you'd get part of a number and you weren't always entirely sure what the score or the time was.

Yet, with all that, do you remember what it said across the bottom of the upper deck and Legion Field? It said, "Birmingham: Football Capital of the South." And we may laugh at that now, but I remember one columnist saying that in the years when the Iron Bowl was a big game and was being played in Legion Field, that was the one time a year that you could actually say that it was true. And that's valid, I think.

Auburn ended the 1982 regular season with an 8-3 record, and their reward was an invitation to Orlando, to play in the Tangerine Bowl against Boston College, with their young star quarterback, Doug Flutie. This would be Auburn's first bowl game since their Gator Bowl win over Texas in 1974. It was the first time the regular season hadn't ended with a loss to Alabama since 1972.

John Ringer

Doug Flutie against Bo Jackson in the Tangerine Bowl on December 18. Two future Heisman winners. And two years before the famous Hail Mary pass against Miami.

Van Allen Plexico

This was very early days for ESPN.

John Ringer
We didn't have cable.

Van Allen Plexico
We didn't either. Probably not fifteen people saw the game on ESPN. I listened to it on the radio.

"Boston College returns to the bowl scene after a fourteen-year absence, led by sophomore quarterback Doug Flutie. Auburn relies on the potent wishbone attack led by freshman running sensation Bo Jackson. You've got a couple of potent offensive teams meeting tonight in the Tangerine Bowl on ESPN.

"Boston College with a multiple offense that Auburn has to stop. This is going to be a problem. They've got to get to Flutie. Flutie, the quarterback, is the key to it. He is only 5'10' but a great football player. What Auburn has to do, number one, is rush this guy. Blitzes. And the other thing I think we're going to be surprised about is we're going to see Auburn go with five defensive backs early in the ballgame, not only on third down but maybe on first down.

"Okay, for Boston College, the problem is dealing with the wishbone offense. They haven't faced it all season long. The wishbone offense is a tough offense. What they try to do with the wishbone is wear a team down. If this is a close game going into the fourth quarter, you got to give the nod to Auburn for one reason: they're going to wear your defense down and they're going to score on you.

"Okay, the stadium is packed, lots of excitement, we'll be set to go in just a little bit with the Tangerine Bowl."
—ESPN pregame

"Boston College is a worthy opponent. Got an outstanding football team. Coaching staff has done a great job. They play with a lot of enthusiasm and a lot of confidence. A big, strong, physical football team on both sides of the ball, and do a great job with their offense. Flutie, a little quarterback as you know, he's amazing."
—Pat Dye, ESPN pregame interview

"We've got to slow down the wishbone, which we haven't played against, and we understand how to play against it but our players haven't recognized it that much. So that's going to be a challenge (to deal with) the wishbone; it's so mental, because the actions and the reactions are so different than with any other offense, where you've got to have somebody on dive, somebody on quarterback and somebody on the pitch.

"And you can't say, 'Well, I thought it was a dive,' and then have the quarterback run forever. So it's a very disciplined approach you've got to have from a defensive standpoint."
—Jack Bicknell, Boston College head coach, ESPN pregame interview

Bo Jackson ran for two touchdowns in the second quarter, powering Auburn out to a 33-10 lead in the fourth. Boston college held Auburn scoreless after that and came back late, scoring 16 unanswered points, but fell just short of a miraculous comeback.

Auburn finished the game with 490 yards of total offense. Randy Campbell was named the game's MVP, hitting 10 of 16 passes for 177 yards.

Even fullback Greg Pratt carried the ball 9 times for 59 yards.

"We had planned to play just about everybody tonight. We wanted everybody to have some fun."
—Greg Pratt, Auburn fullback

Senior safety Mark Dorminey was the defensive MVP, playing brilliantly in limiting Flutie's passing and BC's rushing attack.

Flutie meanwhile completed 22 of 38 passes for 299 yards and accounted for three touchdowns.

"Flutie is more than pretty good. He's unreal. He gave us trouble in a lot of ways. It felt like a track meet. We'd run 30 and 40 yards on every play. I felt like every play lasted five minutes."
—Mark Dorminey, Auburn safety

Van Allen Plexico

Auburn won, 33-26. Bo had a pretty good game. Interesting to note our starting left tackle was none other than Jay Jacobs, future AU Athletic Director.

We pretty much held Flutie in check, and we ended the season ranked no. 14. Not too bad. We ended up tied for third in the SEC, believe it or not, with Vanderbilt. This was one of their more decent years; they finished 8-4, 4-2 in the SEC.

John Ringer

They were at their peak. One of the last times they went to a bowl game before James Franklin took over there.

Van Allen Plexico

I remember thinking one of the best things about Auburn being 9-3 was that Alabama was 8-4. Winning the Iron Bowl gave us a better season record than them, and that hadn't happened in quite a while.

1983

As 1982 ended and the players, coaches and fans faced a long offseason, the entire Auburn Family was just buzzing. It had been years since Tigers fans felt such excitement, such anticipation for an upcoming season.

The starting quarterback, Randy Campbell, was coming back as an experienced senior. Lionel James would be back as a senior, too, and his new partner in the backfield, Bo Jackson, looked to be an unprecedented talent. There was great depth behind them, too, with Brent Fullwood, Tim Jessie, Collis Campbell and Kyle Collins, not to mention incoming freshman fullback Tommie Agee. The Tigers still had Chris Woods and Clayton Buford at receiver, and excellent tight ends like Ron Middleton and Ed West. The offensive line would feature Steve Wallace, who went on to win multiple Super Bowls blocking for Joe Montana and the 49ers. The reliable kicker, Al Del Greco, was a senior, too. Special teams were good all the way around. The defense was rock solid, with Donnie Humphrey and

Doug Smith on the line. Tremendous optimism abounded, going into the 1983 season. Auburn was on the rise. What could possibly stop the Tigers now?

And then the 1983 schedule came out. And it was absolutely insane.

The schedule comprised a perfect storm of strong, traditional SEC foes mixed with non-conference opponents that would be having all-time seasons.

After opening against Southern Miss, who had come so close to beating the Tigers in 1982, game two would be against Texas. In 1983 Texas under Fred Akers was a powerhouse, sitting in the top 3 in the AP Poll most of the season.

For game three, the Tigers would have to travel to Knoxville to face old rival Tennessee in Neyland Stadium, where Auburn had only won once since 1971.

Game four would be against Florida State, a program just then emerging under head coach Bobby Bowden as athletic, fast, and fully capable of whipping even the best teams. They particularly relished doing so on the road, and they'd be coming to Jordan-Hare.

Games five and six would be on the road, against Kentucky and Georgia Tech. Then the Tigers would get Mississippi State at home, just before an extremely strong, top 5-ranked Florida came to town.

Game nine should have been something of a break between the Gators and the Georgia/Alabama finale. In 1983, it was anything but a break. While not a traditional football power, Maryland that year featured future NFL star Boomer Esiason at quarterback, with a solid supporting cast around him.

The season would end with Georgia on the road, in Athens, and Alabama in Birmingham.

Van Allen Plexico

That 1983 schedule was just mind boggling. How did we end up with that schedule? Who could've possibly thought that was a good idea? And yet we won every game but one.

Four of our opponents were ranked in the top 10 in the country. Bear in mind, this is in an 11-game regular season. Throw in Michigan in the bowl game and it's five! Three of our regular-season opponents were in the top 5.

Texas was ranked 3rd. Georgia was 4th. Florida was 5th. Maryland was 7th. Michigan was 8th. That's five top-ten teams. Alabama was the lowest-ranked of the many top 25 teams we played, at 19th. Tennessee finished 9-3 and won their bowl. FSU finished 8-4, another bowl-winning team. They should've both been ranked, too.

John Ringer
Talk about a murderer's row.

Somebody did a historical analysis of teams and schedules, and I think this was rated one of the toughest schedules in the history of college football.

Herman Wilkes was a walk-on player for Pat Dye's Auburn teams in 1982 and 1983:

Herman Wilkes
In my junior year of high school, I was a second-team "all-state" linebacker in Georgia. I was a good high school player but not Division 1 caliber. I had a scholarship offer from the Naval Academy and Georgia Southern but my dream was to play for Auburn. In the spring game of my junior season, I had a severe knee injury that precluded me from playing my senior year and the fall of my freshman year at Auburn. Coach Dye had recruited my father in high school, so he invited me to join the team as a walk on. Coach Dye let me go through non-contact practices for the lead up to the 1982 Citrus Bowl game. I did the full winter workouts, spring training, A-Day game and summer workouts at Auburn. Three points stood out about that 1983 team:

1: The team was really hard-nosed; mentally tough. That's a reflection of Coach Dye in those years.

2: The level of relative talent was really high. Twenty-two players from the team went on to professional football stints.

3: The hardest/most physically demanding training evolutions that I've ever gone through were USMC Officers Candidate Course, USMC Bootcamp and Auburn University winter workouts. We were really pushed hard and the team responded.

I was a walk-on as a defensive back but was asked to switch to scout team running back. It was good for the team but bad for me. I had never played offense in my life and I hated it. I quit football after the Sugar Bowl and focused on graduating. Luckily, I got the 1983 SEC Championship ring.

More on the talent level of the team: Bo Jackson was a transformational player. Keven Greene was an amazing athlete. But I'm not sure if any other modern AU team had this depth of talent, to have so many players go to the next level.

What separated this 1983 team, and made them so special? The 1982 team established a really solid work ethic that led to the success of the 1983 team. Work ethic plus talent was the real difference. (AU defensive back) David King told me once that in previous years, I would have gotten some playing time, but in 1982-83, the roster was just too strong and fast. I wasn't alone, though. Another forty teammates were just like me, slugging out every practice against the (statistically) best defense in the country.

Coach Dye once told us, "The only time to be scared is when you're not prepared. Nerves are fine but never be scared if you've put in the work." That mentality carried me through Marine Corps training, Naval Aviation flight school, and carrier-based operations, flying an F/A-18 and combat ops in Afghanistan.

Van Allen Plexico

There was so much buzz in the offseason before 1983; so much excitement and positivity—and then in practice, Gregg Pratt, our starting fullback, collapsed and died in the heat.

I feel like if it had happened just a few years later, it would have been a much bigger scandal. But this was still a time where you're coming out of the day and age where football coaches would work the players so hard, maybe with no water to drink, and it was all considered a sign of "toughness" and "manliness" to withstand all that.

There was a certain amount of concern and worry and it was a big story, but I think today it would be a huge scandal, and people might even get fired, and you'd have drastic rules changes and so on. Back then, it was seen as a tragedy, and the players dedicated the season to him, but then it seems like we just moved on. And I feel bad about that now. But it was a different time.

"I can't speak for the rest of the guys but it (Pratt's death) changed me forever. At that age you never think about death and dying. It's something that you never forget."
—*Auburn kicker Al Del Greco*

John Ringer

It did get forgotten, unfortunately, by a lot of fans. At the time, programs were more open, but at the same time, there wasn't as much reach; a story like that wouldn't have legs, and it would just kind of fade away, and people would try to be respectful towards the family, so it wouldn't get dragged out.

Clearly, that shouldn't have happened. It was a time when we didn't take players' health as seriously. I think back to the Junction Boys and some of that kind of silliness. In terms of taking care of player safety and keeping players hydrated, and the way they'd exercise and so on, it was different back then.

It was a terrible tragedy, but it does seem like it helped mentally jell this team and all the talent and potential they had. They wanted to win for him, in his memory.

Van Allen Plexico

Yeah, I think that's true. I hate to segue from a player dying to football, but that's kind of how things went back then. Greg Pratt passed away and the team mourned, and then they pulled together and went out and had an amazing season; one of the greatest seasons in Auburn history.

We had a freshman fullback that stepped into Pratt's spot in the lineup in Tommie Agee. He went on to be our starting star fullback for four years, and then played for the Dallas Cowboys, blocking for Emmitt Smith.

The 1983 season was in some ways similar to 2004. In 2004, Auburn made their way up to no. 3 and could never get past the top two. In 1983, similarly, the Tigers went into the bowl season at no. 3

and won, and both of the top two teams lost, and yet somehow Auburn still ended up third after it was all over.

The season opened up September 7 at home against Southern Miss.

"The field at Jordan-Hare Stadium was beautifully trimmed for the (opening) game. The grass is new. The old grass was plowed up in May, and new Bermuda was sprigged. The same was done to the three practice fields, and each field was reshaped and given its own irrigation system. Two light towers also were added on a practice field to allow nighttime practices. Total cost of improvements was $100,000."
—Montgomery Advertiser

One scarcely had to look hard that day to see the impact the success of Pat Dye's teams was having on the Auburn Family; on their enthusiasm and willingness to come out and support the squad. The previous year, attendance for the USM game had been 55,000. For 1983, the university expected as many as 70,000 fans, but the crowd ended up surpassing even the capacity of the stadium, setting an opening-day record. Jordan-Hare at that time held 72,169, but for the game against the Golden Eagles, 73,500 fans passed through the turnstiles.

A good, traditional opponent; Auburn played Southern Miss quite often in the Seventies and Eighties. The year before, they'd wanted to kick a field goal at the end that could've won the game for them, but the clock ran out before they could attempt it. They weren't happy about that; they felt the referees had allowed time to expire without forcing the Auburn players to line back up. This time, Auburn left no doubts. The Tigers won, 24-3.

"They'll get my vote as one of the top teams in the country. They are quite a bit better than they were last year. Offensively, they are more polished. They have no ragged edges. They ran the pitch well, and their halfbacks really knocked us down on the corners."
—Jim Carmody, USM head coach

Notable in the game: Lionel James broke loose for a 94-yard touchdown run that was called back on a penalty. Even without that play, he still finished with 172 yards rushing on 16 carries. Without the penalty, he'd have gained nearly 300 yards. Bo Jackson added 73 more, on 11 attempts, and caught a late touchdown pass for 44 yards. That pass aside, Randy Campbell only completed three other passes, for a total of 18 yards.

"We talked about it yesterday. We all loved Gregg, and decided to sign the game ball and send it to Mrs. Pratt and her family."
—Pat Dye

And then came Texas.

The Longhorns were ranked no. 3 at the time, but would soon move up to no. 2. As the season had begun, the two teams that were poised to dominate college football that year were Nebraska and Texas. Nebraska opened up the season in the Kickoff Classic in the Meadowlands in New Jersey against Penn State, the team that had won the national championship the year before. Nebraska crushed them. After that, and the way the Cornhuskers proceeded to utterly dominate the other teams on their schedule, some were hailing them as the Team of the Century; possibly the greatest college football team ever. They featured Mike Rozier, who would win the Heisman Trophy that year, at running back; Turner Gill at quarterback; and future NFL star wide receiver Irving Fryar. They were coached by the legendary Tom Osborne.

Fred Akers' Texas team was expected to be almost as good, and they would go on to spend a good portion of the season ranked second behind that Nebraska team.

Auburn had to play them at home in week two.

"When the job came open at Auburn, I knew that it was a perfect setting for my background and for me. I grew up in the South, and with the exception of a short stay in Wyoming have always worked in the South."

"He's quite comfortable with the southern roads and highways. He is a well-traveled recruiter down here. Indeed, recruiting may be

140

Pat Dye's number one asset. Some down here went so far as to say Bear Bryant was a little worried about his former student coaching in the Southeastern Conference, because Dye was such a good recruiter. Dye takes a more modern view... In his two years at Auburn, Dye has already put together a program strong enough to place high in the rankings. ...He's a great organizer. He's intelligent, he's an innovator. He's a great coach.

"If one word could describe Pat Dye, it might be work. He loves to work, loves to make people work, loves to watch them work, and loves to talk about work. You've got a real work ethic down here."

"Well, you know, I was a 190-pound guard. And I couldn't even have played football if it wasn't for work."

"Perhaps the one athlete who personified Dye's theory of working was Gregg Pratt, who was a walk-on with no scholarship, who earned himself a top position on the team. Tragically, Pratt collapsed during a preseason session in what is still referred to as a 'freak accident.' He died of a heart attack. So how did Pat Dye get his team through this ordeal?"

"I think that our players and our assistant coaches did a great job of working through that time period and not losing sight of our goals, and realizing that, you know, that's what Gregg would have wanted the team and the coaches to do."
—CBS intro with Pat Dye, Auburn vs Texas, 1983

Auburn lost to Texas, 20-7. It's one of those handful of games Auburn fans wish they could go back in time and play again, and somehow change one little thing here or there. The game turned on a few key moments, with most of Texas' points coming from a couple of big plays.

Early in the second quarter, the Longhorns intercepted Randy Campbell throwing a rare deep ball, and they took over at their own ten yard line. Two plays later, their backup quarterback stepped in for one play and hit Kelvin Epps for an 80-yard touchdown, assisted by an Auburn defensive back falling down as he went for the ball.

Other than that, it was a defensive slugfest. The starting quarterback for Texas only completed three passes the entire game. Both teams netted about 130 yards on the ground, both fumbled once, and time of possession was pretty even. Bo Jackson only carried the ball seven times, and Lionel James only ten; after the game, Auburn assistant coaches speculated that they had been "bluffed" by Texas into avoiding the sweep and having quarterback Randy Campbell keep the ball and run too many times.

"They tried to make Randy (Campbell) run the ball on the option, and we couldn't get the ball to our halfbacks. We wanted to establish the fullback early and get into a slow, methodical game. We were hoping to get into the fourth quarter in a low-scoring game but it sure as hell didn't work out that way."
—Jack Crowe, Auburn offensive coordinator

Even so, Auburn shut Texas out in the second half and scored a touchdown themselves on a long drive. Clearly Auburn wasn't entirely outclassed by Texas; they simply got caught up in a bad game plan and didn't execute properly during the first two quarters. It was one of those games where, if you play it five times, a different team wins each time, back and forth—but it's always close.

"There's no question they have one of the two best teams in the country. There were no surprises. They didn't do anything we hadn't prepared for. They have players on their second and third teams who could start for a lot of teams."
—Jay Jacobs, Auburn offensive guard and future athletic director

The outcome was disappointing at the time. A few months later, Auburn fans would come to realize it had been far bigger—and far more damaging—than that. It was nothing less than one of the most crucial losses in the history of Auburn football. An undefeated, 12-0 Auburn couldn't have been voted lower than no. 1 in the polls after the bowl games were over. But a 1-loss team? By losing to Texas, Auburn had put left that question in the hands of, and to the judgment of, a bunch of poll voters across the country. It remained to be seen how those people would respond.

Lionel "Little Train" James, by Jarrod Alberich

Van Allen Plexico

Our next several games were not on TV, including big wins over Tennessee, Florida State and Georgia Tech. I mention that, and it's important, because this was still the age of sports reporters ultimately deciding which teams got to play for the national championship. Looking good on television mattered a lot. There simply weren't as many chances to play quality teams in an eleven-game regular season, with no conference championship games. When you had those rare appearances on a national network, you had to look good and impress the voters.

We were 6-1 on October 22, but the only game of ours the national audience had seen by the time we played 5th-ranked Florida the following weekend was us getting beaten up by Texas. So that's why we were lower-ranked and didn't even climb up to no. 3 until November 5. All that people remembered was that Texas loss. I remember people saying this at the end of the season: None of the poll voters remembered Florida beating Miami. But everybody remembered Texas beating Auburn. And that's what ended up getting us, I think.

John Ringer

I think you're right because, again, we're on TV five times that year including the bowl game, and the Texas game was a big early impression that stayed stuck in people's minds.

Van Allen Plexico

And Texas didn't lose until the Cotton Bowl.

After the Texas loss, Auburn went to Knoxville the next week to play Tennessee. The Tigers proceeded to administer a violent beatdown on the Vols. In the fourth quarter, with Auburn already ahead, freshman receiver Trey Gainous received a punt, appeared to duck underneath two Tennessee players who converged on him as he caught the ball, and from there he slipped past them and returned it for a touchdown.

"We had a return right called, but all I saw was orange jerseys. I remembered what Coach Wallace told me. If you can't get it going east and west, then just go north and south and get as much as you can.

"When I broke open, I thought if I could pick up a block I might score. When I did, the feeling was indescribable. I don't know if I've ever felt any better."
—*Trey Gainous, Auburn wide receiver*

After that, it was all Auburn, with the final score 37-14.

"I'm just glad to be a part of this one. I've been thinking about this game for two years, ever since I left this dressing room a loser the last time."
—*Gregg Carr, Auburn linebacker*

"There were a whole lot of people who were down. We knew we didn't play well against Texas and we knew our goals were still the same. We knew what had to be done.

"The Texas game is over with. I heard somebody say that if you're going to lose, it was best to lose in September. We feel like everybody is going to lose. I'm just glad to get ours overwith and I'm looking forward to getting our ten."
—*Doug Smith, Auburn defensive lineman*

Florida State came to visit Jordan-Hare on October 1. Always a tricky matchup for the Tigers, games against the Seminoles often devolving into a track meet up and down the field. This game would prove to be no different.

Auburn scored first, going 85 yards in just five plays, mostly on the arm of Randy Campbell. The touchdown came on a 6-yard pass to tight end Jeff Parks.

Florida State came right back down the field when it was their turn. They had the third-ranked offense the country, and it showed for most of the game. They scored on a short field possession to tie the game at 7-7.

"They're like a pro team (on offense)."
—Donnie Humphrey, Auburn defensive lineman

"You just can't shut them down. No way."
—Frank Orgel, Auburn defensive coordinator

The two teams traded field goals after that, and then Al Del Greco added another one to put the Tigers up, 13-10. Auburn cashed in one more touchdown just before halftime; freshman fullback Tommie Agee took a pass from Campbell and raced 27 yards into the end zone as the clock hit 0:00. At the half, Auburn led, 20-10.

The previously maligned Seminole defense cranked things up in the third quarter, shutting Auburn out for that entire fifteen minutes of play, while their offense—ranked third in the country—scored on a short Kelly Lowrey run to pull within 3 at 20-17. As the game moved into the fourth quarter, Lowrey snuck in for another short TD and suddenly the visiting Noles had surged ahead for the first time, 24-20.

"It was a game filled with memorable moments, with great plays and individual heroics. But it boiled down to three passes thrown in the final 3:14—two by Campbell, one by Lowrey. Auburn caught all three."
—Bob Mayes, Montgomery Advertiser

The Tigers responded with one more scoring drive—although things appeared grim just before the score. Auburn faced fourth down twice on the drive. The first time, at the FSU 32, Campbell hit reliable tight end Ed West for a 15-yard gain to keep the chains moving.

A few plays later, the Tigers found themselves looking at another critical down, this time a fourth and 8 at the FSU 15. They had to find a way to get the first down; they knew they had little hope of getting the ball back in the time remaining if they failed to convert or score. Trailing 24-20, a field goal would do them no good. It was touchdown or bust on that drive.

Randy Campbell asked the coaches for a particular play he favored—"89"—and it worked, resulting in a 15-yard pass to Lionel

James, who took it down the left sideline and in for the touchdown. Auburn had regained the lead in the final moments, 27-24. The Tigers had scored on their last offensive snaps of the first and second halves.

FSU was not done, though. They came right back down the field. Lowrey connected with receiver Weegie Thompson to set the Noles up at the Auburn 26 with less than a minute remaining. But on the next play, big Tiger lineman Donnie Humphrey blasted up the middle and pressured Lowrey, whose errant pass landed in the hands of Auburn's Gregg Carr at the 22 yard line.

"I was in the clouds, even though I was on the ground. It's something I'll always remember, but I really can't explain how I felt."
—Gregg Carr, Auburn linebacker

"Give the linebacker credit. He made a great play."
—Kelly Lowrey, Florida State quarterback

"I felt we had it in the bag. I didn't think they could stop us."
—Roosevelt Snipes, Florida State running back

Randy Campbell converted two fourth-downs with *passes* on the final drive, and threw for three touchdowns—both absolutely remarkable occurrences for a team so built around the option run game.

"Our defense played nearly well enough to win. That last play was sad. And then we had time to win it at the end and we gave it up on first down. We had plenty of time. Dadgumit, that just makes you sick.
"I feel bad. I'm upset. I can't wait until next year. I don't want to play 'em again next week, but I can't wait until next year."
—Bobby Bowden, Florida State head coach

This game would prove to be merely a prelude to the great Auburn-FSU rivalry that would continue to be played, every season but one, through the rest of the decade. Auburn, incidentally, would win that rematch in Tallahassee the next year, in what Jim Fyffe would call a "wild and wooly shootout." They'd win the year after that, too.

Meanwhile, next up for the 1983 Tigers squad was Kentucky. Auburn had beaten them the previous year, 18-3, by way of nothing but six Al Del Greco field goals—a feat not duplicated by any team in the SEC until 2016, when Auburn's Daniel Carlson kicked the same number through the uprights to beat LSU. In 1983, however, the Tigers found a good deal more offense, ringing up the Wildcats in Lexington for seven touchdowns and a 49-21 win.

Victories followed over Georgia Tech, 31-13, and Mississippi State, 28-13. After trailing 10-7 at the half, Auburn's defense totally shut the Yellowjacket offense down in the third and fourth quarters as the offense found its footing and roared back.

"In the first half the defense just stood around, but in the second half they got after them and set them down. In the second half we played like Auburn is supposed to."
—Pat Dye

The next week, against the Bulldogs, Lionel James again ripped off a long touchdown run, something he was making into a habit. This one came from 74 yards away, to get the scoring started in the first quarter. Reserve running back Brent Fullwood saw some action late and scored another touchdown.

Then it was October 29 and time once again to play the Gators.

"The preliminaries are over, the breathers a thing of the past.

"Auburn's football season has come to its moment of truth. Are the Tigers good enough to represent the Southeastern Conference in the Sugar Bowl? Are they good enough to actually challenge down the stretch for the national championship?

"The answers start coming Saturday when Florida comes to town."
—Phillip Marshall, Montgomery Advertiser

By this point in the season, the Tigers had climbed back from 11th, where they had dropped after the Texas loss, up to 4th. Florida was ranked 5th and undefeated (they had tied Southern Cal in the

L.A. Coliseum). The Gators were on a roll; they had opened the season with a big 28-3 win over the Miami Hurricanes (about which, more later, unfortunately) and whipped 16th ranked LSU 31-17 in Baton Rouge. It looked to be a big-time matchup on CBS. The game lived up to the hype.

Van Allen Plexico

That was as big an Auburn-Florida game as there has ever been.

Charley Pell was still the Florida coach—though not for much longer! Wayne Peace was their star quarterback. Up until then, the Gators had only won at Jordan-Hare twice in their history—1973 and 1975—believe it or not.

The game went back and forth and back and forth. Bo had a couple of huge runs, 80 and 55 yards. Just amazing.

"Campbell split to the side and Ed West to the left, and flanked to the right is Buford. Campbell pitches to Bo on a sweep on the short side—he broke a tackle—he's at the 45, 40, Jackson looks for running room. He's in a footrace at the 20, the 15, the 10— Touchdown Auburn! You can get excited if you want to, but I am, because that was a great run by Bo Jackson!"
—Jim Fyffe, Auburn radio broadcast

Bo Jackson's 80-yard run came with 8:20 to go in the third quarter and put Auburn ahead by a score of 28-7. The touchdown came one play after Florida running back (and future Chicago Bears star) Neal Anderson appeared to have scored on an 8-yard run, which would have narrowed the score to 21-14. Instead, the ball was stripped and rolled out the end zone, giving Auburn a touchback. Florida coaches and players were livid; they were certain Anderson had crossed the plane of the goal line before fumbling.

"I thought we scored the touchdown. I'm disappointed in the officials and in the conference. ... If I see the game film, and I am wrong, I will apologize."
—Charley Pell, Florida head coach, after the game

"In viewing the video tape this morning, it was obvious that Neal Anderson did fumble the football before he went across the goal line. The official made a good call. And I'll personally write him a note to congratulate him on that good call. But there were many judgment calls in the game that went Auburn's way; none went our way."

—Charley Pell, Florida head coach, on his TV show the following Sunday

"I think there's no doubt that we pulled together a lot closer as a team."

—Dowe Aughtman, Auburn nose tackle, after the game

"Very good blocking by the offensive line. I haven't thanked them yet, but I may buy all of them dinner. Buy them a candy bar or something."

—Bo Jackson, after the game

The Gators put together two very impressive touchdown drives late in the fourth quarter. Quarterback Wayne Peace connected on 6 of 8 passes for 69 yards on the third scoring drive, including converting a fourth-and-15. Florida narrowed the score to 28-21 with just 2:54 remaining. The Tigers were able to hang on and finish the game off after that.

"The Good Lord put some sun on us yesterday.

"Florida deserves a lot of credit for not giving up and for coming back and having a chance to win at the end. It was a classic from the beginning to the end. ... Our players wanted to play and win this game as much as any game since we've been at Auburn.

"I think you can see physically, from a contact standpoint, I don't think there's any we've played that compared with it except the Alabama game the last two years. Kids just laying their bodies on the line, and their heart and their soul and their guts, and that's what it took to win the football game. Because Florida is a very good football team. But they weren't good enough yesterday."

—Pat Dye, Auburn Football Review

Auburn gained 316 yards rushing against the SEC's no. 1 defense against the run; a defense that had shut them down quite effectively the year before. Florida had been giving up just 100.7 yards rushing per game before facing Auburn. The Gators, meanwhile, managed only 74 rushing yards.

"Auburn (7-1) moved into a first-place tie with Georgia in the SEC, each with 4-0 (conference) records, and Florida (6-1-1) fell into second place at 3-1 after the first of three consecutive weeks of matchups involving those three teams."
—AP wire report

The Tigers didn't get much of a break the following weekend. On November 5, in came the Maryland Terrapins.

In the vast majority of years, playing Maryland at football would be considered something of an easier week; certainly not as challenging as most of the teams on the 1983 schedule.

Of course, because Auburn had scheduled them and, given the luck of the Tigers in such things, Maryland brought one of their best teams ever to Jordan-Hare that season. The Terrapin squad was led by future NFL great Boomer Esiason at quarterback, and was ranked 7th in the country.

"This is another step toward the Sugar Bowl; another step in that direction. But we've got a very difficult situation coming up this week. It's gonna be difficult on you; it's gonna be difficult on me. I'm gonna ask the senior leadership to do their part... to get this team ready to play.

"First of all, you've got to come down off of today. That's gonna be tough enough as it is. The next thing is, you cannot be looking beyond Maryland to playing Georgia. I don't know if they (Maryland) won today, but they could very easily come in here a 7-1 team just like you are. Now, we don't have to beat Maryland to go to the Sugar Bowl. But we got to beat Maryland to have a chance to win the national championship down the road."
—Pat Dye, in the locker room after the Florida game

Maryland came into the game apparently determined to focus all their defensive attention on stopping Bo Jackson and Lionel James, and they had a remarkable degree of success in doing that. Unfortunately for them, they failed to take into account Auburn's freshman fullback, who would run wild on the Terps that day, scoring on runs of 61 and 44 yards.

Van Allen Plexico

The Maryland defense just keyed on Bo almost every snap. They all jumped on him whether they had the ball or not. He and Lionel James both had over 100 yards, but the unexpected hero was fullback Tommie Agee. Campbell started leaving the ball with Agee and he'd burst up the middle for ten yards, fifteen yards; he just ate them up and they never would or could adjust. He finished with over 200 yards. At fullback!

"As the last few seconds in this game today ticked away, the sellout crowd of 75,600 was chanting "A-gee . . . A-gee . . . A-gee" in appreciation of the 219-yard rushing afternoon turned in by this 5-foot-11-inch, 210- pound freshman fullback from Maplesville, Ala."
—NY Times

Van Allen Plexico

There was a radio show in Birmingham back then called the "Mark and Brian Show." You may not have ever heard of them, not being in Alabama, but they got to be very popular and went off to do a TV show on NBC later. But they started out in Alabama. I even met one of them at a high school function—Mark Thompson. The two of them had this little skit every week where they would make fun of Bo, because he'd become quite a celebrity and folk figure in the state, particularly after the previous Iron Bowl. They created a caricature version of him that was egotistical and conceited— really the opposite of Bo himself—just for laughs. After the Maryland game, they said the crowd was cheering "Agee— Agee—Agee," and they had their character version of Bo respond to that with, "No, the crowd was chanting 'AG' for 'Always Great', as in 'always great Bo Jackson.'"

"Agee's heroics obscured a brilliant day by the Maryland quarterback Boomer Esiason, who completed 23 of 37 attempts for 355 yards. Esiason was sacked four times, yet always seemed to make a comeback and complete a long pass that made Auburn's fans uneasy.

"Auburn scored its final touchdown on the last play of the game when Esiason was hit and fumbled while trying to pass. The defensive tackle Donnie Humphrey fell on the ball in the end zone."
—NY Times

"Auburn going to the prevent defense. They've got five defensive backs in. Snap of the ball from the Maryland 14, Esiasion is hit—he drops the ball! Auburn falls on it in the end zone! Touchdown Auburn! Donnie Humphrey! Big Donnie Humphrey, who has played a marvelous defensive game, blindsided him and then fell on the ball!"
—Jim Fyffe, Auburn radio broadcast

"Auburn has a great future. We have all kinds of running backs, and the freshman offensive linemen are going to be great. I believe Auburn is going to be the next team of the decade."
—Lionel James, Auburn running back, after the Maryland game

With Boomer's Maryland disposed of, 35-23, the Tigers prepared to travel east in the direction of Clarke County, Georgia, for a titanic showdown with the Bulldogs on November 12.

John Ringer

This was a big win for the orange face masks!

Georgia came into the game as the reigning SEC champs three years running. They hadn't lost a conference game since November 17, 1979, and that loss had come against Auburn. They were on a twenty-three-game conference winning streak. They were ranked fourth in the country. Auburn was 8-1 after the win over Maryland, and was ranked third.

Georgia fans were incredibly confident in their team at this point; probably obnoxiously so. One of the best-selling records in the state at that time was a collection of (their radio play-by-play announcer) Larry Munson's greatest calls.

Auburn was averaging running the ball 54 times a game for 297 yards. Georgia only allowed around 100 yards per game rushing, but Auburn finished with 261. Lionel James scored Auburn's only touchdown and finished with 84 yards, slashing through the Georgia defense. That score came on a short field drive after a fumble caused by Auburn nose tackle Doug Smith in the first quarter.

Bo Jackson finished with 115 yards rushing, but also made many key blocks in the game, including one on the James touchdown run. (We don't always think of Bo as a blocker but, due to his size and strength, he was very effective in this role). Randy Campbell was 12 of 15 passing in the game and also rushed for 33 yards. Many of Campbell's throws that day were key first downs for Auburn.

Both teams entered the game in the top five in the nation and this game was clearly for the SEC title. Auburn's defense shut down the Georgia offense. UGA only crossed midfield three times the entire game. They scored with two minutes left and recovered the onside kick but Auburn stopped them to preserve the win.

The score is not indicative of how much Auburn dominated this game. Auburn moved into scoring position two other times, but Al Del Greco missed two short field goals in the second half. Georgia was completely shut down on offense and Auburn controlled the ball with its rushing attack. With the wishbone offense moving the ball and controlling the clock, Georgia had few possessions to try to come back.

John Ringer

Vince Dooley said after the game that this was the finest Auburn team he had ever seen. And he'd seen a lot of Auburn teams, including the ones where he was the quarterback.

Perhaps most remarkably of all, the SEC was founded in 1933, and this 50th anniversary season was the first time Auburn and Georgia ever finished 1-2 in the conference standings.

I would also note, the kicker matchup in this game was one of the best ever, with Kevin Butler for UGA against Al Del Greco for Auburn.

Van Allen Plexico

They had broken our hearts the year before with Herschel. By this point he was playing in the USFL, but everybody else was back from that great team.

I still remember the TV shots of those Georgia cheerleaders on the sideline crying at the end of the game. The UGA fans and players really wanted to be able to say they'd won the SEC all four years in a row, and we messed that up for them. Instead, it clinched the title for us, for the first time twenty-six years.

It was a game of steel; a game of trench warfare; of smashmouth football. And the good guys won.

"I thought we would have scored more, but it is to Georgia's defensive credit we did not."
—Pat Dye

"Auburn, which only three years ago was on probation and not winning often, played its way into the Sugar Bowl by beating previously undefeated Georgia, 13-7, before a crowd of 82,122 today in Sanford Stadium.

"Al Del Greco, who missed three field-goal attempts, booted two field goals in the first half to provide the margin of victory for Auburn after Lionel James scored the Tigers' only touchdown on a 3-yard run in the opening quarter.

"Auburn (9-1) has no conference defeats but must play Alabama in the traditional season finale Dec. 3. And even though Alabama, Tennessee and Georgia have only one loss each in the S.E.C., the Sugar Bowl's president, Bill Martinez, told reporters shortly after the game ended that his bowl would take Auburn as the host team no matter what happens.

"Auburn entered this game No. 1 in the computer ranking of The New York Times *and third in both news-service polls behind Nebraska and Texas."*
—Gordon S. White, Jr, NY Times

"When I was in high school, I saw Alabama and Penn State play in the Sugar Bowl. I knew at that time that I was going to Auburn, and when I saw that game, I told myself that I would make it to New Orleans someday. Looks like I finally did."
—*Randy Campbell, Auburn quarterback*

Auburn didn't play again for three weeks. When they did, it was time for the Iron Bowl, against a 7-3 Alabama team. And things got a little crazy.

Yes, a force of nature descended on Birmingham on December 3, 1983.

Well, actually, *two* forces of nature struck Legion Field. One was a string of storms across the area that spun off deadly tornadoes, some striking nearby during the game.

The other force of nature was called Bo Jackson.

Channel 6 in Birmingham interrupted the ABC broadcast of the game to issue a tornado warning, and then interrupted themselves live on the air to show Bo breaking off a long touchdown run, before resuming the tornado warnings. That's how big this game always is, and how huge it was when Bo did something unbelievable during it. Even during a tornado.

Van Allen Plexico

I still can't quite believe that game was allowed to continue in those weather conditions. There were literally tornado sirens wailing right outside the stadium. Many of the fans left early, and quite rightly so. But, as we've said before, it was a different time.

It seemed like Alabama really outplayed Auburn in most phases of the game. This was a new Alabama, no longer coached by Bear Bryant. Ray Perkins, an old Alabama wide receiver, had been brought in as the new head coach and he was trying to modernize the offense. Their defense was still strong, and of course they got up for us. Particularly after having lost to us the previous year. It was an odd-numbered year so Auburn was designated the home team, but that never made any difference—not that very many fans were left in the stands anyway. Alabama put up a heck of a fight and played well enough to win.

156

The Tide led 14-10 at the half, on the strength of Walter Lewis touchdown passes to Joey Jones and Joe Carter. Bo Jackson, however, started off and finished up the scoring in the game by tearing loose for a couple of long touchdown runs of 69 and 71 yards, and that made the difference.

"There was an awful lot at stake. I think the conditions of the weather made me look stupid out there at times. The wind was swirling and it was hard to make a decision on the field goals. I think the decision to take the football in the first half was very vital. What it did was give us the wind in the third quarter. When the fourth quarter came, the bad weather came and the wind shifted. Alabama was actually going into the wind in the fourth quarter."
—Pat Dye

Auburn rushed for 355 yards in the game, more than 200 above the average Alabama had been giving up.

"Outside in the driving rain, the Auburn fans were going bananas. In the Tiger dressing room, the happiest place this side of heaven, the smell of cigar smoke filled the air.

"Auburn football is finally king of the hill, in Alabama and in the Southeastern Conference.

"It didn't come easy... but when Bo Jackson was finished destroying Alabama's defense, the scoreboard said Auburn had won, 23-20."
—Phillip Marshall, Montgomery Advertiser

So, for the second year in a row, Auburn had beaten Alabama— something that would've been almost inconceivable just a few years earlier. For the second year in a row, the Tigers had scored 23 points and had held the Tide to no more than two touchdowns. It truly felt like the power, the momentum, the dominance in the state were all sliding east, away from Tuscaloosa and toward Lee County.

With the SEC Championship in hand—the Tigers' first since 1957–and the state championship safely locked away for a second consecutive year, a one-loss Auburn, playing what was clearly the most difficult schedule in the country, could turn its attention to going for a larger championship.

John Ringer

Auburn remained ranked third in the country behind undefeated Nebraska and Texas, 10-1 and undisputed SEC Champions. There was no conference championship game, no BCS, nothing but the bowls with their specific conference tie-ins. Auburn would have to go to the Sugar Bowl and play the runner-up of the Big Ten. There was no choice about it. The voters—the AP and UPI or the coaches poll voters—had to decide comparatively, after all bowl games had been played, who was no. 1, no. 2, no. 3, based on just their opinions, because none of them really played each other.

Van Allen Plexico

The SEC champ had to go to New Orleans, so that's where we went. We drew Michigan as our opponent, which wasn't the ideal matchup for impressing voters. They'd had a mediocre year, at least for them, and had lost to Ohio State, who were consequently headed to the Rose Bowl. But their defense was very good. Their backup quarterback that season, by the way, was Jim Harbaugh.

Texas meanwhile would play Georgia in the Cotton Bowl, and that presented a real opportunity for Auburn. Georgia's only loss all year had been to the Tigers. Auburn fans knew the Dawgs could hang with Texas and maybe do the Tigers a big favor and knock them off, allowing AU to move up at least one spot closer to the top.

Then there was the Orange Bowl. Nebraska at no. 1, coming out of the Big Eight, was contractually obligated to go there. But the other slot in that game was open to anyone, including independents. Howard Schnellenberger's Miami Hurricanes, ranked fifth and with just the one early loss to Florida, were the highest ranked team available. They were invited, and accepted, and would play the alleged "greatest team of the century" in a bowl game *played in their own stadium.*

It's worth noting that the two bowl games that consistently were able to invite independent (non-conference-affiliated) teams during the 1980s-1990s got to decide the national championship an inordinate number of times. The Sugar Bowl had been the premiere bowl during much of the 1970s, as Alabama had often been the dominant team and challengers had to go there to face them for the title. As of about 1981, with its Clemson-Nebraska matchup, the Orange Bowl (and later the Fiesta Bowl) unofficially claimed that designation, because they had the Big Eight winner—Nebraska or Oklahoma—and could also invite emerging and rising independent powers like Miami and Notre Dame. So it was in some ways a perfect storm for the Orange Bowl, and in 1983 that storm was a bunch of Hurricanes from right down the street.

Van Allen Plexico

The Orange Bowl and NBC billed their game, this Nebraska-Miami matchup, as *the* game for the national championship, as if none of the other teams mattered, and none of the other bowl games were happening. It was nothing of the sort, but that's how they promoted it.

There *was* no national championship game. There were no Playoffs. Not even the BCS.

Meanwhile, Auburn was no. 3, playing in the Sugar Bowl. And Texas was no. 2, playing no. 4 Georgia in the Cotton Bowl. So it really was a great semifinal round or quarterfinal round. It wasn't a national championship round at all. But it was the only thing we were going to get.

"After an early loss to Texas, Auburn won nine games in a row including seven against teams headed for bowls.

"The regular season came to a close last weekend against archrival Alabama. Auburn prevailed, 23-20, and is bound for the Sugar Bowl as the third-ranked team in the country. But the outstanding job Pat Dye has done holding the team together and finishing the toughest schedule in the nation at 10-1 got Dye named the 1983 NCAA Coach of the Year."

—ABC announcers prior to the Sugar Bowl broadcast

The Sugar Bowl was a grind-it-out kind of game. Michigan scored early and led at the half, 7-0, but that would be all the points they would score that night.

After halftime, Auburn essentially abandoned the pass and just gave the ball to Bo Jackson, Lionel James and Tommie Agee nearly every play. The Tigers controlled the ball for 23 of 30 minutes in the second half. Bo finished with 130 yards; Agee had 93 and James 83.

All-American linebacker Gregg Carr, who had preserved the win over Florida State earlier in the season with a late interception, recovered a fumble by quarterback Steve Smith at the Michigan 41-yard line, leading to the second of Al Del Greco's three field goals.

Auburn's winning drive started on their own 39-yard line and consumed seven minutes and twenty-one seconds, culminating with the third of Del Greco's kicks, with just twenty-seven seconds remaining in the game.

That was all the scoring we'd see, and all we'd need. Auburn won a defensive battle, 9-7.

Bo Schembechler's defense did a good job of holding Bo Jackson in check, at least in the first half, and certainly in the red zone. But when the game was on the line, the trio of Auburn backs accounted for more than three hundred yards of rushing. The Auburn defense never allowed Michigan to sniff the end zone again, after that early score.

While this was transpiring on ABC, the Orange Bowl was playing out on NBC. Playing in their home stadium, before their own crowd, the Miami Hurricanes held Nebraska's awesome offense in check just enough, scored when they needed to, and stopped Nebraska's 2-point conversion attempt at the end that would have won the game for the Huskers.

Viewers and poll voters saw the Heisman Trophy winner, running back Mike Rozier, mostly shut down. They heard the NBC commentators saying they were watching the "national championship game."

Van Allen Plexico

We only needed nine points to win the Sugar Bowl, but we surely needed way more than that to win the public relations battle. Hardly anyone was watching our game, because it was on at the same time as the Orange Bowl. The ratings difference between the two games was like 35 to 10. There were only a few VCRs and no DVRs back then. Everyone was watching Miami upset Nebraska. Poll voters probably checked the Sugar Bowl score, saw "Auburn kicked three field goals to win, 9-7," yawned, and happily voted for Miami. Heck, they voted Nebraska no. 2, and kept us at 3!

John Ringer
Nebraska came back at the end and scored a touchdown to pull within one of Miami. Tom Osborne could have kicked the extra point, tied the game—there was no overtime yet, not till 1996—and Nebraska would've been national champions at 12-0-1. (They had played an extra game, the Kickoff Classic, against Penn State.)

Van Allen Plexico
But Osborne being Osborne, he's like, "No, I want to win it and go undefeated." So they go for two and Miami knocks Turner Gill's pass down. And immediately Schnellenberger and the media all declare Miami the national champions.

"We're number one. No doubt about it."
—Howard Schnellenberger, Miami coach, just after the Orange Bowl

"It's cut and dried. If there's going to be a no. 1 in America and have any credibility, if you are going to have any credibility in scheduling...
"I don't know what you'd have to do to win a national championship, but I guarantee you can look back in the history of collegiate football and nobody played a more difficult schedule than Auburn did."
—Pat Dye, just after the Sugar Bowl

Van Allen Plexico
But Auburn was like, "Well, hold on a minute, because—what happened in the Cotton Bowl?" This is another really important part of the puzzle.

Just like Auburn against Michigan, Texas was winning the game after kicking three field goals. They were up, 9-3, late in the fourth quarter.

They stopped Georgia yet again, and the Bulldogs punted to Texas. The Longhorns coach, Fred Akers, later said he didn't believe Georgia would actually punt, given they were down six points with little time left on the clock. At the last second, he ran a punt returner, Craig Curry, out on the field, and Curry muffed the catch and gave the ball back to the Bulldogs. Georgia quarterback John Lastinger ran in a seventeen-yard touchdown to give the Dawgs the win, 10-9.

So Georgia, a team we'd beaten in their own stadium, pulled out a narrow win against second-ranked Texas, which knocked another obstacle out of our way. Or so we thought.

"As Auburn fans partied on Bourbon Street and at Toomer's Corner like it was 1957, Auburn coaches quickly became aware that their low-scoring win was getting much less attention than Miami's Orange Bowl upset of the team some were calling the greatest ever. So in his post-game press conference, Dye turned up the heat.

"'I don't know what you've got to do to win a national championship,' he said. 'But there's nobody that's ever played a tougher schedule than Auburn.'

"He backed the claim up with the numbers: Auburn's 1983 opponents had won 69.5 percent of their football games. Miami's opponents? 51 percent.

"'If they are going to have a No. 1 football team in America, and it's going to have any credibility at all—if there is any credibility in scheduling—there's no way Auburn shouldn't be No. 1,' Dye said.

"The voters didn't even have the decency to vote Auburn the No. 2 team in the nation. That (somehow) went to Nebraska, a team whose opponents had won only 52 percent of their games... and, you know, a team that had just lost their bowl game.

"To Pat Dye, the injustice was easy to explain: 'Miami put on a campaign,' one the media was more than willing to embrace following the thrilling end to the Orange Bowl, which by the time it ended was the only game left on TV."

—*Jeremy Henderson, in the War Eagle Reader, January 1, 2017*

Mike McClendon

Pat Dye got robbed of a national championship (although it was not a real won-it-on-the-field championship) in 1983. It was stolen from Dye and Auburn by a marketing campaign put on by NBC to promote the Orange Bowl as a championship game. If we had played Miami, it would not have been close.

"I thought logic was on our side. We were no. 3. Both no. 1 and no. 2 had lost. We all thought that we could move up to no. 1 after winning the Sugar Bowl.

"I kept wondering if there was something more we could have done. But I finally decided there was not. It was just the perfect storm. Miami benefited from it and Auburn did not. That run deserved a national championship, but it just wasn't to be."
—David Housel, former Athletic Director

"That was a good—a great—group of men who made up their minds that they were going to win a championship. We almost got the big one but came up a little short. That doesn't take anything away from what they did for Auburn. I was proud to be their coach."
—Pat Dye

John Ringer

Miami did what they had to do, and I think the biggest thing was not just that the media were on their side, but also that the Sugar Bowl was a defensive slugfest, while the Orange Bowl was a much more entertaining and exciting football game. But if you look at the entire season and the resumes of both teams, Auburn played nine bowl teams and five Top 10 teams.

Van Allen Plexico

Schnellenberger gave that succinct statement: "We're no. 1, no doubt about it," right after they'd knocked off Nebraska. Pat Dye, after the Sugar Bowl, gave more of a paragraph about the schedule and "If you look at this and that." I'm not blaming Pat Dye at all. I just think we would have been better served if he'd simply said, "We're no. 1. We earned it." Not that it probably would've made any difference.

In hindsight, we probably would have ended up higher-ranked if Nebraska had beaten the stew out of Miami. We'd have been second instead of third.

Our schedule was so much tougher than Miami's, it wasn't even funny. We were no. 3, they were no. 5. We beat the team that beat them. And we played a much harder schedule than they did.

I mean, is the national championship an award for one game? Or is it for a season? Because if it's for a season, I'm sorry, Miami, you played this one game that was admittedly great. Congratulations. You get the Orange Bowl trophy. You get to know you knocked off Nebraska. Meanwhile, we went 11-1 against the hardest schedule in college football history.

The *New York Times* computer looked at it all and said, "Oh yeah, Auburn's no. 1." I mean, if we don't raise a banner in the stadium before I'm dead for the 1983 national championship, I'm going to haunt the athletic department for the rest of eternity. Alan Greene, when he's eighty years old and still AD, he'll be sitting at his desk and I'll be a voice behind him going, *"Ooooohhhhh... Alan... raise the banner for '83! Wooooooooooo!"*

John Ringer

Green would be like, "What is that? What is that? Oh, it's that Plexico guy again."

Van Allen Plexico

"Get an exorcist in here. We gotta get rid of him."

So this is what I mean when I say, for Auburn, it seems like every silver lining has a dark cloud to it. It seems like if we've just gone 11-1, won the SEC, won the Sugar Bowl, for the first time in decades, we should be filled with joy. And instead we end this season frustrated again. We look back and we love this season and we love those players and coaches and everything but, my goodness, there's also that sour taste in your mouth again.

164

John Ringer

And especially because it wasn't just that we didn't win. It's that Alabama and Georgia had just won national titles a couple of years earlier in the Sugar Bowl, and we went and did the same thing, and this happened to us. It didn't happen to them.

Van Allen Plexico

Yeah. And I'm going to speak back in time to the Van and John of 1983 now. "You guys, if you can hear me from here in the future—you better get ready, because this won't be the last time this kind of thing happens. Be prepared for more frustrations of this type to come."

That's Auburn football and life in the Auburn Family.

The 1983 season was over, and it had been a sweet one indeed; Sugar-sweet, one might say, despite its controversial ending. But, as always with Auburn people and football fans in general, hope springs eternal. Tigers fans looked ahead to the team that would be returning in 1984 and were filled with optimism. The schedule was a tiny bit easier, though Auburn would be opening against Miami and Texas, both away from Jordan-Hare. But those games seemed more like opportunities for revenge and vindication than contests to be feared. Texas had given the Tigers their one loss and Miami had stolen Auburn's national title. How often do you get to open up a season against two non-conference teams that you feel did you so wrong the previous year?

Everything was trending upwards. Recruiting was going well. Auburn could now boast of being the most recent SEC champions. They'd won two Iron Bowls in a row. Pat Dye looked like a proven winner. The Tigers were losing Lionel James and Randy Campbell and Al Del Greco, as well as some great senior defensive players and others, but Bo Jackson still had two more years of eligibility. He was Superman, right? As long as Auburn had him and as long as he stayed healthy, the Tigers would be fine—and in the hunt for SEC and national championships. Auburn folks just *knew* it.

165

John Ringer

I have to say, 1983 really felt like a huge breakthrough, and it was one of the greatest seasons in Auburn history. Absolutely.

Van Allen Plexico

It was one of our greatest seasons ever, and it really showed that Pat Dye had made Auburn a force to be reckoned with, and that this would be the decade of Auburn in the SEC.

1982:

9-3 overall; 4-2 SEC

Date	Opponent	Result	Score
9/11	Wake Forest	W	28-10
9/18	Southern Miss	W	21-19
9/25	Tennessee	W	24-14
10/2	Nebraska	L	7-41
10/9	Kentucky	W	18-3
10/16	Georgia Tech	W	24-0
10/23	at Miss State	W	35-17
10/30	at Florida	L	17-19
11/6	Rutgers	W	30-7
11/13	Georgia	L	14-19
11/27	at Alabama (Bham)	W	23-22
12/18	Boston College*	W	33-26

Tangerine Bowl, Orlando, FL (Final AP Ranking: 14)

1983:

11-1 overall; 6-0 SEC
National Champions*; SEC Champions

Date	Opponent	Result	Score
9/7	Southern Miss	W	24-3
9/17	Texas	L	7-20
9/24	at Tennessee	W	37-14
10/1	Florida State	W	27-24
10/8	at Kentucky	W	49–21
10/15	at Georgia Tech	W	31-13
10/22	Miss State	W	28-13
10/29	Florida	W	28-21
11/5	Maryland	W	35-23
11/12	at Georgia	W	13-7
12/3	Alabama (Bham)	W	23-20
1/2	Michigan**	W	9-7

(Final AP Ranking: 3)

*New York Times Poll ** Sugar Bowl, New Orleans, LA*

- 3 -

DEFENSE, AUBURN, DEFENSE
Pat Dye, 1984-1988

"Third down and six. Pat is going to leave it with Bo. He breaks another tackle, thirty-five, forty—down the sideline, it's a footrace to the forty, the thirty, the twenty—BYE BYE, BO! Touchdown Auburn!"

—Jim Fyffe, Auburn radio broadcast of the Georgia Tech game, 1985

Jeremy Henderson

Bo Jackson was like "He-Man" or something. It was almost like a toy universe. I mean, he was just so rare. He was like a superhero.

My dad actually checked me out of school to go meet him. He was interning with a business that happened to be working with the business where my mom was at the time. This was in the 1984 preseason; I think it was before school started up. We went and they took a Polaroid of me and I was sitting in Bo's lap. I took that picture to school for "show and tell."

I honestly felt, growing up, that because I had this picture and I had sat in Bo Jackson's lap, it felt like I had been blessed. This was a conversation starter for me until I was probably a teenager, you know? I had sat in Bo Jackson's lap.

The 1983 season had come to an end on the night of January 2, 1984, when the third-ranked Tigers defeated the Michigan Wolverines in the Sugar Bowl, 9-7, on the strength of three Al Del Greco field goals, the running of superstar Bo Jackson, and the stout play of the Auburn defense—a defense that would go on to dominate the SEC over the remainder of the decade.

Unfortunately for the team in burnt orange and navy blue, while we were watching the Sugar Bowl on ABC, the rest of the college football world was tuned in to NBC, to see what was being billed as "the national championship game" between no. 1 Nebraska and the no. 5 Miami Hurricanes. What they witnessed was a huge upset, as Miami—playing in their own stadium—held off the Cornhuskers to win the Orange Bowl. And, as we all know, Miami jumped from fifth to first in the major polls the next day, claiming the national championship.

Many Auburn fans had expected the Tigers to be no. 1 when the dust settled. Many others had expected, or at least suspected, this very thing might happen. There was disbelief, anger, outrage, depression, and eventually maybe a little acceptance. Maybe. But whether it came as a surprise or not, Miami's seeming usurpation of the title brought the Auburn Family together in one simple desire: Revenge.

And the opportunity to take those frustrations out on the Hurricanes would come in the Tigers' very next game, just eight months down the calendar and a couple thousand miles away from either team's home.

1984

"The 1984 college football season begins tonight. Two top collegiate teams face each other in the Second Annual Kickoff Classic, live from the Meadowlands of New Jersey. The Kickoff Classic features the no. 2-ranked Auburn Tigers against the no. 1 Hurricanes from the University of Miami. (Editors' note: In the AP Preseason Poll released prior to this game, Auburn was ranked no. 1; Miami was ranked no. 10. We are not sure what rankings Curt Gowdy was looking at here.)

"Giants Stadium on a gorgeous August night; temperature in the mid-seventies. Just a perfect night for football between two exceptional college football teams. I'm Curt Gowdy.... We have two teams, no. 1 Miami of last year and no. 3 Auburn, both back with a strong nucleus." (Editors' note: Here Gowdy is referencing the 1983 final AP rankings.)

"Miami throws the ball about as much as they run the ball. On the other hand, you've got Auburn, a great running attack with Bo Jackson there, they'll run the ball four times more than they'll pass it. So you're going to see a passing team against a running team. Both teams have some problems or question marks. Miami on defense. Auburn with a starting quarterback.... Miami (has to) stop Bo Jackson and that running attack they're going to do it with inexperienced linebackers. On the other hand, a great running attack for Auburn, but their quarterback is very questionable. Mike Mann is starting for the first time since he graduated from high school. And that was five years ago."

—Curt Gowdy and Len Dawson, Kickoff Classic television broadcast, 1984

Van Allen Plexico

In some ways I think Auburn's success under Pat Dye came earlier than expected. We quoted one of the players earlier, from Dye's second season, as predicting we'd have a national championship team in four or five years. Instead, it happened the very next year—in year *three*. It seemed like he was

171

building towards something. Even before reaching championship caliber, he was making them tougher. Tough as old leather. You might still beat Auburn, but they wouldn't be an easy out anymore.

We knew the 1983 team could be special, but I don't know that we thought it would be *that* special. The schedule they faced was so tough, but they got through it with a record of 11-1, and very arguably should have been national champions. Going into 1984, the key players they lost included the quarterback, Randy Campbell, the talented halfback, Lionel James, and the kicker, Al Del Greco. Now, you should be able to replace a kicker, and I would argue Auburn has had as great a streak of dependable kickers as any program in the country over the past five decades or more. James was an awesome talent in a pint-sized body, and you hated to lose him, but you had Brent Fullwood and Collis Campbell and Tim Jessie and a stable full of other backs waiting to step up there next to Bo Jackson, as well as the great young fullback, Tommie Agee. The quarterback position, though, is often more problematic. You have to find someone who has the physical and mental attributes, the skills and tools on the field, and also the leadership qualities that great quarterbacks possess. One could argue that a wishbone or option system doesn't require a great passer, but there are other qualities the position calls for, like great decision-making on the fly. Campbell—never a great athlete, to be fair—had those qualities where it counted. I don't know that we fully appreciated what we were losing when he used up his eligibility. His record as starting quarterback, 20-4, speaks for itself.

John Ringer

For whatever reason, the quarterbacks who came just after Campbell seemed to struggle. It would be a couple of seasons before we felt comfortable at that position again.

There was a lot of hype going into 1984 because of the way the previous season had ended, and because we felt like we should have been national champions. There were very high expectations heading into 1984. And we knew we would be starting the season off in the Kickoff Classic against the team that had stolen the national title from us, so it was a revenge thing, as well.

Auburn clashed with the team that had been unfairly gifted with the 1983 national championship on the evening of August 27, 1984, before 51,131 spectators in Giants Stadium in East Rutherford, New Jersey.

Howard Schnellenberger had left the Hurricanes after the 1983 season to become head coach and part-owner of a new USFL franchise in Miami—a deal that later fell through, and resulted in his taking the Louisville Cardinals job the following year. In his place, Miami's new head coach was Jimmy Johnson, brought over from Oklahoma State to take over a suddenly-prominent Hurricanes program. Johnson would later famously lead Emmitt Smith's Dallas Cowboys team to two Super Bowl wins. On this night, however, his job was figuring out how to contain Bo Jackson while scoring points on the Auburn defense. It didn't hurt that Johnson had an experienced quarterback in Bernie Kosar, with other future NFL players all around him.

Miami took an early 7-0 lead on a 17-yard pass from Kosar to Stanley Shakespeare. Entering Auburn's red zone again a short time later, a Kosar pass was deflected and intercepted to prevent the Tigers from going down 14-0.

"Their mistakes kept us in the game the first half."
—Pat Dye

Sylacauga's Mike Mann, who had held the ball on Al Del Greco's kick to beat Michigan in the Sugar Bowl the previous season, was given his first start at quarterback for Auburn, but was 0-1 passing in the first quarter. Pat Washington came on in relief at the start of the second, and threw an ugly but successful 31-yard touchdown pass to Clayton Beauford to tie the game at 7-7.

Miami came right back with another touchdown pass to Shakespeare, but then a fumble by the Hurricanes' running back, Alonzo Highsmith, allowed Auburn's Robert McGinty to kick a 42-yard field goal. A bad snap on a punt by Miami resulted in a safety and brought the Tigers to within 2 points, 14-12, at halftime.

Auburn finally took the lead, 15-14, on another McGinty field goal in the third quarter, set up by big runs by Brent Fullwood and Bo Jackson. But the Miami defense largely kept Auburn's stellar backs under control most of the game; Jackson finished with 96 yards on 20 carries, and fumbled the ball away on Auburn's own 31 in the second half, leading to a Miami score.

"Highsmith got about 130 yards, but if Bo had the holes he did, (Bo) would have run for 300."
—Pat Dye

The teams traded field goals in the second half, resulting in Miami going ahead, 17-15 and 20-18. The final Miami kick came from 25 yards away with 6:08 to go in the game. That score would hold up to the end, after Auburn's final drive ended on a botched pitch from Washington to Fullwood that turned the ball over to Miami near midfield.

Auburn missed a chance to increase its lead on its final scoring drive when Bo Jackson was tripped up by the last man who had a chance to stop him, with only green grass and the end zone ahead of him. The Miami player who knocked him down was Ken Calhoun, the same player who had knocked down Turner Gill's attempted two-point conversion pass for Nebraska in the Orange Bowl the previous season.

"At this moment, I'm as proud as I've ever been in my coaching career."
—Jimmy Johnson, Miami head coach

"Miami, the no. 1 team last year, has defeated Auburn, the preseason no. 1 this year, by a score of 20-18. Jimmy Johnson, a successful effort in his first game (at Miami). He can be happy given the pressure on him; he came in to replace Howard Schnellenberger who guided Miami to a miracle season last year, and Johnson did it and his team did it."
—Curt Gowdy, Kickoff Classic television broadcast, 1984

174

"Auburn had a very experienced secondary and they were disguising their defenses real well. They made me work. Nebraska couldn't stay on the field with Auburn, defensively."
—Bernie Kosar, Miami quarterback

John Ringer

It was so frustrating, because Miami was given the title that we should've won after the 1983 season, and then we lost the game where we could've gotten some payback on them. I think this is a theme we will return to in later seasons, which is Auburn starting a season highly ranked and with high expectations. It doesn't always work out the way we want it to.

Van Allen Plexico

No. It seems like we have to sneak up on our best seasons. We can't be predicted to win before the first game, and then go wall-to-wall with victories—with perhaps the exceptions of 1988 and 1989, where we pretty much did what we were expected to do. Other than those, it seems like it's always the seasons where we're not expected to do great things that we have the best years.

There was a lot of buzz in the air going into the 1984 season, but the quarterback situation was a question mark, and some would argue that's what ultimately cost us the most. Nowadays, the '84 season is mostly remembered as a disappointment. Should it be seen that way, though? Auburn finished 9-4, which is not bad at all.

John Ringer

And to break it down further: If we hadn't played in that extra game, the Kickoff Classic, we would've finished 9-3. Two of our losses were out of conference, in the first two weeks of the season, away from home, against top ten teams. Another was to a great Florida team on the road.

Van Allen Plexico

I can't remember many teams that started a season 0-2 and didn't drop out of the Top Twenty polls. But Auburn in 1984 was still ranked going into week three—after losing to Miami and Texas—and would be ranked every single week of the season. That shows how much regard the voters had for the schedule the Tigers were playing. If only they'd shown that much regard for it the *previous* season.

So maybe 1984 is only disappointing in the sense that we didn't do as well as we had in 1983. It didn't help that we lost a baffling Iron Bowl to Alabama, and we ended up in the Liberty Bowl instead of the Sugar Bowl. Those kinds of things will definitely leave a bad taste in your mouth, even with all the other accomplishments of the year.

John Ringer

I think it just shows, number one, the schedule was very different at the time. But also, it was obvious we were a really good team. We just happened to play two other really good teams to start the season.

Van Allen Plexico

This Kickoff Classic game featured the team that was *given* the national championship versus the team that thought they had *earned* the national championship, so it appeared to be a great matchup. The only problem was that Miami brought basically their whole team back, while we were still figuring out who our quarterback should be. Ultimately that season it was Pat Washington. I think Pat was underestimated and underappreciated in his two seasons. Unfortunately, we lost four games each of his two years, including losing to Alabama both times, and that's terrible for an Auburn quarterback's legacy.

John Ringer

No, that's not good. And I think he suffered by comparison to the quarterbacks before and after him.

Van Allen Plexico

The numbers for Washington that season aren't particularly good, though. I know this Auburn team wasn't built to be a passing team, but he completed only forty-five percent of his passes and threw nine interceptions against four touchdowns.

176

He actually had a geography class the period before I did, in 1987. I don't think he found it particularly interesting, because I would be standing outside the door waiting to go into the room, and he would come stumbling out, and I guess it was his girlfriend who was always with him and would be waking him up and helping him out of the room. He seemed to be in a stupor from, I guess, a not very exciting class.

John Ringer

You brought up the quarterback issue and that was definitely a problem. The team wasn't as efficient at quarterback as it had been before. But the biggest difference was Bo Jackson getting hurt that year.

Van Allen Plexico

Ah! You *say* that, but—what was Auburn's record when Bo Jackson was out with injuries those six games? 6-0. Now you can argue, "Well, those six weren't the hardest on the schedule." He suffered a separated shoulder at the hands of Jerry Gray in the game at Texas in week two. He missed the next six games, in which we went 6-0. Then he returned against Florida and we lost. So the funny statistic that year is, after nine games, we were 0-3 with Bo playing and 6-0 without him. Which just sounds crazy, but it was true.

Of course, the three that he played in were against Miami, Texas and Florida, so come on. It's a funny statistic but it doesn't tell the whole story.

We were still running the wishbone that season and we were not throwing the ball very well at all. So, if you could shut down Bo, then it was fairly easy to stop this offense. "Shutting down Bo" sounds like an insanely hard thing nowadays, but when he was the entire focus of our offense, teams with really good defenses were able to do it, especially when he wasn't a hundred percent healthy.

By the time we got to the 1986 season, Bo was gone and Pat Dye finally said, "Forget the wishbone and the pure running attack. We're going to try to be more sophisticated on offense." Teams like Miami and BYU were making the passing game more fashionable during that decade. Dye had said that when you run the wishbone, you spend all week working on getting better at running the wishbone, rather than preparing for your specific opponent. He wanted to move toward an offense where you actually take game plans into consideration and actually mold your offense to match up with the team you're playing that week. So, beginning in 1986, we would become more of a passing team, although still not doing it a tremendous amount, compared to nowadays.

John Ringer
It was like we'd found this new wrinkle in football nobody ever heard of—the forward pass! Crazy town! —and we were going to do it a lot more than before.

Van Allen Plexico
It would require a different type of quarterback. When Randy Campbell would throw a long pass, he looked like Atlas trying to heave the Earth off his shoulders. Not the strongest arm ever. He looked like he was doing the shot put.

Back to our timeline. We had lost to Miami, 20-18, in a very tough game in the Meadowlands. I just hated losing that game, because we desperately wanted some revenge on the Canes, even though it wouldn't have given us the national title back. But still, you just wanted to smack them for having the temerity to think they could steal it in the first place.

But they won. And then we turned right around and faced *another* potential revenge game, because Texas had given us our only loss on the field the previous season.

Miami went up to no. 1 in the AP rankings after they beat us. That meant we started the 1984 season by playing the team that was about to be no. 1, and then the team ranked no. 4, both away from home. It's interesting to note that Miami that year ended up 8-5. They finished with a worse record than we did. That was the Miami team that later lost to Doug Flutie on the famous last-second Hail Mary pass—the pass that probably won him the Heisman.

Auburn's second stop on the 1984 Revenge Tour took the Tigers to Austin to play fourth-ranked Texas, the team that had occupied the no. 2 spot in the polls most of the previous year.

The Longhorns roared out to a big 14-0 lead by the end of the first quarter. Auburn was able to mostly contain the Texas rushing attack, but Todd Dodge took to the air and moved the ball well at quarterback. Auburn fought back with a touchdown and two field goals to pull the score to 14-13 Texas at the half.

The two teams traded touchdowns in the third quarter, but Auburn attempted a 2-point conversion and failed. Going into the fourth quarter, Texas now led, 21-19.

Two big Texas touchdowns by Jerome Johnson in the final frame put the Longhorns up, 35-19, and all seemed lost for the Tigers. Pat Washington responded, however, driving Auburn to a touchdown with 2:33 to go, and then scoring the 2-point conversion on a QB keeper.

On the ensuing kickoff, Robert McGinty executed an onside kick up the center of the field, and Auburn recovered, giving the Tigers one more chance with two minutes remaining. An errant pass from Washington, however, was intercepted by Texas, who ran out the clock. The final score was Texas 35, Auburn 27. The finish was in some ways eerily similar to the game the previous week, as Auburn was again fighting back at the end but gave the ball away before they could score.

For such a run-heavy team as 1984 Auburn was, the stats for this game are remarkably balanced. The Tigers ran the ball 57 times for 247 yards, but also passed the ball 27 times with 14 completions, for 226 yards.

In addition to the loss, Auburn suffered another setback on that trip. Longhorns defensive back Jerry Gray separated Bo Jackson's shoulder during a run. Suddenly the Tigers were without their Mr. Everything on offense. Bo would miss the next six games.

Auburn went on to win unmemorable games against Southern Miss, Tennessee and Ole Miss, with backup runners Brent Fullwood, Colis Campbell and Kyle Collins filling in admirably for the injured All-American. And then the Tigers traveled to Tallahassee, for a game that would go down in Tigers history.

Van Allen Plexico

The Florida State game was not on television! Can you believe that? Auburn was ranked no. 16 and FSU was ranked no. 9 in the AP Poll. Two Top Twenty teams, and no television.

I remember listening to it on the radio. It was a night game. I was lying on the bed and I had a notebook open in front of me. I was very crudely diagramming the possessions so that I could keep track of the flow of the game on paper. My paper ended up looking like zig zags back and forth, because this game was a track meet. It was a ping pong match.

Auburn led at the end of one quarter in Doak Campbell Stadium, 10-3, after a 2-yard Brent Fullwood touchdown run. Florida State tied the game at 10-10, thanks to a 7-yard pass from Eric Thomas to tight end Pete Panton.

The Tigers answered with two touchdowns of their own. Collis Campbell broke loose for a 69-yard gallop to the end zone, and then Brent Fullwood cashed in from 5 yards out. Robert McGinty missed the extra point on the first of those scores, and the 2-point conversion attempt on the second one failed. Even so, it was starting to look like Auburn had taken control of the game.

The Seminoles weren't done, however. Not by a long shot. Thomas connected with Devin Hester on a 73-yard bomb to pull FSU within 5 at the half, 22-17.

In the third quarter, FSU fumbled the kickoff and Ed Graham of Auburn picked up the ball and returned it 60 yards for a touchdown, as Jim Fyffe famously tried to get a handle on what was happening, over the radio broadcast.

Van Allen Plexico

Neither team played a whole lot of defense and there were also big plays on special teams, including a kickoff return that was fumbled and then picked up and run back. I remember Jim Fyffe on that play yelling, "Can he go? Can he go? He can go! Touchdown Auburn!"

With that return, the Tigers had miraculously extended their lead to 29-17, and once again appeared to be in charge of the contest.

Again, the Seminoles came right back. Darrin Holloman carried the ball in for a touchdown from 10 yards out, and then Hassan Jones caught a 13-yard pass for another score, as well as tacking on the 2-point conversion. Suddenly FSU had taken the lead, 32-29.

As the fourth quarter of this "wild and wooly shootout" got underway, FSU tacked on a field goal, and now it was 35-29, Noles.

Auburn needed to stop the bleeding. They needed to get back in the game before FSU could nail the victory down. The Tigers responded. They drove down the field and scored on a Kyle Collins 10-yard run to retake the lead, 36-35.

Van Allen Plexico

Kyle Collins and Collis Campbell and Brent Fullwood all had big games that night, standing in for the still-injured Bo Jackson. Freddie Weygand caught some big passes. They had to, because FSU was scoring just as quickly as we were. Back and forth the game went.

Surely, Auburn fans thought, that Kyle Collins touchdown would do it. Surely 36 points would be enough. Surely the defense would rise up and stop the Seminoles now.

That did not prove to be the case. Try as they might, the Auburn defense couldn't quite stop FSU's powerful offense, led by future NFL stars like Jessie Hester and Hassan Jones. The Seminoles went right back down the field and scored yet again, and with only a couple of minutes remaining on the clock, they were back ahead, 41-36.

This was when, as Jim Fyffe famously put it, the Tigers found themselves with "their backs to the wall, their feet to the fire." He described the finish of the drive thusly:

"Auburn trailing by five. Washington looking, throwing. This one is complete inside the twenty and out of bounds at the Florida State 14 yard line. Washington hitting tight end Jeff Parks. Driven out of bounds by Mike Hayes. That will be another Tiger first down.

"Can it come down to this? Can you stand *a finish like this? What an exciting finish it's been.*

"The pitch to Fullwood, got a block on the outside. Brent turns the corner to the ten, broke a tackle at the five, goes out of bounds at the five yard line of Florida State. With 1:13 to play, 41-36, the Tigers trail Florida State. The last time Auburn was in this situation they ran the option with Kyle Collins who got it in over here on the left corner. Let's see what they do.

"Two tight ends for Washington. He's going to pitch to Fullwood. He tries to get outside. He dives for the pylon—he's in! He's in! He's in! Touchdown Auburn! Touchdown Auburn! Touchdown Fullwood, from four yards away. And the Tigers... the Tigers... have done it! They've marched literally the length of the field and gone ahead, 42-41!"

—*Jim Fyffe, Auburn radio broadcast at Florida State, 1984*

John Ringer

Just an all-time call by Jim Fyffe. I was listening on the radio, too. My memory is that it's one of those games that people talk about later. One of the craziest and most exciting games in Auburn history, that very few people saw and that there are not a lot of copies of.

"It was just like last year. They just came back and snatched the victory. It was no broken play this year, or broken coverages. They just did it. I thought we had it. We had the game won in the last two minutes and they got us again."

—*Bobby Bowden, FSU head coach*

"This was a big one. It might be the biggest one since we've been here. You can't imagine how good Florida State played. We're not a bad defensive team and we were maligned out there. I mean maligned. But these guys fought and they came from behind. I've never, ever been prouder of a bunch of young men than I am of this football team tonight."

—*Pat Dye*

Van Allen Plexico

There is a highlight VHS tape, put out several years later, but before YouTube, which I have around here somewhere. I remember buying it because I was like, "Oh, man—there's actual footage from the '84 FSU game! I gotta have this." It was the first time I'd ever actually seen anything from that game, outside of the brief coach's show highlights.

"Would the TV folks have loved to have this one!"
—Pat Dye

Van Allen Plexico

I seem to remember that this was the game in which Jim Fyffe pointed out that Burt Reynolds had paid for Florida State's jerseys. He'd been embarrassed by their uniforms and wanted them to have better ones, so he wrote them a check. But they were still plain garnet shirts. Which is a look, by the way, I actually prefer to their fancier ones nowadays. That's all a far cry from where their program would be just a couple of years later, when they got Mickey Andrews to shore up the defense and they started winning a lot, and the money started pouring in.

The next week Auburn hosted old non-conference rival Georgia Tech, in a game that seemed very lopsided in the Tigers' favor at first, but grew increasingly interesting in the second half:

Van Allen Plexico

I know that you have a particular affinity for the Auburn-Georgia Tech series, growing up in Atlanta and having a lot of friends that went to Tech, so I'm sure you remember this game.

We were just killing them in the first half. We were up 41-0 at halftime. We felt as good about things as you possibly could. This was one of those Bill Curry Georgia Tech teams, and we never, to the best of my recollection, felt like they were all that dangerous—at least, not going in.

In the second half, I don't know if our guys went to sleep or Curry lit a fire under his guys in the locker room or what

183

happened, but Tech scored, and scored again, and scored again, and suddenly it's 41-21. Then it's 41-28, and you start thinking, "Good lord—we're going to lose a game we led 41-0 at halftime! Is that even possible?"

We got a late score and held on and won, 48-34. But it was pretty weird.

John Ringer

I remember that game. And that is one hundred percent the nature of the Georgia Tech rivalry. That's our rivalry with them in a nutshell. We don't take them as seriously as we probably should, and it comes back to bite us in the rear end again and again.

We used to have a great rivalry with them. We used to play in Atlanta a lot, and there are a lot of Auburn fans in that area who enjoyed seeing our team coming over to play there.

We had the game in hand and we were coasting. Coach Dye was pulling out the starters early. Then Tech got on a roll and we had backups in and we couldn't stop them. It got a little stressful there for a while, yeah.

Van Allen Plexico

Entirely too close for comfort. And just wait until we get to the 1987 game. I know you remember that one!

On November 3, 1984, we went to play no. 13 Florida in Gainesville. In this game, and the one against them the next year, both teams had so many future NFL players all over the field.

John Ringer

The 1985 Florida game is the peak, yes. Just loaded with NFL players. Probably forty guys at least, on the two rosters, who went on to play serious time in the NFL in that game. It was amazing.

Bo came back from his separated shoulder for this game. We had just won six games in a row without him, but he wasn't able to do much against Florida. Their defense was stifling. We couldn't get anything going on offense and they scored basically a score every quarter and they won, 24-3. That ended our ten-game SEC win streak, which had started with the 1982 Iron Bowl win.

The game was tied 3-3 midway through the third quarter, when future Chicago Bear Neal Anderson scored the first of two touchdowns to put the Gators up 17-3. Lorenzo Hampton added another in the final minute to make the results look even worse. Bo Jackson finished with only five carries for 16 yards, along with one catch for 15 yards.

After the game, some in the media whispered that maybe Bo Jackson wasn't all that tough. It was an infuriating insult that Bo would have to refute multiple times over the remainder of 1984 and on into 1985, by his gritty performances on the field.

"I don't think anyone has shut Auburn down like that this year."
—Galen Hall, Florida head coach

Van Allen Plexico
The Florida rivalry was always streaky. They won three in a row starting that season, and then we won three in a row from 1987-89. Then they brought in Steve Spurrier and back it went for three years, before Terry Bowden won two in a row off of them. Then back to them for a while, then we dominated for a while. Very streaky.

John Ringer
This Florida defense was amazing. They were led by Wilbur Marshall, who went on to play for the Chicago Bears. That next year the Bears almost went undefeated and won the Super Bowl. So yeah, just a great defense. Shut our running game down and we didn't have much of a passing offense.

Van Allen Plexico
The next game we beat Cincinnati, 60-0, in the biggest blowout I'd ever seen. Then we welcomed Georgia to Jordan-Hare, and they were ranked 15th, a few spots ahead of us at 18th. That's so frustrating, by the way, considering we'd started the season ranked no. 1.

John Ringer

We beat Georgia in a night game on ESPN, in another hard-fought Auburn-Georgia, Pat Dye-Vince Dooley game, played in Jordan-Hare. During that time, and for a while afterward, we would usually win in Athens and they would usually win in Auburn. So it was especially good to get a home win over them.

In fact, this game was Auburn's first win over Georgia *in Auburn* since 1974!

Before and during the game, ESPN's announcers kept talking up the fact that the winner of the game could play in the Sugar Bowl, which at that time was the reward for the team that won the entire SEC—the equivalent today of "guaranteed spot in the College Football Playoffs." Georgia would get in if Florida was not allowed to go, due to rules infractions that were being investigated (and which would ultimately result in Charley Pell's resignation and in probation for Florida's best teams in the mid-1980s). Auburn would go to New Orleans if they won the game that night, and Florida was disqualified, and Auburn then went on to beat Alabama the following game.

Two of those three things happened, but not all three. As it turned out, neither team would be going to the Sugar Bowl.

"I think you can take what happened last week in our games and throw it out the window, because this is Auburn-Georgia and the emotions will run so high on each side, with the players and the fans, that anything can happen. The game the last three years has been decided on turnovers. In fact, I think we have outgained Georgia statistically in each of the last three ballgames, but only won only once, and that was last year, when they had two turnovers and we didn't have any."
—Pat Dye, before the 1984 Georgia game

Auburn's stifling defense held Georgia in check for most of the game, and the Tigers sent a stable of backs charging at the Dogs all night. Bo Jackson, Collis Campbell, Reggie Ware, Brent Fullwood—they all got yards against Georgia, and fullback Tommie Agee had over a hundred yards before halftime, on just five carries. Reggie Ware and Pat Washington punched in short touchdowns after long, time-consuming drives. On a third visit deep into UGA's red zone, this time led by QB Mike Mann, the Tigers were stopped on fourth and one.

At halftime, Auburn had twelve first downs to Georgia's four, and had 203 yards rushing to Georgia's 38, and the Dogs had turned the ball over once, yet the Tigers only led 14-0.

In the second half, Georgia's defense held Auburn to just one more touchdown, but all the Dogs could put on the scoreboard were four Kevin Butler field goals. Final score, 21-12, Auburn.

Van Allen Plexico

Two weeks later... I hate to bring this game up. I hate to have to remember it at all.

We had moved up to no. 11 after beating Georgia, and we had to go up to Legion Field to play a bad Alabama team. Ray Perkins, in his second year as head coach, had them at 4-6 coming into this game. I guess our guys just thought they'd roll their helmets out there and get a big win. But it didn't work out that way.

Alabama led 17-7 in the fourth quarter, thanks to two touchdowns by the Tide's Paul Ott Carruth and a Van Tiffin field goal of 52 yards. Auburn's players, coaches and fans could see the Sugar Bowl, not to mention the Iron Bowl, slipping away.

The Tigers rallied late. They came back with a 60-yard touchdown run by Brent Fullwood and a 2-point conversion by Bo Jackson, narrowing the score to 17-15 with more than nine minutes remaining to be played. Unfortunately for Auburn, two more trips into Alabama territory late in the game came up empty.

Facing fourth and goal at the Alabama one, Coach Dye opted for a run play instead of a short field goal that would've given the Tigers the lead.

"The whole idea was: We're going to go for the touchdown, if we don't get it we're going to have them down here on the 1. We're going to hold them; we'll get it back and we'll get a chance to kick a field goal and win anyway. It gives us two chances to win instead of

one. At that point in the game, I thought we had so much momentum it wouldn't have mattered. But the thought was, if they break a kick and get out to the 40, hit one pass and the way (Tiffin) was kicking the football, they could kick a field goal and beat us."
—Tracy Turner, Auburn offensive lineman

"So now it's fourth and goal. And Pat Dye has to make the decision: Do you go for what figures to be the sure field goal and go up by a point, or do you try for the touchdown? That's his decision right now."

"I think I'm going for the short field goal."

"I do too with all that is at stake. Fourth down and goal. Inside the one yard line. Bennett has come back in defensively. And Dye has elected to go for it. To go for the touchdown. This is the critical play of the game right here.
"It's Fullwood! And he is stopped! And they will talk about that play for years!
"With 3:27 to go in the game, Rory Turner ran him out of bounds, and that will be forever ingrained in the lore of this rivalry. If this final score doesn't change, they'll be talking about that from now until the year 2020."
—Al Michaels and unnamed color commentator, 1984 ABC TV broadcast

It is beyond 2020 as this is being written, Al, and Auburn folks are *still* talking about it.

Quarterback Pat Washington pitched the ball to Brent Fullwood even as Bo Jackson, who had misheard the play call, ran the wrong way on his blocking assignment. Without a lead blocker, Fullwood was knocked out of bounds and Alabama took over at their own one yard line.

"We're going to call the play at the line of scrimmage in that end zone down there that wasn't even our end zone. It was all full of Alabama students. That's just not a good idea. Bo didn't hear the

call. So he wasn't there to be the lead block for Brent, and there was Rory."

—*Tracy Turner, Auburn offensive lineman*

Auburn did get the ball back for one final attempt at victory, but Robert McGinty missed a 42-yard field goal attempt.

Dye would later say he blamed himself for that Iron Bowl loss, saying he was "too light" on the team in the week leading up to the game, causing them to come out flat.

John Ringer

We lost. 17-15. To an Alabama team that, coming in, was 4-6 overall and 1-4 in the conference.

On their goal line, did we give the ball to Bo to dive over the top, like in 1982? A play nobody had stopped before? No. The ball went to Fullwood and he got stuffed on the sweep. Bo was supposed to block for him but he ran the wrong way.

But the game wasn't over yet. We stopped them and got the ball back and went down the field on them again at the end, and that time Pat Dye went for the field goal that would've won the game, but Robert McGinty missed it.

Van Allen Plexico

We had so many chances to pull that game out and we just couldn't do it.

How did we lose to that team?

"I did a poor job getting across to our players the kind of effort it was going to take to beat Alabama. The game meant more to their fans, their coaching staff and their players than it did to ours. We were in a talking stage and they were in a playing stage. They played with more purpose than we did. That's the thing that I've had a hard time dealing with."

—*Pat Dye*

Van Allen Plexico

If we had won this Iron Bowl, we would be a 1985 Van Tiffin field goal away from *eight straight wins over Alabama* in the 1980s. And that's one of the things that's always eaten me up: We won in 1982 and 1983 and we would go on to win four more after Tiffin. If we could have just won in 1984 and 1985, we would've made up almost that entire 1970s Bear Bryant run of nine wins over us in one shot, and gotten back on par with them. And we let two games get away, cancelling out the two we had just won. It just galls me. It burns me up. I remember Pat Dye saying this one kept him up at night and gave him hives.

I believe Dye pulled Robert McGinty's scholarship after he missed that kick. He certainly made it very clear to him he wasn't particularly welcome on the team anymore. Dye was going to look for other kickers. So McGinty transferred to Florida. And just to add extra salt to the wound, two years later McGinty kicked a 55-yard field goal to give the Gators the points they needed to beat us in the Swamp. He can make a 55-yarder *against* us, but he can't hit a chip shot to win the Iron Bowl for us. This is the roller coaster we ride John. This is what it's like to be Auburn fans.

Many of those Auburn fans were grumbling even before the Iron Bowl, given the losses to Miami and Texas early and then later on to Florida, after the team had been ranked no. 1 in the pre-season. The loss to a poor Alabama team only raised the volume level on the discontent coming from the orange and blue fan base.

Pat Dye heard it, and he addressed it the week of Auburn's bowl game.

"I know how to win and I know what it takes to win. I know how to get it done. I don't think our program is going backwards.

"When I analyze our program, I go back to four years ago. You look at it from an overall standpoint, and you have to be pleased. You look at our current season and you'd have to say it's been disappointing.

"It doesn't matter who's playing quarterback, who's coordinating the offense or who's coordinating the defense. It's my football team and I'm responsible for the whole deal. We haven't been as good as we'd hoped to be and that's my fault.

"We've got to go back to basics and build a football team. I am very, very excited about our future. It's not just talent and ability. It's the kind of people and kind of character we have in our program."
—Pat Dye

Auburn finished the 1984 regular season at 8-4 and were invited to play Arkansas in the not-terribly-prestigious Liberty Bowl in Memphis, in what is usually one of the coldest bowl games of the year. Arkansas was not yet a member of the SEC—they were still in the Southwestern Conference with all the Texas schools—so this was a more interesting matchup than it first sounds.

John Ringer

My family and I went to Memphis for this game, and it was miserable. It was Memphis in December. A miserable week. It was cold with freezing rain. My parents were stuck with my two brothers and me, three young boys, in a hotel room most of the time. We were going crazy because it was too yucky to be outside running around.

The one thing I remember from this game is, there was a guy in our section who was an Auburn fan and he was so drunk, he said some curse words I had never heard before. The stadium security came and took him away. That's what I remember about the 1984 Liberty Bowl, more than the game itself and beating Arkansas.

Arkansas, coached by Ken Hatfield, ran the "flexbone," a modification of the wishbone attack Auburn was still running—though this would be the last game the Tigers ran it.

Auburn's offense was controlled much of the evening. The Tigers played three different quarterbacks at different times—Pat Washington, Jeff Burger and Mike Mann—and together they completed just 5 passes, all of them thrown by Pat Washington.

The swarming AU defense shut the Arkansas flexbone down pretty well. Bo Jackson was named the game's MVP, but he tallied a relatively modest 88 yards on 18 carries, though he did find the end zone twice. The third Auburn score was a pick six by Kevin Porter, one of four interceptions claimed by the Auburn defense in the game. The final score was 21-15, Auburn.

191

Auburn had won their ninth game of the season, marking three years in a row with at least nine wins. The Tigers very nearly played in a completely different bowl game, however.

"All of football history would have been different if not for LSU. We had a deal and we voted as a team that we wanted to go to the Holiday Bowl and play BYU in sunny, warm San Diego. We would have whipped their butt and they never would have won the national championship. But LSU (who would've gone there if Auburn had beaten Alabama and had been invited to the Sugar Bowl) said that was too far for their fans to travel. So instead of the deal being Holiday Bowl-Sugar Bowl, it became Liberty Bowl-Sugar Bowl. Somehow, we lost and wound up having to go to Memphis and play Arkansas." (While BYU beat Michigan in the Holiday Bowl, instead of playing Auburn or LSU, and won the 1984 national championship.)
—Tracy Turner, Auburn offensive lineman

Van Allen Plexico
You think of Memphis in May and you think of yummy barbecue. Memphis in December? The Liberty Bowl? You think of how you can't even leave your hotel room because it's so nasty outside.

We still ended up third in the SEC that year, so it wasn't horrible. The top team in the SEC was Florida, at 9-1-1, but they were on probation for violations under Charley Pell. LSU was second, so they got to go to the Sugar Bowl, where they got demolished by Nebraska. We won our bowl, so we ended up with more wins and a higher final ranking than LSU, and the same number of wins as Florida.

John Ringer
That is a lot more wins than Alabama had. Georgia, too.

The important thing there is that, back then, those preseason Kickoff Classic-type events were extra games. They weren't part of your regular eleven-game schedule. Nowadays we have games similar to them, but they count as part of your regular schedule in terms of number of games. So nobody besides Miami and Auburn played thirteen games that year.

Van Allen Plexico
And in fact, I've always pointed out that in the calendar year 1984, Auburn played fourteen football games, because the previous year's team played in the Sugar Bowl on January 1, and then we played the Kickoff Classic in August, and then an eleven-game regular season, and then a December bowl game. That was pretty much unheard of, for a team back then to play fourteen games in one calendar year.

1985

The 1984 season had been an odd one in numerous ways. Because of his injury in week two, the legendary Bo Jackson missed six games and ended up as only the third-leading rusher on the team, behind Brent Fullwood and Collis Campbell and just ahead of fullback Tommie Agee. Mike Mann started off the season at quarterback, but Pat Washington took over for him pretty early on, and freshman Jeff Burger also appeared in a few games. We would see a lot more of him in the not-too-distant future.

Meanwhile, the 1985 season would turn out to be another moderately disappointing year, after huge preseason expectations. Of course, this is all relative; under the previous staff, an 8-4 season and a bowl game of any kind would've been cause for great celebration.

Oklahoma began the year ranked no. 1, with the Tigers one spot below them, at no. 2. As we know, Auburn teams do not typically perform up to expectations when they are highly-ranked at the start of the season.

Ultimately, the 1985 season would be another four-loss campaign, with Auburn finishing somewhere in the middle of the conference standings. It would be remembered mainly for Bo Jackson winning the Heisman Trophy. Pat Dye changed the offense in the offseason to the I-formation, to better feature and spotlight Bo in his senior year and increase his chances of winning the prestigious award. As far as that went, it worked: Against Southwestern Louisiana in game 1, Bo gained 181 yards and scored three touchdowns—*on his first six carries!* He finished with 290 rushing yards total. After the first two games, he had amassed almost 500 yards rushing.

> *"It's hard to compare Bo to anybody we've played against."*
> *—Sam Robertson, head coach, Southwestern Louisiana*

Against teams with weak run defenses, the new Auburn offense was devastating. Against solid competition, however, the Tigers' one-dimensional attack remained a serious problem—one that would be exposed in week three by Tennessee.

Following the massive rushing performance in week 1, Auburn replaced idle Oklahoma as the no. 1 team in the AP Poll. They kept that position after a 29-18 win over Southern Miss in week 2. Then came the annual battle with old foe Tennessee, and with perennial Auburn foil, Johnny Majors.

The Tigers traveled to Knoxville on September 28 and the Volunteers were lying in wait. Pat Dye later called it an ambush. Auburn was riding high atop the polls, and Tennessee relished the opportunity to bring it all crashing down.

> *"Not only did Tennessee overwhelm top-ranked and previously unbeaten Auburn, 38-20, today before almost 95,000 at Neyland Stadium, the Volunteers did it with stunning simplicity.*
>
> *"In fact, the most difficult problem Tennessee seemed to face all afternoon was keeping its frantic swarm of fans off the field and away from the goal posts before the horn sounded ending the game.*
>
> *"'Beautiful, beautiful, the whole thing was beautiful,' Tennessee Coach Johnny Majors said when it was over. 'It was just about the greatest thing I'd ever seen.'*
>
> *"The truth is, this nationally televised matchup between two of the toughest and best members of the Southeastern Conference wasn't even close. In leading Tennessee to its first victory of the season (the unranked Volunteers, now 1-0-1, tied UCLA two weeks ago), quarterback Tony Robinson danced and passed and danced and passed, and had just a fine time.*
>
> *"He completed 17 of 30 passing attempts for 259 yards and four touchdowns, overshadowing the play of Bo Jackson, the great*

Auburn running back who gained only 80 yards on 17 carries and watched most of the final period from the sideline."
—John Ed Bradley, The Washington Post, September 29, 1985

"We played awfully, awfully hard and awfully, awfully well. This was one of our biggest wins at UT."
—Johnny Majors

Tennessee led 14-0 after one quarter. They led 24-0 at the half. As the fourth quarter began, astonishingly enough, they were still holding the Tigers scoreless. In that final frame, Auburn managed to score three touchdowns—but the Vols scored two more, as well, keeping the game completely out of reach.

In addition to the 259 yards in passing by Vols quarterback Tony Robinson, UT tailback Keith Davis amassed 102 on the ground. Future NFL receiver Tim McGee caught six passes for 163 yards and a touchdown.

Auburn managed just 252 yards of offense, 170 below its season average. Bo Jackson left the game in the third quarter with a knee injury.

"We ran into an extremely emotional Tennessee team today. Obviously, we have not played an offensive team like theirs. It was just a good, old-fashioned whipping in every area. We brought everything we had with us and it didn't work. I just hope we're not as bad as we looked today."
—Pat Dye

That Tennessee team would go on to finish the season with only one loss—a 17-10 defeat to the Gators at Florida Field—along with two ties. While Pat Dye later gained a reputation among some people for loving tie games, mainly due to the outcome of the Sugar Bowl after the 1987 season, Johnny Majors always seemed able to maneuver his teams into them—and more often than Dye.

The 1985 Vols later faced the Miami Hurricanes in the Sugar Bowl and destroyed them, beating them even worse than they had beaten Auburn. The final score there was 35-7, in favor of the Vols.

Prior to the Auburn-Tennessee game, *Sports Illustrated* had planned to feature Bo Jackson on the cover the next week. Instead, it was Tony Robinson who graced the cover for Tennessee. Robinson would go onto a checkered career in the pros, eventually landing in prison for a drug conviction and later turning up as a replacement player for the Redskins during one of the NFL strikes.

Auburn tried three different quarterbacks during the game—Pat Washington, Jeff Burger and Bobby Walden—and none seemed able to get the job done, together completing just ten passes and throwing three interceptions. Before the season was over, Dye would settle on Washington as the starter. But the coaches never seemed happy with him or the others, and the question at quarterback would linger until the end of the year.

Van Allen Plexico

As bad as the Tennessee game was, we then played a truly memorable game at home against Florida State on October 12; a game that was the polar opposite of the UT game in every way.

The Seminoles were ranked no. 4, while we had fallen all the way down to no. 12. This was a game that was so close most of the way. And then, as the *Birmingham News* headline the next morning stated, "The Dam Breaks and AU Wins by 32."

Bo had some long runs, but we also forced them to turn the ball over and we ran back some easy fumble recoveries.

For three-and-a-half quarters, Auburn and FSU traded scores, back and forth, up and down the field. At the 6:21 mark of the fourth quarter, Auburn led, 31-27, but there was a sense among those watching that the game was far from over—that anything could still happen.

What *did* happen was absolutely astonishing.

First, fullback Tommie Agee took the ball 68 yards to the FSU 12, where Freddy Weygand would carry it in on a reverse.

It was 38-27, Auburn.

"Yeah, that was it. That was the dam-breaker."
—Bobby Bowden, on the Agee run

196

Next, Kevin Porter ran back a 33-yard interception of a Seminole pass for a touchdown.

It was 45-27, Auburn.

"For us, that was when the fat lady sang."
—Bobby Bowden

Then, Ron Stallworth picked off another FSU pass and cashed it in after dashing 22 yards into the end zone.

It was 52-27, Auburn.

But there was yet more amazing action to come!

Freshman Chip Ferguson, on for a "dizzy" Danny McManus at quarterback, fumbled the snap on the next FSU possession and Auburn's defense recovered at the Seminole 27.

"I asked (McManus) how he was. He wanted to stay in. He finally said he was a little dizzy. You can't be a little dizzy, and beat Auburn. You gotta be no dizzy."
—Bobby Bowden

Tiger back Demetrius Threatt punched it in from eight yards away.

59-27 Auburn.

And that was the final score.

No team had ever scored 59 points on FSU. Combined with the previous year's outcome in Tallahassee, Auburn had scored 101 on them in two games.

Bo Jackson had scoring runs of 53 and 35 yards prior to the fourth-quarter chaos.

"I cannot believe how good (Bo Jackson) is. When he wants to do it, he can do it.

"Auburn is a lot better football team than I thought."
—Bobby Bowden

"After it was all over, Bo Jackson described things perfectly: 'It just went haywire in the fourth quarter. And it was like the Twilight Zone.'

"As for Florida State, no excuses were necessary or offered. 'I thought we'd win the ball game [said FSU Coach Bobby Bowden]. The game for the first fifty-five minutes, we were behind seven points or something like that, or four points or something. So we were in it for fifty-five minutes and then they busted it wide open.'

"The Seminoles fall to 4-1 and surely out of the top 10."
—Bob Warren, Channel Six Eyewitness Sports, Tallahassee

"'Bo Jackson was the difference in the game,' Bowden said. 'He's one of the greats of all time. I think if we would have had him, we probably would have won the game. The teams were fairly even. He's the difference.'

"Jackson, the nation's leading rusher, reeled off touchdown runs of 53 and 35 yards, helping the Tigers ease ahead in the third quarter, and the Tigers' defense turned the game into a rout in the final period, running back two interceptions for touchdowns.

"'In the fourth quarter, we made them make their own mistakes and then we took advantage of them,' said Jackson, who gained 176 yards on 30 carries.

"'This was a typical Auburn-FSU game for three quarters,' Tiger Coach Pat Dye said, 'but the mistakes and turnovers caused it to break open.

"'This is one of the biggest wins since I've been here,' he said. 'I don't know when I've had this much fun.'"
—Los Angeles Times, October 13, 1985

John Ringer
It was close for so long, and then it all just kind of fell apart for them. But yeah, Florida State was on the verge of getting it together as a program.

Van Allen Plexico
They were playing really well. They still didn't have the defense thing figured out. Not until the next year when they

hired that great defensive coordinator, Mickey Andrews. But yeah, this game was close right up until the fourth quarter, when Bo went off on them. And they kept throwing interceptions and fumbling. We went on to win, 59-27. Just an amazing shellacking of a very good team. There were some really strange games between Auburn and Florida State during this decade, and every one of them had at least one weird thing happen. But this one took the cake.

After wins over Georgia Tech and Mississippi State, Auburn rose to no. 6 in the polls as the month of November began. That meant it was time to play another powerhouse.

Into Jordan-Hare came no. 2 Florida, whose only blemish to that point was an inexplicable, early-season tie with Rutgers. The *Birmingham News* called this AU-UF contest "The Game of Steel," because of the great players and strong defenses on the field for both teams that day. It was covered by ABC, who had previously broadcast the Tigers' loss at Tennessee.

Auburn's defense dominated early, holding Florida to just 1 yard of offense and no first downs in the first quarter. Auburn meanwhile connected on a 46-yard Chris Johnson field goal to take an early 3-0 lead.

Florida responded in the second quarter with a touchdown drive that put them ahead at halftime, 7-3.

Neither team could score in the third quarter.

In the fourth quarter, Florida got the ball back with just over nine minutes left to play. Quarterback Kerwin Bell—a player Auburn fans would come to dislike over the next couple of seasons—led the Gators down the field, eventually connecting with Ray McDonald for his second touchdown catch of the day. That put the Gators back ahead, 14-10.

Auburn attempted to mount two more scoring drives at the end, but Brent Fullwood was stopped on a fourth-down dive on the first effort, and Pat Washington's fourth-down pass fell incomplete on the second.

"This was a great victory for everybody—the team, the school and the administration. For me, there's no doubt it's the biggest."
  —Galen Hall, Florida head coach

"We knew Florida was great and they proved it today. And I think we proved we're just short of being great."
—Pat Dye

"For the third time in four years, the Florida Gators tormented Bo Jackson. The No. 2-ranked Gators stretched the nation's longest unbeaten streak to 18 games with a 14-10 victory against No. 6 Auburn Saturday as Ray McDonald caught two touchdown passes from Kerwin Bell.

"Florida (7-0-1) played inconsistently on offense but used a strong defensive effort—helped by an injury to Jackson—to drop Auburn to 6-2. Jackson, who came in leading the nation in rushing with an average of 200 yards per game, suffered a right thigh bruise midway through the second period and carried just once after halftime. He finished with 48 yards in 16 carries.

"It was a rare victory for the Gators at Auburn, where they had won only three times in 24 games."
—LA Times Archives

Bo Jackson was criticized by some in the media for apparently subbing himself out of the game in the second half, due to an injury. He hadn't been accomplishing much against the rugged Gators defense up to that point.

"It was very frustrating to lose this game. I thought both teams played very well, and both teams have stingy defenses. I really wanted to get back out there and play the second half, but I started to have spasms. A helmet hit me in the thigh."
—Bo Jackson

"You saw two of the finest football teams in the nation today. This is the biggest win we have had. It hurt Auburn when Jackson went out, but Fullwood is a great back."
—Florida coach Galen Hall

"It was a close game, but we didn't do what we needed to do to win it. This game boiled down to the fact that Florida is a better football team. They are a first-class team."
—*Pat Dye*

John Ringer
I have to take a minute to talk about the players that were on Auburn's defense in 1984 and 1985. Kevin Greene, Gregg Carr, Gerald Robinson, Tommy Powell, Tracy Rocker, Harold Hallman, Ben Thomas, Gerald Williams. There were so many great players on those two teams.

A lot of guys went on to play in the NFL from that offensive line, too. Steve Wallace, Ben Tamburello, Yann Cowart, Stacey Searles; great, great offensive linemen. We also had a run of tight ends who went on to the NFL during this time, like Jeff Parks and Ed West, and a little later Walter Reeves.

Van Allen Plexico
The 1984 Auburn roster listed *thirteen* different players at running back, and five of them went on to careers in the NFL. That's just incredible.

Florida in 1985 not only had a great defense, they also had great running backs like Neal Anderson, who had a good career with the Bears, and John L. Williams, who was the man for the Seahawks for years. Two big NFL backs on that Florida team.

This game was an absolute slugfest. We held them to 14 points, but they held us to 10. I mentioned earlier that the Florida series back then was streaky, and here we are in the middle of a three-year Florida streak. We hated losing this one, but it felt fair and square. The kind of game Pat Dye relished, where you line your guys up and they line up theirs and you "see who's the better man, the tougher guys." The 1986 game would play out a little bit differently.

And I still can't stand Kerwin Bell.

A 24-10 win in Athens over a higher-ranked Georgia team on November 16 righted the ship a little. It also put Bo Jackson firmly back in the Heisman Trophy conversation. Afterward it was revealed that he'd played the game with cracked ribs. Earlier in the season, some had absurdly whispered that Bo wasn't tough enough, after his less-than-stellar outings against Tennessee and Florida. Consequently, his stock had seemingly dropped a bit. This performance pretty much put such talk to rest.

Auburn had fallen from no. 6 to no. 14 in the rankings, two weeks after the loss to Florida. Georgia was ranked no. 12. The Dogs had only lost once, to Alabama in week one, but had been tied by Vanderbilt. Even more surprisingly, they were coming off a huge upset win over first-ranked Florida the previous week, 24-3, in one of the classic outcomes in that famous series.

After a scoreless first quarter, kicker Chris Johnson put the Tigers on the board with a 50-yard field goal. He'd missed from 51 earlier in the game.

Georgia responded with a short QB keeper by James Jackson for a touchdown, to cap off a ten-play, 68-yard drive, nine minutes before halftime.

Bo Jackson's first nine carries went for just 36 yards, but then he took a pitch from Pat Washington to the right side of the field, cut back to the middle, got a great block from Trey Gainous and, 67 yards later, walked into the end zone. Auburn was back on top, 10-7. Perhaps as importantly, a whole lot of Heisman voters had just watched Bo do what Bo did best: smash his way through a defense and take it the distance.

Georgia attempted a long field goal on their next possession, but Kevin Porter blocked it and Aundray Bruce ran it back to the UGA 38. Running behind fullback Tommie Agee in a preview of the 1986 first-team offense, Brent Fullwood carried it deep into UGA territory. A couple of plays later, Bo took it to the UGA 1 yard line with 47 seconds to go, but the run was called back for holding, so Auburn took a time out and came up with something unexpected for third and long: Washington pitched to Freddie Weygand on the end-around and the speedy receiver dived for the corner of the end zone, landing on his head in paydirt. Now it was 17-7, Auburn, as halftime arrived.

At the half, Georgia led in only two statistical categories: first downs (10-7) and passing yards (UGA had a whopping 65, while AU

202

had only 15!). As Coach Dye had predicted the previous year, the team with the fewest turnovers was winning—Georgia led there, 1-0.

Then the third quarter got underway, with Georgia taking the opening kickoff and moving the ball far enough on a time-consuming drive to allow their kicker to knock through a 50-yard field goal. When Auburn took over possession, Washington connected with Trey Gainous on a long pass into Bulldog territory. A few plays later, Washington tossed a screen pass to Bo Jackson, who carried it inside the Georgia 5. The Bulldog defense bowed its collective neck and stopped Bo on first down and Fullwood on second down. On third down, Pat Washington could get nowhere on the QB keeper, and the Tigers brought out the field goal unit—only to have the attempt blocked. As the fourth quarter approached, the Dogs were down only seven and had seized all the momentum in the game.

Auburn's defense responded as Auburn's great defenses of the Eighties usually responded. They stepped up and stopped Georgia cold, forcing a punt.

The fourth quarter began with the Tigers moving the ball again. On third and long, Washington found tight end Jeff Parks for the first down. A couple of plays later, under extreme pressure from the UGA pass rush, Washington lobbed a short pass to Bo, who wove his way through the Georgia secondary all the way down to the Dogs' 27.

"Jackson, who had not caught a pass in nine games this season, has caught two in this half."
—Al Michaels, ABC broadcast commentary

On second and two at the Georgia 6, Bo took the pitch and absolutely ran over three Georgia defenders, blasting the first one onto his backside and dragging the other two into the end zone for the touchdown. He did it so quickly, you couldn't be entirely sure what you'd just witnessed until you saw the replay. If there had been a camera angle showing Bo bulldozing his way into the end zone, there would be paintings of it the way there are paintings of Ronnie Brown doing something very similar at Tennessee in 2004. With 11:45 to go in the game, Auburn was up, 24-10.

Georgia tried to respond, but QB James Jackson was picked off by Kevin Porter at the Auburn 23. The resulting Auburn drive yielded little, and the Tigers punted.

Now Georgia had to take to the air—an unfamiliar environment for this Bulldog team. Benefiting from a pass interference penalty on Tommy Powell, the Dogs made it to Auburn's red zone, but on fourth down, a pass from James Jackson was bobbled and dropped in the Tigers end zone—helped a bit by Jimmy Warren banging into the receiver from behind.

Taking over on downs, Auburn tried to run the clock out, but couldn't make a first down and punted. Georgia started their final drive on Auburn's side of the field, and James Jackson took numerous shots at the Auburn end zone in the final two minutes, but the Dogs couldn't score. As the clock expired, Auburn had won, 24-10.

"Bo Jackson, bothered by a deep thigh bruise, did a masterful job, scored twice, caught a couple of passes. We can write a finish to this one.

"A very happy Pat Dye. In his fifth year, a man who has taken the Auburn program and turned it into one of the best in the country."

—Al Michaels, ABC broadcast commentary

"Jackson helped provide the Auburn Tigers with a tidy 24-10 victory over the Georgia Bulldogs and, in the process, solidified his status as the most deserving of the Heisman Trophy candidates. Two touchdowns, both of them impressive, and 121 yards of rushing against the nation's third-ranked run defense should lessen the criticism heaped on Jackson in recent weeks.

"'We just did what we had to do,' Jackson said. Then, looking at the small branch he took from the hedges that surround the Georgia playing field, Jackson said: 'This is something I can put in my trophy case.'

"Soon he may be able to add a stiff-arming statuette, though Jackson declined to become involved in conjecture.

"'It's in the back of my mind and that's where it will stay,' he said. 'I didn't come into this game running for the Heisman. I didn't go out there to better my stats for the Heisman.'

"He could have fooled Georgia, which was a spectator during a 67-yard Jackson touchdown run and later a six-yard scoring effort that included the planting of defensive back Miles Smith into the stadium turf. 'I ran over someone,' Jackson allowed."
—Gene Wojciechowski, LA Times, November 17, 1985

The win over Georgia would be Bo Jackson's final win as an Auburn Tiger.

Victory over the Bulldogs in hand, the Tigers had to wait two more weeks before facing Alabama in Birmingham, for what was to be the fiftieth Iron Bowl.

The Tide had certainly improved from their dismal record of the previous year, but at 7-2-1 they were unranked, while Auburn at 8-2 had worked its way back up to no. 7.

Alabama was still coached by Ray Perkins, and their quarterback was future Tide head coach Mike Shula.

It would turn out to be another memorable—perhaps legendary—contest, though not in a positive way for Auburn fans.

Van Allen Plexico

The Van Tiffin field goal game. I don't even want to talk about it.

It was Bo Jackson's birthday, and the cheerleaders sang to him before kickoff. The memories of the previous year's Iron Bowl debacle were still fresh in everyone's minds. We were confident we'd learned all the right lessons and this year would be different. Hadn't we seized control of this rivalry? Weren't we now the team that was supposed to win? Wasn't Alabama now the little brother, hoping for the big upset? It couldn't happen in back-to-back years. Surely not.

Alabama held Auburn scoreless in the first quarter while piling up 13 unanswered points.

After Bo Jackson finally put the Tigers on the scoreboard in the second quarter with a 7-yard touchdown run, Van Tiffin connected on his third field goal, increasing the Alabama lead to 16-7. Auburn was able to get a critical Chris Johnson field goal from 49 yards away, just before halftime, to pull the Tigers within six, at 16-10.

In the third quarter, neither team could manage a score. The fourth quarter, however, would be completely different.

Late in the game, Auburn led by two different famous scores from games the Tigers had won in the recent past: 17-16 (1972) and 23-22 (1982). But neither would stand up as the final score.

Auburn started off the scoring in the furious fourth quarter by marching down the field and sending Bo Jackson over the top at the goal line for a touchdown, just as he'd done to win the Iron Bowl his freshman season. Auburn led, 17-16, stirring the echoes of "Punt, Bama, Punt."

Auburn fans breathed a sigh of relief. That had surely been the game-winning touchdown. All the Tigers had to do now was play great defense, hold Alabama in check a couple more minutes, force one more punt, and go home with the big win.

Tide running back Gene Jelks—who would land the Tide program in hot water a few years later, over admissions of recruiting violations—had other ideas. He ripped off a 74-yard run for a touchdown. (After the game, he told reporters, "I made up my mind to outdo Bo.") The two-point conversion failed, but suddenly Alabama was back ahead, 22-17.

Again the Tigers went on the march, mixing the run and the pass. They chewed up most of the remaining time in the game and capped off the drive with a short plunge into the end zone by fullback Reggie Ware.

Yes, they chewed up *most* of the remaining time. Unfortunately, not *all*.

Auburn now led, 23-22, stirring the echoes of 1982 and "Bo Over the Top," and Alabama only had 57 seconds to work with. Auburn's defense held the Tide in check on three consecutive plays, but Mike Shula converted on fourth down. Now time was exceedingly short. Surely there was no way the Tigers could lose; not after fighting back and scoring on back-to-back desperation drives late in the fourth quarter.

It should have worked out that way. Alabama had no time outs left. The last thing they needed to do was throw the ball over the middle. And yet that's exactly what Shula did: he passed to receiver Tony Richardson on a completion near the center of the field that should have resulted in a quick tackle and the last few seconds slipping away. But the larger Richardson was able to drag undersized

Auburn defensive back Luvell Bivins all the way out of bounds, stopping the clock with six seconds to go and with the Tide now on the Auburn 35 yard line.

Van Tiffin trotted out on the field. The rest, unfortunately, is history.

Van Allen Plexico

Bivins jumped on Richardson's back and Richardson just carried him out of bounds to stop the clock and set up the 52-yard field goal. I remember watching Tiffin kick it while Keith Jackson on ABC announced it and hollered about it. And I remember just saying out loud, over and over, "Unbelievable. Unbelievable. Unbelievable."

And when the *Birmingham News* came out the next morning, the headline of their Sports section was one word: "UNBELIEVABLE."

John Ringer

It *was* unbelievable.

Van Allen Plexico

Sickening. It was just absolutely sickening.

"If my kick had beaten LSU or Mississippi State, it would have been a big moment. But I don't think it would have had the import (of beating Auburn). Typically, when I get outside the state, there's not much said about it. But things are different in Alabama."
—Van Tiffin, quoted in Sports Illustrated, 2015

"It was an all-out war between two groups of young men who were willing to give it all and then some more."
—Phillip Marshall, Montgomery Advertiser

"It didn't bother me too much. I just didn't think about it. I had a job to do."
—Bo Jackson, Auburn running back, on playing with broken ribs against Alabama

Pat Dye later said he had hives after the 1985 Iron Bowl. He couldn't sleep. He decided to make changes to the team's philosophy and approach going forward. The Tigers would have to, because after the bowl game, they wouldn't have Bo Jackson to turn to anymore. By the end of 1985, Auburn's coaches realized they desperately needed a more diversified offense.

Eight days later, at the annual ceremony at the Downtown Athletic Club in New York, Vincent "Bo" Jackson won the 1985 Heisman Trophy.

In his acceptance speech, the famously shy and quiet Bo was surprisingly gregarious and easygoing. He encouraged young people to pursue their dreams, admitted he didn't always go to class, and called Georgia's Herschel Walker up to the podium to compare their abilities and accomplishments, pointing out how they were so similar. "The only way I can see that I'm different is, I'm prettier," he told the Bulldog legend. Then he added, "You can sit down now." The place erupted in laughter and even Walker grinned.

"Auburn running back Bo Jackson tonight was awarded the Heisman Trophy in the closest voting in Heisman history. Jackson beat Iowa quarterback Chuck Long."
—CBS Sports

Van Allen Plexico

It's almost inconceivable today to imagine that Bo could have lost the Heisman that year. After everything he had accomplished over four years at Auburn, and all the legendary, near-mythical things we saw him do during and after that time, to think that he almost lost the Heisman to a quarterback who put together *one* flashy game on television, at the end of his career... Astonishing. But it almost happened.

Almost.

"Bo Jackson, Auburn University running back."
"Yes sir. And this year's Heisman Trophy winner. He is some kind of open field runner. He is really tricky. In fact, he's so tricky, on the instant replays he's doing something else!"
—Bo Jackson and Bob Hope, 1985 Bob Hope Christmas Special

Jerry Hinnen

I remember going to the Florida game that season. We had Florida fans behind me, which I feel like was the first time I really grasped the fact that there were fans of football teams other than Auburn; that people existed who didn't want our team to win football games. That wanted Auburn to lose! And so that was kind of mind blowing. And unfortunately, Auburn did lose that game. If I remember correctly, Bo didn't play much or at all in that game.

But then, you know, the first individual play I can remember watching as a football fan was against Georgia. It was a Bo Jackson touchdown run. A sixty- or seventy-yard run where, after he'd gotten into Georgia territory, he cut back all the way across the field. And I just remember thinking, "I've never seen anyone do that before. I didn't know you could run one way and then run all the way the other way across the field. This is—oh my gosh—*mind blowing*." Even then, as a little kid—I guess I had just turned seven—I had the understanding that the guy who was carrying the ball was an exceptional football player, and not like all the other football players that were on the field.

It sounds like a cliche to say, "Oh, I'm an Auburn fan and the first thing I remember is watching Bo."

But I'm an Auburn fan and the first thing I really remember is watching Bo.

Auburn had played in the 50th Sugar Bowl after the 1983 season, and their previous game was the 50th Iron Bowl. With the 1985 regular season over, they accepted a bid to play Texas A&M in the 50th Cotton Bowl.

If he hadn't already decided to do so, Pat Dye made up his mind to radically change the offense after this game. Because things did not go well for the Tigers in Dallas that day.

Van Allen Plexico

Jackie Sherrill's Texas A&M just ran all over us in the Cotton Bowl.

Two moments stand out in this game for me. Bo caught a short pass and took it the length of the field for a touchdown. The Aggie coaches still talk about that play, about being shocked at how fast he really was, as they watched him zoom by. And then, later in the game, trailing 21-16, Auburn got to the goal line and ran the famous Bo Over the Top play, and the Aggies stuffed it on fourth down. Right after Bo had won the Heisman Trophy. That was frustrating in the extreme.

"I think if we had scored on that fourth-down play, we would have won the ball game. But when they stopped us, it gave them the edge and the momentum."
—Pat Dye

Bo did accumulate 129 yards rushing on 31 carries, as well as 73 yards receiving and two touchdowns, but the Aggies went on to win the game, 36-16.

Van Allen Plexico
Our final record for 1985 was 8-4 overall, 3-3 in the conference, putting us right in the middle of the pack in the SEC standings. But at least Bo had won the Heisman.

He played in a couple of postseason all-star games and did really well, especially in the one played in Yokohama, Japan—the Japan Bowl. I remember the headline in one paper was, BO RUNS WILD IN JAPAN.

Bo Jackson ran for 171 yards on 18 attempts in the 1986 Japan Bowl, scoring three touchdowns; one came on a classic Bo 57-yard breakaway run, and another was a 69-yard pass reception. He was named the game's MVP.

By that point, his NFL stock was through the roof and he would be the first overall pick in the 1986 NFL draft, chosen by the Tampa Bay Buccaneers. Of course, with Bo, that didn't necessarily mean he would sign the contract with the lowly Bucs or ever play a down for their new coach—who just happened to be one Ray Perkins, late of Tuscaloosa. No, he turned them down flat. Instead, of course, he chose to play baseball with the Kansas City Royals, going on to do amazing things there, including being named MVP of the All-Star

Game in 1989. George Brett and other great Royals players still tell stories of the astonishing feats they witnessed their teammate from Auburn perform.

"This is not a normal guy."
—George Brett, Kansas City Royals, on Bo Jackson

"You know what? I really did play baseball with Superman."
—Kansas City Royals Hall-of-Famer Frank White, on Bo Jackson

"Neither of us is very easily amazed."
—NBA great Michael Jordan, on Bo Jackson's casual attitude toward his remarkable feats

Meanwhile, the Los Angeles Raiders kept an eye on Bo and, the following year, used a late-round pick to select him—just in case he decided to play football again.

He did.

As a "hobby."

The Raiders seemed to him to be a much better option than playing for Perkins at Tampa Bay. He therefore ended up wearing the black and silver, sharing the backfield with the legendary Marcus Allen, and going on to the 1990 Pro Bowl, even as he continued to play Major League Baseball. Critics taunted him for his claim that football was a hobby—right up until they saw him play the game, and excel at it the way he had in college.

Van Allen Plexico

The sports media and opposing fans both love to jump on someone who makes wild claims and can't back them up, or someone about whom wild claims are made. The wilder the claims, the more they all relish tearing that person down; just ripping them to pieces, as soon as that person reveals they can't do what people have said they could do.

Bo perplexed his detractors. He sent them into fits of apoplexy. And that was because he backed up everything anyone had ever said about him, and more. Much more.

The sports media and opposing fans went after him hammer-and-tongs when he started playing pro football with the Raiders while he was still playing baseball with the Royals. When he called it a "hobby," they doubled down, just savaging him on the air and in print. And then they all saw that he could do exactly what people had been saying he could do. He could dominate at both sports. They were shocked.

Once they realized he really was that good, almost all of his detractors—at least the ones I heard—flipped 180 degrees and became his most vocal cheerleaders for the rest of his career in both sports. He won them over. What else could they say? They had to acknowledge what was obvious to everyone. His astounding feats on both the football field and the baseball diamond changed their hearts and minds, and his worldwide prominence and fame as not just an athlete but a celebrity grew in direct proportion to how much they'd ridiculed him before that.

Perhaps Bo Jackson's career highlight with the Raiders was the Monday Night Football matchup on November 30, 1987, with the Seattle Seahawks and their flamboyant star linebacker, Brian Bosworth. A former Oklahoma All-American, Bosworth was used to winning and liked to talk big before a game. The much quieter Bo did his talking between the hash marks. And on that particular night, he certainly did that. He rang the Seahawks up for 221 yards and three touchdowns, including two scores that became absolutely iconic. One was a 91-yard blast in which he shot like a rocket down the sideline, through the end zone and beyond, into the stadium tunnel, finally lost from view. Those watching at home might well have wondered, had we seen the last of him for the night? Was this his "dropping the mic" moment? Would he come back at all?

He did, in fact, come back—and would score an even more famous touchdown soon after.

This one was a lot shorter than 91 yards, but in at least one way it was even more dramatic. In order to get into the end zone, he had to get past one Brian Bosworth, who stood in his way. Bo proceeded to run the Boz over like a Mack truck, bulldozing through and over the flattened former Sooner. Bosworth—and his once-fearsome reputation—never seemed the same again.

1986

Van Allen Plexico

Going into the 1986 season, Bo Jackson was no longer on the Auburn football roster. And we'd finished 8-5 with him on the team the year before. Pat Dye made it clear that big changes were coming. Auburn was going to be a different team. It would *have* to be a different team. And we had a much better year as a result of that decision.

This was Jeff Burger's team. He turned out to be a very solid passing quarterback for us. Later on, he told the story that, when he was being recruited, coaches would ask him if he preferred the passing game or the option attack. He said that he would tell them what they wanted to hear; whichever one he thought they liked to run the most. So he had told Pat Dye he was an option QB, and he ended up at Auburn in that role. Then, going into 1986, we became more of a passing team, with Coach Dye even bringing in Pat Sullivan to be the new offensive coordinator and Larry Blakeney to be receivers coach, and Dye asked them to cook up more of a passing attack. We kept the I-Formation, more or less, but with more of a "throw the ball" approach to it now. Burger shrugged off the change; now he was a passing quarterback.

I remember Aubie at one of the games that season, running around in his big airplane he could sit inside, and it said "Air Auburn" on the side. Throwing the ball: such a revolutionary concept for a Pat Dye team in the mid-Eighties!

John Ringer

It was exciting. We had been "tailback, tailback, tailback" forever. Now suddenly we had this whole other way of scoring. We threw the ball a lot, relatively speaking, and threw it deep. The defense was great that year, too. They absolutely crushed most teams. Nobody scored more than fourteen points against us until November. We held five of our first seven opponents to single digits.

The offense was rolling up and down the field and really opening things up. Teams didn't know what to expect from us now. We had a lot of talent on the roster. Our opponents would bring everybody up into the box to stop the running backs, and that made for some easy throws for Burger. When they backed out of that, he could hand it off to Brent Fullwood and Tommie Agee and keep chewing them up.

Van Allen Plexico

This was the year that the backfield duo of senior runners—Tommie Agee and Brent Fullwood—really exploded. They were just a great running duo at fullback and tailback. Fullwood had played behind Bo since 1983 and we had seen glimpses of what the two of them could do together. This year was Fullwood's chance to shine, and with Agee clearing the way, he took advantage of it.

You're absolutely right about that defense not getting enough credit. Everybody remembers the defenses the next three years being so great, but it really began here. Georgia scored twenty points on us and nobody scored more than that all season.

Auburn came out throwing the ball early and often in blowout wins over Chattanooga and East Carolina, winning by a combined score of 87-14. Then, in week three, the Tigers welcomed Johnny Majors and Tennessee to Jordan-Hare. Everyone vividly remembered the "ambush" at Neyland the previous season, and fans desperately wanted payback against the Vols.

They got it, and then some.

After using the first two games as opportunities to test out the newly-installed passing attack that featured Jeff Burger at the controls of "Air Auburn," Pat Dye and Pat Sullivan returned to basics in week three. Burger gave the ball to Brent Fullwood, and Fullwood delivered. He racked up 207 yards on 18 carries, including an 85-yard blast that set up a score. The Tigers obliterated Tennessee, 34-8.

"Everybody thought we couldn't run the football. Well, we proved them wrong today."
—Brent Fullwood

Jeff Burger, by Jarrod Alberich

Lopsided wins followed, as the Tigers trounced Western Carolina, Vanderbilt and Georgia Tech.

On October 25, Auburn traveled to Starkville to face 6-1 and 13th-ranked Mississippi State, coached in his first season by Rockey Felker. During this decade, seeing the Bulldogs ranked at all was an unusual sight. Seeing them with only one loss, this far into the season, was truly remarkable. What was perhaps even more amazing was how they'd gotten to 6-1: they'd knocked off Syracuse, Tennessee and Florida. ESPN televised the Auburn game and hyped it up as a potential barn-burner, with what they expected would be two evenly-matched teams.

That did not turn out to be the case.

Recovering from the flu, Brent Fullwood received IV fluids at halftime. On either side of that treatment, though, he ran for 179 yards and 3 touchdowns, including a long of 88 in the second quarter. Jeff Burger was only called upon to throw 12 passes, of which he completed 6 for 125 yards. Auburn won easily, 35-6.

"Brent Fullwood is a fast piece of work. I'm mighty proud of this football team. We've got an unselfish offense. We're happy with whoever gets the ball or the points. These kids have worked hard to get where we are."
—*Pat Dye*

"There's not much you can say about this game. We got beat fairly convincingly in all phases of the game."
—*Rockey Felker, MSU head coach*

Van Allen Plexico

We started out by winning seven in a row and worked our way up to no. 7 in the country. Our seventh opponent was Mississippi State, and believe it or not, they were also undefeated and ranked thirteenth. It was one of those years

216

where the Bulldogs from Starkville thought, "This is our big chance!" And it just never is.

By the way, that was also the game that got mentioned by *Saturday Night Live* during a skit. They did a thing where Kevin Nealon and another guy—maybe Dana Carvey—were in the basement watching TV, and they were bored and trying to find something to watch, and they noted that Auburn was playing Mississippi State—as if that was the most awful, boring thing you could possibly do, to watch that game. I guess to the rest of the country, it might be.

Also of note: this game was being played at the same time as the famous Mets-Red Sox World Series game where the ball rolled between Bill Buckner's legs.

The game was on ESPN and Brent Fullwood ran wild on the Bulldogs. He took a pitch from Burger and went 88 yards down the sideline for a touchdown. We killed them, 35-6. That's one of those times that the State fans just kind of shake their heads and say, "It's not easy being a Mississippi State fan."

After seven decisive wins, this undefeated Auburn team found itself ranked fifth in the country. But the level of competition was about to rise, as the Tigers traveled south to Gainesville to face the Gators. Florida had won the two previous years with an ultra-stout defense and a strong running game. Many of those players had moved on to the NFL, though, and the 1986 edition of the Gators would prove to be a slightly different animal. This Florida team relied heavily on the play of quarterback Kerwin Bell. Unfortunately for Florida, Bell had injured his knee in an earlier game and didn't start against Auburn.

The Gators were not operating at peak efficiency for much of the game, as Bell's backup, Rodney Brewer, turned the ball over four times in the first half. Auburn meanwhile got off to a solid start and the two teams went into the fourth quarter with the Tigers up 17-0. It looked to Auburn fans as if the game would turn out to be just another lopsided blowout win.

In desperation mode, Florida's coach, Galen Hall, inserted the injured Bell at QB in the second half, and immediately the game turned around. Bell led the Gators to two quick scores and suddenly

Florida only trailed by seven, 17-10. The 51-yard field goal on that second drive was delivered by one Robert McGinty, the former Auburn kicker who had transferred after missing the potential game-winning kick against Alabama in 1984. Salt in the wounds.

Auburn still led by a touchdown, though, and methodically moved the ball down to the Florida 34 yard line with 1:31 remaining in the game. Another score here—even a field goal—and it would be over.

Unfortunately, that was when usually-dependable fullback Reggie Ware fumbled the ball, and Florida recovered.

Bell led the Gators back down the field, hit Ricky Nattiel for the touchdown with barely thirty seconds left, and then somehow, miraculously hobbled his way into the end zone for the two-point conversion to give Florida the improbable comeback win, 18-17.

"Kerwin Bell made some great plays and completed the passes he had to under pressure. They did it when they had to. We didn't.

"The loss is tough on our players, coaches and fans, but we want to run the whole race before we give it up. Sure, it's disappointing, but we'll be back next week."
—Pat Dye

Van Allen Plexico
That game was a nightmare.

Florida turned the ball over seven times, trailed 17-0 in the fourth quarter, and they still won. Heck—we were deep in their territory with a touchdown lead and less than two minutes to go in the game, and they still won!

Florida had won the last two against us, so we owed them, and we really wanted to keep our win streak and top five ranking alive.

Stop me if you've heard this song before, but this is one of those games where Pat Dye was very conservative. We should have been leading by more than 17-0 in the fourth quarter. Then again, given how little the Gators had been able to accomplish in the first three quarters, I guess there was no reason to think they'd totally flip the switch there at the end—especially with Bell playing hurt. But, somehow, they did.

I always like to say Kerwin Bell wheeled his wheelchair into the end zone for that two-point conversion and we couldn't stop him.

"We knew (Auburn) hadn't had to play hard in the second half all year. We felt if we could come back and make it close, we could win it. That's the good thing about playing such a tough schedule, it gets us ready for a game like this.

"I was trying to get the ball to Ricky again (on the 2-point conversion), then I saw the left side of the field was open so I just headed that way. I was just hoping I would get there, it seems like it took me all day to get into the end zone."
—*Kerwin Bell, Florida quarterback*

John Ringer
I hated that guy.

So after a win over Cincinnati, Auburn was 8-1 overall and ranked ninth, and hosted Georgia in the infamous "Nothing Stinks Like a Wet Dawg" game.

Georgia was ranked in the top twenty but they had just lost their starting quarterback and had to play their backup against this Auburn defense, so we felt pretty good. We were big favorites and we felt like, "This is a year we're going to get Georgia. We're going to take it to them."

With Georgia's starting quarterback, James Jackson, unavailable to play due to attending the funeral of his grandmother, backup Wayne Johnson got the start. Johnson ran for one touchdown and threw for another, as the Bulldogs put 20 points on the scoreboard by the fourth quarter.

Auburn's offense was unable to do much for most of the game, but it found some life late as a young receiver named Lawyer Tillman emerged onto the stage in a big way for the first time, catching numerous passes from Burger, including a 13-yard touchdown with three minutes remaining to pull the Tigers within four. On an earlier Auburn possession, Brent Fullwood appeared to have scored what would've been the game-winning touchdown, but the officials ruled they had blown the whistle before Fullwood broke loose and scampered to the end zone, so the touchdown was brought back. Bulldog linebacker Steve Boswell intercepted Burger to stop Auburn's final drive, and the Dogs held on to win.

"I'm very proud of Wayne Johnson, who came in and was unbothered by the situation. First of all, he's a marvelous athlete and is always plugging away. And, secondly, he did not get rattled in starting against one of the top teams in the country."
—*Vince Dooley, Georgia head coach*

"They just lined up and whipped us. This is a mighty disappointing loss, and I will lose a lot of sleep from it."
—*Pat Dye*

The loss knocked Auburn out of contention for the SEC title and a trip to the Sugar Bowl. LSU would go instead, as they had in 1984. (And again they would get thrashed by Nebraska.)

John Ringer

Georgia had a great game. They pulled it out in the end, 20-16, and Auburn was devastated. The Georgia fans were going crazy in the stadium. Some went down on the field, and some of them stayed in the stadium celebrating for a long time. Finally the Auburn public address announcer asked them to get off the field and leave the stadium, but they didn't. So we turned on the sprinklers on the field, turned on the hoses on the fans in the stands, and they got wet that day. This was at night in November, and it wasn't hot outside, and they sprayed the Georgia fans down, wet them down. The Georgia fans were not happy about that.

So the next year when we went to play them in Georgia, we were looking for payback for the way the game went, but the Georgia people were more upset about the water, and were acting like it was a huge scandal. Some of my relatives and some of my nearby neighbors were Georgia grads, and they were all outraged about it.

Can you imagine if that happened today? Oh lord, if you hosed down the other team's fans after a win in your stadium? Can you imagine that? They were so mad about it.

Van Allen Plexico
Yeah, well, they should have gotten out when they were told to. They were ripping up the turf, from what I understand. Damaging the field.

Not that we would ever mess with their hedges.

John Ringer
No comment.

Van Allen Plexico
We won't go on the record about that.

But, hey, it sold a few T-shirts. And Aubie came out the next season with a garden hose wrapped around his shoulder and the little sprayer gun in his hand. It was hilarious.

One of the noteworthy things about that game was that we were trailing late, 20-16, and Brent Fullwood scored a touchdown. But the refs called it back. They ruled that he had been whistled down, even though he had never been stopped or down. It was one of those deals where the ref blows it, literally, and there's nothing you can do.

So, without that referee's phantom whistle, we would have won, and been 9-1 going into the Iron Bowl, and still been alive for the SEC title.

This was also the game where we couldn't get much of anything going on the ground before that, so we had to pass the ball more. Here came Lawyer Tillman, catching everything that Jeff Burger threw anywhere near him. I remember Vince Dooley after the game saying, "I didn't think we'd ever stop Tillman. He was killing us."

For some Auburn fans, this amazing performance in a losing cause against Georgia was the first time they'd become aware of Lawyer Tillman. But just one game later, the lanky receiver would etch his name into the Auburn history books forever.

On November 29, the Tigers made their way up the highway to Birmingham to play Alabama in Legion Field.

Alabama came into the game ranked seventh in the country, while Auburn was fourteenth. Both teams had two losses. Both teams had won their first seven games. Mike Shula was still the quarterback and the star player on their defense was linebacker Cornelius Bennett, in his senior year, along with sophomore Derrick Thomas— both future NFL stars. Ray Perkins was in what would be his final year as Alabama coach before bailing on the Tide and heading down to Tampa Bay.

The outcomes of the previous two years weighed heavily on the minds of all the players and fans. Media personalities around the state had begun to speculate that the wins by Auburn in 1982 and 1983 were just an aberration; that dominance in a series that had begun to move Auburn's way with the arrival of Pat Dye and the departure of the Bear was now sliding back toward Tuscaloosa. There was talk—some of it from Perkins himself—that former UGA player Pat Dye just didn't care as much about the Iron Bowl rivalry as he did about beating Georgia.

It was all nonsense, of course. But it was *everywhere*.

The idle chatter had to stop. Reality had to be reasserted into this series.

Auburn wanted a win. Auburn *needed* a win.

Some way, somehow, the Tigers had to get it done in 1986.

Van Allen Plexico

I remember clearly that Brent Fullwood scored on the first play of the second quarter and the first play of the fourth quarter. I also recall him injuring his knee and appearing to be in agony on the sideline, before coming back in and racking up more yards against this strong Alabama defense. He was just a tough back.

John Ringer

He was.

Bobby Humphrey had a big game at running back for Alabama, too. He ran for 207 yards, which was the most an Auburn team had given up in a long time. It would be two and a half years before another running back rushed for more than 100 yards on us.

It was a game filled with drama and with memorable moments.

Auburn moved the ball well enough in the first quarter, mixing the run and the pass, but Jeff Burger threw an interception in the Alabama red zone. Alabama came right back down the field with Humphrey running the ball and scored a touchdown.

Then Auburn drove back down the other way, relying mostly on Fullwood running and catching, and on the first play of the second quarter, he took it around left end for the score.

On the next Auburn possession, after a great punt return by little receiver Trey Gainous, another Auburn receiver, Scott Bolton, took the ball on the reverse and picked up a big gain down into the Alabama red zone. Both of those players—as well as Bolton's signature play, with him carrying the ball on the reverse—would figure prominently in the way the game's climactic moments would pan out.

That possession looked promising, with Fullwood even finding his way into the end zone at one point, but that run was brought back on a holding call. Eventually Chris Knapp missed a field goal from just 29 yards out and the game remained tied at seven.

Humphrey carried Alabama right back down the field for a touchdown on the next drive. Then, forcing an Auburn punt, they looked to score yet again. Fortunately, defensive back Kevin Porter intercepted Shula in the Auburn end zone. The half ended with Alabama ahead, 14-7.

Auburn's first two drives of the second half ended in an interception thrown by Burger and a fumble by Fullwood, but all Alabama could manage out of those two turnovers was a single Van Tiffin field goal. Still, the Tide now led by double-digits, 17-7, and Auburn fans were starting to squirm in their seats.

Auburn's offense had looked effective for most of the game, but turnovers and penalties had taken their toll. The Tigers finally got their act together late in the third quarter, with a drive that was aided by a personal foul call on Alabama, and Fullwood scored on the first play of the fourth quarter.

Yet again Alabama responded, marching right back down the field, and it looked like running back Gene Jelks—he of the "outdo

223

Bo" comments the previous year—had taken the ball very close to the Auburn goal line before going out of bounds. A score from there would've probably iced the game for the Tide. The referees, however, stepped in and called clipping on Alabama, backing them up. The drive sputtered and ultimately ended with the hated Van Tiffin missing a relatively short field goal.

Still only down 17-14, Auburn got the ball back and moved down the field with a gutsy drive that included multiple third-down conversions. Once they reached the Alabama red zone, however, Burger threw another interception. It felt like the end of the Georgia game all over again. With only seven and a half minutes remaining in the game, one might well have wondered if the Tigers had just squandered their last chance.

The Auburn defense had other ideas. They held Alabama and got the ball back. The offense came out on the field with one last opportunity. If they were to score, though, they would have to go nearly the length of the field in under three minutes.

With 2:18 remaining, Burger scrambled for his life on third down and only made it back to the line of scrimmage. Now Auburn faced a fourth and three, just across midfield, trailing by three. Surely Pat Dye would order a Brent Fullwood run here, right? And it would go directly into the teeth of Alabama's defense, with Bennett and Thomas just waiting. Surely that's what the Tide players, coaches and fans expected.

But that's not what happened.

Burger took the snap, dropped back, held the ball only a split second, and hit little Trey Gainous— "Old Reliable," as ABC's Keith Jackson described him—coming across from right to left at the Alabama 40. A pass! A first down!

Now suddenly all the momentum seemed to swing toward Auburn. Pat Dye motioned confidently toward the Alabama end zone. Previous Auburn drives that had made it farther than this, however, had ended in turnovers. What could the Tigers do differently this time?

Fullwood ripped off a run down to the Alabama twenty. Agee blasted his way to the ten. The folks in the stands wearing orange and blue were going crazy.

Facing second and goal at the 8, and with the clock ticking, the call came in for a very specific play. One that involved receiver Scott

Bolton, whom we had last seen in the first half, running a reverse for about twenty yards. But Bolton wasn't on the field, and wasn't directly at hand on the sideline, either.

Lawyer Tillman *was* on the field. He saw the play call, realized it was not one he usually participated in, and started off the field. The coaches frantically waved him back on. He appeared confused, but also seemed determined to do the best he could with it.

Indeed he did.

"Burger's gonna pitch to Jessie, gonna give it to Tillman on the end around. The ten, the five, Tillman—he's in! Touchdown Auburn! Lawyer Tillman on the end around reverse! Thirty-two seconds left! And Auburn has gone ahead, 20-17!"
—Jim Fyffe, Auburn radio broadcast

Burger took the snap and pitched the ball to backup running back Tim Jessie, who handed it to Tillman on the end around. Tillman made one good cut at about the 5 yard line and stumbled into the end zone for the winning score.

What could've been a disaster—running a play featuring a player who probably hadn't practiced it much, if at all—proved instead to be a stroke of inadvertent genius. Defenses often key on the particular personnel who are sent in before a play, and Alabama's defense could not have been looking for the reverse with that particular set of personnel on the field.

Knapp knocked through the extra point and Auburn now led by the last- second- field- goal- proof score of 21-17. There would be no Van Tiffin heroics for the Tide this year.

The ghosts of "Unbelievable" in 1985 might not have been *entirely* put to rest, but "Reverse to Victory" went a long way toward making the entire Auburn Family feel better.

A *very* long way.

John Ringer

Tillman was a much bigger receiver than Scott Bolton. There was some contact as he got close to the goal line. I think his size helped him get into the end zone.

You and I both later worked at the AU Bookstore in Haley Center, where our boss was Scott Bolton's brother.

Van Allen Plexico

Yes, we did. We could write another whole book about those days.

There was enough time left after Alabama got the ball back at the very end for them to run three or four plays. I was still scared to death after what had happened the year before. It felt like Shula had some kind of hex on us. I didn't feel entirely confident and really able to celebrate the win until we knocked down Shula's final desperation Hail Mary pass. That was like an exorcism.

I remember an anchorwoman on Birmingham television that night, who had only lived in the state and been around the rivalry for a couple of years, saying on the air how the ending of this game was so disappointing compared to the previous year. I thought, "Good lord. She must be saying that as a newly-minted Alabama fan, because that's the only way I can see the end of this game as being disappointing. If the 1985 ending is the outcome and the benchmark we're holding every future Iron Bowl to, fans like her are going to be pretty disappointed almost every year. Or, at least, I hope they are."

Auburn, with those two narrow, frustrating losses, did not win the SEC and would not be going to the Sugar Bowl. LSU, a team Auburn had not played, got that honor. Again, as had happened two years previously, they faced Nebraska, and were once again butchered.

Auburn was invited to the Orange Bowl in Miami.

"Wait," one might say. "Auburn went to the *Orange Bowl* that year? Why don't I remember that?"

It's a fair question. The Tigers were, in fact, *invited* to the Orange Bowl; they just didn't *go*. Because, you see, Pat Dye had made a *promise...*

Van Allen Plexico

The Citrus Bowl in Orlando had already asked us, and Coach Dye had promised them that we would come. We hadn't been to the Orange Bowl in forever, if ever. Then they called Auburn up and invited us to come down and play in

Miami, which would've been incredible. But Coach Dye wanted to keep his word, so we had to tell the Orange, "No."

I appreciated his attitude in doing that, and I agree it was the honorable thing to do, but I've always regretted that we missed our one chance to play in the Orange Bowl. Our opponent would have been a 10-1 Oklahoma team whose only blemish was an early-season loss to Miami. (Arkansas got the spot opposite them instead, and got killed.)

So a 9-2 Auburn team went to the Citrus Bowl to play Southern Cal, coached by Ted Tollner, who had been fired by USC before the game but coached in it anyway. Take a note, Terry Bowden.

"We're excited to be playing in a New Year's Day bowl game. And to be facing such a strong team like Auburn will certainly be an exciting challenge."
—Ted Tollner, USC head coach

"I realize they (USC) have a lot of young players, but they have a lot of potential. The strength of their defense is the linebackers. They've got good pursuit. It's going to be up to us as an offensive line to get on them and stay on them. You've got to play with no mistakes."
—Ben Tamburello, Auburn center

"I rate them high. They are real physical. But I've been against some that were a little better than them. Right now, the best (pass defense I've faced) was Florida. They were a nasty type. They would hit you whether you had the ball or not."
—Lawyer Tillman, Auburn receiver

"I basically just handed the ball off to Bo (last year). Other teams knew what we were going to do. If we had thrown more, I think Bo would have been even more effective.

"We're not as predictable (this season) and that's when we are at our best. We've had a good pass-run mixture. Looking at us last year you'd see a very physical offense, just pounding and pounding."
—Jeff Burger, Auburn quarterback

Burger was asked about his relationship with first-year passing game coordinator and Auburn legend Pat Sullivan:

"I hadn't lost confidence in myself, but I felt the coaches in previous years had lost confidence in me. I was the starting quarterback last year at the beginning of the season, and then I got pulled. Even when I was the starting quarterback, I never felt like I was.

"He (Pat Sullivan) approaches me on a player-to-player basis. It's like talking to a roommate.

"We're going to have the same game plan against (USC) as we did against Alabama. We want to make USC realize that we can throw the football.
—Jeff Burger, Auburn quarterback

John Ringer
That was a brutal game. Very physical. Rodney Peete was the USC quarterback in that game. They had a number of guys on defense who went on to play in the NFL.

Southern Cal's only score came on an interception return in the first quarter, when a USC lineman had fallen on the ground during the play but popped back up in between Burger and Tommie Agee in the flat, just as Burger threw the ball toward Agee. Burger didn't see him until it was too late.

That was it for the Trojans. Auburn scored two touchdowns in the second quarter. The only scoring by either team after halftime was Tracy Rocker's safety on Rodney Peete early in the fourth quarter. The defenses scored as many times as the offenses in a game filled with turnovers and fourth down stands. The final score was 16-7. Linebacker Aundray Bruce was named MVP. Brent Fullwood gained 152 yards and scored a touchdown in his final outing as a Tiger.

This game marked Auburn's 500th football win.

"(This win) was one of my most satisfying, because they were rude. They were one of the rudest teams we've ever played. Instead of playing ball, they wanted to fight."
—Brent Fullwood, after the 1987 Citrus Bowl, quoted in the New York Times

Van Allen Plexico

They weren't quite what they had been a few years earlier, or what they'd become starting in 2002, but it was still a good feeling to beat USC.

There was a controversy over Brent Fullwood playing in this game. He was the fourth-leading rusher in the country coming into the bowl game, but it turned out he hadn't been going to class toward the end of the year. Coach Dye received some criticism for allowing him to play. I can certainly see that side of it. But I also know that, after everything Fullwood had done for the team that year and over the course of his career, if Dye could find a way to allow Fullwood to play in that one last game, he was going to do it, no matter what.

We ended 1986 with just two losses, which was fewer than any other team in the SEC. LSU and Alabama both ended up with three.

1987

With the 1986 season behind them, Auburn fans looked to the coming of the following year with great anticipation. The passing game under senior-to-be QB Jeff Burger, throwing to receivers like Lawyer Tillman, seemed to have radically transformed the offense from somewhere in the Stone Age to new heights of glory and possibility. The defense appeared absolutely rock-solid—or maybe *Rocker*-solid. There was an excitement and an anticipation around the program that hadn't been felt quite that fully since perhaps before the 1983 season. Big things, everyone was sure, waited just over the horizon.

Jordan-Hare Stadium looked a bit different when the 1987 season began. A second upper deck had been added, this one on the East side of the stadium, complete with luxury suites. The facility's capacity was now up to 85,214.

In order to make the first game in the expanded stadium a more memorable one, Auburn persuaded Texas to come back over for a return visit. The two previous games against the Longhorns had not ended well, with losses in 1983 and 1984. This, however, would be a different Texas team—not as powerful as the ones led by Fred Akers. They'd changed coaches to David McWilliams, who wouldn't last long in Austin.

It would also be a different *Auburn* team—one with a veteran quarterback who could throw the ball, receivers capable of doing something with it when they caught it, and a defense that was beyond stingy.

It was not immediately clear that Texas understood either of those facts.

Van Allen Plexico

Auburn was ranked fifth in the country coming into this season, and we wanted a big name to open up play in the expanded stadium with the new deck. Texas turned out to be the perfect choice, because they brought the name brand and reputation, but they weren't quite what they'd been before. There was of course the revenge factor. We were still plenty mad that Texas had spoiled our national championship season in 1983 and then dislocated Bo's shoulder in 1984.

For some reason, in this game, Texas thought we were still a running team. They geared everything to stopping the run. It looked like our passing game caught them completely by surprise.

Brent Fullwood and Tommie Agee had moved on to the NFL after the 1986 season, and we would miss their toughness and breakaway ability in the run game. But the passing game was much improved, with Jeff Burger having a year of experience as the starter and with a whole group of excellent receivers, led by the amazing Lawyer Tillman, speedy Alexander Wright, dependable Duke Donaldson, as well as powerful tight end Walter Reeves—and all of them joined again by fast Freddie Weygand, who had played on the team in 1984 and 1985 before taking a year off in 1986. I always suspected he saw how much better the passing game had become while he was gone, and he probably couldn't wait to get back on the field.

Most everyone else was back, as well, including Tracy Rocker and Aundray Bruce, on a defense that was rapidly becoming known as one of the best in Auburn history.

We had also found a kicker in Win Lyle, who proved to be super-accurate and reliable. Pat Dye hadn't been particularly fond of Chris Knapp, the kicker in 1986, even going so far as to respond to a Citrus Bowl reporter's question of, "What is your team's main weakness?" with the one-word reply, "Placekicking." *Ouch*.

Lyle ended up serving as our kicker for only three years because, somehow, it was determined that he'd lost a year of eligibility along the way. So he kicked for us from 1987-1989—three extremely successful seasons.

I was at the Texas game. I was still out on summer break; Auburn under the quarters system used to play the first two or three games every season before students came back for fall quarter. I wanted to see this game, though, so some of my high school friends and I stopped there on the way down from Sylacauga to Panama City for the weekend. It was a great experience. It was the first football game in the state of Alabama to have more than 80,000 fans in attendance.

"Pat Dye enters his seventh year with a 52-20 record at Auburn and a veteran ballclub that has a chance to win it all. The Tigers are led by quarterback Jeff Burger, and the senior's passing ability will be needed more this year. He has a great corps of receivers led by Lawyer Tillman, a tremendous leaper who averaged more than twenty yards a catch in 1986. But a championship for the Tigers will depend on the defense, led by All-American Tracy Rocker, one of eight returning starters."
—Mike Patrick, ESPN broadcast, September 5, 1987

Van Allen Plexico

It was spectacular. A 31-3 shellacking of Texas. That win exorcised a lot of demons.

Jeff Burger threw the ball all over them. And our defense didn't let them have anything. They were lucky to get out of Jordan-Hare without being shut out.

Two moments still stand out in my memory from this game. One was when Greg Staples, our safety, intercepted a Bret Stafford pass. But it wasn't just any interception. The Texas receiver caught the ball and Staples came out of nowhere and collided with him in midair, like a guided missile, and the two of them sort of spun around each other from their momentum, and when they separated again, Staples had the ball. He had just taken it away from the guy in midair. It looked like something out of the Matrix.

The other moment was something unexpected our great linebacker, Kurt Crain, did:

"That was the game where I hugged the referee."
—Kurt Crain, Auburn Network video interview

"Auburn, which recovered two fumbles and picked off two passes in the first half, capitalized on an interception by Alvin Briggs and a fumble recovery by Robert Goff to score the first two times it had the ball.

"(Auburn) Quarterback Jeff Burger passed for 269 yards and 2 touchdowns."
—From wire service reports

Having disposed of the overmatched Longhorns, no. 3 Auburn traveled to Knoxville on September 26 to face no. 14 Tennessee in front of nearly 94,000 spectators. The previous trip to Neyland Stadium had proven to be a costly one, with Bo Jackson held in check and the UT offense rolling, and Auburn wanted revenge. Instead, the game ended in a result that left neither team particularly happy.

Win Lyle kicked two field goals of more than fifty yards in the first half, including one from fifty-five, giving Auburn a narrow, 6-0 lead at halftime. Tennessee back Reggie Cobb scored in the third quarter to put the Vols ahead, 7-6, and they later added a field goal to increase their advantage to 10-6. Auburn retaliated with two long touchdown drives to take a 20-10 lead with just over seven minutes to go in the game.

With ninety seconds left, Cobb found the end zone again and Majors elected to kick the extra point rather than going for two. It succeeded and the game ended, 20-20, but it was a controversial call.

Van Allen Plexico

This was back when Auburn played Tennessee every year, and it was a pretty big rivalry. It was basically what the LSU rivalry has become today. They used to say it was virtually impossible for the loser of this game to go on and win the SEC. That meant both Pat Dye and Johnny Majors were deeply concerned every year about *not losing* it. Somehow that resulted in way more ties than you might expect in an intense series like this.

In this game, I think Majors felt it was smarter to play things safe, and not risk a loss by going for two at the end. He probably thought Tennessee could win the SEC with a tie but not with a loss in this game. Unfortunately for the Vols, that decision came back to haunt him, because the tie helped Auburn as well. Tennessee ended up losing to Alabama, and the Tigers would go on to win the conference.

After wins at North Carolina (20-10) and at home against Vanderbilt (48-15), the Tigers were ranked fifth, and traveled to Atlanta for the last game in what had always been an annual series against Georgia Tech that had begun in 1892.

The last couple of minutes of this one turned out to be far more memorable and exciting than anyone could've dreamed.

The final score was 20-10, but few games in history featured a final score that was more deceptive of how things actually played out.

John Ringer

The game was played at Georgia Tech in Atlanta in October, and Auburn was ranked fifth. Georgia Tech was 2-3 and they weren't ranked at all, and we were expected to kill them. But Tech played a really good game. I was sitting in the Georgia Tech student section with some of our other Auburn friends and a lot of my Georgia Tech friends. We were wearing the Tiger Rag shirts for that game: "Catch a Buzz in Hotlanta."

The Tech defense limited Auburn to only 54 yards rushing for the entire game. On the final drive, Auburn abandoned the run entirely and went strictly to the passing game. Jeff Burger, on that drive alone, completed 11 of 17 passes for 91 yards, including the game-winning touchdown. On the day, he passed for 265 yards on 30-of-46 passing; quite the unusual stat line during the Pat Dye era.

Aundray Bruce had three interceptions and three sacks, forced a fumble and recovered another one. Auburn's first touchdown came on a fumble recovery by Kurt Crain in the Tech end zone, after Bruce crushed the Tech quarterback and forced him to drop the ball.

The Tech defensive backs taunted Auburn's receivers the entire game.

"We had them intimidated big-time. I was taunting them a little, and maybe I shouldn't have. But everybody taunts us. Once I hit Weygand and he stayed down. I told him, 'You're out of here, buddy,' and pointed at him. I came over to the sideline, picked up the phone and told our coaches upstairs, "Weygand's out."
—Sammy Lilly, Georgia Tech defensive back

John Ringer
Georgia Tech played a great game. They led 10-7 with very little time left. Auburn got the ball back at the nine yard line and had one last chance to win. They marched to the Tech four yard line and, with twenty-four seconds left, Jeff Burger passed up a potentially more open receiver at the goal line and fired a pass to Lawyer Tillman, who was double covered in the end zone but who was able to outleap both of the defenders to grab the ball for the score.

"Here's motion by Donaldson to the near side and now reverses his field goes back to the wide side of the field. Burger sets up to throw—OH MY! TOUCHDOWN AUBURN! TOUCHDOWN AUBURN! TOUCHDOWN AUBURN! TILLMAN TILLMAN TILLMAN! At the baseline of the end zone! A bullet by Burger! Auburn goes ahead! Unbelievable! Unbelievable! Tillman from Burger. Touchdown Auburn! Tigers lead, 13-10, with thirteen seconds to go!"
—Jim Fyffe, radio broadcast of the Georgia Tech game, 1987

Sammy Lilly sat alone in the end zone after Tillman made his game-winning touchdown catch. Tillman had made the catch by outleaping Lilly for the ball.

"I don't know how he caught it. I can't see how he did it."
—Sammy Lilly, Georgia Tech defensive back, on Tillman's touchdown catch

Tillman took the ball over to Lilly after the play.

"Their defensive backs had been calling us all kinds of names. So I just took the ball over to him and said, 'Here's what you've been asking for all day.'"
—Lawyer Tillman, Auburn wide receiver

So now Auburn led for the first time, the extra point pushing it out to 14-10, with mere seconds remaining. But the strangest part was still to come.

John Ringer
This was a one-man kind of wrecking crew game for future no. 1 NFL draft pick Andrey Bruce. He had an absolutely dominating game with multiple sacks and turnovers.

At the very end of the game, after Lawyer Tillman's score, Georgia Tech needed a touchdown. Their quarterback threw a desperation pass. Bruce intercepted it and returned it for a touchdown. Auburn won, 20-10, in a game they trailed 10-7 just a few seconds earlier. The Tech fans were all in shock. But it was a lot of fun for us.

235

You have never seen a fanbase that looked like they'd had the rug yanked out from under them like this. We were no. 5 in the country and they were unranked. They were beating us the whole game. Our offense hadn't scored on them for almost the entire game. They could taste it. They wanted to beat us so badly. And at the last minute we won that game and their entire fanbase was just devastated, that whole night. They could not handle it. And they didn't win another game the rest of the year.

This was also the game where all the Atlanta Falcons scouts must have been in attendance, because it was played in Atlanta, and it caused the Falcons to pick Bruce with the no. 1 pick in the NFL Draft the next year.

We're Auburn fans and even *we* didn't think that was a good pick.

The following Saturday, Auburn delivered a beat-down to Mississippi State, 38-7. Backup quarterback Reggie Slack received extensive playing time. Once the maroon Bulldogs had been disposed of, it was time to welcome in the team that had beaten the Tigers—and beaten them in absolutely excruciating fashion—the past three seasons in a row.

John Ringer
Florida. Halloween night on ESPN. The t-shirts said, "A Nightmare in Jordan-Hare."

Van Allen Plexico
We were ravenous for a win over Florida. Just rabid. I wanted to see Kerwin Bell crumpled into a ball and tossed in the trash. I wanted to see Emmitt Smith totally shut down. I wanted to *beat* them, finally!

ESPN billed the game as "the irresistible force meets the immovable object." The irresistible force was Florida's freshman running back, Emmitt Smith, who had been tearing up defenses across the league. And the immovable object was Aundray Bruce, believe it or not.

John Ringer
The whole Auburn defense was an immovable object.

Van Allen Plexico
As it turned out, yes.
Stop me if you've heard this one before, but there was a big controversy on campus in the week before the game, and it looked like our quarterback might not get to play.

The week before the Florida game, starting quarterback Jeff Burger was accused of accepting improper benefits and was ruled ineligible. He had gone on a hunting trip with offensive lineman Jim Thompson, and a friend of the Thompson family had flown the two players to the hunting reserve in his private plane.

Prior to the season, two other incidents involving Burger had come very close to derailing his senior season. He was involved in a scuffle outside an Auburn restaurant late at night and was arrested, and quarterbacks coach Pat Sullivan had paid the $700 to bail him out—which to the NCAA constituted another improper benefit. In addition to that, he was also accused of plagiarizing a paper in a psychology class.

"'I made a mistake with the quotation marks and I didn't write a good paper,' Burger said. 'That's my fault, but I was never dishonest.'

"The academic committee upheld the plagiarism charge, but reduced the suspension to two quarters. Auburn vice president Warren Brandt agreed with the committee's decision of guilt, but removed the suspension and lessened the punishment. Burger received an 'F' in the course and was required to take an English composition course along with the psychology class. His transcript also was marked 'Academic Dishonesty', which will be removed if he passes the psychology class.

"Burger said he feared the worst. 'They were talking about taking away something that is my life,' he said. 'Football and school both mean a lot to me.'

"Although he is eligible to lead Auburn's offense, and the team is expected to be among the country's best, Burger's slate has not

237

been wiped clean. He declined to appeal to Auburn President James Martin, who could have removed the 'Academic Dishonesty' remark from the quarterback's transcript—or increased the penalty. Burger, unwilling to gamble with the partial decision in his favor, said he is content to postpone the matter of clearing his name until after football season.

"'I don't think I'm compromising by not doing that right now,' he said. 'It will be cleared off the record in the winter quarter when I retake the class. I don't even think of it as clearing my name, because everybody knows I wasn't being dishonest. I'll just be clearing my record.'"

—Keith Dunnavant, Dallas Times Herald, 1987

The Auburn campus was divided between those who felt Burger's alleged plagiarism infraction was not serious enough to warrant severe punishment, and those who felt football players shouldn't be getting any special favors or having anyone look the other way on their behalf.

"Burger was so besieged by the press and fans during all this that he chose to live for a time at a hunting camp ten miles outside town. But his troubles may have served to bring the Tigers closer together. 'I found a lot of people standing behind me and beside me,' says Burger. 'The pressure's off now because I'm back where I belong.'"

—Hank Hersch, Sports Illustrated, October 5, 1987

It's worth noting that even a one-semester suspension would have effectively ended Burger's football career, because he was a senior. Brandt may have taken that fact into account when reducing the punishment.

With regard to the fistfight, eventually the NCAA decided that Sullivan paying Burger's bail represented something any professor might do for a favored student, and that incident went away.

As punishment for the hunting trip, Coach Dye announced that Burger would not start the Florida game. He then proceeded to hold Burger out for precisely one play. Reggie Slack took the first snap, bobbled it, fell on it—and that was it for him. Out he went and, as the crowd roared, in came Burger for the second play. So, technically, Dye did what he said he would: he didn't allow Burger to start the game. But by putting him in on the very next play, it came across to some as almost a nose-thumbing to the NCAA and the rule book. As with allowing Brent Fullwood to play in the previous season's bowl game after he had stopped attending classes, Dye appeared to be asserting that football came first, and that nothing was going to stop him from playing his best players. Many of the fans loved him for that attitude. Many others criticized him heavily.

Van Allen Plexico

As it happened, I had taken a class with the professor who chaired the academic honesty committee the previous spring—the one who came down so hard on Burger—and he had been one of my favorite teachers I ever had. I understood that plagiarism was a super-serious infraction and that Burger, if guilty, deserved punishment. But I also felt that taking away his entire senior season over it seemed a bit excessive. I also have to be honest and admit that, as a young guy at the time and as a huge football fan, I desperately wanted to see Auburn do big things in 1987, and we all knew Burger would be the key to that happening. So, like many students at the time, my sympathies were divided pretty evenly as well. Today, of course, as a college professor myself, I would not be so forgiving of academic infraction in the name of sports. But the question does remain: What is the appropriate punishment for that alleged crime? In this case, it was never really resolved, because the whole thing became so politicized, with major players like the vice-president and the head football coach and the head of the academic honesty committee all going to war over it. It was just an unfortunate situation and the outcome left too many issues unresolved.

I do recall that the professor was so disappointed with the way things played out, he left Auburn for a job at another university.

The situation with the hunting trip before the Florida game wasn't nearly as gray to me. I understood that football players were not supposed to receive special benefits not available to other students, but Burger going on that trip had nothing to do with him being a football player. Any student could've gotten invited to go hunting and could've been carried on that plane. Thompson just happened to invite the quarterback of the football team. He could just as well have invited *me*.

All the controversies faded away, at least down on the field, after Burger came in on the second play. Auburn went out and manhandled the Gators, winning a game that was never close and in which freshman star running back Emmitt Smith accomplished very little, failing to rush for a hundred yards, after lighting up other SEC defenses in previous weeks.

"Jeff Burger, who regained his eligibility last Thursday, passed for 218 yards and a touchdown to lead Auburn to a 29-6 rout of Florida in a Southeastern Conference game tonight.

"Burger had taken a free plane ride on a dove hunt in Alabama Oct. 11 in violation of the extra-benefits rule. The NCAA declared him ineligible last Wednesday, but he won an appeal. He did not start tonight because he did not cooperate with school officials investigating the matter. But when his replacement, Reggie Slack, fumbled early, Burger was rushed into the game.

"Burger, who completed 18 of 29 passes, provided a 15-3 lead 23 seconds into the second half when he hit Lawyer Tillman on a 21-yard touchdown.

"Auburn limited the nation's leading rusher, Emmitt Smith, to half his average, 72 yards on 21 carries. It ended the freshman's string of six 100-yard performances."
—AP report

Van Allen Plexico

This was not a very creative Florida team on offense. They mostly hammered Emmitt Smith at us and we stopped him. We also shut down ol' Kerwin Bell, which was immensely satisfying. I know I screamed myself hoarse every time they snapped the ball. This was as loud of a game as I ever attended at Auburn.

The final score was Auburn 29, Florida 6. And it felt like an even bigger beat-down than that. I remember being so happy that we had crushed them after three straight years of frustration.

The attendance was 85,187–the largest crowd to ever see a football game in the state of Alabama to that point. The record wouldn't be broken until the Georgia game a year later.

John Ringer

The crowd was as loud as it's ever been. A home game at night on TV against Florida, where we beat the crap out of them and their All-American running back and held him down. That really was one of the most fun games in Jordan-Hare I ever attended.

Van Allen Plexico

Yeah, it really was. And then the next week was the exact opposite.

On November 7, Florida State came to town, and they absolutely killed us. We self-destructed against a very tough opponent that didn't need our help beating us. It was our only loss all year.

"On a beautiful day, with Jordan-Hare Stadium crammed with 85,000 fans, the Tigers immediately self-destructed. Jeff Burger, who has been unflappable through three declared ineligibilities this season, may have wished at least one of those NCAA sanctions had stuck. His pass on the first play of the game was fumbled by Duke Donaldson, right into the hands of Florida State's Terry Warren. The Seminoles scored directly.

"Auburn trailed, 17-0, after little more than the first quarter, when Reggie Ware fumbled into Warren's hands and led to a Derek Schmidt field goal. Donaldson would later fumble a punt return and Burger would throw three interceptions, one converted into a 20-3 score, McManus hitting Herb Gainer for one of his two touchdown catches two plays later.

"Schmidt became college football's all-time leading scorer when he booted the extra point that put the Seminoles ahead, 27-3."

—Richard Hoffer, LA Times

Florida State went on to win, 34-6, in a game that could have been even worse for Auburn. It was in some ways the polar opposite of the two teams' previous meeting, in which the Tigers had romped to a big win in the fourth quarter.

Van Allen Plexico

This is the game where we found out that Aundray Bruce didn't know Florida State was not in the SEC. After the game he expressed his concern that we'd just lost our chance to win the conference. A reporter had to explain to him that it didn't affect the standings because the Seminoles were not in the SEC, and Bruce replied, "They're not? Why not?"

It's not surprising we came out so flat in this game. I'm sure the players were coming down from an emotional high after that huge win against Florida. This was when Pat Dye first started referring to our last four games as "Amen Corner," the football equivalent of the last four holes at Augusta. It was just tough for them to get up to play Florida, then usually a very good non-conference opponent, and then Georgia and Alabama, all back-to-back. That's an insane stretch of football every year. Especially when the non-conference opponent in the middle of that is a team like Florida State.

The game was televised on CBS, so of course we were going to lose it. That's the way it was going back then. We played so well at night, but during those afternoon games in daylight, we seemed to be a different team. We struggled just like we had against Georgia Tech.

On the very first play, Burger took the snap and threw the ball out to the receiver on a quick screen. Duke Donaldson caught it and went about ten yards and it looked like he was going to make a first down, and then he fumbled it and Florida State got it and a couple of plays later they cashed it in, and immediately we were in the hole. Momentum swung to the Seminoles from that point onward, and we could never do anything.

The other important incident in this game happened on the very last play. We were down 34-6, and Pat Dye didn't want Florida State to score again, so we put the first team defense back out for the final series. As the last play was happening, I

242

was dejectedly filing out of the stadium, not really paying any attention anymore, and I heard what remained of the crowd gasp. I looked back and saw the stretcher cart being rolled out there. Someone was lying on the field, unable to walk. At first, we couldn't tell who it was. Then we saw. It was Tracy Rocker. Our great, All-American defensive lineman. He had torn up his knee. It was just a sick feeling to see it.

John Ringer

Yeah, that was an all-time not good coaching decision right there. No, your All-American, the guy that would go on to win the Outland and Lombardi awards the next season as the best defensive lineman in the country—you had him in on the last play of the game, in a game that you were losing 34-6.

Van Allen Plexico

At least he came back and had a stellar season the next year, won those awards and made it to the NFL. Later on, of course, he served as our defensive line coach during the 2010 National Championship season.

The next week we went over to Athens to try to improve our fortunes against the Bulldogs. We had won the last two games in a row in their stadium and felt pretty good about our chances. We went on to win that day, too, 27-11.

The score was close for most of the first two quarters, with Auburn's Win Lyle kicking a 34-yard field goal with three seconds remaining in the half, to send the Tigers into halftime with a 10-3 lead. Georgia, though, was still in it.

The game turned on a few plays in the third quarter. James Jackson fumbled at the UGA 37 and the ball was recovered by Auburn's Carlo Cheattom, leading to another Lyle field goal. Then Nate Hill intercepted Jackson to set up Alexander Wright's 28-yard reverse for a touchdown, on a play where Wright bobbled the ball and nearly fumbled it away before scoring.

"The ball takes some funny bounces in this game. Last week, we didn't get any of the breaks and tonight it seemed the ball bounced our way a number of times."
—*Pat Dye*

"I really thought we wanted to win this game. We were very excited; we just didn't play very well. We weren't very consistent."
—*Vince Dooley, Georgia head coach*

The loss eliminated Georgia from the conference title chase. It also evened the series in the Deep South's Oldest Rivalry, at 42-42-7.

Van Allen Plexico

I remember this game being one where everything was going our way, to the point that our speedy young receiver, Alexander Wright, was running a reverse, and he bobbled the ball in midair, turned around, caught it, and scored a touchdown. My roommates and I were laughing that when you can fumble a reverse, catch your own fumble in midair, and score a touchdown, you know things are going your way.

John Ringer

I went to this game. This was the game where the Georgia fans wanted revenge for the hosing they got in Jordan-Hare the year before. They all showed up with water pistols and stuff, and a bunch of our fans wore ponchos. The Georgia fans were grousing about the hoses and they were trying to spray us with their water guns. It was crazy.

Lawyer Tillman had a big catch in this game to put it away, and I got a big piece of the hedge.

Van Allen Plexico

Didn't you ring a bell or something, too?

John Ringer

I did! There's a victory bell on Georgia's campus. They ring it after big games, big wins, yeah. We were walking back across the campus that night and I asked my Georgia friends what it was and they said, "That's the victory bell—students and fans ring it after games." So I sprinted across the lawn. I grabbed the rope and rang that sucker.

The Georgia fans were so mad, but it was a great victory. Why shouldn't we celebrate?

Van Allen Plexico

I love it.

The Alabama game that year was the first one I ever attended in person, and the last one where the crowd was allegedly split, 50-50.

Alabama came into this game with a 7-3 record and ranked 18th. Somehow they had managed to lose to Memphis State in Liberty Bowl Stadium in Memphis, as well as to Florida and Notre Dame. The real mystery is what Alabama was doing playing Memphis State *at Memphis* to begin with.

Our defense was suffocating and Alabama could never get anything going on offense. Jeff Burger hit Lawyer Tillman with a long bomb down the right sideline to set up the one touchdown of the game. Overall, we did just enough to win. That's the kind of offensive performance from a Pat Dye team in the Eighties that would sometimes come back to bite us, as with Florida the year before and LSU the following year—we would get a couple of early scores and try to play defense and shut out the other team the rest of the way. But we managed to hold on, this time, and it was such a great feeling to shut them out.

"The Auburn Tigers have shut out the Alabama Crimson Tide by the score of ten to nothing, here at Legion Field in Birmingham. The clock running down, seven, six, five, four, three, two, one, it is over, ladies and gentlemen, hail to the champions of the Southeastern Conference! The Auburn Tigers have defeated the Alabama Crimson Tide ten to nothing here at Legion Field! War Eagle!"
—Jim Fyffe, Auburn Network commentary

"I'm so happy for you to win (the SEC) outright. We've only got one champion in the conference. You are the champions of the best football conference in America."
—Pat Dye, locker room after 1987 Iron Bowl

Van Allen Plexico
I was actually standing in J&M Bookstore a day or two later, when the owner was discussing with his employees what should go on their Iron Bowl bumper stickers, and they settled on, "Shut down, shut out, shut up!"

Auburn had finished the 1987 season with just one loss—to FSU, which was out of conference, despite what Aundray Bruce might have thought—and one tie, and so they won the conference outright. It would be the first of three straight SEC titles for Auburn. In the locker room after the Iron Bowl, Coach Dye accepted the invitation to play in the Sugar Bowl for the second time in five years.

The opponent would be undefeated and fourth-ranked Syracuse, a team with very heavy designs on claiming the national championship.

John Ringer
We played Syracuse in the Sugar Bowl.

Their quarterback was Don MacPherson and their coach was Dick MacPherson. No relation. I remember they were good. They had some good players. The quarterback was very good, and they had good defensive players.

"There may be some doubters out there that think we're not a good enough team to be national champion. We want to go out there and beat Auburn bad just to show people we are deserving of the national championship."
—Syracuse punter Cooper Gardiner

"We'll have one advantage (playing in the Superdome). Auburn has been throwing the ball on a field with a crowned surface. But indoor football is played on a flat field—and that's what we have at

home in the Carrier Dome. It can make a difference—if we throw it straight."
—Dick MacPherson, Syracuse head coach

With the score tied 13-13 with 2:05 to go in the game, Syracuse faced a fourth down and short yardage at the Auburn 22 yard line. MacPherson opted to kick the field goal rather than going for the first down. He later explained:

"I told my guys a field goal was like a touchdown. I told them if we made it, Auburn would have to go for the touchdown (to win). If I had thought in my wildest imagination he'd go for a field goal, we would have gone for a first down."
—Dick MacPherson, Syracuse head coach

Auburn came back down the field. On that final drive, Jeff Burger completed 11 of 12 passes, in a performance reminiscent of what he'd done at the end of the Georgia Tech game. He converted one fourth down at the Syracuse 30, connecting with Stacey Danley for 8 yards.

A few plays later, the Tigers found themselves looking at another fourth down. This time, though, it was fourth and goal at the Orangemen's 13, with only four seconds left in the game. The down no longer mattered; it was fourth and goal to go, with time enough remaining for just one more play. The two possibilities appeared to be either score a touchdown and win or fail to score a touchdown and lose. As it turned out, a third option was on the table.

Pat Dye had a decision to make.

"I was hollering for us to throw the ball and win the game. We were busting our butts the whole game. We wanted to go for the win."
—Stacy Searels, Auburn offensive lineman

John Ringer

The game was close all along. We faced fourth down at their end of the field in the last few seconds of the game, and we could've tried for a touchdown that would have won it, but

Pat Dye chose to kick a field goal and tie the game rather than throwing the ball into the end zone. He felt that the Syracuse defensive players were holding Lawyer Tillman and that the pass had little chance of working, and he later said he didn't want all the effort the players had put in to go for nothing. So we kicked the field goal and the game ended 16-16.

The Syracuse coaches and fans were really mad about it.

"You win some, lose some and some end in ties. I made up my mind early on (during the final drive) what I was going to do. I wasn't going to let my team get beat. If they (Syracuse) wanted to win, they should have blocked the field goal."
—Pat Dye

Van Allen Plexico

I've never known who ended up with the trophy that year— them, or us, or neither. But apparently Dick MacPherson was carrying it around with him while doing interviews after the game. I don't know if they let him take it home or took it away from him later.

Jeremy Henderson

If you look closely at the trophy, you'll notice that, no, Auburn didn't TIE Syracuse in the 1988 Sugar Bowl—we CO-WON.

We're assuming the Orangemen have their own version— all that angst, all those ties in the mail-all for (Windsor) naught—up in Syrexcuse.

"I was very proud of our football team and the courage and the character they displayed. And I didn't want to take a chance on them losing that at the end of the game.

"Syracuse is a great football team. This is not the way we wanted it to end and it's not the way Coach McPherson wanted it to end. But it came down to four seconds and we've got one play to not get beat, that's what we did."
—Coach Pat Dye

The Tigers came into the game ranked sixth and didn't have anything on the line in the game beyond the Sugar Bowl trophy. Syracuse, on the other hand, was ranked fourth and hadn't lost, so they thought they had a shot at the national championship if they won against Auburn and other things broke their way. Unfortunately for them, nothing broke their way.

Undefeated Miami played undefeated Oklahoma in the Orange Bowl and Miami won. They claimed the national title. One-loss FSU beat Nebraska and moved up to second. Oklahoma, losing to Miami, fell one spot to third. Poor Syracuse, still undefeated but with their Sugar Bowl tie, remained fourth.

Van Allen Plexico

Their game with us accomplished absolutely nothing for them. They didn't get the Sugar Bowl win, they didn't get the national championship, they didn't end the season without a blemish on their record, and they didn't even move up a single spot in the polls. No wonder they were so bitter afterward.

Dick McPherson, their coach, came out to shake hands with Coach Dye after the game, but instead he slapped at Dye's hand and ran off the field. Dye's reaction as he stood there on the turf morphed quickly from surprise to laughter as he watched the other coach run away.

Syracuse later vented their frustration by collecting tons of ugly ties and shipping them to Auburn. Pat Dye autographed them and sold them to raise money for charity and scholarships. Then we sent a bunch of sour grapes to Syracuse. We could've also sent them some cheese to go with their whine.

I've never known exactly how to feel about this game. On the one hand, I totally agree with Coach Dye that we were not going to get the calls at the end; that the likelihood of scoring a touchdown was extremely low; that if you're in a position to score an almost sure-thing field goal and to avoid a loss, you might as well take it. On the other hand, though, this was a bowl game, not the Tennessee game in September where a tie actually can (and did!) help you win the conference and get to the Sugar Bowl in the first place. It's not the FSU game, a couple of years later, where tying the score puts more pressure on the other team to take more risky chances when they get the ball back—because this was the final play. Beyond even strategies like that, it was essentially a meaningless exhibition game. If you're going to bother to show up and give effort for four quarters, why not try to win at the end? What did a tie really accomplish for us? If we'd lost, this team would've ended up with two losses, the same as the team the year before, and the same as the next two teams after it—all remembered as very good or great Auburn teams. Instead, we ended up with two ties, which is very strange.

John Ringer
The other great thing about this year is Alabama finished 7-5. They had lost to Memphis State, but came back to beat no. 8 Tennessee and no. 5 LSU, and things looked to be going well for them, at 7-2. But then they dropped their final three games, losing to Notre Dame, Auburn and Michigan in the Hall of Fame Bowl. Not a good first year for Bill Curry!

Auburn ended the 1987 season ranked seventh in the country, with a record of 9-1-2. They had as many wins as the 1984 team but three fewer losses. It was indeed strange.

The Sugar Bowl had been Jeff Burger's final game in an Auburn uniform, but Reggie Slack was waiting in the wings to take over at quarterback. Most everyone else was returning for 1988, including those great players on defense. The future looked very bright.

1988

John Ringer
I love the 1988 team. I was a sophomore and I went to every game that I could. That was a great team. I love defense and this was, in my opinion, the best Auburn defense we've ever had. They were amazing. They were dominating. They shut other teams down. They didn't allow an inch if they could, and really destroyed a lot of teams that year. And they

came so close to winning the national title at the end of the season, that it's just agonizing.

Van Allen Plexico

Here are the scores we allowed our opponents in 1988: 10, 7, 6, 21, 7, 0, 0, 0, 8, 10, 10, 13. That sounds more like the 1957 team than a team in the 1980s. They averaged allowing 7.7 points per game, which was first in the country. Tracy Rocker, Ron Stallworth, Benji Roland, Quentin Riggins, Craig Ogletree, Carlo Cheattom, Greg Staples, Shan Morris... so many great players on that defense.

The game where we allowed 21 points was against North Carolina, when we played the backups in the second half. Interesting note: That team was coached by Mack Brown, in his first season at UNC. They only managed to win one game all season, but they did score some points on people.

Of course, we lost two of those games. We lost games where we gave up seven and thirteen points. The problem on that team was not the defense. And the offense wasn't bad. The passing game was better than it had been in ages and the running game was decent. But it lacked a consistent big play threat in the mold of a Bo Jackson or Brent Fullwood. We'd gotten spoiled the previous few years. The 1988 team had a stable of decent running backs including Stacey Danley and James Joseph, but no true homerun hitter.

We steamrolled Tennessee at home early in the year, 38-6, and that was one of those games I thoroughly enjoyed. Shan Morris had a huge hit on the Tennessee running back— probably Reggie Cobb—way behind the line of scrimmage and put him down. Alexander Wright caught a pass from Reggie Slack on a crossing route, turned up field and lit the afterburners, and raced 75 yards for the score.

Our main problem in 1988 was that, against the better teams, our offense either wasn't quite enough, or wasn't allowed to be. We just weren't very free-wheeling and open on offense. Coach Dye knew he had a great defense and so he played a very conservative strategy on offense all season. For most of the year, it worked. But in one key game, it blew up in

251

our faces at the end, and cost us a chance at the national championship.

It was the night of October 8. Auburn was undefeated and ranked fourth in the country. LSU, coached by Mike Archer, was unranked after back-to-back road losses to Ohio State and Florida. But Tiger Stadium in Baton Rouge has a reputation—or, at least, LSU fans like to promote the idea that it does—for being an incredibly difficult place for road teams to play and to win. Especially at night.

"Stadiums don't win ball games. Stadiums don't block or tackle; teams do all of that. So what's the big deal?"
—Pat Dye, before the LSU game in Baton Rouge

"LSU and its highly rated quarterback, Tom Hodson, have fallen short of expectations. Hodson was benched during the Florida upset, and he is not among the nation's top 40 quarterbacks in passing efficiency. He was expected to be among the top two or three for the season."
—Gordon S. White, Jr., New York Times

For most of the game, neither team could do a lot on offense. Auburn managed a Win Lyle field goal just before halftime and another early in the fourth quarter, and was clinging to a 6-0 lead with less than two minutes remaining in the game. The Bengal Tigers had one last chance to make something happen. Their offense, which had done absolutely nothing for 58 minutes, finally woke up. LSU began to march down the field, barely keeping the drive alive on multiple occasions, only to face fourth and ten in the Auburn red zone. As time ticked away, LSU's quarterback dropped back, threw the ball… and the ground shook.

"Tommy Hodson capped a 75-yard drive with a fourth-down, 11-yard touchdown pass to tailback Eddie Fuller with 1 minute 41 seconds to play tonight, and David Browndyke kicked the extra point that gave Louisiana State a stunning 7-6 victory over Auburn.

"Until the late 15-play drive, on which Hodson completed 6 of 14 passes for 74 yards, L.S.U. had crossed midfield only once against an Auburn defense ranked third nationally."
—From AP Wire reports

John Ringer

Tommy Hodson, in the last two minutes of the game, hit Eddie Fuller in the end zone, and they beat us, 7-6.

The crowd was cheering and jumping around so loud that it registered on the seismograph in one of the campus labs, so it's called the Earthquake Game. It was a devastating loss.

And that was not a great LSU team. They ended up 8-4.

"It's as big a win as I've ever been around."
—Mike Archer, LSU head coach

"I'm mighty disappointed because we had a very effective offense and couldn't score any points. We kind of self-destructed."
—Pat Dye

Jeremy Henderson

The 1988 LSU game. I mean, we were doing so well. And we were obviously so good. And I'm sitting there with my dad and my uncle, and we've got a Pizza Hut pizza spread out on the footstool, Dad's college footstool. We're sitting there eating and watching the game, and we lose at the end. And I was just so devastated. I couldn't... I couldn't believe it, because we were so good. This was gonna be a great year. I'd been thinking, "This is it. This is the year. This is it."

And I straight up went upstairs and threw up. At eight years old. I was so upset.

Van Allen Plexico

Here's a little story—kind of funny, kind of horrible—about me and that LSU game. Many years later, in 2005, I was flying on American Airlines from Dallas to Tokyo, on my way to Singapore. And they offered passengers, at that time, several viewing options on the little screen on the back of the seat in front of you. You could watch a movie, you could watch a sporting event, or you could watch the radar of the plane on a map of the globe. Just a handful of options. One of the options they offered was a college football game. So I clicked on that, and lo and behold, it was the 1988 Auburn-LSU game. And I was thinking, "Why in the world did they choose *that* game to offer to us to watch on this flight?" It seemed like a strange choice, because it was *seventeen years* later. And it was honestly a boring game, unless you were an LSU fan—and even then, only exciting at the very end! What an odd choice to show on a flight. I suspected the pilot of that flight was an LSU fan. It was the only thing that made any sense.

I watched a little bit of the game, because it had been seventeen years since I'd seen it. And I was like, "Ugh—this is as horrible as I remember." So terribly depressing. I finally turned it off and read a book.

I stayed in Singapore for two or three months, and then it was time to head back to the States. So, months later, I'm flying back home on an American Airlines flight from Tokyo to Chicago—not to Dallas, so it wasn't even the return leg of the same flight. It was a completely different route, to a different city, months later. Again they offered a movie, a sporting event, or the radar view.

Guess what sporting event they were showing?

Yes. Auburn-LSU 1988. The Earthquake Game, from seventeen years earlier. *Again.*

I started to think I was trapped in some kind of nightmare loop like the Matrix or Inception or something.

All I can assume is that whoever runs American Airlines is either a huge LSU fan or just really, really hates Auburn.

Auburn finished the regular season 10-1 and shared the SEC title with LSU, who was 8-3 overall but, like Auburn, only had one loss in the conference (to Florida).

There was no tiebreaker in terms of head-to-head competition—Auburn and LSU shared the conference title. The Sugar Bowl was allowed to pick whatever team it wanted as the SEC's annual representative, and Auburn received the invitation because of their higher national ranking; LSU was 16th in the polls while Auburn was 7th.

Over the next three weeks following the LSU loss, Auburn shut out all three opponents, Akron, Miss State and Florida, defeating them by a combined score of 91-0. When Southern Miss QB Brett Favre threw a touchdown pass in the fourth quarter at Jordan-Hare on November 5, it represented the first points the Auburn defense had given up since the Earthquake Game; the first points in almost a month of play; the first after fifteen quarters of shutouts.

Before that game against USM, though, the Tigers traveled down to Gainesville to play Florida on their "Gator Growl" homecoming.

Van Allen Plexico

Despite beating the Gators in Jordan-Hare the previous year, we were still frustrated with that 18-17 game in the Swamp in 1986. We went back down there in 1988 on their homecoming and shut them out, 16-0. It was remarkably similar to that 1986 game, except without the annoying fourth quarter comeback. This time, we took the game and the shutout into the fourth quarter and kept it going.

The first quarter was scoreless. Midway through the second, Win Lyle came on and connected on a long field goal to put the Tigers ahead, 3-0. That score held up through halftime, and the Tigers still had not allowed an opponent to score a touchdown in the first half all season. Nevertheless, the lead was only three points, and it was starting to feel a bit like the LSU game all over again.

Early in the fourth quarter, Auburn drove deep into Florida territory but had to settle for another Lyle field goal. Now it was 6-0, and the Earthquake Game truly had to be on everyone's mind.

A touchdown finally was scored in the game, but it wasn't by Florida on some miraculous, last-second, fourth-down play. Instead, Auburn linebacker Quentin Riggins picked off a Florida pass at midfield and took it back deep into Florida territory. A facemask penalty, tacked on at the end, put Auburn in business at the Gator nine yard line. Two plays later, Auburn cashed the turnover in as Stacey Danley took the handoff from Reggie Slack, recovered from a stumble and burst into the end zone.

A late Auburn drive, featuring the runs of Stacey Danley and James Joseph, took the Tigers inside the Florida 5, and Lyle added one more field goal. The Tigers intercepted a last-ditch deep pass by Florida at the Auburn 5 to preserve the shutout, 16-0.

Over the space of eight quarters of football played between Auburn and Florida in Gainesville in 1986 and 1988, Florida had managed to score any points at all on the Tigers in only one quarter—the fourth frame of 1986. This time around, the Tigers blanked the Gators all the way to the end.

Following the aforementioned win over Southern Miss, ninth-ranked Auburn welcomed no. 17 Georgia to Jordan-Hare.

"Reggie Slack threw for two touchdowns on bootleg rollouts as Auburn knocked Georgia out of the Southeastern Conference race and kept its title hopes alive with a 20-10 victory today. Slack completed 20 of 34 passes for 263 yards, and Stacey Danley rushed for a career-high 172 yards, bettering his previous best of 157 against Alabama last year.

"The Tigers, 9-1 overall and 5-1 in the SEC, can gain a share of the conference championship with LSU by beating Alabama in Birmingham on Nov. 25.

"Auburn denied Vince Dooley's bid to become only the tenth coach in Division I-A history to reach the 200-victory plateau, using its best-in-the-nation defense to shut down Georgia (7-3, 5-2). Auburn had been allowing only 68 yards rushing a game and 210 total yards a game."

—From AP Wire reports

Georgia managed to tie the game at 10-10 in the third quarter, but then Reggie Slack connected with Walter Reeves to push the lead to 7. In the fourth quarter, Win Lyle tacked on a late field goal to seal the deal.

Tracy Rocker, by Jarrod Alberich

"Auburn is the truly great team in our league.

"I thought we fought hard, but what I saw confirmed this is the best Auburn team I've ever seen. They won the game soundly. They dominated. Our team played hard, but we were beaten by a better football team."
—Vince Dooley, Georgia head coach

"He's probably right."
—Pat Dye, on this being the best Auburn team

And then there was a fairly nondescript win over 17th ranked Alabama.

Alabama had a good team, with stars Derrick Thomas and Bobby Humphrey. But they just were not going to score many points against that Tiger defense. The question was, could Auburn score anything against theirs? Fifteen points turned out to be more than enough.

Tracy Rocker opened the game with a huge sack on Alabama quarterback David Smith. Ron Stallworth sacked him four more times. It was reminiscent of the 2005 "Honk if you sacked Brodie" game.

Lawyer Tillman emerged as one of the main weapons for Auburn on the day, with 104 yards in pass receptions. He caught a long pass from Reggie Slack deep in Alabama territory, but Stacey Danley fumbled it away on the next play. But then Ron Stallworth sacked Smith in the Alabama end zone for a safety. Later Quentin Riggins made a touchdown-saving interception at the Auburn goal line, and Greg Staples grabbed another in the third quarter. There was that Auburn defense coming up big again, over and over.

Alabama would net a grand total of 12 rushing yards in this Iron Bowl. You read that correctly: they rushed for 12 yards on 27 attempts.

Van Allen Plexico

The only real controversy in this Iron Bowl came midway through the third quarter, and it was possibly the single worst call by a referee I have ever seen in all my years of watching football. Auburn had the ball on the Alabama 31 yard line.

Reggie Slack took the snap, dropped back, rolled to his right under pressure, and threw the ball while standing on the 39, 8 yards behind the line of scrimmage and at least three or four yards away from the near sideline. The pass was completed for a first down, but the referee blew the play dead and claimed Slack went out of bounds before he threw the ball. It wasn't even close, and Slack and the Auburn coaches went nuts, but the ref wouldn't listen. The astonishing thing is that none of the other officials corrected him. Looking at it now, in a time of instant replay, it is beyond unbelievable to see that call not overturned. On the next play, now needing many more yards to get the first down, Slack dropped back for a deep pass and was sacked, basically ending a drive that should've yielded points.

Eventually Auburn scored a touchdown to go with the safety and the two field goals. Alabama scored a late touchdown to make it closer than it really was. Final score: Auburn 15, Alabama 10.

"The matter is no longer in question. Auburn commands the state of Alabama in college football. The Tigers left that message in the Legion Field scoreboard lights here Friday."
—*Phillip Marshall, Montgomery Advertiser*

This game marked the ninth consecutive time Bill Curry lost to Pat Dye.

"Players have success, not coaches. I don't think he was the reason they lost tonight. Their kids played as well as they could play."
—*Pat Dye*

This season marked the first time Auburn had ever won back-to-back SEC championships.

"The (SEC) co-championship is important and big and we're proud of it. But winning this game (the Iron Bowl) is more important than Sugar Bowls or championships or whatever. It's the real deal."
—*Pat Dye*

Alabama was designated the home team in Legion Field for this game and the tickets were distributed like a normal game for the first time, rather than being split 50-50, as they had been for so many years, going back to the resumption of the series in 1948. Auburn got 10,900 of the tickets to the game.

Van Allen Plexico

People forget that was part of the agreement that got the next year's game down to Jordan-Hare Stadium: Alabama got to be the home team in 1988 and receive the vast majority of the tickets. The other part of the deal was that Auburn would have to go back to Birmingham again for our home game in 1991, which was even more ridiculous.

John Ringer

At the end of the year, we ended up playing a very tough, fourth-ranked Florida State in the Sugar Bowl in New Orleans. But if not for that one-point loss at LSU, we would've been playing undefeated Notre Dame for the national championship.

And we would have killed them.

Van Allen Plexico

Oh, man. I wanted to play them so bad. Instead, we end up playing a meaningless game against Florida State. That year was one of only two seasons between 1983 and 1990 that we didn't have them on the schedule already, and we ended up playing them in a bowl game.

Here's the unbelievable thing about how the regular season ended: Auburn was ranked 7th in the AP Poll. There were four teams with one loss ranked above us. *Four.* We were SEC champions, with the best defense in the country by most measurements, and our only loss was on the road, at LSU, at night, *by one point.*

If there had been a four-team playoff in 1988, Auburn would barely have been in the conversation. Notre Dame and West Virginia were undefeated and would've been in. Miami was ranked second, with a road loss by one point to top-ranked

260

Notre Dame. They would've been in. Auburn—the SEC champs, with just one loss by one point on the road—would have had to fight for that final playoff spot against FSU, USC and Nebraska, each of which also had only one loss and two of which were also conference champions. Again—one loss, by one point, on the road at LSU, and we were *seventh*.

We could've seen a scenario similar to 2004 play out back in 1988, where a more-than-deserving, SEC champion Auburn team is left out entirely, even with four teams going to a playoff. It's astonishing.

But this was still the old bowl system, so Auburn was the home team in the Sugar. If we'd been undefeated, Notre Dame would've come to us, because they didn't have a specific bowl commitment and would've gone wherever they could've played the highest-ranked opponent. As it was, with one loss, our opponent was then-independent Florida State.

John Ringer

My family and I went to the game in the Superdome. And we all know what Florida State fans can be like. I wasn't happy with them to begin with because I had sat through that 34-6 game the year before in Auburn. If you've never been in a stadium when FSU is playing that stupid war chant for hours and hours, you have no idea how annoying it can be. And let me just say that, in an indoor dome with that chant, it's ten times worse.

The game was low scoring and very tight. It saw FSU's Sammie Smith become the first opposing running back to gain over 100 yards on the Auburn defense since Bobby Humphrey in 1988—a span of twenty-four games.

FSU scored 10 points in the first quarter, capitalizing on Auburn mistakes, then added a field goal in the second to push the Seminoles out to a 13-0 lead.

"I've never been in a football game like this before. The things in the first quarter totally shocked me. Three seniors got personal fouls. That was totally uncharacteristic."
—*Pat Dye*

Reggie Slack hit Walter Reeves for a 20-yard touchdown to bring the Tigers back within a score at halftime.

In the second half, both teams would threaten but both would go scoreless.

Still trailing 13-7 in the fourth quarter, but driving for a potential game-winning touchdown, Slack completed three fourth-down, do-or-die passes to keep the chains moving. As the Tigers entered the FSU red zone, he then threw a pass over the middle toward Freddie Weygand that should've been an easy completion; one that would've set the Tigers up for the potential game-winner.

It didn't happen. Dedrick Dodge of FSU hit Weygand from behind and drove his helmet into the turf before the ball even got there.

John Ringer

It was the easiest pass interference call you could ever imagine. And the referee didn't call the penalty.

"(Second and ten,) Slack throwing—knocked down! Oh, that looks like interference initially. Oh, Weygand the intended receiver and Dodge covering. Looks like Dodge made contact before the ball got there. I think we're gonna have to look at this. You be the judge.

"That's Dedrick Dodge coming in from behind. That is interference.

"Did you see that on the board right here? Dedrick Dodge gets away with manslaughter. They'll be talking about this one in Alabama for a while."

—ABC announcers, 1988-89 Sugar Bowl

John Ringer

On the next play Deion Sanders intercepted the ball in the end zone to end the game. He then ran down the Auburn sideline individually taunting everyone on the team, including the coaches and Bo Jackson, who was on the sideline.

Auburn had held Florida State scoreless in the second half, but the missed call on the blatant pass interference in the FSU red zone meant Auburn wouldn't be scoring, either.

In three Sugar Bowl appearances under Pat Dye—1983, 1987 and 1988—Auburn had scored a total of two touchdowns. Both of them came on passes. It's hard to imagine Auburn never scored a single rushing touchdown in a Sugar Bowl under Pat Dye.

"I'm extremely proud of our kids for playing hard and not giving up. This game will make me and our staff better coaches. I know it will make me a better coach.

"Our defense was put in some tough situations. They were the best defense in the nation tonight, giving up only 13 points to an offensive team like Florida State."
—Pat Dye

Van Allen Plexico
This was Reggie Slack's last game. We haven't really talked about Slack, but he came in after Jeff Burger graduated and got to play two years. And Reggie Slack, I think, is one of our more underappreciated quarterbacks. I thought he was a great quarterback for us for those two huge years, 1987 and 1988.

John Ringer
He was steady. He was productive. And he was good in tight situations and important situations. He really played well.

As the 1988 season came to an end, Auburn had won the SEC in back-to-back years and played in two consecutive Sugar Bowls for the first time ever. And the 1986 team had come within a point in Gainesville of making it three straight. The program was at its all-time high in terms of sustained success over multiple years at the very highest level. With all the players who would be returning for 1989, it was hard to imagine the good times would be ending any time soon.

Van Allen Plexico

Auburn was doing so well back then, going to the Sugar Bowl so often, I didn't even make an effort to get tickets and go down to New Orleans in 1988. I just said to myself, "We'll be back again next year, so I'll wait and go then."

We didn't go back for sixteen years.

As the 1989 season approached, in addition to a loaded Auburn roster of returning veterans, it also promised one additional bonus: Alabama would be coming to play Auburn in Jordan-Hare for the *First Time Ever.*

Jerry Hinnen

Were Auburn fans spoiled by the success of those (late 1980s) years? It's certainly possible. I think that probably is something of an issue for Auburn fans in my particular generation, where we grew up in the Pat Dye years. And you know, I still remember being sort of vaguely disappointed on a couple of occasions. I was a big *Sports Illustrated* reader, and I very clearly remember the Tennessee quarterback appearing on the cover, under the headline, "The Tennessee Waltz," after the Vols had completely stomped Auburn that season (1985), with Auburn coming in as the no. 1 team in the country. Even though we came up (to national prominence) during those years, we still remember being disappointed.

I do think there's something to the idea that Auburn fans in my particular generation were raised on, "Okay, we're going to go to the Sugar Bowl every other year, pretty much whenever we feel like it," and now we know that wasn't always going to be reality. I think that probably has colored our perceptions somewhat, as opposed to the folks who came of age in the late Sixties and Seventies.

But for all the disappointments, you still had those huge triumphs every year. And obviously, in some ways, that entire era culminated with the 1989 Iron Bowl.

John Ringer

I think the most important thing from that era was that we won the SEC three years in a row, and beat Alabama four years in a row. But there's also this kind of bittersweet taste because I believe the 1988 team was the best team in the country, and they had one of those "night game in Baton Rouge" situations where LSU pulled a miracle out of their rear end at the end of the game and won, and denied us a shot at the national title.

People also forget, there were no divisions at the time. LSU was not an every-year opponent for us. We played Georgia and Florida and Alabama every year. We did not play LSU every year. They had rotated onto our schedule instead of Vanderbilt or Ole Miss. We could have been playing Ole Miss, but instead we played them. And they were really good. They pulled out a miracle at the end and beat us, and that was tough. That was a tough loss. And then the Florida State loss in the Sugar Bowl was a tough loss. I really feel like in both those games we had really good chances to win and we didn't.

I still love that team though. I mean, they were tough. They had a great defense and they were really fun to watch.

"There has been considerable drama here in Legion Field today.

"With this win today, Pat Dye has moved ahead of Georgia coach Vince Dooley and into eighth place on the scroll of the nation's winningest active coaches in terms of winning percentage.

"After one year at Wyoming he was offered the head job at Auburn. He called Bear Bryant, his former boss at Alabama, and said, 'Should I take the Auburn job?' And Bear said, 'No, I wouldn't do that if I were you. Because if you take it, I'm gonna whip you.' And Pat said, 'Well, Bear, that may be true, but whoever follows you, I'm going to whip them like a stepson.' And he took the job.

"But he does have a 4-3 edge and he's made major progress. They've made the stadium larger. They're trying to move the game to a home-and-away series and will have Alabama play them in Auburn.

"The program has not only arrived but it continues to get better. And he has given Auburn supporters a kind of pride that they did not enjoy during all of the years that Bryant and Alabama were able to dominate them and the great Shug Jordan in the Sixties and Seventies."
—*CBS broadcast, 1987 Iron Bowl*

Van Allen Plexico

I look back at those great seasons we just covered, and for me, that's just the heart of the experience of being an Auburn person, of being part of the Auburn Family. From Bo Jackson winning the Heisman Trophy, through back-to-back Sugar Bowls, and having an unbelievable defense and dominating Alabama.

That stretch of seasons took us both from high school through most of our undergraduate years. It was such a great time to be associated with Auburn. It was really the first time that Auburn people could stand up in the state and say, "We're every bit as good—or—better at football than Alabama." There was no more looking at this behemoth lording it over us from the other side of the state. Bear Bryant was gone, Alabama was somewhat flailing around, looking for a coach who could do even some of what he had done, and meanwhile we had Pat Dye in his prime.

Alabama fans hated Pat Dye. But they hated him because they feared him and they respected him. They wished he was *their* coach instead of ours. That's the best kind of hate.

Auburn fans were walking around a little taller, holding our heads up a little straighter, looking those Alabama fans in the eye and giving it back to them, measure for measure. Before that, we couldn't really deny that the Bear was kicking our tails. Now the *new* "Auburn mindset" was that we were just as good as anybody on the football field, and better than most. We felt like Pat Dye would inevitably win us a national championship, and sooner rather than later. I was sure it was going to happen. I had no doubt. I also kept in mind Coach Dye saying that if we won one outright, he would go back and claim the 1983 title as well. That sounded great to me.

That made this era, psychologically, a very important period for Auburn fans, because I would argue it laid the foundation not just for us having a great program, but also for us having the confidence to *believe* our program is as good as any in the country. It's why it just seems so ridiculous to us nowadays when Alabama fans act like we're somehow second- or third-class football citizens. We *know,* after the Eighties, we're on the same plane as anybody else. Auburn is on that heavyweight contender level with the very best.

Those Dye seasons in the Eighties were the years that sealed that deal. Our wins during this period weren't flukes. There was no luck involved. There was no "Kick Six," no "Miracle in Jordan-Hare," no "Punt, Bama, Punt." These were the years we beat the snot out of Alabama and Georgia and Florida and everybody else by just being so good on defense and with that hard-nosed running game and just being tough in general. That's why people still love and respect Pat Dye. It wasn't razzle-dazzle and trickery or anything like that. Don't get me wrong, that kind of thing has its place. But this was just going out there, man-to-man, and punching each other in the nose and seeing who gets up. And more often than not, it was *us* getting up.

John Ringer
That's a good way of putting it.

And the very next season, as if their degradation were not manifest enough in the wake of three straight Iron Bowl losses, the Alabama team and the Tide fans would have to make a journey that the Bear and Ray Perkins had both assured them they would never, ever have to make. They would have to pack their bags and leave Tuscaloosa and Birmingham and travel in a southeastern direction, toward Lee County, in order to play a football game in the Loveliest Village on the Plains.

"It won't happen," Perkins famously said.

It happened.

1984:

9-4 overall; 4-2 SEC

8/28	Miami*	L	18-20
9/15	at Texas	L	27-35
9/22	Southern Miss	W	35-12
9/29	Tennessee	W	29-10
10/6	at Ole Miss	W	17-13
10/13	at Florida State	W	42-41
10/20	Georgia Tech	W	48-34
10/27	at Miss State	W	24-21
11/3	at Florida	L	3-24
11/10	Cincinnati	W	60-0
11/17	Georgia	W	21-12
12/1	at Alabama (Bham)	L	15-17
12/27	Arkansas**	W	21-15

*Kickoff Classic, E Rutherford, NJ
**Liberty Bowl, Memphis, TN
(Final AP Ranking: 14)

1985:

8-4 overall; 3-3 SEC

9/7	SW Louisiana	W	49-7
9/14	Southern Miss	W	29-18
9/28	at Tennessee	L	20-38
10/5	Ole Miss	W	41-0
10/12	Florida State	W	59-27
10/19	at Georgia Tech	W	17-14
10/26	Miss State	W	21-9
11/2	Florida	L	10-14
11/9	East Carolina	W	35-10
11/16	at Georgia	W	24-10
11/30	Alabama (Bham)	L	23-25
1/1	Texas A&M*	L	16-36

*Cotton Bowl, Dallas, TX

1986:

10-2 overall; 4-2 SEC

9/6	UT Chattanooga	W	42-14
9/17	East Carolina	W	45-0
9/27	Tennessee	W	34-8
10/4	W Carolina	W	55-6
10/11	at Vanderbilt	W	31-9
10/18	Georgia Tech	W	31-10
10/25	at Miss State	W	35-6
11/1	at Florida	L	17-18
11/8	Cincinnati	W	52-7
11/15	Georgia	L	16-20
11/29	at Alabama (Bham)	W	21-17
1/1	USC*	W	16-7

Citrus Bowl, Orlando, FL
(Final AP Ranking: 6)

1987:

9-1-2 overall; 5-0-1 SEC
SEC Champions

9/5	Texas	W	31-3
9/12	Kansas	W	49-0
9/26	at Tennessee	T	20-20
10/3	at North Carolina	W	20-10
10/10	Vanderbilt	W	48-15
10/17	at Georgia Tech	W	20-10
10/24	Miss State	W	38-7
10/31	Florida	W	29-6
11/7	Florida State	L	6-34
11/14	at Georgia	W	27-11
11/27	Alabama (Bham)	W	10-0
1/1	Syracuse*	T	16-16

Sugar Bowl; New Orleans, LA
(Final AP Ranking: 7)

1988:

10-2 overall; 5-1 SEC
SEC Champions

9/10	Kentucky	W	20-10
9/17	Kansas	W	56-7
9/24	Tennessee	W	38-6
10/1	North Carolina	W	47-21
10/8	at LSU	L	6-7
10/15	Akron	W	42-0
10/22	Miss State	W	33-0
10/29	at Florida	W	16-0
11/5	Southern Miss	W	38-8
11/12	Georgia	W	20-10
11/25	at Alabama (Bham)	W	15-10
1/2	Florida State*	L	7-13

Sugar Bowl, New Orleans, LA
(Final AP Ranking: 8)

- 4 -

THE LAST BRICK IN OUR HOUSE
Pat Dye, 1989-1992

"From the cradle to the grave, football borders on religion in the state of Alabama. This timeless phenomenon solidified some seventy years ago. It was during the Depression of 1929 and on into the Thirties when the hopeless Alabama citizens looked with pride towards the great Crimson Tide teams. In this era Wallace Wade and Frank Thomas won four national championships, soothing the desperate times.

"When America rebounded, Alabama football continued to be the toast of the upper crust. The state's doctors, lawyers and bankers sent their children on to Tuscaloosa to be educated. Auburn University was an agricultural and engineering school, attracting the state's middle class. Auburn always felt it was being shunned by the University of Alabama followers, and Auburn knew the one place to gain respect from Tuscaloosa was on the football field.

"For the past forty years, these social wars have been settled on a battleground in Birmingham. These two teams have battled on the last weekend of their seasons to settle 364 days of impassioned arguments over who has the better team, and the better way of life.

271

"When Alabama and Auburn play, the goal is to win. But the fear is of losing, and having to tolerate your arch rival fans and their incessant torture for an entire year.

"People said it would never happen. Today it will *happen. Second-ranked Alabama against 11th ranked Auburn—in Auburn, for the first time ever."*
—*CBS Sports voiceover, prior to 1989 Iron Bowl*

Reynolds Wolf

Oh gosh. First time the Iron Bowl was on the Plains, I couldn't believe it. I remember being there—I was a freshman at Jacksonville State University and was with a buddy of mine named Carl McRae. We were there in the stadium and just thinking, "Dude—this is *real*. This is *happening*."

"A full spectrum of football heroes from Bear Bryant to Bo Jackson have been a part of this glorious series, yet many of them never would have believed that this game would one day shift to this site.

"Good afternoon, everybody. I'm Jim Nantz, and welcome to the southern plains of Alabama where, for the first time ever, the Alabama Crimson Tide comes in to challenge the Auburn Tigers. Clearly today the objective for these teams is to win the state title, but there is certainly much more at stake than just that. In fact, by the end of the day, the Southeastern Conference title will be finalized, as will the conference representative in the Sugar Bowl in New Orleans.

"Now, Alabama can win the conference outright and go on to New Orleans undefeated with a victory today. However, Auburn could spoil those plans, and we could even see a three-way tie by the end of the day if Tennessee can claim victory against Vanderbilt. The national championship picture is also in focus here. The Crimson Tide, ranked second in the country; however, obviously needing a victory today to keep any hopes at all alive of winning the national championship.

"Yesterday, Alabama made its first journey ever from Tuscaloosa to Auburn, and many of their fans tagged along. They went through

272

the towns of Centreville and Maplesville they all came; 160 miles they traveled to a new world. Meanwhile, here at Auburn all week, it's been a celebration."
—Jim Nantz of CBS Sports, 1989 Iron Bowl broadcast

Jerry Hinnen

Being eleven at the time, I didn't understand the full significance of that game. I didn't understand that playing in Legion Field every year was a kind of slap in the face to Auburn, or at least it was to a lot of perfectly sensible Auburn people. That this had been such a sticking point, that the game just wasn't played in Auburn, and that was how it was supposed to be, until 1989. I didn't understand how cathartic that game was at the time. But that's the nice thing about growing up is you can read things and learn things.

And now, obviously, I think about that as the culmination of the Dye years. Maybe Auburn never won the national championship—obviously should have in 1983, which is another season, unfortunately, I don't remember. But they kept winning big games, they kept going to Sugar Bowls, and finally kind of built up, I think, to a game that really changed the dynamic of Auburn football from everything that came before to everything that came after.

Even if I didn't understand its importance at the time, I think I'm not overstating its importance. Beating an undefeated Alabama team fairly comfortably, from what I remember, watching at home. It was a seismic event and to say that was the culmination of the Dye years—I don't think it's overstating it.

The Auburn Tigers accomplished quite a bit during the 1989 season. They defeated LSU, Florida, Georgia, Alabama and Ohio State. They claimed a share of the SEC Championship—something Auburn had accomplished only four times before that. They even won double-digit games in back-to-back years—the only Auburn team ever to have done so. Beyond those great accomplishments, however, they will always be remembered for one single, shining achievement; one that overshadows everything else about the 1989 season; one that meant more to Auburn fans than any of the others.

273

They were the team that played Alabama in the "First Time Ever" Iron Bowl played in Jordan-Hare Stadium, and they were the team that won it.

That day was about more than just another football game; it was about more than just another Iron Bowl. It was personal, and it was history.

"It was, for Auburn, a day that signified acceptance, if you will. It was a day that said no one can ever again deny this school and this football program its rightful place."
—*Phillip Marshall, Montgomery Advertiser*

1989

Van Allen Plexico

The 1988 team came so close to winning it all. We had just suffered through that with the 1983 team, as well. There was frustration that Auburn ended up playing a meaningless Sugar Bowl against Florida State, when we should have been undefeated and playing Notre Dame for the national championship.

We knew that we were losing some great players off that 1988 team, but we were also getting a lot of really good players back for at least one more year. We lost Tracy Rocker to the NFL, but we had his brother David coming back. The defense still had great talent, but it lost some of that front-line, All-American talent from the 1987 and 1988 squads.

What were your expectations going into 1989, particularly knowing that we would be witnessing Alabama's first ever visit to Auburn?

John Ringer

Coming off two SEC titles in a row the expectations were high. We had a returning quarterback in Reggie Slack. We had lost a lot of talented defensive players, but we had a lot coming back in Quintin Riggins and Craig Ogletree, David Rocker and some other guys. We had James Joseph and Stacey Danley returning at running back. We also had a few good players on the offensive line like Ed King, John Hudson and Rob Selby.

Our schedule had some tough spots on it; we had to play some tough road games. But knowing that we were getting Alabama at home for the first time ever was huge. It made you think about the season in a different way. You knew that game was coming up at the end of the season, you looked forward to it, and you hoped the team would be peaking by the time November and December came around.

We had a lot of confidence and high expectations going into the season, because we felt we had a good team. It was going to be a tough schedule, but we knew we had a good team and firmly believed it would be competitive.

Van Allen Plexico

This is interesting: What team scored the most points against this Auburn defense all season?

John Ringer

Tennessee? Louisiana Tech?

Van Allen Plexico

Louisiana Tech! It was very similar to North Carolina scoring the most points on us the year before. It's one of those games where we were looking past them and probably played the backups a lot, resting up to go to Georgia the next week.

The character of that 1989 team was revealed over the course of September through December. I mean, I honestly can't remember any other season like this. And I think Pat Dye even mentioned this in the locker room after the Iron Bowl.

"Tonight is what our program is all about. I want you to think about it and let it sink in deep. This is the reason we work you in the summertime, in January, in February, in the spring. This is the reason we push you beyond what you think you can do, is to experience moments like this. Yes. Ain't no easy way in life. And it wasn't easy out there tonight, but you were prepared for the task at hand. Everyone of you players, I mean, No way. No way—I ain't smart

enough to tell you how I feel about you. I mean, it's family, every one of you. I mean, you know it. Shoot, I'd like to be 11-0, but I'm gonna tell you something: I wouldn't swap this year for any year that I've been at Auburn. I wouldn't swap it, men, because I've watched you struggle, and I've watched you wrestle with those angels and demons, and I watched you grow up and become men. I watched you become men."
—Pat Dye, the locker room after the 1989 Iron Bowl

Van Allen Plexico

He's saying that all season long, this team was struggling with itself. It always had great potential, but it was having trouble putting it all together on a consistent basis in every phase of the game. It was a good team. A team that *wanted* to be great and *could* be great. Earlier in the year they couldn't quite come together and gel and get over the hump and whatever other euphemisms you want.

We need to talk for a minute about the two losses that came in the first half of the season, on either side of a big win over LSU. After the second loss, our record was 4-2, which was not where this team expected to be.

The first loss was to Tennessee. Neyland Stadium had been a "house of horrors" for us during most of the decade. Afterward we and our friends called this the "Blame it on the Rain" game, as we sang along to that Milli Vanilli song of the same name.

After destroying Pacific and Southern Miss by a combined score of 79-3, the Tigers had to travel to Knoxville to take on the Vols.

Auburn hadn't had much luck in Neyland Stadium during the 1980s. Arguably Tennessee, along with FSU, were the Tigers' most difficult opponents throughout the decade—and the toughest SEC foe. The Vols had won a hard-fought affair in 1981, and after losing to Auburn in 1983, they'd sprung the ambush on Bo's 1985 team and come from behind to tie the Tigers in 1987.

For the 1989 game, Vols coach Johnny Majors decided he needed to slow down Auburn's speed advantage. His plan was to pound the ball at Auburn with Reggie Cobb and Chuck Webb, while limiting the Tigers' wide receiver corps. With rain already falling on Knoxville since the Friday before game day, Majors had the Neyland Stadium sprinklers cranked up to add even more water to the mix. By the time the two teams took the field, Neyland was a quagmire.

What resulted was the most lopsided game imaginable, in terms of rushing yardage, in the Pat Dye era—and certainly among his better teams, as the 1989 squad surely was.

The Auburn defense had held Pacific and Southern Miss to a combined 56 yards rushing in the first two games (and the Tigers' Lamar Rogers was named National Defensive Player of the Week after the game against Brett Favre's Golden Eagles). Tennessee players and coaches, however, felt they could see vulnerabilities when watching game film.

"We thought we could run on them. They're not supermen. You can see on film how good a team is. The films don't lie, and we felt we could move the ball.

"Against Southern Mississippi, they (Auburn) made some big plays, but I didn't see the (USM) offensive line getting crushed."
—Charles McRae, Tennessee offensive lineman

"Auburn coach Pat Dye had an uneasy feeling going into the game. Still, Dye felt confident of one thing: His defensive line would dominate. No question.

"But something went awry, beginning with Tennessee's second possession, when the Volunteers' offensive linemen—most notably right guard Eric Still—began driving the Tigers off the ball. Tailbacks Cobb and Chuck Webb were biting off huge chunks of yardage right up the gut of Auburn's defense."
—Austin Murphy, Sports Illustrated

Reggie Cobb ripped off a 79-yard touchdown run early in the second quarter, sandwiched between two safeties—each coming as a different Auburn long-snapper sent the ball over the head of punter Chris Dickinson.

"I wasn't careful enough. The ball in the game was dry. We had been practicing with a waterlogged ball in warmups. The (dry) ball

just took off. I've been snapping since junior high and it's the first time this has ever happened to me."
—Travis Galloway, one of Auburn's long-snappers

After that, the teams swapped field goals, and Tennessee led at the half, 14-3.

Neither team found the end zone in the third quarter. With 11:15 to go in the game, Reggie Slack hit Alexander Wright for an 83-yard touchdown and Stacey Danley took it in for the two-point conversion. (Wright had made big plays against Pacific, and this bomb in Neyland would not be the last time we'd see him change the course of a game in 1989.) Suddenly the Tigers were back in business, down only three, at 14-11.

Auburn's defense stopped the Vols and got the ball back. Then the offense started to drive for what could've been the game-winning touchdown. (Given that it was Johnny Majors against Pat Dye, maybe it would have been a game-tying field goal.) With about seven minutes to go, Reggie Slack's pass was intercepted by Shazzon Bradley at the Auburn 42. Five plays later, Chuck Webb carried it in from the eight, pushing the Vols' lead back out to 10. A late Win Lyle field goal kept hope alive a little longer, but Tennessee held on for the 21-14 final score.

Being beaten by the Vols was bad enough—up until that season, the loser of this game had never gone on to win the SEC—but the way Tennessee's backs had run roughshod over a proud Auburn defense was both astonishing and deeply troubling.

The numbers were eye-popping: Reggie Cobb gained 225 yards rushing on 22 carries, with a long of 79. His freshman backfield partner in the "Cobb-Webb Connection," Chuck Webb, gained another 95 yards on 19 carries. Meanwhile, Auburn's duo of Stacey Danley and James Joseph combined for just 92 yards.

Cobb had been suspended prior to the 1989 season for drug use, but Johnny Majors had reinstated him in time to do what he did to Auburn. The following week, he helped the Vols eke out a close win over a mediocre Georgia squad—only to be kicked off the team again, for a drug offense. Playing without him the week after that, the Vols lost to Alabama. That Tide win ended up being as important to Auburn as anything Alabama ever did, because it dropped Tennessee back into a tie for the SEC title.

"We're not the same team they beat 38-6 a year ago. They made some remarks during the week, saying I wasn't going to be a factor in the game.
"I don't really think they took us serious."
—Reggie Cobb, Tennessee running back

Reggie Slack attempted 40 passes in the downpour, completing 18 of them for 285 yards, though 83 of that was the one long pass to Wright. Tennessee's two quarterbacks, meanwhile, completed a total of four passes in seven attempts, for a grand total of 66 yards. Passing, though, wasn't really needed—not when "the Cobb-Webb Connection" was amassing nearly 350 yards on the ground.

It should also be mentioned that Tennessee defensive end Marion Hobby batted down five of Slack's passes, including three in the fourth quarter when the Tigers were trying to come back.

"I can't believe we are as bad as Tennessee made us look."
—Pat Dye

"They beat us at our own game. They kicked our butts."
—James Joseph, Auburn running back

Pat Dye called a timeout with seven seconds remaining in the game, trying to force the Vols to run a play on fourth down. The students, however, thought the game was over. They stormed the field and began tearing down the goalposts. Seeing this, Dye decided to let it go, and walked to midfield to shake Majors' hand.

John Ringer

Reggie Cobb just destroyed us that day. The other games that year, I think you pointed out we struggled on offense and didn't score enough. This was a game where the *defense* let us down and Tennessee ran over us. They had some great offensive linemen and Cobb was excellent at running back and they took it to us in the rain up there.

Van Allen Plexico

Alexander Wright caught an 83-yard bomb from Reggie Slack, so we did have at least one good play.

It was a strange score in that 21-14 looks like there were five touchdowns, but actually field goals and safeties and a two-point conversion were involved.

Other than the one long play, Tennessee's defense pretty much kept our offense under control the whole game. We weren't going to be a great team as long as we were struggling to score 10-14 points on the likes of Tennessee, LSU and Florida. I mean, they all had good defenses, but to be a real contender, we needed to be able to score more points than that, and that's coming.

Understand, though—the main thought underlying Auburn fans' hopes and expectations for this particular season wasn't "What bowl will we get to?" or "Will we win the SEC?" or "Can we play for the national championship?" The three previous seasons had taught us all that just a couple of points here and a score or two there would have us in the conversation for the national title. What we were most concerned about during the 1989 season, though, was simply, "When Alabama comes to town on December 2, will we be able to give them a game? Can we *win* that game?" That thought—that worry; that concern—hung over everything else all season long.

The loss in Knoxville dropped Auburn from no. 4 to no. 11 in the AP rankings. After a relatively easy win against Kentucky in Lexington, the Tigers came home on October 14 for a redemption game against LSU.

The loss to LSU in "the Earthquake Game" in Death Valley in 1988 has rightly been called one of the costliest defeats in Auburn history. It quite possibly knocked the Tigers out of a national championship matchup with Notre Dame. The need to exact some measure of revenge from the Bayou Bengals burned brightly in the breasts of every Auburn fan when October of 1989 rolled around.

"LSU entered the 1989 season No. 7 in the AP poll. The team returned its leading passer (Tommy Hodson), leading rusher (Eddie

Fuller), its leading receiver (Tony Moss), and its leading tackler (Verne Ausberry). This was a loaded squad ready to build off of last year's success to even greater heights.

"And then the bottom fell out.

"Let's not sugarcoat it, nothing good happened in the 1989 season, the worst season in LSU football history."

—andthevalleyshook LSU blog, 2018

The game was another hard-fought contest, but as it progressed it took on the air of a "grind-it-out" affair—few fireworks, just hard-fought battles in the trenches. As they'd done the previous season, Auburn managed to score only twice against LSU. This time, however, one of those scores was a touchdown—with LSU ahead, 6-3, late in the game—giving the Tigers in blue enough of an advantage to hang on for the win over their Cajun opponents, who were only able to match Auburn's scoring output from that previous contest of just two field goals.

John Ringer

The LSU game wasn't the same as the year before. It wasn't quite what we thought it was going to be—a huge revenge game. I think LSU was good that year, but they weren't *great*. They had lost some good players, I believe, from the previous year. And we did want revenge. I wanted to beat them and get them back.

Their defense was again excellent, as it always is, and it was a slugfest, just like the more recent Auburn-LSU games where the two defenses dominated. The score was 6-3 going down the stretch. It didn't help that Auburn had lost two weeks earlier, so it didn't quite feel like a game for the national championship.

Van Allen Plexico

Right. If we had been undefeated and it had felt like winning that game was going to help get us to the national championship or something, then maybe it would have been bigger.

It was tough game. I remember James Joseph plunging in for the touchdown that ended up winning the game. It was kind of like the previous year in reverse, in terms of scoring and everything. We got the late touchdown instead of them.

The final score was 10-6 Auburn, in a game that was mostly dull but ultimately satisfying. That LSU team would go on to finish only 4-7, but they certainly played hard against Auburn and, at the time, it felt like a legitimately big win. More than that, it felt like a measure, however small, of revenge for the night the ground shook in Baton Rouge.

Then came Florida State.

The Tigers had played home-and-home games with FSU in 1983/1984 and 1985/1987, as well as the Sugar Bowl after the 1988 season, so these two teams were very familiar with one another, for two out-of-conference opponents.

For the 1989 game, Auburn met the Seminoles in then-decrepit Doak Campbell Stadium on the cool, humid night of October 21.

The first quarter saw only an exchange of field goals, with the two teams tied at 3-3 going into the second frame.

In the second quarter, Florida State appeared to seize control of the game. Peter Tom Willis drove the Seminoles down the field and Edgar Bennett scored the first of his two touchdowns of the quarter, from one yard out. A few minutes later, Bennett scored again, this time from 7 yards away—the Noles missed the extra point—and FSU now led, 16-3. They tacked on a field goal a minute before halftime and went into the break safely ahead, at 19-3. Auburn had a shocking grand total of only 55 yards of total offense at that point.

Auburn came out in the second half determined to get back in the ballgame, and they very nearly pulled it off, outscoring the Noles 11-3 before the end. After one more FSU field goal, pushing them out to a seemingly unassailable 22-3 lead at the end of the third quarter, Auburn took over and owned the final stanza.

Reggie Slack led the Tigers on a 75-yard drive that produced another Win Lyle field goal. Moments later, Slack was the recipient of a roughing-the-passer penalty after an incomplete fourth down throw that kept the Tigers alive. James Joseph took it in from four yards away, and Stacey Danley added a two-point conversion.

Suddenly the deficit had narrowed to just 22-14, with more than seven minutes remaining.

Florida State turned to freshman running back Amp Lee to drive the Noles down the field and use up the remaining clock, and he nearly succeeded. On Auburn's 5 yard line, however, Craig Ogletree knocked the ball out of Lee's hands and the Tigers recovered. They'd get one more chance to make it happen.

Alas, it was not to be. They drove part of the way toward the FSU end zone, but time—and the Noles defenders—caught up with them, and Slack was sacked one final time, bringing Auburn's comeback attempt to an abrupt ending.

"Just about like the Sugar Bowl, wasn't it? You get where you think you're going to eat them up, relax a little bit, and all of a sudden, they're driving for the win... uh, tie. I thought we had the game wrapped up about three different times."
—Bobby Bowden, FSU head coach

"They had the momentum and were probably playing better than anybody in the country. I've watched Notre Dame and (FSU) may be playing better than them."
—Quentin Riggins, Auburn linebacker

The *Miami Herald* reported the next day that Auburn and FSU had agreed to a new ten-year home-and-home contract with Auburn, with the 1989 game being the first of the ten. The two teams met again in Auburn the following season, but they didn't play again after that until the final BCS National Championship Game on January 6, 2014. The series ending so abruptly when it did, after the 1990 game, probably had to do with the imminent expansion of the SEC in 1992 and the addition of more conference games to all the teams' schedules, as well as FSU joining the ACC in 1991 and therefore picking up their own conference schedule. The two teams nearly played one another in 1999, in an effort to pit father Bobby Bowden against son Terry Bowden, but that contract was canceled by Auburn after Terry resigned as Auburn's coach, late in 1998.

Van Allen Plexico

I was there in Tallahassee for that FSU game. My two roommates and I and some other friends made a caravan down to the panhandle to see it.

First—Doak Campbell Stadium back then was nothing like it is now. It was terrible. The end zone seats were bleachers with long wooden planks to sit on. It was worse than you'd find at most high schools. In fact, at one point in the game, a wooden plank snapped in half and the two jagged ends flew up in the air like seesaws and hurt at least one person.

It was a cool but humid evening. I was coming down with my traditional fall bronchitis, and really shouldn't have tried to go. Yelling at a football game was the last thing I needed to be doing. I was feeling worse and worse as the night wore on, and Florida State was getting farther and farther ahead. At least we did rally late, but then we came up short.

Leaving the stadium, some of their fans ran in circles around us, taunting and doing war cries at us. I remember after the game in Auburn the following year, Florida State fans complained about how scared they were of Auburn fans when they were leaving our stadium, and I was thinking, "You must have no idea how your own people treat visitors to Tallahassee!"

Another thing they did that annoyed us involved their marching band. Now, understand that opposing fans already despise that band because they play the FSU "chopping" war chant over and over, even more often than the Tennessee band plays Rocky Top. Well, they exited the field after halftime and passed directly below us, where we sat in the visitors' section of those cheap wooden bleachers. We didn't know they were beneath us until, all of a sudden, they smashed their drums and cymbals and blasted out their war cry, directly under us, to try to scare us. And it did cause some folks to jump! But the band got their just desserts. Now, I'm not condoning the following behavior at all, but karma can be unpleasant. Right after the band startled our section, I witnessed a number of Auburn fans dumping their cokes between the cracks in the bleachers, straight down onto the Florida State marching band.

With the loss to Florida State, Auburn's record stood at 4-2, and they had fallen to 16th in the AP Poll. They'd suffered two one-score road losses against teams on five-game winning streaks, with a combined record going into that weekend of 9-2.

Clearly something was wrong. The question was, with that big historic date looming on the horizon in early December, could the ship be righted in time, if at all?

Van Allen Plexico

This Auburn team just wasn't firing on all cylinders until the Georgia game—which we're getting to—or maybe our last offensive play in the Florida game, which seemed to unclog the pipes and get things rolling. And just in time, because you know what game was coming up at the end of the season.

We had that great defense, but the offense just wasn't clicking. We had lost a good bit of our receiving corps from the last few years: Tillman, Weygand, Donaldson, and the great tight end Walter Reeves were all gone. The main receivers that year were Alexander Wright, Greg Taylor and Shayne Wasden. Our running game was okay, but just *okay*. It wasn't what we had gotten used to in that decade. Stacey Danley and James Joseph were fine, there was nothing at all wrong with them. They just weren't Bo Jackson and Brent Fullwood, or Brooks and Cribbs and Andrews. They were serviceable backs who could get the job done, but neither of them, as of 1989, was a game-breaker of the magnitude we'd gotten accustomed to in previous years.

As a consequence, the offense was having a hard time getting going. It bit us at Tennessee on September 30th. It meant we only scored 10 points at home against LSU; fortunately, we won that game by holding LSU to just 6.

John Ringer

It sounds like a lot of Auburn-LSU games, though.

Van Allen Plexico

Yeah, it does.

It meant that we could hold Florida State in their own stadium to 22 and still only score 14. And, I think most importantly, it meant that in that November 4 game against 19th-ranked Florida with Emmitt Smith and that great Gators defense, we had to find a way to score on our last offensive play of the game.

"(Against FSU,) our offense had been stalled. I was determined we were going back to basics. All the next week, we just practiced three plays: the sweep, the sprint draw, and the counter. That was it. That was about all we ran against Mississippi State. We won the game, 14-0. We only passed for 37 yards. We ran for 241. James Joseph ran for 172 yards. We ran 59 running plays, 35 of 'em by James, who was a man in every sense of the word."
—Pat Dye, In the Arena

After that grind-it-out, back-to-basics win over Mississippi State on October 28, the Tigers turned their attention to Florida.

The 1989 season marked the 50th anniversary of Jordan-Hare Stadium. Play had begun there in the fall of 1939, when it was known as Cliff Hare Stadium. Before kickoff, the 1939 Auburn team was introduced, and quarterback Dick McGowen recreated the first touchdown ever scored in the stadium, throwing an 11-yard pass to C.H. "Babe" McGehee. That re-enactment would prove to be eerily prescient later that evening.

Auburn had thrashed the Gators the two previous seasons, first at home on Halloween in 1987 and then on the road for Florida's Gator Growl homecoming weekend in 1988, shutting them out. The 1989 contest would be much closer. It would also be the final chance for the great Florida and future Dallas Cowboys running back, Emmitt Smith, to get a win against Auburn. While running roughshod over the rest of the conference, Emmitt had been held entirely in check in his two previous games against the Tigers. This would be his final opportunity to show what he could do against a great defense.

As it turned out, he did very little at all.

In Florida's game the previous week, Emmitt had rushed 31 times for 316 yards. On this November evening, his output would be substantially less.

Neither team could move the ball on their opening possessions; this would be a recurring theme for much of the game. On Auburn's second possession, Reggie Slack fumbled the ball at the Tigers own 5-yard line. The Gators took over in sublime field position, and Emmitt Smith punched it in to give the Gators a 7-0 lead. This marked the first touchdown scored by the Gators against Auburn in three years, and Emmitt's only career score against the Tigers.

How focused was Florida on feeding the ball to Emmitt? The Gators didn't even attempt a pass until just over eight minutes remained in the half. Even so, the Auburn defense was shutting the Gators down completely. The problem was, their defense was doing the same to Auburn's offense—and the Gators had that one cheap touchdown in their pocket. The game was starting to look like one of those soccer matches where the first team that manages to score has achieved a fabled "insurmountable 1-0 lead."

The one bright spot for Auburn in that quarter was a huge, 50-yard touchdown pass from Slack to Alexander Wright. Why don't you remember this play? Because it was called back on a facemask penalty—against the *offense*! The score remained 7-0 Florida.

In the third quarter, both teams punted back and forth, but the Gators managed to keep the Tigers backed up just enough to avoid any danger of a score. Near the end of the quarter, Auburn finally made it to Florida's 30-yard line, but had to settle for a 47-yard Win Lyle kick that hit the crossbar and bounced through. As the game moved into the final quarter, the Gators still led, but the margin had shrunk to just 4 points, at 7-3.

At last Auburn began to get its offense together. They marched the length of the field, helped along by James Joseph converting a fourth-and-inches at the Florida 23. Slack hit tight end Victor Hall for another first down to the 7. But then the resilient Gators defense stiffened again, and Lyle came out to attempt another field goal—which Florida promptly blocked. With less than six minutes remaining in the game, Auburn still trailed by 4 and now the Gators had the ball. The Tigers defense would have to hold the Gators in check just one more time.

The defense held. They stifled Florida and forced a punt, handing the offense one last opportunity to shine.

The Tigers started from their own 47 with less than four minutes left. After driving Auburn into the Gators' red zone, Reggie Slack was sacked all the way back at the Florida 38, forcing Coach Dye to burn the Tigers' final timeout. A 15-yard pass to Greg Taylor brought the Tigers back into striking range, but the clock was still ticking away.

The Tigers attempted to run the ball again, but could get nothing going on the ground, and faced 4th and 11 at the Florida 25. With less than a minute remaining, Slack dropped back, surveyed the field, and saw that the safety who should be covering Shayne Wasden was shading over on Greg Taylor instead. Slack responded by lofting the ball to Wasden, uncovered and running into the right corner of the end zone. Wasden spun around, caught the ball over his head and stumbled backwards to the ground for the winning score.

"Fourth down and 10 with 45 seconds on the clock, it is still on the move and Auburn can't stop it, they can't call time. 4th down and ten. This could be the last play of the game for Auburn. They trail 7-3. Slack has one setback and four wide receivers. Desperation play. Slack is gonna throw in the end zone, got a man wide open— Wasden—and he's got it! Touchdown Auburn! Touchdown Auburn! Touchdown Auburn! Slack threw it to Wasden! Wasden wide open in the end zone. Shayne Wasden! Touchdown Auburn! Reggie Slack a desperation heave and it is an Auburn touchdown! Tigers lead with 26 seconds to go! 9-7! Unbelievable!"
—Jim Fyffe, Auburn Network broadcast

Amazingly, astonishingly, the Tigers led, 10-7, with mere seconds to go in the game.

The crowd in Jordan-Hare Stadium went nuts.

"We've had to play against that play 300 times since I've been at Florida. All of a sudden, the guy's awfully open. It wasn't even that hard a throw."
—Gary Darnell, Florida interim head coach

Florida was not quite finished, though. While the Auburn faithful celebrated in the stands, plastic cups flying everywhere, Florida's quarterback scrambled to near midfield. On the final play of the game, he threw a deep pass to his receiver, who bobbled and dropped it as he neared the goal line and crashed into a bevy of Tiger defenders. Auburn had held on for a tremendous victory.

Van Allen Plexico

The Florida receiver was running right at me, in the corner of the end zone, as he almost caught that final Hail Mary pass at the end. I was sure he was going to catch it and Florida was going to win. I couldn't believe it when he bobbled and dropped it. On the television broadcast, it looks like he never had a chance at it, but I'm telling you, I wasn't that far away from him and had my eyes right on him, and it was close. Everyone else around me was going crazy celebrating, not even paying any attention, as if the game was already over. Meanwhile, I was just staring at the spot where they had almost salvaged a miracle play, twenty seconds after our miracle play!

"For Slack, it was a sweet ending to a trying week. It had been rumored during the week that Slack had been kicked off the team for failing a drug test. Slack shunned the rumors and responded with a strike to Wasden to win over the fans and keep the Tigers in the race for the SEC championship.

Slack, the subject of several boos in the first half, left the field to a chorus of 'Reggie, Reggie.'"
—Mike Easterling, Montgomery Advertiser

"When I was in the huddle, the guys had a look in their eyes. Nobody gave up. That was the difference in the game. I went into that last play with the attitude that I was going to make something happen."
—Reggie Slack, Auburn quarterback

"You coach and preach and teach, and you don't know if you're getting the message totally across until you see it surface right out there on the field in front of your eyes."
—Pat Dye

As the two teams exited the field amid chaotic celebrations, a tearful Emmitt Smith fell to his knees on the sideline and pounded his fist on the ground in frustration.

How dominant was the Auburn defense that night? The future NFL star carried the ball 27 times for a net of 86 yards rushing. He ended his Florida career never having gained 100 yards on the Tigers. Gator QB Donald Douglas attempted five passes in the game. He completed one of them, for a total of 6 yards.

After the game, Slack said the Auburn offense was finally becoming what it was supposed to have been all season.

"We got what we've been trying to do all year. We wanted to get a balance (of rushing and passing). We finally got it."
—Reggie Slack, Auburn quarterback

Even so, the numbers were pretty grim. Auburn rushed for a net total of 109 yards on 43 attempts. Slack completed 12 of 19 passes for 143 yards. The two teams together punted 16 times.

With the win, Auburn's record against Florida in games played in Auburn improved to a remarkable 21-4-1.

John Ringer

The visiting team exit and entrance was in the student section area and some of our friends got into it with the Florida coaches after the game as they were leaving the field.

Florida's defense was excellent. They had a ton of great talent and they were really tough. At the end of the game, we drove down the field and Reggie Slack hit Shayne Wasden going into the end zone, and he was kind of falling backwards as he caught the ball. It was a huge moment. That stadium went absolutely bananas.

Van Allen Plexico

This was Emmitt Smith's third and last try to beat us. And he ended up 0-3. You and I have talked before about how his recruitment came down to Florida and Auburn, and allegedly his mom said he would not be going north of the Florida state line. But if he'd chosen Auburn, you and I agree we'd have won one, maybe more than one national championship during those years. Adding his abilities to the running game we had with Danley and Joseph, and that passing game with Slack and those receivers, and that defense. They would've scored more

290

than six points on LSU in the Earthquake Game. There wouldn't have been any earthquake!

If I remember correctly, one of the people who ended up down on the field after that Florida game was my good friend and roommate. He and a bunch of other students got in a screaming match with Gary Darnell, Florida's interim coach. I remember thinking that Darnell had no class and was pretty dumb to stand there yelling at a bunch of students from the opposing school. I think my friend ended up getting zip-tied by the AU campus police during that melee. People were screaming and running around, and those plastic drink cups were flying everywhere. It was crazy.

It was a huge relief to win the Florida game and to win it in such a dramatic style, but afterward we were thinking, "If we can only score one touchdown against Florida, what will the Georgia game be like? And what about that big one looming at the end of the season?"

And then we played Louisiana Tech. We won it, of course, but with a score of 38-23, and with La Tech scoring more points against us than anyone else all year, it started making some of us nervous all over again.

At that point, our record was 7-2, ranked 11th in the country, and Alabama was undefeated and ranked second. We were looking ahead to that gigantic date of December 2 in Jordan-Hare and feeling gut-wrenching agony and wondering, "Do we even have a prayer?" We'd waited for years and years to finally get Alabama to come to our town, to our stadium, to play the Iron Bowl—and it looked like they would be bringing their best team in a decade. We were like, "Of all years, why does it have to be this year they're so good?"

John Ringer

I remember I kept pointing at Alabama's win-loss records in the years leading up to this, and they were usually kind of mediocre. So why couldn't we have had them visit Jordan-Hare in one of the seasons when they were mediocre?

Van Allen Plexico

At the time, the anticipation was just gut wrenching, as we waited for that game to come around. Looking back on it now, though—their being undefeated and apparently on the way to playing for the national championship, it just makes beating them sweeter, doesn't it?

John Ringer

Yes. A hundred percent.

Before playing that long-anticipated Iron Bowl in Jordan-Hare, however, the Tigers had to travel to Athens, Georgia to take on the Bulldogs. In new head coach Ray Goff's first season in charge, the Dogs came into the game with a record of 6-3. But they had just beaten Florida the week before, and featured a powerful running game led by Rodney Hampton. If ever in history there could have been a "look ahead" game, this would've been it. With the "First Time Ever" Iron Bowl next on the schedule, the Tigers could perhaps have been forgiven for not devoting all of their attention to Georgia; for not taking this Bulldog team as seriously as they should have.

That did not happen. Auburn came out focused against Georgia and absolutely dominated the game. The Dogs had to kick a late field goal to avoid being shut out. Reggie Slack's touchdown pass to Greg Taylor provided all the points the Tigers would need, but "Lectron" Williams added another, to go along with two Win Lyle field goals.

Van Allen Plexico

We went to Athens and beat Georgia 20-3. That's a good score to beat Georgia by: 20-3. I like that we held them down; the defense was really rolling then.

John Ringer

Yeah, this was one of the few times in history where we dominated them in the series and dominated them in Athens. We have this game and the Ronnie Daniels game, but there's not a lot of other games where we so thoroughly dominated them. But we absolutely kicked Georgia's rear end that year.

292

"We beat Georgia for the third straight year. Craig (Ogletree) made eleven tackles. John Wiley intercepted two passes. We held their great back, Rodney Hampton, a first-round draft choice by the Giants, to 29 yards. And Darrell 'Lectron' Williams had his first big impact on a game. He ran for 128 yards and scored once."
—Pat Dye, In the Arena

"As a team, Georgia gained 48 yards rushing, its lowest (total) in 146 games. Its 173 yards passing was its lowest in eight games. Its total offense of 221 yards was its lowest since gaining 210 in the 1985 opener against Alabama. The last time the Bulldogs scored fewer points was 62 games ago."
—Thomas O'Toole, Atlanta Constitution

Auburn, meanwhile, amassed 468 yards of total offense against the Dogs, rushing 52 times for 248 yards and passing for 230. The Tigers held the ball for a whopping 40:22 of the game. Georgia had the ball for less than 20 minutes.

"They took away our running game and when we went to our passing game, they took that away, too. You can't feel good about this. They shut us down every way. They stayed after us, and we didn't respond."
—Greg Talley, Georgia quarterback

"The way the Auburn center (John Hudson) plays—he's good. He tries to annoy you. You have to try and get through, and that back (Darrell Williams) cuts so well. I'd cut across, going for him, and he would cut right back behind me. It was a frustrating thing the whole time."
—Robert Bell, Georgia nose guard

"For the first time this season, Auburn looked like the team that was picked to challenge for the national championship."
—Phillip Marshall, Montgomery Advertiser

In the locker room after the game, some of Auburn's defensive players explained that they'd found extra motivation in the statement of a Georgia player that was reported earlier in the week.

"They're getting ready for the Alabama game. We can be the spoilers. I'd like to see somebody other than Auburn win the title."
—Kurt Mull, Georgia offensive tackle

"In the locker room before the game, I thought we were the most pumped up of any game since I've been here. One of their players said he wanted to win this game for Alabama. That just made me mad. Why would you want to win it for someone else? You should want to win it for yourself."
—Quentin Riggins, Auburn linebacker

"That (the Mull comments) just made us that much madder. We were ready to go out and do something about it.
"Everybody expects to get hit when they play Auburn. We didn't want to disappoint them. And I don't think we did."
—Craig Ogletree, Auburn linebacker

Van Allen Plexico

I don't remember a lot of the details of that game. I just remember thinking that maybe we finally got it together. The offense went out and scored some points. The defense looked ferocious. I was thinking afterward, "Maybe we do have a chance in the Iron Bowl, because we're getting our act together at the right time."

"The question was when we were going to come together, not if. Evidently it happened against Georgia today. We're going to enjoy this one, but now we have to get ready for Alabama and try to win another championship."
—David Rocker, Auburn defensive tackle

Then, finally, at long last—it was time for the Iron Bowl.

But not just any Iron Bowl. This was the Iron Bowl that would be remembered by the words printed on the oversized commemorative tickets—tickets showing Aubie rolling out the red carpet for his visitors from Tuscaloosa: FIRST TIME EVER.

Alabama played many of its home games in Legion Field in Birmingham in those days. Auburn had too, for a while, mainly because it wasn't believed that the City of Auburn was big enough—in terms of infrastructure, restrooms, hotels, restaurants—up through the 1960s and 1970s, to accommodate such large crowds.

As Jordan-Hare kept expanding, though, it eventually became the largest football stadium in the state—and certainly a much nicer facility than Legion Field ever had been. Over the years, Auburn began pushing to move all its home games to the Plains. Some opposing programs resisted. Georgia Tech gave in and came to Jordan-Hare in 1970. Tennessee didn't come to Auburn until 1974. Eventually, only Alabama remained as the lone holdout.

When Auburn was still playing a number of its home games in Legion Field, the arrangement with Alabama didn't seem so strange. By the late Eighties, though, with Alabama being the only team Auburn still played in a faraway stadium for its home games, the oddness of the situation became overwhelmingly apparent. Alabama didn't care, though. They knew they had an advantage playing every year in Birmingham, and they meant to keep it.

"When I saw Coach Bryant when I first got to Auburn, the first thing he said to me, very first thing, he said, 'Well, I guess you're going to want to take that game to Auburn.' I said, 'We're going to take it to Auburn.'

"He said, 'Well, we've got a contract through '88. ... I said, 'Well, we'll play '89 in Auburn.'"
—Pat Dye

One way Alabama's advantage in playing every year in Legion Field was camouflaged was that the tickets to the game were divided equally between the two universities. That helped bolster the Tide's shaky claim that Legion Field was a "neutral site."

"No question from a financial standpoint it would make a great deal of difference to both schools (to move the Iron Bowl to Auburn and change the ticket allotment). Tickets to the game had always been split 50-50. It was pretty obvious if we started splitting the tickets like a regular home game, giving Alabama 10,900 tickets as visitors, we would be able to sell thousands more season tickets. And we've done that....

"Don't think the idea of changing the ticket split didn't appeal to Alabama. We were already selling more season tickets than they were."
—Pat Dye, In the Arena

In addition to the money side of it, there was also a general dislike of having to travel all the way to Birmingham to play what was supposedly a "home" football game. There was also a fair amount of dislike of Legion Field in general. By the 1980s, nobody honestly considered it a neutral site anymore.

"Morris Savage, one of our trustees who played on the 1957 national championship team, said it best. He said, 'Legion Field was as neutral a location as Normandy was on D-Day in 1944.'

"I think Auburn developed a complex about going to Birmingham. I don't necessarily think that spilled over into the team, but Auburn's fans sure had a complex about going. We played Oregon State up there in 1973, and we played Louisville up there in 1974, and a lot of Auburn season-ticket holders just said they weren't going."
—David Housel, quoted by Creg Stephenson

One Auburn trustee reportedly said that if Alabama didn't show up at Jordan-Hare for the 1989 game, Auburn would consider the Tide to have forfeited the game! Now Auburn was playing hardball, indeed.

With all the other series having moved to Jordan-Hare—with Legion Field no longer being one of the places Auburn played home games—Legion Field looked less and less like "Auburn and Alabama both choosing to play the game there, at a neutral site" and more and more like "Auburn having to play its home game in the series at Alabama's preferred venue." When the perception shifted in that way, it became only a matter of time until the inevitable happened—no matter what Ray Perkins or anyone else said to the contrary.

By the mid-1980s, an Auburn official was rumored to have stated that Auburn would soon "demand" the game be moved to a true home-and-home arrangement.

"Demand? That's pretty strong, isn't it? I'm not going to worry about it. I've said in the past that the game traditionally has been played on neutral turf and that it should stay that way. They can demand anything they want, but that doesn't mean they are going to get it."
—Ray Perkins, Alabama head coach, as quoted by Creg Stephenson

Ray Perkins said, "It won't happen." But it *did* happen. And it didn't just matter to Auburn people. It opened the eyes of Alabama fans to the possibilities that could exist, if the game could be moved away from that decrepit old metal monster on Graymont Avenue in Birmingham.

"Alabama didn't like it. But when Alabama folks came down and saw the atmosphere, and the tailgating and things going on in and around the stadium ... I knew that they would have to take the Auburn-Alabama game to Tuscaloosa."
—Pat Dye, quoted by Creg Stephenson

Eleven years later, Alabama moved *their* home games in the series to their own stadium as well. The first Iron Bowl played in Tuscaloosa in a century took place in 2000.

"I think it's very, very important that Auburn said the 1989 game would be played at Auburn. Alabama wanted to play in Birmingham in '89 and then come to Auburn in '91. But Auburn said 'No way.' We said 'It's going to be in Auburn in '89, and we'll go to Birmingham in '91.' So it all balanced out, but perception-wise, because Auburn got '89, it appears as though Auburn got the upper-hand on them."
—David Housel, quoted by Creg Stephenson

Alabama *did* come to Auburn to play the Iron Bowl on December 2, 1989. It *did* happen.

Van Allen Plexico

This was a truly special day. You and I and our friends all went to this game together.

I have to tell this quick story, though: I almost missed out on going at all. And I totally blame my roommates at the time for this!

December 2, 1989 was the Saturday of the game. But on Friday, December 1, I was as sick as I've ever been in my life. I got food poisoning, probably from one of my roommates leaving my pine-orange-banana juice carton out on the counter for hours and then putting it back. I kid you not—it would be seventeen years before I was able to drink that stuff again. It was either that or something I ate at a buffet in Opelika. That kind of food poisoning doesn't just make you throw up a lot, it makes you barely able to move. It's like every muscle in your body has been poisoned. I could barely get out of bed, all day on Friday.

I was terrified I wouldn't be able to go to the game. I was all feverish and kept imagining what it would be like to try to sit inside Jordan-Hare when I couldn't keep anything on my stomach. The thought of having to miss being at that game, that huge, historic game, when I lived right there in town, a mile away from the stadium, was overwhelming.

My roommates were horrible that year and wouldn't even run to the store to get me something to drink. My girlfriend at the time, who was a student at UAB, came down that afternoon and took care of me; she made me soup and helped get me rehydrated.

The morning of December 2, I woke up at dawn, and quickly decided I was a lot better. I think the relief I felt at knowing I'd be able to go to the game was much greater than the relief I felt at not being on death's door anymore!

We left our little house on the far end of Magnolia and walked with some other friends toward the stadium. I think we stopped at McDonald's for breakfast on the way. It was about seven o'clock in the morning, and the game was in the afternoon, but we wanted to be there as early as possible.

John Ringer
I didn't go to McDonald's. I feel like we met up outside the stadium.

Van Allen Plexico
All of us congregated at the student entrance to the stadium. The gates weren't going to open until maybe one o'clock so we had to sit there all morning.

Our friend Kristin brought a big white bedsheet that she'd painted to say "CBS: Can Bama Survive?" and we hung that in the corner of the stadium.

John Ringer
The student section seating was always first come, first served. And because it was Alabama and it was the "first time ever," we were *not* going to get bad seats. No, we had decided earlier that we were willing to do that—that we would sit outside the stadium all morning. Normally we would go to my parents' tailgate and other tailgates before the game, hanging out to watch earlier games, but we didn't do it on that day. We got to the stadium very early and were first in line at that gate. We brought some playing cards and we just sat on the ground and played cards and hung out all morning until the gates opened, and then we rushed in and we got great seats as a group.

There were about twenty of us that were together there, in a really good spot in the student section. We were a couple of rows above the middle walkway area and toward the 30-yard line, as far towards the 50 as the student section went over.

Van Allen Plexico
Yeah, we claimed that spot as our official seating position for the next couple of years. In 1990 we sat there the whole season, because we figured out that the Baptist Student Union and the fraternities had blocks reserved just below there, but the top two rows above the Baptists and below the walkway

railing was actual general admission. Nobody had claimed it, and very few people tried to sit on those two rows because I think everyone assumed those rows belonged to the BSU. So we would go and get that very top corner up against the fence to our right, with the walkway right behind us.

John Ringer
Yep, they were good seats. A really good view. Good location.

The SGA had put orange and blue shakers—the old paper kind—in every Auburn seat in the stadium. I mean, every single seat had one. Basically, we had a budget for this kind of stuff, and they had intentionally stopped putting out as many shakers for the other games in order to save some of them up for this game. Pretty much every seat in the stadium had shakers, other than the corner wedge where the Alabama fans sat. In the pregame warmup time, everybody got their shakers out and shook them, and there was this haze from the paper shakers over the crowd and over the stadium, from everybody shaking them so hard. It was there the whole way through to the end.

"They were shaking those damn shakers so hard it was like a blue smoke, a blue fog, rising up out of the stadium."
—Pat Dye

Van Allen Plexico
We've always said we all probably got lung cancer at that game, but it was worth it.

John Ringer
Absolutely. And I still have that paper shaker. It's in a sealed plastic bag.

Van Allen Plexico
Oh, man. I'm so jealous. I had like five of them, because so many were available inside the stadium, and I had their sticks all decorated with orange and blue Sharpies to give the score, the date, all that. And they're all long-gone.

The game mattered so much to Auburn in a historical and emotional way, in addition to trying to win the state championship and a share of a third straight SEC championship. It meant a great deal to others, too, though. Alabama was undefeated and looking to play for the national championship in the Sugar Bowl. They had all the motivation they could ever need, right there. All they had to do was beat an 8-2 Auburn team that had lost to a team they'd beaten. Quite a bit rode on the outcome of this game.

"Finishing at 11-0 and having a chance for the national championship would be a fantastic accomplishment by a great group of men. We want to go to the Sugar Bowl. We want to go down to Auburn and take the decision out of somebody else's hands."
—Bill Curry, Alabama head coach

"We will have two people at Auburn, two at Knoxville watching Tennessee-Vanderbilt, and the rest at a television 'watch party' in our offices. If we have to break a tie, there will be number of factors that will influence us: the teams' overall records, their national rankings in the polls, how they've done in head-to-head competition, their strengths of schedules and the progress the teams have made over the season."
—Mickey Holmes, executive director, Sugar Bowl

"I have never been involved in a game that's as exciting as this one. You can put all the Super Bowls together and they're not as exciting as this."
—Bill Curry, Alabama head coach

Prior to kickoff, the Auburn players—who had spent the previous night in a hotel in Georgia—made the "Tiger Walk" to the stadium.

Before 1989, Tiger Walk was a nice little tradition. Fans would line both sides of the street and cheer for the players as they casually walked along to the stadium entrance.

But the sight that awaited those players on the morning of December 2, 1989, was unlike anything they'd experienced before.

Fans filled the streets, to the point that players and coaches could only move single-file through the teeming crowd, buffeted by well-wishers and encouragement every step of the way. It definitely got their attention. It reminded them—as if they needed any reminding—just how big and just how important this game was to the entire Auburn Family. And it changed the tradition of Tiger Walk forever. It would no longer be a "nice little gathering of fans." From that point on, Tiger Walk became one of Auburn's biggest and best-known traditions, and a cannot-miss event on game days.

"As the challenge of an undefeated Alabama football team finally arrived here - here, for the first time in 54 meetings over 97 years - the football players from Auburn University set out late this morning on their Tiger Walk.

"The ritual, a stroll of no more than three football fields in length through an adoring crowd from their home at Sewell Hall to Jordan-Hare Stadium, had been followed here before: onto Donahue Drive, a right turn onto Roosevelt Street, in single file because the crowds could not help but push close. But the Tiger Walk had never been quite like the one on this Crimson Tide morning."
—Malcolm Moran, NY Times

"We had to leave town that day. We had to go to a different state. We went to Georgia to stay the night and we came back. The Tiger Walk seemed like it took an hour to get from Sewell Hall to the stadium. When we got onto the field it was just awesome."
—John Wiley, Auburn defensive back

"Walking single file down the line in Tiger Walk. We'd never done that. It was just in the air that night."
—Corey Barlow, Auburn defensive back

"The fans, the look in their eyes, some people were crying with joy that we had gotten that game there finally, and what it meant to the Auburn people."
—Win Lyle, Auburn kicker

"The day of the game, and seeing the crowd for Tiger Walk, and going through Tiger Walk, it was over. The game was over that morning at Tiger Walk. It wouldn't have mattered who we played. If we played the Dallas Cowboys that day, they were going to be in for a run for their money."
—Stacey Danley, Auburn running back

"Wednesday was almost like game day. So many RVs, jam-packed. The Tiger Walk, it was like a tunnel. It was so tight. Tiger Walk was so pumped up. It was like a pep rally. I remember Coach Dye telling us, 'Keep it down, keep it down, not yet,' because we were ready."
—Ed King, Auburn offensive lineman

"I don't think there's no way to describe the feeling that football team must have gotten when they walked through that crowd to the stadium today. I'm sure that it must have resembled what went on the night the wall came down in Berlin. I mean, it was like they had been freed, and let out of bondage, just having this game at Auburn. I can't imagine what it must have done to our players, and the effect it must have had on their emotions."
—Pat Dye

After the Auburn players completed that monumental and historic Tiger Walk, the Alabama players arrived at Jordan-Hare—and they received quite the reception from the Auburn Family.

"Auburn fans naturally surrounded the (Alabama) buses and began chanting and hitting the sides of all the buses. As if it were choreographed, the buses began rocking back and forth, back and forth, back and forth as Auburn fans had totally engulfed them.

"Finally realizing that it was impossible to let the Bama players off at that spot, each bus had to individually pull into the stadium, unload, and back out before the next one could pull in. Because of my vantage point, I got to see the players' eyes when they stepped off. It was a deer-in-headlights look, if there was ever such a look."
—Rusty Robinson, Auburn athletic trainer, quoted in 2019 by Evan Woodbery

The two teams prepared to come onto the field for warm-ups. The way the Alabama players did it, though, was... *odd.*

Reynolds Wolf

Alabama, coming onto the field, came through—if memory serves—the south end zone, and they split in two and they paraded around the sidelines in this weird formation, as though they were giving the middle finger to the Auburn people. They came up each sideline and it was like they thought they owned the place.

They had this great quarterback, Hollingsworth, who seemed to do no wrong, and Bill Curry had these guys firing on all cylinders—but there was something about that day. You could feel it just wasn't going to be their day. Especially after Reggie Slack stepped up to drop a laser beam down the sidelines, hitting Alexander Wright, and I can still see Wright running to this day. And just the eruption! The party started then and never ended.

Van Allen Plexico

I remember that very clearly. The Alabama players emerged from their tunnel in pairs and proceeded to jog in formation all the way around the boundary of the field, two-by-two. It was so strange and I've never seen another team do it. I wasn't sure how we were supposed to take it. Ultimately it didn't work out too well for them.

John Ringer

We wanted Alabama to be good when we played them, but not *that* good. But they were. They were undefeated and no. 2

in the country. It was a really good Alabama team. A great defense. Excellent skill positions.

It was a game where, emotionally, the Auburn crowd was as ready as they have ever been for a game, and they were not going to be denied. They were not going to let the team falter. They were not going to let Alabama come into our stadium without knowing where they were and how we felt.

Van Allen Plexico

If they'd been coming in with the same record we had, and it looked like an even match up, sure. That would've been fine. Let's go out there and it's fifty-fifty and we will rely on our players being jacked up and our crowd making the difference and we'll win.

Instead, we had this juggernaut of a Tide team coming in. We'd wanted them to come to Auburn, but there was almost a tiny sense of, "Maybe this wasn't the best year to do this, after all!" It was kind of a feeling of, "Be careful of what you ask for!"

But, again, that just made it all the sweeter, as things played out. Getting a shot at knocking off an undefeated and national-championship-bound Alabama team is something Auburn fans and players always relish. See 2013! We simply didn't want to lose the first Iron Bowl played in Auburn. We in the crowd understood we had to energize ourselves and the team as best we could.

You could feel that outside the stadium before we went inside. The single word I hear most used when people describe that day is "electric." And it's true. Take the anticipation you had as a kid on Christmas Eve, when you knew the next day was Christmas and you were going to get some awesome presents. Then multiply it times a hundred. And then add in a nice dose of concern: After all this build-up, all it took to get the game moved here—what if things don't go our way? The Christmas analogy is more like, "I can't wait to get that big present! But—what if I get a lump of coal instead?"

We'd been waiting our whole lives to be on an equal footing with those guys from across the state. We'd been going to school with them, dealing with their fans, putting up with them thinking they were better than us, looking down at us, being condescending and arrogant towards us. We'd been waiting our whole lives to finally stick it to them. Beating them several times already in that decade had been great, but *this*...! This was making the bully come over to *our* house so we could take a club to him in our own living room. This was him coming to our house, only to have us take away his weapon and beat him down with it.

That being the case, there was an incredible electricity in the air, on the surface of your skin and in your mind that this could be the greatest moment any of us had ever seen as Auburn fans—or it could be an utter disaster. It was like we were floating over the edge of the blade and we didn't know which side we were going to come down on. It was just this incredible scene and an incredible feeling. I mean, people were running around yelling "War Eagle!" constantly and un-self-consciously, all morning long.

Back then, on game days, we students would try to be very nondescript. We would go to home games wearing colors that weren't orange-and-blue because, if you dressed like an Auburn fan, other students would say to you, "You look like you're from out of town." We tried to play it cool, usually.

But there was nothing about playing it cool on December 2, 1989. You let your orange-and-blue Auburn flag fly, metaphorically, very proudly, and everybody was yelling "War Eagle" and everybody was screaming and doing spontaneous cheers. I've never before or ever since seen anything like that. In terms of an experience as a fan, even being in Arizona in January 2011, about to play for the National Championship, it was not quite what this was like, because this was so *personal*. That trip to Glendale, Arizona, was profoundly important because we had never in our lifetimes had that experience. But that was still like a "business trip." December 2, 1989 wasn't a business trip. As CBS put it in their TV intro that day, "All week long it's been a celebration." It was so intensely personal. It was a family affair, all the way down. And it is just impossible to put into words what it felt like. You just had to be there.

306

John Ringer

I think you're doing a good job of it. I think usually, for home games, I would go to Tiger Walk. And we didn't that day, because we were at the stadium too early to go, but I talked to people who were there. My parents, other people who were at Tiger Walk said afterward, they said it was the most crowded and intense Tiger Walk that Auburn has ever had. It really was single-file for the players the whole way, because there were so many fans on that street. All those fans that wanted to tell them how they felt, and go kick Alabama's ass. Yeah.

The game was a back-and-forth game, and Alabama was really good that year. But the crowd was not going to sit down. They weren't going to be quiet. They weren't going to let the team falter. I think that was really important. The crowd was determined to do whatever they could do to lift the team up.

Van Allen Plexico

Yeah, absolutely. The crowd was utterly determined to insert itself into the drama and be a part of it and not just a witness.

John Ringer

Yes, and we did. A hundred percent. We were part of the outcome.

Van Allen Plexico

What did that game mean to you as an Auburn person that it took place at all, and that we got to be there?

John Ringer

I think it represented a change in the rivalry and how we saw each other. We joked earlier about how Legion Field was divided 50-50 but all the ushers were in Alabama hats and shirts. This was a huge change in how we perceived the rivalry, because we finally felt like we were on even footing. It felt like we had been fighting uphill for years, and now we were in a place where we were on even footing with Alabama. We had a great stadium. We had a great coach. We had a great team and a great crowd, and now Alabama would have to come to our stadium every other year, and we knew that gave us a better shot.

Van Allen Plexico

It changed the whole complexion of things. And it had been building for a while already. I mean, it's not like this was 1982 and Alabama had been winning every year, and then suddenly this happens and changes everything. We took the better part of a decade to build up to the point that, when that day finally came, when "it happened," we were a team, a program that was already on an even keel with Alabama. And this 1989 game was, in fact, our *fourth* win in a row over them.

So, did that change things? We were on a level playing field with Alabama after this game, right?

Reynolds Wolf

Well, we weren't quite yet. We should have been on a level playing field, but we weren't quite because you'll remember that the only way Alabama would agree to come to Jordan-Hare Stadium was if we played the 1991 game, our next home game in the series, back at Legion field—which was an absolute cesspool. The idea that we needed to go back up there and to play those guys there again two more times; are you kidding me?

Ah, but at the end of the day, it was well worth it. And it was Pat Dye. The guy who made it happen. I will always be grateful.

"The compromise was worked out between our lawyers, Alabama's lawyers, and the City of Birmingham's lawyers. And the City of Birmingham is the reason we ended up playing our home game in Legion Field one last time, in 1991. By all rights, that game should have been played in Auburn.

"Well, everybody had to prove a point, everybody had to win something. Birmingham felt we were obligated to play the game there every year. Alabama didn't want us to move it at all. We intended to move the game. So we compromised. We moved the

1989 game to Jordan-Hare Stadium...(but) we agreed to play one more home game in Legion Field in 1991. It was a fair compromise."
—Pat Dye, In the Arena

Van Allen Plexico

I don't think people now can fully appreciate how strange it was to see a bunch of Alabama fans walking around our campus that weekend, because you see them on our campus every two years nowadays. Back then, of course, there were *individuals* who would wear Alabama stuff on campus. We went to class with people that were Alabama fans who just happened to be going to school at Auburn, because they wanted a better education. But how weird was it to see the Alabama fan base descend *en masse* on the Auburn campus for the first time? Red t-shirts and hats everywhere?

John Ringer

It was weird. It was weird to hear their band play in our stadium. It was really strange to see their fans. I think that was it. In their minds, our campus and our stadium were too small. To them, it wasn't worth playing the game there. But I think, once they got to Auburn and saw the campus and experienced Jordan-Hare Stadium, it changed their perceptions a little bit.

Van Allen Plexico

Back then, Alabama was still playing their big home games in Legion Field. Bryant-Denny Stadium in Tuscaloosa wasn't seen as big enough or nice enough for them. Now compare Legion Field in 1989 to what Pat Dye had Jordan-Hare looking like during those years. For one thing, Jordan-Hare was bigger than any other stadium in the state. I don't know if people now realize this, but during the Eighties and well into the Nineties, Jordan-Hare was the biggest stadium in the state of Alabama. When it was full, it was "the fifth largest city in the state of Alabama," bigger than the city of Tuscaloosa! They had the hedges, the flower beds, everything looked nice and neat. The stadium had just been renovated and expanded with the East Upper Deck in 1987. So there was no competition. We had the biggest and the nicest stadium. And it just took away any credibility to them saying, "Oh, we can't go down there. We're too big a program to go play in that stadium." I mean, it was the biggest stadium in the state, bigger and nicer by far than yours, Alabama. You have no more excuses.

I remember, the week before the game, seeing on the roof of one of the ticket office buildings a hand-painted banner that said:

"It won't happen." —Ray Perkins, 1985.
"It happened." —Phi Kappa Tau

John Ringer
No, they had said for years, "It'll never happen." They threatened to end the series rather than come to Auburn and play us there.

People don't realize this but Auburn and Alabama haven't played anywhere near the same number of times as Auburn-Georgia, for example. The Auburn-Alabama rivalry was on hold from 1908 through 1947, because of a dispute about officiating, money, and where we were going to play; that kind of stuff. And the rivalry was so bitter, they couldn't agree on the fundamental rules about the games and how they were going to be played. It took the state legislature finally stepping in and making them play again. That meant we haven't played them nearly as many times as we've played teams like Georgia.

So, the precedent was there for the series to end over a disagreement like this. It wasn't beyond the realm of possibility.

In the end, of course, Alabama—in the form of Athletic Director Steve Sloan and Coach Bill Curry—conceded that they couldn't control where Auburn chose to play its home games. Today, the very idea that Alabama once thought they could tell us where to play seems laughable.

It was not laughable at all back then. Far from it.

"That (playing the game in Auburn) was by far more important than the outcome of the game. Just the fact that we were going to

310

play our home game at Auburn every other year was monumental to Auburn and our program."
—Pat Dye

December 2, 1989, therefore represented a kind of Independence Day for the Auburn Family. Complete with a battle, sixty minutes long, and with fireworks—fireworks on the football field.

Unfortunately, Alabama had brought a loaded team with them.

"Leading Alabama offensively has been Siran Stacy, who has run for 1,023 yards and 18 touchdowns, and Gary Hollingsworth, who has completed 178 of 290 passes for 2,039 yards and 12 touchdowns.

"Auburn (8-2-0) has succeeded mainly with its defense, which has given up only 9.7 points a game. Its offense has been led by Reggie Slack, who has completed 134 passes for 1,722 yards and 10 touchdowns."
—Thomas Rogers, NY Times

Auburn came out of the gate hot, scoring on their first possession. With the ball near midfield and facing third and five, Auburn's Reggie Slack threw a bomb deep to Alexander Wright for a 44-yard gain to the Alabama 7.

"Reggie Slack needing five yards on third down. He's going to throw long to Alexander Wright— Oh, a great catch over the shoulder inside the 10 and down at the seven yard line, as he beat Ephraim Thomas, who made the tackle at the 7. Reggie Slack threw a beautiful pass and Wright took it over his left shoulder as he raced down that eastern sideline."

"When Reggie Slack came to the line on 3rd and 5, he saw that Alabama was playing man to man in the secondary. They were in a blitz situation, they had Keith McCants coming toward the quarterback. Auburn's offensive line needs the credit. The pass protection was there."
—Jim Fyffe and Charlie Trotman, Auburn Network broadcast

James Joseph capped off the drive a few plays later, vaulting over the goal line from the full-house-backfield formation, and Auburn led, 7-0.

Two Auburn turnovers allowed Alabama to roar into the lead in the second quarter: freshman running back Darrell "Lectron" Williams fumbled a handoff from Reggie Slack on Auburn's second possession, and then Alabama star linebacker Keith McCants intercepted a tipped pass from Slack. Alabama's Gary Hollingsworth connected with Marco Battle for the touchdown, putting the Tide ahead at the half, 10-7.

Alabama's lead probably should have been larger, though. On two of the Tide's first three drives, they moved the ball inside the Auburn 10, only to settle for a measly 3 points in total. On their first trip there, Alabama attempted a fake off the field goal formation, but Auburn stopped them cold and turned the ball over on downs.

In the third quarter, Alabama moved the ball down the field, but their exceptional kicker, Philip Doyle, missed only his third field goal of the year. After that, Auburn established its offense at last, and put enough points on the board to win the game.

Reggie Slack found Shane Wasden in the open field and hit him for a 59-yard gain. The speedy receiver almost scored, but he was pulled down from behind by McCants.

"Shayne Wasden could run, now. He was a good player and could run, but to see that big man (McCants) go and get him? It was an unbelievable play."

—Dabo Swinney, Clemson head coach, and freshman receiver on the 1989 Alabama team

James Joseph punched it in, giving Auburn the lead again, at 14-10.

On the following Auburn possession, Slack directed another solid drive that ended with a Win Lyle field goal to put the Tigers up, 17-10.

The next time the Tigers had the ball, Slack again connected with Alexander Wright for a long gain, and then Stacey Danley ripped off a big run inside the Alabama 15. From there, Darrell "Lectron" Williams took a pitch from Slack and raced to the end zone, giving

Auburn a 24-10 lead as the fourth quarter got underway. The Auburn faithful were ecstatic.

On Alabama's next drive, Hollingsworth's pass was intercepted by Darrell Crawford on a controversial call where Crawford might not have had possession of the ball when he hit the ground. This, however, made up for an earlier call where the Tigers recovered an Alabama fumble that was whistled dead by the officials, when it shouldn't have been. Lyle kicked his second field goal of the game to push the lead to 27-10 with 9:36 to go.

Alabama finally responded, putting together a drive that ended with a Doyle field goal. Now it was closer, at 27-13, but the lead still felt safe.

It was not.

The Tide got the ball back and drove down the field. Hollingsworth capped it off by hitting Marco Battle for his second touchdown, pulling the Tide to within one score, at 27-20. But it had all taken too much time for Alabama. The clock revealed that only 1:49 remained in the game. Alabama attempted an onside kick, but Auburn recovered at the Tide 47. At that point, Pat Dye turned to Stacey Danley to work the clock. Danley ran three straight times for 32 yards total and two first downs, forcing Bill Curry to burn two timeouts.

"That was our philosophy. We're going to hit 'em in the mouth and hit 'em in the mouth and, in the fourth quarter, they'll start finding a way to miss you."
—*Stacey Danley, Auburn running back*

A couple of plays later, Win Lyle kicked his third field goal, making him 3-for-3 for the day, and putting the game out of reach.

"I don't need to tell you the magnitude of this Lyle field goal of 34 yards. Angle to the left, the ball will be placed down on the near side hash mark by Dickinson. There's the kick. The kick is away. Kick is Good!!! Auburn 30, Alabama 20. 33 seconds to go. Let the celebrating begin!"
—*Jim Fyffe, Auburn Network broadcast*

On the following possession, Auburn's Dennis Wallace intercepted Hollingsworth to seal the deal for good.

Both teams had over 400 yards of offense in the game. The difference was that the Tigers were able to score at the end of their drives. Alabama ended up paying the price for netting only 3 points out of their first two trips inside the Auburn 5; how big that failed first-quarter fake field goal loomed at the end.

"Final score here is Auburn 30, Alabama 20. The Tigers have captured a share of the SEC championship with the victory over archrival Alabama."
—Jim Fyffe, Auburn Network broadcast

Reggie Slack finished the game having completed 14 of 26 passes for 274 yards, with long completions of 44, 58 and 60 yards. He was not sacked during the game.

"Our offense was rebuilt in the Mississippi State game, and I think it has come a long way."
—Reggie Slack, Auburn quarterback

"It's not difficult to see or describe what happened today. We got beat by a better football team. We were pressing. We were struggling to do things that normally come easy for us."
—Bill Curry, Alabama head coach

Speedy Alexander Wright caught seven passes for 141 yards.

"We came in with the plan to throw it. We didn't care how good they were. We knew how good we were. And any receiver with a great quarterback, with great protection to give him time—he can get open and make some catches."
—Alexander Wright, Auburn wide receiver

"To me, he (Wright) is the difference in the ballgame. We felt like we could throw any way we wanted to throw on them, if we could protect Reggie."
—Pat Dye

"On a day when Alabama (10-1) most needed to justify its No. 2 ranking and add to its 12-game unbeaten streak, the Crimson Tide crumpled under the pressure of the nation's meanest and most intense intrastate grudge match.

"Since 1892, the Tigers had tried to persuade Alabama to visit the Auburn campus. Alabama, being Alabama, always said no.

"Auburn being Auburn, it didn't forget the annual slights. If anything, it used the bad blood, as thick as honey after a 97-year wait, to its considerable advantage."
—Gene Wojciechowski, LA Times

"Bo Jackson didn't get to play Alabama at home. Gregg Carr didn't get to play Alabama at home. Joe Cribbs. None of those guys. Pat Sullivan. We got to play Alabama at home. We couldn't lose that first game."
—Quentin Riggins, Auburn linebacker

"There was no way in hell we were going to lose that game. That's just the bottom line. Whatever it took. That was our motto that day: whatever it took."
—John Wiley, Auburn defensive back

"We were excited that we won, but I think there was a feeling of relief as much as there was being excited about winning the game. We were relieved that we were the first team that played Alabama in Auburn, and we won the game."
—Shayne Wasden, Auburn receiver

"It was a very emotional day. Coach Dye said earlier on that it would be the most emotional day in Auburn history, and he was right. It was."
—David Housel, former Auburn Athletic Director

"There will never be another 1989. In any discussion of the greatest Iron Bowls of all time, it stands alone, never to be approached, let alone equaled or surpassed, for reasons that eclipse the game itself. ...When it comes to changing the future, to changing the very nature of the game itself, Iron Bowls don't get any bigger than 1989."
—*Kevin Scarbinsky, longtime state of Alabama sports reporter*

After the game, Coach Dye told the players he'd watched them grow up and become men during the 1989 season. The team then learned their next game would be the Hall of Fame Bowl in Tampa, Florida.

"If we'd have grown up to be men a little earlier, maybe we would be going (to the Sugar Bowl). But we're thrilled to death to be going to the Hall of Fame Bowl in Tampa."
—*Pat Dye*

An Alabama team that had come to the Plains riding a long winning streak and eyeing Alabama's first national championship in a decade instead found themselves only one of three co-champions of the SEC, and only hoping to be spoilers as they faced Miami in New Orleans. Bill Curry understood that Tide fans weren't particularly interested in a group of players that "only" accomplished that much.

"They have done some things that are absolutely remarkable, and it would be wonderful if they could be recognized for them. I don't hold out high hopes for that. But that's life."
—*Bill Curry, Alabama head coach, on how Alabama fans would probably think of his players, after the game*

After losing that Sugar Bowl to the Hurricanes, this once-fearsome Alabama squad finished the season with the same won-loss record as Auburn, and three spots lower than the Tigers in the AP Poll.

Bill Curry immediately packed up and left Tuscaloosa for the University of Kentucky job.

John Ringer
There had been some concern before the game about what might happen at Toomer's Corner if Alabama won. People had vowed to fight to the death to defend the Toomer's trees from Alabama fans. Some said the Alabama fans were bringing red toilet paper to throw into our trees after the game. It didn't prove to be a problem that year, though. They cleared out of town quickly.

Van Allen Plexico
If there's one thing Alabama fans are good at, it's clearing out of a road opponent's stadium in the fourth quarter when they're losing. They know when to hit the on-ramp onto the highway. I don't think I saw *any* Alabama fans at Toomer's Corner.

That was the first time I can remember Toomer's Corner looking like a snowstorm from one end of College Street to the other. Up and down Magnolia, too. In the past, we'd roll the two big oaks. Maybe, if it was a *big* win, a couple of other trees would get it. But this time, it was just everywhere. If you stood still too long, *you* might get covered!

John Ringer
This time it seemed like the whole town was covered.

"I have never again or since seen that much toilet paper. Standing there in that crowd, it felt like January in New Hampshire. It was just so white!"
—Jerry Romine, Auburn fan, quoted in 2019 by Evan Woodbery

John Ringer
The only other thing I want to say about this game is, there was a player who had one of the best nicknames of any Auburn player on this team. There was a young running back that got a bunch of playing time down the stretch and made a

bunch of big plays against Georgia and Alabama, and that was Darryl "Lectron" Williams.

"There were many stars today. This was won as part of a team effort. But perhaps the icing on the cake was Auburn's final touchdown by the freshman from Pritchard, Alabama, Darryl 'Lectron' Williams."

(Recording plays) "Second and 9 at the Bama 12. One running back is 'Lectron' Williams, behind Reggie Slack. He'll toss it to Williams to the short side! He's at the 10! He's at the 5! He's in! Touchdown Auburn!"

—Jim Fyffe, Auburn Network broadcast

"To Auburn fans, playing the Iron Bowl in our stadium was somehow tangible proof that we were as good, as important, as the school in Tuscaloosa. I will never forget the euphoria of that day. You hear the term 'emotional high' all the time. The 1989 Iron Bowl was the ultimate emotional high for the Auburn family."

—Laura Spencer, Auburn fan and 1989 graduate, quoted in 2019 by Evan Woodbery

"Auburn goes on to a 30-20 victory over the Alabama Crimson Tide. Hello again, everybody, I'm Jim Fyffe with Charlie Trotman, back at Jordan-Hare Stadium—the scene of the first on-campus game between the two arch-rivals after 54 years.

"Second-ranked Alabama came in undefeated today for the first time, and the Auburn Tigers came back from a 10-7 halftime deficit, to win it in the second half impressively 30 to 20, over their arch rivals. Charlie, I don't think a single Auburn fan has left this stadium."

"Well, it is definitely a jubilant atmosphere, Jim, and the fans, I think first of all, were excited to have Alabama here, playing in Auburn for the first time and to play this well against an Alabama team that is truly outstanding. It has so many weapons I think it really has excited this crowd, and they're showing their appreciation for the effort today because they're still in the stands cheering, and they want the players and the coaches and the administration,

everybody, to know that they appreciate what is taking place at Auburn."

"What a victory this is. This ranks right up there with the biggest of all."

—Jim Fyffe and Charlie Trotman, Auburn Network broadcast

"Some Auburn people were openly fearful as the season unfolded. Alabama was rolling and Auburn was struggling. But Saturday, supercharged by the noise, the emotion that filled the air, Auburn did the rolling."

—Phillip Marshall, Montgomery Advertiser

"One for the ages—the first ever at Auburn yesterday, and Auburn beat Alabama 30-20 and Pat Dye took his place alongside Neyland and Bryant and Dooley with three straight conference championships."

"Oh, I'm not believing what I just looked at on the screen. It was amazing. There's some things about life that you just can't... It's been 50 years since there were three champions in the Southeastern Conference. The last year was 1939. Our stadium is 50 years old, (built in 1939). I'm 50 years old and I just looked at the screen and the score was 30-20 - a total of 50! I mean, it's absolutely amazing. Maybe Alabama didn't have a chance after all."

"And Auburn played in the Cotton Bowl and the Sugar Bowl 50th anniversaries."

—Phil Snow and Pat Dye, The Auburn Football Review, December 3, 1989

"But it has been a great year for our football team. The things that this football team has gone through—I talked about it a little bit in the dressing room, but—it's been one of the most satisfying years that I have ever seen.

"You know I got a kick out of fussing at our people through the course of the year, the way they got on our team, but they brought it home yesterday. I can be in coaching the rest of my life and I won't ever witness anything like yesterday. And anybody that was on that field that was a player from Auburn or a player from Alabama—you

know you can talk about a home field advantage if you want to, but what happened yesterday at Auburn lifted our players to another level, and and there's no question that our fans had a lot to do with the outcome of the ball game yesterday."
—Pat Dye, The Auburn Football Review, December 3, 1989

After the Iron Bowl, Alabama dropped from 2 to 7 in the AP Poll, with 1-loss Tennessee at 8 and 2-loss Auburn at 9. Despite losing the Iron Bowl, Alabama still received the invitation to play in the Sugar Bowl against Miami, due to their having the highest ranking of the three. (There was no official tie-breaker for such a scenario within the conference—all three teams were considered equal co-champions.) Tennessee would play Arkansas in the Cotton Bowl, and Auburn would play Ohio State in the Hall of Fame Bowl in Tampa.

Van Allen Plexico

I always like to point out that the "First Time Ever" Iron Bowl was Auburn's last football game played in the decade of the 1980s. I think that's fitting.

Our bowl game was played on January 1, 1990, and it was the last game for a lot of the players that had made the late Eighties so huge for Auburn.

Our players were calling it the "fame game," and we played Ohio State, coached by John Cooper. It's best remembered for the incredible lick one of the Buckeyes put on Stacey Danley—and how Auburn responded after that.

"Slack throws the quick pass—and there is the biggest hit maybe of the 1989-90 bowl season. Danley down as he was struck by Zack Dumas.

"Zack Dumas. A fellow that came to this university as a running back, and said, 'You know, I don't like to get hit, what I like to do is hit people,' and he put a knockout blow on Danley that time. Hardest tackle I've seen in years. ... Just about the time that ball hits his hands, Dumas just unloads on him."
—NBC TV commentary

John Ringer
I remember that hit. It was just gigantic.

Van Allen Plexico
They floored him. Pat Dye told Danley to get up and run off the field. Danley I think said later that he didn't know who he was or where he was, but he got up and ran off the field because we didn't want to look bad in front of the Ohio State players.

"Auburn tailback Stacey Danley...couldn't see what 52,535 others could. Ohio State defensive back Zack Dumas was going to play the role of a speeding Mack truck. And Danley was going to be Dumas' road kill. About the time the ball reached Danley, Dumas placed a square lick under his chin, lifting Danley into the air and backward on his head. With the Buckeyes winning the game on the scoreboard (14-3) and winning the battle of most impressive hits, it seemed as if Auburn's hopes collapsed with Danley to the turf.

"But Auburn, instead of playing dead, turned the moment into its favor and roared to life for a 31-14 victory here Monday in the Hall of Fame Bowl at Tampa Stadium."
—Mike Easterling, Montgomery Advertiser

"It woke us up. We were all looking around at each other, and we knew we didn't want to get embarrassed on national TV. We knew we couldn't let it go on."
—John Hudson, Auburn center

"Everybody was telling me it got them mad. And it made me mad. I came back strong after being unconscious against Alabama two years ago. I wanted to come back strong today. If I can get the team fired up, I'll give up my body. But I would just as soon leave that out of the game plan."
—Stacy Danley, Auburn running back

Reggie Slack hit Greg Taylor with the first of his two touchdowns just before halftime, cutting the Buckeyes' lead to 14-10. Ohio State would not score again. The Tigers stormed back in the second half, racking up three more unanswered touchdowns, and won, 31-14.

Slack finished with 16 completions in 22 attempts for 141 yards. He passed for three touchdowns and ran for another. He took home the game's Most Valuable Player award in his final outing as an Auburn Tiger.

"He's (Slack) up there with all the big quarterbacks we've played against this season. It's hard to make a comparison. Auburn played well in the second half. You've got to give them credit. They won today, but I'm not going to concede that they are better."
—Bo Pelini, Ohio State defensive back and future Nebraska head coach

"I'm proud of Reggie Slack. He's had a fine two-year career as the starter. Reggie did more personally this year than any quarterback that I can remember at Auburn. He carried this team when we were struggling offensively.

"Reggie, for two years, was probably better than any at Auburn. I think he's probably the best we've had."
—Pat Dye

Meanwhile, a small footnote in the same *Montgomery Advertiser* issue that covered the Hall of Fame Bowl also mentioned the recruitment of a "highly-sought quarterback from Naples, Florida" who had "strong ties to Auburn."

"Before Florida hired Steve Spurrier, Auburn was considered the leader for (Terry) Dean, who passed for 1,400 yards as a (high school) senior. All of that changed when the Gators hired Spurrier Saturday."
"'Right now, Florida is my No. 1 choice,' Dean said... (and) added that Florida wouldn't have been among his top five schools if Florida hadn't hired Spurrier."
—Montgomery Advertiser, Jan. 2, 1990

One can't help but wonder what Terry Dean could've accomplished as an Auburn quarterback, playing between 1990 and 1994, for Pat Dye and Terry Bowden—and challenging Stan White and Patrick Nix for the starting job. At Florida he certainly had his highs and his lows, with many of the lows coming at the hands of the Auburn defense.

Watch this space—we will see the name "Terry Dean" again!

Van Allen Plexico
During the NBC broadcast of the Hall of Fame Bowl, a TV reporter went up into the audience and interviewed Twilita Ramsey, wife of Auburn defensive back Eric Ramsey. We knew little about him and nothing about his wife at that point.

In the brief interview, Twilita talked about her son being named Eric Ahmad Rashad Ramsey. Ahmad Rashad, the famous Vikings receiver, was doing the color commentary on the game, which is why they brought it up and did the interview in the first place. That was our first experience with Mrs. Ramsey, but it would not be our last.

1990

Van Allen Plexico
We started the Nineties off by beating Ohio State but, after that, unfortunately, the cracks in the program started to show, the dam started leaking a little bit. The following season, 1990, was still respectable. In the preseason, it might have been *Sporting News* that even had us ranked No. 1 in the country. In the AP Poll, we were no. 3 in the pre-season and rose as high as no. 2 in week 3. It all started out so well, and then things kind of fell apart.

When you look back at 1990 now, what do you think of it?

John Ringer
When I look back at 1990, I think about the beginning of the end of the Dye era, the start of the downhill part of the Dye era.

Two games come to mind from the 1990 season, and they're both losses.

One was the game at Florida. Steve Spurrier was the brand-new Florida coach. Good gosh. We played them in Gainesville. I was with my wife's family and I had to go over to somebody else's house because they didn't have ESPN. Auburn had an old school SEC defense with a bunch of bigger, heavier, slower guys. This was the very first kind of iteration of the Spurrier "Fun and Gun" offense. In modern terms it was like a Big 12 kind of offense against a bigger, older, slower defense, and they absolutely shredded us in that game. It was a complete annihilation. It was 48-7, and honestly it didn't feel *that* close from an Auburn fan perspective, you know? And that was when we were like, "Wow—who is this guy Spurrier?" It looked like the future of football against the past of football, and we were the past.

We came back from that game and the next week, after getting just curb-stomped at Florida, we played Southern Miss with a quarterback named Brett Favre. Maybe you've heard of him. They had a wide receiver named Michael Jackson who was a high draft pick, and a running back named Tony Smith, who got drafted by the Falcons. That year, 1990, Southern Miss beat both Auburn and Alabama with Favre at quarterback. We lost to them, 13-12. It was one of the most frustrating games I can remember, but they had some really good players. Plus, I think we were kind of in a shell shocked, hungover state from that Florida ass-kicking we'd taken the week before.

Van Allen Plexico

I look at 1990 and it really is a tale of two seasons. I think it's a watershed moment for Coach Dye and for our program, because, going into it, we thought, "Hey, good times! Just keep on rolling. Right? We had a great 1986, '87, '88, '89, and we thought we were going to keep it rolling, baby. Let it ride.

We came out and had big wins and against Cal State-Fullerton and Ole Miss. We moved up to no. 2 in the country in the AP Poll.

Then No. 5 Tennessee came to town.

324

Stan White, by Jarrod Alberich

That game stands out in my mind because we had to fight back from a deep deficit. This was Stan White as a freshman, our starter that year. He'd been chosen as a freshman to start over several older players, and he would go on to be the only four-year starting quarterback in Auburn history. To this day that's still true.

Tennessee dominated the game early, kicking two field goals and scoring a touchdown behind the passing of Andy Kelly to future NFL star Alvin Harper, along with miscues by Auburn that gave the Vols a short field twice in the first quarter. Tennessee failed on a two-point conversion, but added another touchdown before halftime. This one came after the Vols defense returned a James Joseph fumble to the Auburn 5 yard line.

Jim Von Wyl hit a 36-yard field goal just before halftime, but the damage seemingly had been done by then. Three catastrophic mistakes by the Tigers had directly resulted in 13 of Tennessee's points, and they led 19-3 at the half.

Auburn came out more composed in the second half, and the two teams stifled one another until the 5:35 mark, when Greg Taylor caught a 34-yard touchdown pass from Stan White. The 2-point conversion failed, but the Tigers were slowly pulling themselves back into it, at 19-9.

Early in the fourth quarter, Auburn looked to have made a huge play when they blocked a Tennessee field goal—but Dennis Wallace was called for roughing the kicker, giving the Vols the ball deep in Auburn territory. They capitalized with a touchdown, and now the lead was 26-9 with only fourteen minutes to go.

Von Wyl added another field goal at the 11:47 mark, making the score 26-12. It still seemed like too much ground to make up, in too little time, but Stan White kept passing, and Greg Taylor and company kept making catches.

Just three minutes later, Dale Overton caught a 13-yard pass from White for a touchdown. Suddenly Auburn was only down one score, at 26-19. But Tennessee ran the clock effectively, and Auburn didn't get the ball back until only two minutes remained in the game. Starting at the UT 43, White drove the Tigers down the field and hit Greg Taylor with another touchdown. Coach Dye opted to go for the extra point, keeping in mind that the loser of the Auburn-Tennessee game usually didn't figure into the conference championship in December. Unexpectedly, almost inexplicably, the score was tied at 26-26.

"The best chance we had of winning it was to tie the game and force their hand. If they throw incomplete passes, we get the ball at midfield with a minute and a timeout left."
—Pat Dye

Indeed, the game wasn't over yet. Unfortunately, Tennessee found some offense for the first time in the fourth quarter and moved the ball to the Auburn 44. A late hit penalty on the Auburn defense, tacked onto a completed pass from Kelly to Harper, moved the ball all the way down to the Tigers' 14 yard line. The Vols' kicker, Greg Burke, came out to attempt the last-second, game-winning field goal.

He missed, wide left. The game was over, with the score 26-26.

"We had put ourselves in a position to win at the end of the game. It's disappointing, to say the least, that the kick didn't go."
—Andy Kelly, Tennessee quarterback

"We should have won this one. It hurts to play yourselves into a position to win and then have it slip away."
—Tony Thompson, Tennessee running back

Stan White's passing statistics for this game are of particular note, as they don't much sound like what you'd expect from an Auburn quarterback in the Pat Dye era. White—a freshman, no less—attempted a whopping 58 passes, completing 30 of them for 338 yards and 3 touchdowns.

Van Allen Plexico

It seemed like we tied Tennessee every other year back then.

I'll never forget how the Vols came down the field at the end and had a chance to kick a field goal to win. But the kicker missed, and his own players and fans started throwing stuff at him. I watched it happen. If you watch a recording of the end of that game, you can clearly see crumpled-up paper cups bouncing off his helmet as he leaves the field.

This one felt like a win, though. It's interesting how the circumstances at the end usually determined whether a tie felt good or bad, back then. This one was about as positive of a tie as I can imagine, considering how far down we'd been with less than a quarter remaining.

The following week, Auburn faced Louisiana Tech in a game that came within a whisker of being a loss for the Tigers.

An oddly sluggish Auburn found itself tied with the Bulldogs at the half, 7-7. A couple of Jim Von Wyl field goals gave the Tigers a 13-7 lead going into the fourth quarter, and Tigers fans believed that just maybe they could start to breathe again.

But then Tech drove down the field and punched in a touchdown to take the lead at 14-13 with less than five minutes remaining. To borrow a phrase from Jim Fyffe, Auburn's backs were to the wall and their feet were to the fire.

Stan White responded. His passing accounted for every yard of offense on the final drive. He took the Tigers 74 yards in 12 plays, setting up Jim Von Wyl at the Bulldogs' 17 with three seconds remaining. Von Wyl nailed the kick and the Tigers had escaped, 16-14, over an absolutely devastated Louisiana Tech team.

"When I saw it (the kick) go through, I felt like I had been shot."
—Myron Baker, Louisiana Tech linebacker, after the game

There were two notable takeaways from this game: One, this AU squad could play very well indeed, but they could also play remarkably poorly at times—and they very much depended on the passing arm of freshman Stan White. Two, Jim Von Wyl could be counted on to make a big kick in a clutch situation. That fact would prove tremendously important just a couple of weeks later.

After that win over Louisiana Tech, followed by a comfortable 56-6 romp over Vanderbilt, Auburn found itself at 4-0-1 and ranked no. 5 in the country in the AP Poll on October 20. That was the day the seventh-ranked Florida State Seminoles came to Jordan-Hare for the second game of what was supposed to be a ten-year series, but what turned out to be the last battle between those two old foes for twenty-four years.

John Ringer

Florida State came to play Auburn in another night game on ESPN, in Auburn. And we had a great crowd, very fired-up. We hadn't beaten them since 1985—we'd lost three straight to them. We had all these bitter feelings towards them from the last few games; the game where they crushed us in Jordan-Hare, and then the Sugar Bowl and the game in Tallahassee. So we had a lot of strong feelings toward Florida State and we really wanted to beat them.

The 1990 Florida State game had the feel of the last game in a seven-game championship series that was tied, 3-3. Auburn had won close games in 1983 and 1984 before blowing out the Noles in 1985. FSU had blown Auburn out in 1987 before winning close games in 1988 and 1989. The balance was perfectly divided between the two programs, and it felt that way to the fans. With the series ending, the 1990 "rubber game" would decide the overall winner between two schools that had risen to prominence in the previous decade and sought to continue that dominance on into the Nineties.

The game was tough, hard-fought, and low-scoring, at least for a while. Auburn took an early 7-0 lead with the only points scored in the first quarter, on a 5-yard run by fullback Tony Richardson.

Florida State surged into the lead in the second quarter with a field goal and then a touchdown run by Edgar Bennett. The field goal came after an Auburn turnover—an FSU interception of a Stan White pass in Tigers territory—very similar to the way the first half against Tennessee had gone. FSU added another touchdown with 1:40 to go in the half, on a long catch and run by Amp Lee, the young running back who had bedeviled Auburn down in Tallahassee the previous season. A close contest had become a double-digit lead for the Seminoles at halftime, 17-7.

As also happened with Tennessee, however, Auburn saved their offensive punch for the second half. After most of the third quarter went by with no scores, a run by Darrell "Lectron" Williams set up Jim Von Wyl for a 37-yard field goal to bring the Tigers to within a touchdown, at 17-10, as the third quarter wound down. That would represent all the scoring in the game for a while. Finally, with 3:47 to go, Stacy Danley found the end zone for Auburn and leveled the score at 17-17.

Pat Dye opted to kick the extra point, figuring he had enough time to get the ball back and score again. Florida State, of course, had other ideas, and began to drive. But as the Noles reached the Auburn side of the field with just over a minute remaining, the Tiger defense clamped down and forced them into a fourth down situation. It was just slightly too far for a field goal, so Bobby Bowden opted to go for the first down. What happened next totally changed the momentum of the game.

"Fourth and five-and-a-half at the Auburn 37. 1:10 to play. We're tied at 17 apiece. Everybody is on their feet in the stadium. 10-12,000 for Florida State. The rest of them for Auburn. This game is a long way from being over with still 1:10 to play, but Auburn's task now is to stop this potent FSU attack. Lining up with Casey Weldon at quarterback, slot formation on the near side, ball on the left side, over the ball is Robbie Baker, the center. Weldon reaches under, takes the snap. Back to throw is Weldon. Weldon chased out of the pocket! He is hit! He stumbles, he falls down! Deep in his own territory! Back at the (FSU) 41 yard line!"

"Jim, the big thing is that Auburn is now only one first down away from their own field goal attempt!"
—Jim Fyffe and Charlie Trotman, Auburn Network broadcast

Van Allen Plexico

We scored late to make it 17-17 and this looked to be another one of Pat Dye's infamous ties. We'd already tied once that season, against Tennessee, so we could have actually had two ties in our first six games. Tennessee *did* do that, that season, tying us and Colorado in their first five games. And we remember our two ties in 1987—one of them against Tennessee.

Coach Dye said he went for the extra point on that last touchdown against FSU because he felt like we could get the ball back and score. When I heard that later, my reaction at the time was: Well, what difference does it make if we're behind by one or if we're tied? I later learned his reasoning. He was thinking a tie score would cause FSU to take more chances on offense and make themselves more vulnerable to turnovers, or at least to throwing the ball and stopping the clock, rather than just running it out. That makes sense.

Florida State got over to our side of the field in the waning moments, and it looked like they were going to kick a field goal to beat us. But we held them and made them go for it on fourth down. Their quarterback, Weldon, dropped back, and Ricky Sutton came blasting up the middle and got pressure on him. As he tried to get away from Sutton, he seemed to trip over his own feet and stumbled backward like another ten yards. He started that play at Auburn's 37 and ended it at Florida State's 41.

John Ringer
He lost about 20 yards on fourth down and gave us the ball on their side of the field. It was great.

Van Allen Plexico
And it seemed like he barely even got touched. Give Sutton the credit, but Weldon basically sacked himself for a huge loss as our guys chased him around. He was trying to get away and he stumbled and he just kept stumbling and stumbling and stumbling, and then finally hit the ground. And I remember Jim Fyffe going crazy, because now we had the chance to kick the field goal. But first we needed a few more yards to get in Von Wyl's range.

The Tigers were unable to gain much on the first three downs, with FSU linebacker Marvin Jones stuffing the draw play on third down. Now Auburn faced a fourth down, still too far away for a field goal attempt. Pat Dye yelled and waved his arms at Pat Sullivan on the sideline, as the old quarterback dialed up a last-gasp play for the current quarterback.

"Fourth down, eight yards to go. Stan White, in from the sidelines, has called his play and here's that double wing. Joseph is

the setback. All or nothing here for White. Throws over the middle. Great catch over the middle to the 20! First down Auburn, with 31 seconds to go!"

"Great catch by Herb Casey! Great throw by Stan White! Pressure throw, great protection Jim! Give credit to the offensive line, nobody in his face."
—Jim Fyffe and Charlie Trotman, Auburn Network broadcast

Herbert "the Weapon" Casey had snagged a smooth-as-silk pass from White across the middle. With the ball now on the FSU 28 yard line, and only three seconds remaining, the Tigers turned to steady and dependable Jim Von Wyl.

"They'll put the tee down at about the 28. So it'll be a 38 yard attempt. He made a 37-yarder earlier. He has kicked from 48 yards. The ball is about 6 or 8 yards in from the right hash mark, there is a crosswind from right to left. Dickenson waits, there's a snap, the kick is away, by Von Wyl—the kick is GOOOOD! IT'S GOOOOD! IT'S GOOOOD! Von Wyl! Two seconds to go! 20-17! How about that kid from Akron, Ohio!"
—Jim Fyffe, Auburn Network broadcast

Florida State players on the sideline pounded their helmets on the ground in frustration and disgust. Auburn players danced and hugged. The Jordan-Hare Stadium crowd exploded.

Van Allen Plexico

Jim Von Wyl came out and hit that field goal to beat them, 20-17, ending three years of frustration. It felt very much like the 1987 Florida game where we had lost to them three years in a row and finally got the big revenge. This time, though, it was a last-second finish—much more dramatic.

Right after the end, you and I and our friends were celebrating so hard, we fell down several rows of bleachers together! We were all hugging each other at once, in a massive scrum, all jumping up and down, and we all together fell down two or three steps. We were all losing our minds and losing our balance at the same time. Since we were all in a big scrum together, though, it didn't matter; we just kind of fell down a couple of steps and bounced off the people below us.

It was an amazing, incredible game and it really ended up being the highlight, I think, of that season.

John Ringer

It was a great crowd and the team played very well that night. And I just remember at the end of that game, the Auburn fans did the tomahawk chop back at the Florida State fans and they ran out of that stadium so fast. We were so mad at them.

Van Allen Plexico

They were scandalized that we would even do that. They wrote letters to the editor of the *Plainsman* the next week, basically saying, "We were worried for our safety—those horrible Auburn fans were doing the tomahawk chop back at us!" FSU fans discovered it's not fun having the tomahawk chop done at you. Well, no kidding. You show bad sportsmanship to your opponent for three straight games, and then you're shocked and outraged when they get you back for it. And they were all clutching their pearls, all riled up about it. And we were like, "Join the SEC and you'll get this every week, you bunch of ninnies."

John Ringer

Their chant was so freaking annoying. It was 1990, and they had won the last three games against us, and we'd had to just sit there and endure it for game after game after game. And at the end of this one, when we won, we just wanted a way to stick it to them, to stick it back at them. So the whole stadium did it back at them, like "Naa naa, you're nothing. Here's your chant." And it was great. It was a really fun time.

The 1990 Florida State game was Pat Dye's final win over a top-ten-ranked team.

After seven games, Auburn stood at 6-0-1, with a huge win over FSU in their pockets. The Tigers jumped up three spots in the AP Poll to no. 2 in the country. The 1990 season looked to be the one

Auburn fans had been waiting for—the one where everything finally came together. Pat Dye looked like a genius for coming back to tie Tennessee in week three. The Seminoles and the Vols had been the two teams to do Auburn the most damage the year before, as well as in previous seasons in the late Eighties. With both of those games in the rear-view mirror now, and neither of them a loss, surely the Tigers could go on to beat everyone else on their schedule—right?

Things began to take a concerning turn the very next week, though, as they barely escaped a tight, 17-16 contest before 39,000 fans in Starkville, Mississippi. The Bulldogs scored a touchdown with 2:33 remaining to pull within one point of Auburn, but linebacker Darrel Crawford preserved the win by blocking the extra point attempt. The warning signs were there, but most fans blamed it on a let-down after the FSU game, or were still riding high from the outcome of that game, and barely noticed—or noticed that Auburn dropped to no. 4 in the AP Poll.

The following Saturday, Auburn headed down to Gainesville to play no. 15 Florida, led by their new head coach, Steve Spurrier. Surely, Auburn fans thought, the Tiger team that beat FSU would show up again to take down the Gators.

Instead, that was when the world came crashing down for the 1990 Auburn Tigers. The game became the perfect representation of the 1980s meeting the 1990s, and the SEC would never be the same again.

Van Allen Plexico

It was my last quarter at Auburn; I graduated in December. I rode down with some friends to the game. I recall the driver got pulled over and ticketed for speeding on the way—which should've served as some kind of warning for what lay ahead. The Gators sped all over us.

We were sitting so far down in the stands that you could barely see the field. It's a crowned field and the entire stadium sits low down in the ground. We were on the bottom row with the cheerleaders and the War Eagle Girls and Plainsmen. We just barely saw Stan throw that first touchdown to Herbert "the Weapon" Casey, to go up 7-0. After that it was literally all Florida—a 48-point shellacking.

Before that Florida game, we saw Steve Spurrier at Florida as an interesting new addition to the SEC, doing some innovative things—but not a juggernaut; not invincible. After that game, we realized we were likely going to be struggling against him for a long time to come. Bear Bryant had always said that Florida would be a monster if they could ever get the right coach that could recruit and then go out on the field and take advantage of the state's great athletes. Before the Nineties and Spurrier, they'd never even won the SEC! Things were about to change in a huge way.

As you said earlier, John, we came home from Gainesville with a bad hangover from that drubbing, and went right out and lost the next week to Southern Miss with Brett Favre. Suddenly we'd gone from no. 2 in the country, 6-0-1, to 6-2-1 and barely in the Top 25, at no. 24. And we still had to play Georgia and Alabama. It was stunning and demoralizing.

Any win over Georgia can go a long way toward reviving the emotions of an Auburn football team. The Tigers did beat Georgia that year, and beat them badly, 33-10. Suddenly the Tigers felt a little bit better about themselves again.

Georgia's loss marked its fourth straight in the series with Auburn. The beat-down began on the first play of the game, when strong safety Dennis Wallace intercepted Georgia quarterback Greg Talley, setting up Auburn's first touchdown. The Bulldogs managed only a measly 41 yards of offense in the entire first half, and trailed 16-0 before they finally crossed midfield.

With the win, and despite the loss to Florida and tie with Tennessee, Auburn headed into the Iron Bowl in sole possession of first place in the SEC. Because Florida was still on probation and ineligible for the conference title, all the Tigers needed in order to clinch a fourth consecutive SEC championship was a win over Alabama in Birmingham. It was a scenario very reminiscent of 1984—and it would play out in a very similar fashion to that year.

"That was the first thing we said when we came through the door (after the game). We whipped Georgia. Now we've got to go whip the Tide."
—Jason Merchant, Auburn linebacker

"It will be the biggest game of our lives. If we can beat Alabama, we will win our fourth straight SEC championship and it will make everyone forget about Florida and Southern Miss."
—*Dennis Wallace, Auburn strong safety*

Unfortunately, that 1990 Iron Bowl didn't work out the way the players hoped and expected it would.

Alabama, under first-year head coach Gene Stallings, had begun the season 0-3, a situation absolutely unthinkable for Tide fans. But then they'd corrected their course and scored a big, 9-6 win in Knoxville over no. 3 Tennessee to gather momentum for the second half of the season. They came into the Iron Bowl on a three-game win streak, with their defense playing lights-out.

Alabama led 10-0 late in the second half, but Stan White connected with James Joseph on a touchdown pass to pull within 3, at 10-7. Alas, those would be the only points the Tigers could manage that day. Two Phillip Doyle field goals pushed the Tide's lead out to 16-7, which turned out to be the final score.

"The past three or four years, things have just been going our way. Today, they just fell their way. It was a defensive battle. You can't really put it on any one thing. There were a lot of factors.

"It's going to be hard (to be fired up for the Peach Bowl), but we've got a lot of strong guys on this team capable of bouncing back."
—*Darrel Crawford, Auburn linebacker*

"We're excited about going to Atlanta, I can assure you of that. We're going to try to make it the best bowl game of the season."
—*Pat Dye*

Tennessee, meanwhile, ended up winning the SEC at 5-1-1, and went to the Sugar Bowl to play Virginia.

One thing included among the game reports on the 1990 Iron Bowl was a brief note about Pat Dye having appointments for medical tests at UAB Medical Center in Birmingham on the following Monday and Tuesday. It is described as "because of stomach problems."

David Housel in the report says "It's a routine thing. There are no serious problems."

In May of 1991, Coach Dye would undergo a three-hour operation that marked the beginning of his coping with hemochromatosis, a condition that caused an excess of iron in his blood. Following the operation, he was told he would have to donate 200 pints of blood over the ensuing three years, to reduce the amount of iron in his system.

Van Allen Plexico

Auburn ended up settling for the Peach Bowl in Atlanta, and a date with an unusually good Indiana team. It wasn't quite what we'd had in mind after coming back to tie Tennessee and beat Florida State! Because the Peach Bowl in 1990 wasn't what the Peach Bowl is today.

John Ringer

No. It was a very minor bowl game. And the Georgia Dome wasn't there yet. It was played in the old Atlanta-Fulton County Stadium, and it was a muddy and rainy outdoor game in Atlanta in December.

Indiana had a really good running back, Anthony Thompson. Thompson was one of the leading rushers in college football history at the time. We beat them but it was not a great game. Stacy Danley and Greg Taylor didn't play. Stan White ran for two touchdowns. Herbert "the Weapon" Casey had a big game at receiver, including converting a third-and-ten on the final drive, taking the ball into Indiana territory.

We got right down to the Hoosier goal line with just a few seconds to go.

"Indiana leads Auburn 23-20 with 43 seconds left in the 23rd Peach Bowl game. And Auburn's got the ball one foot away from a possible victory. Well, anybody who thinks that Pat Dye will go for the tie—he's not going for the tie, he is going for the win."
—Jim Fyffe, Auburn Network broadcast

"We knew Pat Dye's history of going for ties. We were hoping they would go for a field goal."
—Trent Green, Indiana quarterback

Stan White ran a bootleg and got into the end zone and the Tigers pulled out the tough victory, 27-23.

He had a good game that day, throwing for 351 yards on 31 completions in 48 attempts.

"This will never make right of the season that got away, but for a year Auburn will stand as champion of the Peach Bowl, whatever that may mean to a War Eagle from Demopolis, and Pat Dye remains a coach who has never lost to a Big Ten team."
—Furman Bisher, Atlanta Journal and Constitution

1991

Van Allen Plexico

Some people describe the Pat Dye era as basically ending after 1990, and say the FSU game was his last great win. It was his final win over a top ten-ranked team.

I don't have a whole lot to say about 1991 and 1992. The highlight of 1991 was going to Texas on September 21, ranked 13, and beating them, 14-10. Joe Frazier at running back had a good game, as I recall. Even so, it wasn't a very good Texas team; they were unranked and ended up finishing 5-6, like us.

We lost to fifth-ranked Tennessee, and we lost to Brett Favre's Southern Miss again. Spurrier's sixth-ranked Florida killed us at home. We ended the season 2-6 after beating Texas. The only wins came over Vanderbilt and Southwestern Louisiana—and we almost lost to Vandy. The season mercifully ended with another low-scoring loss to Alabama in Legion Field.

On October 26, 1991, Auburn played Mississippi State in Jordan-Hare Stadium. The Tigers came into that game unranked. It marked the first time Auburn had been unranked in the AP Poll since the end of the 1985 season—a *six-year span*. It was only the second time they were unranked since the day they played and upset Alabama in the "Bo Over the Top" game in 1982.

John Ringer

We had the First Time Ever Iron Bowl in 1989, so obviously we'd started the home-and-home series with Alabama, the back-and-forth arrangement. But Auburn had to give away the 1991 home game as the price to pay for making the deal. So the 1991 game was still played in Birmingham, even though it was Auburn's home game.

Van Allen Plexico

It was the "throw Bama a bone" game. I think it definitely worked out; I'm glad we played in Auburn in 1989 and not 1991. That's undoubtedly one of the biggest things to come out of how Dye and the AU administration stood up to Alabama and said, "We're playing the game in Auburn in 1989." Imagine if 1991 had been the "First Time Ever" game.

I was at that 1991 Iron Bowl, and it was absolutely surreal to see that crappy artificial turf painted to look like an approximation of Jordan-Hare's grass, complete with the AU logo on the fifty yard line. They had the Legion Field scoreboard flashing Auburn home messages throughout the game, but it was an old, low-tech design and it was never intended to display the color orange, so our graphics on it looked like hot pink or something. And, as always, bulbs were burnt out all over it. It was terrible.

Overall, 1991 was just a tough season.

John Ringer

We had lost a bunch of talent, and the last of the great, really great players from the 1988-89 teams were gone. The team wasn't the same. At the same time, I think some of our rivals had gotten better. Florida in particular. I think Alabama had improved, and at the same time we took a real step back. Defensively, yes, but offensively, too. Defensively we were really, really sliding, and we didn't have the great difference-makers on offense like we'd had in years past.

Van Allen Plexico

By the end of 1991, we were on a slide from 10-2 to 8-3-1 to 5-6. Did you think Pat Dye could still salvage things and turn the program around again? Or were you thinking maybe this was it?

John Ringer

No, in my mind at the time, I was thinking, "He's won the SEC three times in a row. He had a bad year. We'll get it back."

Van Allen Plexico

Pat Sullivan was leaving to be head coach at TCU, so we brought in Tommy Bowden as our new offensive coordinator. We still had Wayne Hall as the defensive coordinator. We felt like we had coaches that knew what they were doing. So maybe we could turn it around.

1992

As it turned out, we would never know if Pat Dye could have adapted again, as he'd done after the 1985 season, and led the Tigers to more big wins and championships. The 1992 season would turn out to be his swan song as head coach on the Plains. His team struggled on the field again, even as his noted health problems increased. Other issues would soon arise, as well.

Van Allen Plexico

You and I had both moved to Washington, DC, by the time the 1992 season kicked off. We were both in graduate school at Georgetown. It was almost like being back in the early Eighties again, in terms of finding some of the games on television. We were having to locate restaurants and bars that were showing the Auburn games. It was hard to be away and to try to keep track of this season that turned out to be the end of the Pat Dye era.

The 1992 season marked Auburn football's 100th anniversary. A special logo, showing the Samford Hall clock tower with the number "100," was used all year long, including at midfield on the grass of Jordan-Hare Stadium. There were hopes among some fans that the historical magnitude of the season might somehow motivate the players and coaches into producing a miracle.

That miracle season was indeed coming, but it was still a year away

Van Allen Plexico

Probably the thing I missed seeing the most that season was when they retired Bo's jersey. I had been wondering for years when they were going to do it, and I believe they finally did it at the Arkansas game that year, in a game that ended up a 24-24 tie.

You knew things weren't going to go well that season when we started out by losing on the road to Ole Miss, 45-21. I've always said, the easiest way to judge an Auburn season is whether we beat the Mississippi schools. In the years where we lose to one or both of them—or to Southern Miss—we generally lose several other games, too. We lost to both of them that season, which was bad enough. To let a poor Ole Miss team ring us up for 45 points, though? That was truly disturbing and did not bode well for the rest of the year.

We beat Samford on September 12, 55-0, which is interesting because we'd be hiring their head coach a few months later. We actually won against LSU, 32-28, with a miraculous, last-second finish. That sounds encouraging until I point out that they ended up last in the SEC that year, at 2-9. We beat Southern Miss for the first time in three years. We got a win over Vanderbilt. And then, guess what? We only won one more game the rest of the season—against Southwestern Louisiana. We ended the season on a 1-4-1 run.

The 1992 Iron Bowl would be Auburn's final game of the year; there would be no bowl for a 5-5-1 team. It would also be Pat Dye's final game as Auburn coach. He announced before the game that he was retiring. The causes included his health issues (mentioned earlier) and allegations swirling around secret recordings made by former defensive back Eric Ramsey involving alleged payments to Ramsey and possibly to others.

Meanwhile, Alabama—also celebrating its 100th anniversary of football that season—was on its way to going undefeated and winning the national championship for Gene Stallings. Their defense had carried them past all opponents for the previous eleven games, but against the Auburn defense in this Iron Bowl, at least for a half, they could do little.

The two teams went to the locker room scoreless at halftime. In the third quarter, though, Alabama's great defensive back, Antonio Langham, grabbed an interception thrown by Stan White and took it to the house, and that seemed to break the game open. Alabama added ten more points before the game was over and won, 17-0. Auburn netted just 20 rushing yards the entire game.

"I told him we would miss him. He's a great competitor. He's meant a lot more to the conference than I have. I've got a little bit of mixed emotions. You can't imagine how excited I am about winning this game. At the same time, I think I'm sad that we're losing Pat Dye in this conference. He's meant a lot to the Southeastern Conference and a lot to college football."
—Gene Stallings, Alabama head coach

The game marked Pat Dye's first time being shut out at Auburn, in the final game of his Auburn coaching career. The game could have been his 100th win on the Plains, but instead the history books show him with 99, tied with Mike Donahue for second all-time behind Ralph "Shug" Jordan.

"The worst thing was not winning the game for Coach Dye. We wanted to get it for him and we couldn't do it. That's hard."
—Thomas Bailey, Auburn receiver

"Coach Dye would never tell us to win a game for him. Any player who cares about Coach Dye would have wanted to win the game for

him. This game wasn't for my family. This game wasn't for revenge. I didn't even want it for myself. He was my first priority. I wanted to win this game for Pat Dye."
—Reid McMilion, Auburn fullback

John Ringer

The specter of the NCAA was swirling. You mentioned the Ramseys earlier, and they provided information to the NCAA that a coach had bought him steaks and other things. Consequently, Auburn was put on probation for 1993 and 1994. That, combined with Coach Dye's health issues and the general downhill slide and declining performance of the team helped to end the Dye era.

"You know, I wish we could have made a better game out of it. But, you know, they just have too many weapons and a little too much ability for us on defense. I really felt like they might be the best team in the country coming in and, defensively, I don't know if I have ever seen a better defensive football team. They can run and they have so much talent....

"I'm mighty proud of our kids, and you know we were in the football game until the interception, and then we just couldn't get anything going offensively. And we didn't give ourselves a chance down the stretch."

"Coach, it's been a great twelve years. Enjoy your hunting."

"Thank you very much and, you know, I hate for it to go out like this, but ... I've been playing or coaching since 1952. And I guess you're never ready for it, but it's got to happen sometime."
—Pat Dye and Phil Snow, on Coach Dye's final Auburn Football Review show

And so, with the end of the 1992 season, and in dizzying fashion, Pat Dye's twelve-year run as the head coach of the Auburn Tigers came to an abrupt conclusion. He had won the SEC in 1983, 1987, 1988 and 1989, and had very near misses in 1984 and 1986. Even the underachieving 1990 team came very close to winning a fourth straight SEC title. He'd ended the 9-year losing streak to Alabama, brought the Iron Bowl to Auburn and then won it, and beaten the Tide in six out of eight years. Beyond that, he'd restored pride and respectability to the program, and toughness to the teams.

Van Allen Plexico

Honestly his only really bad seasons, record-wise, were the first one and then the last two. Nine out of his twelve years were really good seasons and championship-caliber seasons. The 1981 team only won five games, but they were a tough group! They were laying down the foundation.

When you look back at the Pat Dye era now, what would you say Pat Dye meant to Auburn? And how should we remember him and his era now?

John Ringer

I think he took Auburn and made it back into a perennial SEC contender. We had fallen away from that, and Dye made Auburn into a program that was known around the country for a great running game and tough defense—tough, hard-nosed defense. Yeah. That's what I think people remember about the Pat Dye teams, and that was the key to their success for a long time.

At the same time, I think football was changing, moving away from the style of play and the types of players that were successful in the mid-Eighties. Those ways of playing the game weren't going to be as successful in the Nineties. You had different types of athletes, faster players and different schemes. And so I think that was part of it as well.

Finally, I think there was a bitter taste in everybody's mouth at the end, because his tenure finished with two poor seasons and with NCAA sanctions.

Jacob "Jboy" Crain

Pat Dye's time at Auburn not only changed Auburn's trajectory as a program, it changed the mindset. Gone were the days of *hoping* to beat Bama and in were the days of earning the right to beat Bama.

Coach Dye almost singlehandedly built Auburn's backbone. Getting the Iron Bowl to be a home-and-home series was huge, but the mentality is what got it over the hump.

My father (Auburn linebacker Kurt Crain) started every lesson he taught me with "Coach Dye used to say," because he was teaching a way of life, not just football.

"Pat Dye really was the kind of guy that probably should have played at Auburn. He had that mentality. He was like an Auburn guy that had played at Georgia and then coached under Bear Bryant for nine years. It was his toughness. He knew Auburn was a gold mine that hadn't really been mined in a number of years. That's why he went after the job so hard and wanted it so badly. That's what made him good."

—Bobby Lowder, Auburn Trustee, interview with Phillip Marshall, 2020

Van Allen Plexico

"Pat Dye football" was really "run and stop the run" football, so big in the Eighties. In the SEC, you could win championships by running and stopping the run. But even as that was going on, teams like Miami had been showing us that you could pass the ball and win championships too. By the Nineties, with Steve Spurrier at Florida, it was clear that the page had turned. If you stopped the run, they'd just throw the ball over your heads.

The other big team in the Eighties that did what we did was Oklahoma, and it was the same thing there: Oklahoma would be killing the lesser teams in their conference every week, and then they'd play Miami and get killed by the passing game. We had expanded in 1986 to be more of a passing team, but even then, throwing the ball was usually our secondary thing. It was not our primary thing.

Steve Spurrier changed football in the SEC in 1990. With that "Fun and Gun" offense at Florida and through the rest of the Nineties, he would terrorize teams. We'll talk in the next chapter about a couple of games where that actually didn't work out so well for him, because we would beat Florida at least as much as anybody did during those Spurrier years, which drove him nuts.

For now, though, the Eighties were an amazing decade, and I'm really happy that I was a part of it. I was down there. I'm glad that you were there, too. And we had a good time, didn't we?

John Ringer
We did. It was wonderful.

Van Allen Plexico
The difference between what it felt like to be an Auburn fan when we were in elementary school, and what it felt like when we were actually going to school at Auburn, is hard to describe. We'd gone from "lovable losers" to "the best and the toughest program in the conference" in just a few years. We could hold our heads high. The AU logo commanded respect from everyone.

It was a great time to be on the Plains. It was a great time to be an Auburn student. It was a great time to be an Auburn Tiger. And it was a great decade.

While the Pat Dye era didn't exactly end on the high note we might have wished for, the "Pat Dye Decade of the Eighties" at Auburn ended with the last game played in that decade, the "First Time Ever" Iron Bowl, and I think that was the true high point we can look back on fondly and proudly.

Auburn understood that. A few years later, we would actually name the field in Jordan-Hare Stadium, "Pat Dye Field." A worthy honor, and well-deserved.

Meanwhile, the 1993 season was just around the corner, and Auburn didn't have a head football coach.

The day after the 1992 Iron Bowl, Ragan Ingram of the *Montgomery Advertiser* listed three names he'd heard circulating about who might be hired by Athletic Director Mike Lude to become the next head coach of the Auburn Tigers. He mentioned Don James of Washington, Pat Sullivan of TCU, and one other, whom he regarded as a long-shot at best:

Terry Bowden of Samford.

Nobody could have ever dreamed that just a few months later, Jim Fyffe would be saying these magic words: "Eleven and oh! *Eleven and oh! ELEVEN AND OH!!"*

1989:

10-2 overall; 5-1 SEC
SEC Champions

9/9	Pacific	W	55-0
9/16	Southern Miss	W	24-3
9/30	at Tennessee	L	14-21
10/7	at Kentucky	W	24-12
10/14	LSU	W	10-6
10/21	at Florida State	L	14-22
10/28	Miss State	W	14-0
11/4	Florida	W	10-7
11/11	Louisiana Tech	W	38-23
11/18	at Georgia	W	20-3
12/2	Alabama*	W	30-20
1/1	Ohio State**	W	31-14

Final AP Ranking: 6
*"First Time Ever"
**Hall of Fame Bowl, Tampa, FL

1990:

8-3-1 overall; 4-2-1 SEC

9/8	Cal St Fullerton	W	38-17
9/15	at Ole Miss	W	24-10
9/29	Tennessee	T	26-26
10/6	Louisiana Tech	W	16-14
10/13	Vanderbilt	W	56-6
10/20	Florida State	W	20-17
10/27	at Miss State	W	17-16
11/3	at Florida	L	7-48
11/10	Southern Miss	L	12-13
11/17	Georgia	W	33-10
12/1	at Alabama (Bham)	L	7-16
12/29	Indiana *	W	27-23

*Peach Bowl, Atlanta, GA (Final AP Ranking: 19)

1991:

5-6 overall; 2-5 SEC

8/31	Georgia Southern	W	32-17
9/14	Ole Miss	W	23-13
9/21	at Texas	W	14-10
9/28	at Tennessee	L	21-30
10/5	Southern Miss	L	9-10
10/12	at Vanderbilt	W	24-22
10/26	Miss State	L	17-24
11/2	Florida	L	10-31
11/9	SW Louisiana	W	50-7
11/16	at Georgia	L	27-37
11/30	Alabama (Bham)*	L	6-13

Final Auburn "home" game in Legion Field

1992:

5-5-1 overall; 2-5-1 SEC

9/5	at Ole Miss	L	21-45
9/12	Samford	W	55-0
9/19	LSU	W	30-28
9/26	Southern Miss	W	16-8
10/3	Vanderbilt	W	31-7
10/10	at Miss State	L	7-14
10/17	at Florida	L	9-24
10/24	SW Louisiana	W	25-24
10/31	Arkansas	T	24-24
11/14	Georgia	L	10-14
11/26	at Alabama (Bham)	L	0-17

- 5 -

ATTITUDE AND AUDACITY
Terry Bowden, 1993-1998

"Two and a half minutes to play; actually, 2:32 to go on a first down play. Up the middle Bostic five yards, ten yards, 45 yard line Bostic, 50 Bostic, racing to the 45, to the 40, breaking a tackle to the 30, to the 20, to the 10, he's gone— Touchdown Auburn!"

"Well, I guess that lets you know that the Alabama defense, Jim, was a little bit tired. Boy, did James Bostic ever break that one. Yeah, three touchdowns against Georgia coming in this week as the SEC Player of the Week offensively; 184 yards in that game. And that big man just broke it over the right side and outran everybody, and broke another tackle around the 25 yard line. Great speed, great power. What great blocking by the Auburn offensive line."

"Seventy yards!"
—Jim Fyffe and Charlie Trotman on the radio broadcast of the 1993 Iron Bowl

Jerry Hinnen

I remember trying to wrap my arms around the ancient stereo that my parents had put in my bedroom. That's where I listened to the 1993 Iron Bowl on the radio. When James Bostic got free for the game-icing touchdown, I was so excited, I put my arms around the stereo. That sounds insane. Well, it *was* insane. But, you know, you're fourteen years old, and you're pretty excited and jumping up and down and screaming.

I understand that Terry Bowden gets the short stick from a lot of Auburn fans; he's persona non grata in a lot of ways. But I remember that Iron Bowl moment, and I remember that season and how magical it was.

In what seemed in some ways like a sudden change, but in others like a move long coming, the Pat Dye era at Auburn had ended. Its final days were marked by three mostly disappointing seasons, three consecutive losses to Alabama, and a decline in Dye's health. After a dozen years of amazing highs—and a few perplexing lows—Auburn found itself needing a new football coach.

This would be just Auburn's third new head coaching hire since 1951. It was hoped the right hiring could bring the Auburn Family together and dispel some of the gloom hanging around the program in the wake of Dye's tumultuous final years. There was also a sense that probation penalties were heading Auburn's way, connected to the Eric Ramsey investigation—and a strong hand on the tiller would be needed to help the program navigate its way through those choppy waters.

The man Auburn chose to captain the ship had a well-known surname in the South and in the football coaching profession, but he himself was something of an unknown commodity. The Tigers hired themselves a *Bowden*, yes—but not *Bobby* Bowden. Not even *Tommy* Bowden. No, Auburn reached down to NCAA division I-AA and chose the head coach at Samford University. Auburn fans, quite surprised at first, warily embraced him and waited to see how this unexpected move would work out.

"On December 17, 1992, a new era began on the Plains. Samford's Terry Bowden was hired as the 23rd head coach in Auburn history."
—*Voiceover, 1993 Auburn Football Highlights Video*

"I want to appeal to all the good people of Auburn; to our alumni; to the Auburn Family; former players; all those who this football program means so much to; to join behind me, and help us take this program not to places where it's never been, but to the levels that y'all have already obtained and want to go back to again."
—*Terry Bowden, at his introductory press conference, 1992*

In the years that followed, Terry Bowden would excite Auburn fans, then frustrate them, and ultimately disappoint them. The "Bowden era" the university had hyped in 1993 turned out to last not even six full seasons before the plug was pulled. (Who actually pulled that plug—Auburn or Terry himself—also became a point of controversy.)

By the time Terry's tenure on the Plains came to its contentious end midway through the 1998 season, Auburn fans had for the most part mentally and emotionally moved on. Attention shifted to anticipating who would replace him (or rather, replace interim coach Bill "Brother" Oliver). By that time, Terry himself had been relegated to a footnote, and soon after would be nearly lost in obscurity between the coach he followed and the one he preceded.

Looking back now, though, more than two decades removed from the events, Terry's time at Auburn doesn't seem quite so negative. The early seasons in particular stand out as a collective high point in modern Auburn football history, filled with big games and big plays and big wins.

The legacy of Terry Bowden demands reassessment on its own merits. Van and John brought in a guest to help them do just that.

Van Allen Plexico

So now we leave the Pat Dye era behind and venture into the middle of the 1990s; the Terry Bowden Era, for all the good and the not-so-good of that time period. Joining us for this portion of the discussion is John's brother, Pat Ringer, who has specific insights into that period.

Pat Ringer

I was four years younger than John, so right when he was graduating Auburn in 1991, I was coming into school. I was there for the end of the Pat Dye era. It was tumultuous and kind of scary. We felt almost like we felt after 2012: Oh my gosh, are we going to be competitive? That was how it felt. Fortunately, it turned out we were competitive.

Van Allen Plexico

I get the sense that many Auburn fans today, perhaps the younger fans, look back on the Terry Bowden years as maybe something of a down period or a little embarrassing. He was there for six years, with Pat Dye on one end and Tommy Tuberville on the other. His tenure represents a kind of interregnum, in a way. But if you look at the Bowden era from our personal perspective of when it was happening, those years didn't seem like a step down or a disappointment. It felt more like we were keeping everything that had made the Dye era so great, and adding even more to it. There was a period there where it felt like we were going to have even *more* success.

John Ringer

I think you're right in the sense that it ended badly, and so that's the taste that was left in your mouth. But he was there six years, and we won the SEC West in 1993 and 1997, and second in 1994. And 1995 wasn't bad, either. It was solid. But that 1993-94 run was special, and I think we should really appreciate it and revel in it.

Van Allen Plexico

We had that 20-0 Streak, which was incredible. And we had "Eleven and oh!" in 1993. So, yes, 1998 was a mess, but those other years stack up well against anyone else who's ever coached at Auburn. And it wasn't Terry Bowden's fault we were on probation for those first two years.

Terry Bowden, by Jarrod Alberich

"I was 36. I was coming from Samford University. People knew of my father, but they really didn't know of me. I was the youngest head coach in the country at that time. It was my tenth year as coach in college. I'd had 10 years to mess up everywhere else to prepare me for that experience. I was a lot more prepared than people thought, just because I'd been a head coach for 10 years in college at a smaller level. Auburn had had two straight non-winning seasons. They were 5-5-1 and 5-6 coming into that year. And Coach Dye is a legend. I was replacing someone who had brought Auburn's program to an equality with, on level with Alabama, getting the game to Auburn and bringing the two programs to a level stage at that point. After a couple bad years, and me being very young, people didn't know what to expect. There was worry, and there was doubt."
—Terry Bowden, 2018 interview with Jeff Shearer

To get more perspective on how the Bowden years should be viewed, Van sat down with Cole Cubelic, now of WJOX and the SEC Network, but a player on the last couple of Auburn teams fielded by Terry Bowden.

Cole Cubelic

Terry was cool as a head coach. He didn't go out of his way to get into your business and didn't try to make life miserable. I feel like he was a bit of a player's coach. There were times when guys on the team felt like he was a little bit caught up with some of the other things that came with being a college coach, and became a little bit disconnected from some of his players. But I think he was someone who understood what he wanted his team to be. He allowed his coaches to coach. He allowed his coordinators to coordinate and he managed that and managed it well. He wasn't an 'in your face' kind of a guy. He wasn't a real "rah rah" guy. He wasn't somebody who cusses you out. But he was direct, and he was blunt. And he let you know, right away, "Hey, we need this from you. We need you to be this, we need you to be that and we need to improve here." And I think because he didn't try to go overboard with how he delivered his message, that made it easier for a lot of guys to get on board with what he wanted to do.

Overall, as a coach in the league, he had obvious success. There were reasons that he got run, but I don't think too many of them had to do with his performance on the field. Did we have a bad year in 1998? We did, but we were in the SEC Championship Game in 1997. And we lost our quarterback and also our inside linebacker; lost our left tackle and our monster fullback. I mean, anybody with football common sense should have known that there was going to be a bit of a rebuild.

I'll always be appreciative to Terry Bowden for giving me a scholarship. And I think he's somebody who was a good head coach and knew how to be a good head coach and just got a little distracted.

Van Allen Plexico

Do you think he's underrated today?

Cole Cubelic

I think he is. I think it's easy. It's low-hanging fruit. People were going to talk about his height and about the bloodlines and say that's the only reason he got the job, was because of his dad; because of his family, and things of that nature. But again, I go back to it just being a part of what he was trying to do, and how he tried to build it. And it made a lot of sense.

He understood how to recruit. He understood how to utilize talent. And he understood how to deliver a message to a guy of, "If you're not going to perform this way, or if you're not going to give us this, then you're not going to be a part of our team, you're not going to play." And I felt like he organized his team fairly well, and his coaching staff fairly well, and I think some of the ways that people do talk about him are inaccurate. But listen, there were things that were going on that led to his dismissal. So you can't just completely overlook those things. And I think Terry would be fair and honest with you, and he would tell you that things got in the way and he got a little bit distracted. But there are a lot of things about him that I think he is unfairly labeled as, and I also don't think he gets enough credit for how good he was early on in his career.

Terry Bowden faced enormous obstacles right from the beginning. As the 1993 season began, Alabama was coming off an undefeated campaign that culminated in a national championship. Auburn, meanwhile, had lost the coach that had rebuilt the program and had brought the Iron Bowl to the Plains. The Tigers were starting over with an unproven young coach. To make matters worse, the NCAA handed down a particularly nasty set of sanctions on the program, stemming from events near the end of Pat Dye's tenure.

No one, it seems safe to say, could have expected Auburn to enjoy a better year than Alabama in football in 1993. When it comes to the Tigers and the Tide, though, things rarely work out the way they one would expect.

1993

Van Allen Plexico

I remember going to the Ole Miss game to kick off 1993. I was back at Auburn after being away for a year or two, working on my Master's Degree. As it turned out, I picked a darned good time to come back.

At the time, though, nobody had any idea what to expect. We had just learned we were on probation. We had just learned we weren't going to be in the SEC Championship Game—not that we thought that was going to be a problem that year, coming in—and we learned we were not going to be shown on TV at all. That was a serious set of penalties that came down at the end of Pat Dye's era. And Terry just got the brunt of it.

But let's back up for a second. How did we get Terry Bowden to be our coach? When we left off in the previous chapter, Pat Dye was retiring, and we were saying how nobody could guess who our new head coach would be. Nobody would have bet a cent on Terry Bowden from Samford. So how did we end up getting him as our head coach?

John Ringer

Bobby Bowden was the dominant force in college football at the time. People forget now how good Florida State was at that time. They finished in the top three for eleven years in a row. He was the great coach of the time, and so programs were trying to hire away people that had a connection to him.

Terry had gone off to Samford and won some games, and it was a small school in Alabama. He was seen as a connection to Bobby Bowden. There was a sense that he must know what he's doing. And also he kept some of the holdovers from the previous staff. He kept Wayne Hall as defensive coordinator, Joe Whitt with the linebackers, and others. So it was one of those things like you see with teams hiring Nick Saban's assistants more recently, where people are trying to recreate Bobby Bowden's Florida State thing at Auburn.

Van Allen Plexico

Terry said that he had the greatest job interview of all time. He told the interviewers at Auburn how he would combine a Pat Dye defense with a Bobby Bowden offense. He mentioned he had a law degree and that he knew how to talk; how to sound good on camera and be good for public relations for the University. And it didn't hurt that he could get on the phone to "Diddy" Bowden and get some game advice if he needed to. "Diddy said to do the fake field goal here!"

Looking back, Terry did have a lot going for him that made him a surprise dark horse candidate and ultimately the guy we hired. But he also tended to rub people the wrong way pretty quickly. He was kind of a motormouth; hyperactive; very different from his older brother, Tommy, who had been our offensive coordinator for a couple of years at that point.

Terry came in and he was bouncy and chattery and in some ways that was a breath of fresh air, after some of the things we'd dealt with the last couple of years. But it got old quickly. When things were going well, we could make excuses and overlook his jittery nature and talkativeness. Unfortunately, when things started going bad, his personality rubbed some people the wrong way and just made it all go downhill that much faster.

Pat Ringer

I think you hit on something there, Van. We were thinking we were getting an upgrade to our program and our offensive system, all of a sudden being able to throw the ball, when we had been this run-first program for so long. And the same thing with the coach as a person, thinking that we're going to get this smooth communicator that the nation would connect with. We'd had this slow-talking Southern guy, and we had failed to appreciate what we had. I think it's easy in hindsight to see Terry's deficiencies, but at the time, we were thinking, "Oh, this guy's fantastic."

Van Allen Plexico

Yeah, that first year, in the flush of victory after the 1993 Iron Bowl, Pat Dye came out and hugged Terry and waved at the crowd with him, and he said something to the effect of, "The great thing about Terry is, he's a young coach, so we can have him at Auburn for many years to come."

John Ringer

I think we need to give Terry some credit for walking into a situation where Auburn was hiring a coach while we were under NCAA investigation. Sanctions were coming.

The penalty phase of the sanctions came out in August. The team learned during fall practice that we were not going to be on TV and that we couldn't go to a bowl. Can you imagine how that affected them mentally and emotionally? But there were a lot of veteran players on that team and they kept the team together. They kept the team focused and motivated and I think Terry did a good job getting them to play for each other and to kind of go, "Okay, they're doing this to us. We've got to show the world that we're good, by going out and taking it to people."

Van Allen Plexico

I think you're right. To me, that's one of the most remarkable things about that 11-0 season in 1993: the circumstances surrounding it. I mean, it's crazy enough to go

11-0 in the SEC West. To do it when you've just found out you're on probation and can't even compete for anything other than trying to win your regular-season games—how does that even happen? And if Pat Dye had come back for another year, I honestly don't know that we would have been any better than 5-6 again.

Pat Ringer

The SEC West was not what it is. Alabama was coming off a national title but, aside from them, it was not at all the same division. Of course, we didn't have Texas A&M in the division and LSU had not quite discovered whatever it is they've discovered. They were a lot less of a team. Arkansas was soft, and the Mississippi schools were soft. I think we ended up beating just two ranked teams that year—Florida and Alabama.

So it was a different time. But it is amazing that they were able to come into the season, having just found out that they really couldn't play for anything, and perform that well. But again, it reminds me of the 2012-2013 thing—how the 2013 team responded after their bad season the year before. "Hey, listen, we've been down in the dumps, so we're just going to go game by game, one game at a time."

I remember going into the first game of 1993, the Ole Miss game, and Ole Miss was not expected to be great. We the fans were thinking, "All right, let's just win this game. I don't care what else happens. Let's just win the game." The Tigers didn't look great in that game, but they got the job done.

Then it was on to the next week, and the next, and that was how that entire season felt. And I think in the vast majority of the games that year, we came from behind to win.

The team had a lot of talent. We forget just how much. The two tackles started for years in the NFL—Willie Anderson and Wayne Gandy.

Van Allen Plexico

Oh yeah. The talent on our roster that year was better than people think. I remember, about a year after that season, having a conversation with a friend who is a big Florida fan. He was saying something like, "I have no idea how you guys went 11-0 with that roster." And I said, "Well, it wasn't a very deep roster, but if you look at the starters on that team, there were All-SEC players at so many positions. You had Stan White at quarterback, as a senior, with Patrick Nix backing him up. That's not bad. Frank Sanders was a future NFL receiver. They had the most effective punter Auburn's ever had in Terry Daniel, plus a really dependable kicker in Scott Etheridge. As you said, the offensive line was solid across the board, and Anderson was a star. The defensive backs on the 1993 and 1994 teams are vastly underrated, and all you have to do to see that is look at the 1994 LSU and Florida games. If there was a weakness on that team, it was probably at linebacker. But every other position—I mean, we had Stephen Davis backing up James Bostic at running back!

John Ringer
Along with Tony Richardson at fullback, who played in the NFL a good while, and Fred Beasley. There were a lot of All-SEC and future NFL players on that team. It's enough to make you wonder how we went 5-5-1 the year before.

Pat Ringer
I think the distractions took their toll that year, and in 1991. The new coaching staff came in and it made for a clean slate.

Van Allen Plexico
We ground out a win against Ole Miss, then beat Samford, Bowden's old team, 35-7. When you beat Samford 35-7, you think, "That wasn't a very impressive win over a lower division team." Maybe Terry took it easy on them.

The game that I think signaled we could be a special team was that next week, when we went down to Baton Rouge to play LSU. A friend and I drove down for that game. While we were there, we caught the Saints-Lions game and got to see Barry Sanders, which was pretty cool, and I won $300 at roulette. That's a whole other story, but it was a good trip.

The best part of the trip, though, was beating the snot out of LSU, 34-10.

After trailing 7-0 for most of the first quarter, Auburn scored 3 touchdowns in the second quarter to take a commanding lead. Stan White had a great game, passing for nearly 300 yards. In the process he broke Pat Sullivan's career passing yardage record.

"Coach, I couldn't have done it without you."
—Stan White, Auburn quarterback, to Pat Sullivan, his former position coach, after the LSU game

Auburn's powerful duo of running backs dueled to see who could do the most damage to LSU. Both performed well. James Bostic rushed 13 times for 110 yards, while Stephen Davis carried the ball 16 times for 95 yards.

"I would've liked to have carried the ball a few more times, but I think I'm still The Man. We both had a good game, but I think I played a little better."
—James Bostic, Auburn running back

It was Auburn's first victory in Tiger Stadium in 54 years. Not that the two teams had played one another all that often before the changes to the conference structure in 1992, but the team in orange and blue hadn't won in Baton Rouge since 1939—the same year "Cliff Hare Stadium" first opened for business on the Plains.

Van Allen Plexico
Unfortunately, the game wasn't on television, because of the sanctions.

John Ringer
We need to set the stage for people who can't appreciate what that was like, not being on TV at all in 1993. Not even any kind of pay-per-view. It was pre-Internet days, too, really. All you could do was listen on the radio.

Van Allen Plexico
At the end of the season, there was a t-shirt someone was selling that declared Auburn the "National Radio Champions."

We already knew Jim Fyffe was a great play-by-play radio announcer, but this season proved how truly great he was, because so much of the Auburn Family depended on him to give them any glimpse of the team and the games. That year, he was all that most people had. And he was so great. He made you care. He was so passionate about the team and the game. There were other years that he made memorable calls, but this was the year everybody really leaned on him.

John Ringer
For the Iron Bowl that year, they had a telephone number you could call in to listen to Jim Fyffe do the play-by-play over the phone. And so many Auburn fans called it, they melted the electronic system down. It even sold out two stadiums, because they showed it in Tuscaloosa on closed-circuit TV, and sold out that stadium too.

Pat Ringer
Compare that to now, where my main problem is wanting to pause the game so I can fast forward through commercials, but it messes up the flow of Twitter and the game. First world problems.

Auburn came from behind to win over Southern Miss. The Tigers trailed in that game, just like most of them that year, but came back to win, 35-24.

Next, they traveled to Nashville to take on Vanderbilt. Auburn was ranked 23rd in the AP Poll. The Tigers ended up winning, 14-10, but they struggled the entire game.

Vanderbilt had a big running back that Jim Fyffe kept referring to as "Big Royce Love." Seemingly singlehandedly, he carried Vanderbilt all the way down the field to Auburn's goal line as the clock was ticking away and the Tigers were clinging to a four-point lead. The Auburn defense responded when they had to: They proceeded to stuff Big Royce Love in a massive goal line stand and held on to preserve the win.

Van Allen Plexico

Just imagine if the only loss we'd suffered that whole season was to *Vanderbilt*. That goal line stand was the closest we came all season to losing, aside from the Florida game, which was nip-and-tuck. That goal line stand in Nashville turned out to be huge.

"Vanderbilt from the Power-I with two tight ends. Again motion out of the backfield. They'll give to Johnson. He's up. Did he make it? I don't think he did! I think they stopped him! Yes! Yes! Yes!"
—Jim Fyffe, Auburn Network radio broadcast, 1993

Pat Ringer

It was the last minute of the game and I believe Vanderbilt had first-and-goal from the one. It was a real goal line stand and it was big time.

Van Allen Plexico

With an Auburn defense that had decent starters across the front and a good secondary, but this wasn't a team with future star Takeo Spikes in the linebacking corps. This was a team with Jason Miska, the kid from Connecticut, starting at linebacker. They were taking pretty much anyone they could get to play linebacker, and they stopped Vandy on four downs from the one.

We had a good, 31-17 win over Mississippi State the next week. That game is totally unmemorable to me, other than Jackie Sherrill claiming we were putting helium in the footballs before Terry Daniel punted them. (The SEC investigated and found no evidence of such a thing.)

"At first I thought it was joke. But when I heard the ball was sent to the SEC, I was kind of surprised. I'm innocent."
—Terry Daniel, Auburn punter

Then comes one of the greatest wins of the year and one of the most famous wins over Florida ever—and I think one of the most exciting games in Auburn history.

Bear in mind, under Steve Spurrier in 1990, Florida had beaten our brains in, and in 1991 and 92 it didn't look like things were getting any better. So, going into the 1993 Florida game, the popular conception was, "Okay, Auburn's gotten lucky and pulled out some miracles to be 6-0, but that's all about to come crashing down because Florida is going to kill them, just like they have the last three years under Spurrier."

Florida went right down the field on us and scored ten points very early on, and they were driving to possibly go up 17-0, still in the first quarter. You can't imagine that team ever coming back from that kind of deficit.

Florida drove to our eleven-yard-line and Danny Wuerffel was throwing into the end zone. We knew that if they scored there, this is going to be a 50-0 kind of game; just a disaster. And then?

"Rhett the setback. It's a second down play for Wuerffel at the Auburn 11. Six-man rush. Wuerffel's gonna throw in the endzone— the pass is intercepted! To the ten, the fifteen, the twenty, he's at the thirty, he's at the forty. Giving chase is Wuerffel, not gonna catch him. At the thirty, at the twenty, to the ten, he is gone! Ninety-five yards! Touchdown Auburn! Calvin Jackson!"

"He's Auburn's best one-on-one cover man and he saw that play coming, Jim, and Danny Wuerffel, if there's been any fault I could say in his play so far this season, it's in the fact that he's been intercepted. He threw it out, thinking that Willie Jackson was gonna be there. Auburn had two defenders actually on the play. Calvin Jackson just stepped in and it was clear sailing. And just that quickly, Auburn is back in the ballgame because of the Florida turnover. That's what's killed Florida; Auburn's taken advantage of it. Tremendous defensive play by Calvin Jackson."

"You talk about igniting a crowd. They're going crazy in Auburn now."
—Jim Fyffe and Charlie Trotman, Auburn Network broadcast

Pat Ringer

Calvin Jackson of Dillard High School. The 95-yard pick-six right in front of the end zone and all the way back the other way. Absolutely amazing.

Van Allen Plexico

That team had a secondary, and in the biggest games in 1993 and 1994, that secondary showed up. They showed up big time. So instead of 17-0, it's 10-7 and now we have all the momentum.

After that, the game swung back and forth. Florida turned the ball over again later, and we immediately gave it to Frank Sanders on the reverse for a thirty-yard touchdown. That was something I don't know that Pat Dye would have done: They turn the ball over, we hit them with the big play.

The game kept going back and forth and back and forth.

Pat Ringer

This era was before the rule that you can't take your helmet off. I haven't seen video of this game in years but don't you recall everybody taking their helmet off as soon as they did anything? People were realizing football players aren't as recognizable. Everybody was taking their helmet off after every play.

And the NCAA was not cracking down on uniforms the same way. Bostic had his jersey tied up like he was wearing a halter practice shirt.

There was a run by Bostic; I think it was fourth down. We were on about the five yard line and we ran a toss sweep and he was trying to get to the corner, but he was not the fastest guy in the world. Florida had a lot of fast guys on defense. And you looked up and there were like three guys that were beating him to the corner. There was no way he could get inside of them. And yet, he did. And then he scored.

"It's four yards to go on fourth down. Two tight ends, White up under center. One wide receiver from the I-set. White's gonna give it to Bostic. Racing to get outside. Won't make it. Broke a tackle—he's gonna go! Touchdown Auburn! They had Bostic, over on the far

flank, trying to turn the corner. I don't see how James broke out of that. He was in the clutches of Ed Robinson and Henry McMillan. They had him by the shirt, wrapped up hopelessly. He was able to spring loose and get a touchdown. Auburn ties it up, 27-all, and a chance to go on top with the point after."
—*Jim Fyffe, Auburn Network broadcast*

Pat Ringer
And then he made this little hula celebration.
If he doesn't score there, I think that's the game.

Van Allen Plexico
It looked like it was hopeless—like he was going to lose yards. And then he cut back at a sharp angle and the Florida players all whiffed on him.

The different ways we scored in that game, with that touchdown and the pick-six and the reverse, I mean, we were just very creative and colorful that year, in ways we hadn't been under Coach Dye. John and I have been talking about how he did so much great stuff for Auburn, but maybe the one thing that always bothered us was how we would be so vanilla on offense. It was like some huge deal when we started throwing the ball about thirty percent of the time in 1986; a huge revelation that we would actually throw the ball occasionally.

Terry Bowden came along and suddenly it was like we were playing modern football, and it was amazing. And that was *him*, not some assistant coach, doing it. I remember someone asking him before that season if he was going to call the plays, and he replied that he didn't think he would want to coach at all if he couldn't call the plays.

Scott Etheridge kicked a field goal with 1:21 to go in the game, to give Auburn a 38-35 lead that would hold up to the end.

For the game, Florida outgained Auburn 560 yards to 383. Errict Rhett of Florida rushed for 196 yards, compared to Auburn's leading rusher, James Bostic, who finished with just 76. Danny Wuerffel won the head-to-head passing battle with Stan White, 386 yards to

267. The Tigers, however, were opportunistic, winning the turnover battle 3-0 and taking advantage when they got them.

"Time is up. Auburn has won! Auburn has won! The Tigers have defeated the Florida Gators. Auburn 35, Florida 35. Can you believe it? This team of destiny has come from behind to upset fourth ranked and previously undefeated Florida. The Auburn Tigers are back! Count on it!"
—Jim Fyffe, Auburn Network broadcast

"I told our team (at halftime), 'Don't quit trying. We'll get a play here and there, something good will happen and we'll go from there.

"All I can say is, it's a big day for Auburn. A big day for our program. A big day for our fans."
—Terry Bowden, Auburn head coach

"This is the one reason I came to Auburn. This is old Auburn football, and I'm glad it's back. It was the biggest win of my life."
—Thomas Bailey, Auburn wide receiver

"Everyone thought nationally, 'Who's this team that's not on television? They're not going to be able to hang with Spurrier and that juggernaut offense. Most people thought, if you get into a Fun-and-Gun type game with Spurrier, you're going to lose. That's exactly what we did, and we won. That put us on the radar. That Florida game was the pivotal moment in that season. I think everybody on that team after that said, 'Okay, here we come. We can do something.'"
—Quarterback Stan White, 2018 interview with Jeff Shearer

"All of a sudden, at that point, everybody said, 'We can do something special here, because nobody was better than Florida that year. That was the point in which we began to look and see ourselves as someone who could really be a contender for the conference, although we weren't eligible for post-season. We weren't eligible for the SEC championship. But we knew we could

win it on the field. We had a chance to be the best in the SEC on the field. There was a point that our expectations changed, it was the day we beat Florida at Auburn."
—*Terry Bowden, 2018 interview with Jeff Shearer*

John Ringer

This is one of those games where they made a collector's edition VHS tape that had just this game on it, with the Auburn radio call dubbed over it. We watched that a lot.

"Everybody here. I can't say offense, I can't say defense, everybody here, great job. Men, you believe in yourself, you can do anything. You're in the top four now—I don't care where they rank us. You're there. They can rank us nothing, I don't care. It's a great win. I'm so proud of you."
—*Terry Bowden, after the 1993 Florida game*

Van Allen Plexico

We also had future best-selling novelist Ace Atkins on that team, playing on the defensive line. He got through and crushed Danny Wuerffel.

Pat Ringer

I actually have the commemorative *Sports Illustrated* issue right here in my office with me. He was a walk-on player. I thought I knew a lot about the team that year, but I'd never heard the guy's name until that moment. And he got two clutch sacks in the closing minutes.

Van Allen Plexico

I remember one of the Auburn beat writers mentioning that backup defensive lineman Ace Atkins had written an unpublished crime novel. And it was always this sort of a joke like, "Oh, right, a football player wrote a book. Hahaha." Well, he's getting the last laugh now, isn't he? He's like John Grisham, Jr. He dominates in the crime fiction literary world. But he absolutely crushed Danny Wuerffel, and I'm a firm proponent of crushing Danny Wuerffel at all opportunities.

That's another thing we need to mention here: In both the 1993 and 1994 games against Florida, the Gators were having a quarterback controversy; not an unusual thing under Spurrier. I think Terry Dean started the 1993 season, but by the time Auburn played Florida, they'd switched to Wuerffel as a true freshman. Wuerffel played QB for this entire game. Then, in 1994, I think Dean started and they were hyping him for the Heisman that year. And then he threw interception after interception against us, so they put Wuerffel back in. So I feel like we faced both of their star quarterbacks in those games and kind of tore them both up. I know we ended Terry Dean's Heisman campaign in '94.

I remember talk about him being an Auburn fan when he was a kid, having Auburn pajamas and stuff. He was planning to come to Auburn until Florida hired Spurrier. I kind of hate that we ruined his Heisman thing after he'd grown up a big Auburn fan, but I guess you can blame Spurrier as much as Auburn for how his career played out.

After a week off, Auburn traveled to Fayetteville to face the Razorbacks of Arkansas. The Tigers had opened the season unranked, then entered the polls at no. 25 after beating LSU. Post-Florida, the Tigers had at last cracked the top ten, rising from 19th all the way up to 9th in the AP rankings.

The game against Arkansas would be yet another oddly memorable contest, this time because of the weather.

Pat Ringer

The Arkansas game was one of the few games I didn't go to in 1993 and '94. We knew it was going to be cold. The story I remember was that Auburn wasn't prepared for the cold, but I recall talking with people beforehand and saying, "I think it's going to be really cold. I don't know if I want to go to this game."

The team flew into Tulsa, Oklahoma, on Friday, then traveled by bus through sleet and snow for two-and-a-half hours to Bella Vista, Arkansas, where their team headquarters was located. They elected not to continue on for another thirty miles to Fayetteville for walk-throughs on the field.

Van Allen Plexico

It ended up being a blizzard, and they had to scrape inches of snow off the field to be able to play the game. Another story floating around at the time was the Auburn equipment managers had to go out and buy lots of extra orange and blue gear for the coaches and staff before the game, because it was so cold when they got out there and they didn't have enough warm clothing.

John Ringer

It was one of the few games I can remember Auburn playing in, where there was snow. Maybe the only one with substantial amounts of snow on the ground.

This was also the game where Reid McMilion had a huge game running the ball for Auburn. Twelve carries for 92 yards, outrushing even Bostic. He was the fullback and was good, but had never put together a huge game because they said he tended to overheat in Auburn in August and September. But in northern Arkansas in late October in the snow? He dominated, with a fourth-quarter touchdown run to cap it off. He'd have been an All-American if he'd gone to Wisconsin.

Pat Ringer

This was also the "Otis Mounds Homecoming Queen" game. We need Jeremy Henderson of the *War Eagle Reader* to tell the story.

Jeremy ran that very story in the *War Eagle Reader* back in 2012. In it, he quotes Auburn's aforementioned defensive-end-turned-crime-novelist Ace Atkins describing the incident first-hand:

"It's funny how the truth vs. the myth is always confused in football stories. Someone told me... that it's a famous story of how Terry Bowden came to the locker room at the Arkansas game and said you guys can be 8-1 or 9-0, or something like that. Anyway, it's told as that being the turning point of that game.

"Not true.

"The turning point came when we had been berated the entire first half by the Arkansas homecoming queen — yep, we were so bad in '92, we were picked as homecoming (opponent for 1993) — and finally... Otis Mounds had had enough.

"He turned around to the young lady – decked out in a fur coat and tiara – and yelled at her in the third quarter, 'Shut up, b——!'

"Now, that is what made the whole sideline pickup, and we won the game. The girl was trying to get down to the field to slap Otis, but she was held back by her court, her tiara falling off her head.

"True tale."

—Ace Atkins, quoted in the War Eagle Reader, October 2012

With the 31-21 win, Auburn moved up to 8th in the rankings, and next faced New Mexico State.

Van Allen Plexico

The thing I remember about the New Mexico State game was that, even though we won pretty handily, 55-14, it was a little harder early on than we expected. And after the game, the New Mexico State players were complaining that Auburn ran a "high school offense"—that Stan and the receivers were doing nothing special at all.

John Ringer

I know that in the run-up to the season, Terry Bowden talked about how he had simplified the offense dramatically. He said something like, they had only fifteen plays total, with maybe six running plays and nine passing plays. Maybe even less than that.

Van Allen Plexico

But they knew what they were doing, though. It's one thing to have a hundred plays in the playbook, but if nobody knows how to execute any of them, what's the point? I've always been a firm believer that you minimize the number of things you try to do, and just get really good at those things.

That was one of the things that was so good about the old wishbone. They basically were doing one thing, and got really good at it.

But I remember the New Mexico State players saying that, and our players responding, basically, "Well, it works," and we were 9-0 doing it, at that point.

Then we went to Georgia.

Auburn was indeed still undefeated, 9-0 and ranked seventh in the country in the AP Poll.

With no bowl game possible, no chance of getting to play in the second-ever SEC Championship Game (the second of two to be played in Birmingham, before the game permanently moved to Atlanta), and no ranking allowed in the Coaches' Poll, Auburn's players and fans increasingly looked to an undefeated season as the one possible grand accomplishment that was still possible for this team.

But the Tigers' two biggest rivals remained to be played. Auburn had to visit Athens to face the Bulldogs—who, at 4-5 coming in, were not having one of their better seasons, it must be said. After that, Auburn would return home to play Alabama in only the second-ever Iron Bowl played in Jordan-Hare Stadium.

Van Allen Plexico

At this point, we were starting to feel like something special was going on because we were going for our tenth straight win. We usually had pretty good luck over in Athens during these years.

Several friends from graduate school and I, along with our girlfriends, got a block of tickets up high in Sanford Stadium. I had a bunch of t-shirts printed up before the game and took them over in a paper bag. They were blue shirts with white letters; the front said 10-0, and the back said, "AND ONE TO GO."

Eric Zeier played well at quarterback for Georgia in the game, and they scored 28 points, but Auburn scored 42, including a late touchdown to seal the deal at the end. At that point, we busted out the t-shirts and started handing them out, and we all put them on, and the Georgia fans around us lost their minds. They couldn't stand the fact that, not only were we beating them, but we'd been confident enough of victory before the game that we'd had the shirts made—and then were able to wear them, right there in their stadium!

With that loss, Georgia's record was 4-6. A Georgia fan behind us yelled, "Well, what bowl are you going to?" And I replied, "The Iron Bowl!" And my friend Dennis added, "What bowl are *y'all* going to?" And that shut the guy right up.

The potentially perfect season—something simply unimaginable just a few short weeks earlier—came down to one last game, and one against a very familiar opponent.

"At a remote outpost in frozen South Korea, an Army sergeant tunes his radio to the Armed Forces Network to listen as he pulls guard duty along the DMZ. A Selma native in Fairbanks, Alaska, is hosting a listening party today with his friends, who will hear the game via telephone, all decked out in orange and blue. A sellout crowd of 85,000 will watch in person, while 44,000 more, who scarfed up all the available tickets, will view a closed-circuit telecast in Tuscaloosa, making this the only game to sell out two stadiums at one time. It impacts the lives of just about everyone who lives here or ever has. If your team wins, seashells and balloons. But losing means a whole year of pure agony. It's the annual meeting between Auburn and Alabama.

"Hello again, everybody. War Eagle! from Jordan-Hare Stadium."
—Jim Fyffe, Auburn Network broadcast, 1993

Van Allen Plexico

Alabama the year before had gone undefeated and won the national championship. This time around, they'd been tied by Tennessee and then lost to LSU, but they were still, at 8-1-1, a very formidable foe. We were ranked sixth, they were no. 11. They were coming into our house. Remember, this was only the second time Alabama had ever played in Jordan-Hare, because we'd had to go back to Birmingham in 1991.

It looked bad for a while.

Pat Ringer

I remember the game started out slow for us. Alabama jumped out to the lead, and we got a safety and a field goal, and it was 14-5. But it was kind of like in 2010, where we knew we'd had a lot of success all season, and we wouldn't be going down that easy. The Auburn fans were into it, and there was a feeling that we were going to hang around and pull the thing out in the end.

Alabama still led 14-5 in the third quarter, when Auburn found themselves facing a fourth and fourteen to go, on Alabama's side of the field. Sacked on the previous play, starting quarterback Stan White was injured and had to leave the field. He would not return—a senior whose team was not eligible for the postseason, he had just played his final moments as an Auburn Tiger.

Now Coach Bowden faced a difficult choice: try a very long field goal, kick a relatively short punt, or go for it, with a backup quarterback who would be taking his first snap of the game on that play. There was still a quarter left to play, but Auburn had not enjoyed much success on offense up until then, and one wondered how many more opportunities they would get in this kind of field position.

"I thought it was too long for a field goal. Terry Daniel was an All-America punter, and he could kick it a mile, but I only needed about a half-mile there. You didn't want to go out there and punt it out of the end zone on fourth down at that important stage of the game.

"At the time, our defense was playing pretty good. It wasn't the most difficult call of my life. Okay, it's fourth-and-15, let's just throw it up. If it's incomplete, (the) defense is in good field position. Who knows? You might get pass interference.

"The stars were aligned and things fell into place.

"(I was) not sure Pat Nix had a strong enough arm to throw the deep takeoff to the field, so I flipped the formation to put Frank Sanders into the boundary, which is very short from the hash, so that Pat Nix would have a shorter throw for a takeoff. Antonio Langham was their star cornerback. And he played on Frank the whole day. That was his job, to play on Frank Sanders. So he always

just goes out to the field and lines up, expecting Frank to come out. That's where he always went.

"Antonio sees it late. He starts to jog across the field, and he got about halfway across, and he just signaled the other corner – stay there – he'll stay out wide. The other guy was a very good player, too. But it took their All-American first-round draft pick, and took him off Frank Sanders for that play. And Frank caught the jump ball, fell across the goal line for a score."
—*Terry Bowden, 2018 interview with Jeff Shearer*

"I did not physically see the play. I basically heard the play. I was laying down with my back on the bench, and I hear the crowd go wild, and our sideline. One of the first ones over there, my roommate, Reid McMilion, saying we just got it.

"Several of them came up, 'This one's for you. We're going to win this for you.' That really made me feel special."
—*Quarterback Stan White, 2018 interview with Jeff Shearer*

"When you think of the season, that play stands out in your mind. The improbable circumstances in a final game of the season. I think that play defined 1993."
—*Terry Bowden, 2018 interview with Jeff Shearer*

"Someone asked me the other day if this kind of game can make or break somebody, and I think I'm living proof that it can. You don't know who it will be in a game like this and who will be remembered. That's what makes this game so special and this rivalry so special... (It's) that big and everyone knows exactly where they are when things like that happen.

"There's been a lot of talk of 'Nix to Sanders,' and it all starts with that '93 game."
—*Quarterback Patrick Nix, 2013*

Van Allen Plexico

We brought in Patrick Nix in, and on his first play, he chucked it to Frank Sanders in the left corner, who caught it, turned around and dived in to score a touchdown. That didn't put us ahead, but it made it 14-12, with Alabama leading by just two, and now you felt like we had the momentum. In the fourth quarter we got a field goal to make it 15-14 Auburn. And that set up the very last big play that I know you guys remember, because it was like third and one on our own 30, and Alabama wanted to stop us and get the ball back and try to kick a field goal and win. And what happened?

Pat Ringer
Bostic busts one.

John Ringer
A big breakthrough run. He comes through the line and just keeps on going.

Pat Ringer
It was particularly dramatic because he's not a breakaway speedster, and was always in danger of being run down from behind, and there was heavy traffic around him the entire way. You didn't know if he was going to make it across midfield, much less all the way across the goal line.

Van Allen Plexico
Bostic didn't run like a sprinter. He ran like an angry boxer coming out of the corner. He seemed more like a puncher than a marathon runner. He seemed more like the kind of running back that comes in to dive into the end zone than run the length of the field, but people somehow kept bouncing off of him all the way down the field. It was one of the strangest runs I've ever seen.

I was jumping up and down so hard in the stands that my radio flew out of my pocket and hit the concrete steps and broke. But it died for a good cause.

"It's an emotional day and it should be for you, from a standpoint of being excited about the events of the day. I wanted to come by the dressing room; win, lose or draw I was going to be here to thank Terry and his staff and all the people—Dr. Muse, the administrative, everybody, for making me feel a part of this football team. You can

imagine how important that's been to me. The players, the same thing—our relationship and it's just made my life a joyous one this fall in watching you play, watching you grow, and being able to pull for you, and knowing the kind of quality and the character we had in this program."
  —*Pat Dye, after the 1993 Iron Bowl*

"Today, and I don't have to tell you, but today you have set the standard. The greatest football team ever played at Auburn University, 11-0. Because of what you did on that field. 11-0, it's never been done before. There's better teams, maybe, but you have done something no one else can do and no one will ever take it from you. You will be the benchmark they look to. And one more thing: Today I became an Auburn Man."
  —*Terry Bowden, after the 1993 Iron Bowl*

Van Allen Plexico

After the game, we went to Toomer's Corner and we were standing up in the air above the street on the black iron railing and seeing just a huge celebration. It was kind of bittersweet, though, because we had gone undefeated, we had done something that just seemed utterly improbable, and by all rights, we should have been in Atlanta, playing Florida again. We'd already beaten them once, and would beat them again the next time we played them. And yet, our season was over. And, I mean, there are worse ways to end your season than by beating Alabama. But it still was kind of bittersweet. And you always wonder, what would it have been like?

I think, John, when we did our previous book, *Decades of Dominance*, one of our "Top Ten Auburn Games that Never Happened" was the 1993 SEC Championship Game, with Auburn playing in it.

John Ringer

That's right. We were on probation at the time, but Alabama ended up having to forfeit their record for most of the season. So, in the history books, they're actually 0-8 in this year in the SEC, which I appreciate, and 1-12 overall.

379

I think we would've beaten Florida again. I think we'd have been really confident if we had gotten to play them in Atlanta. It really was the kind of thing that happens to Auburn, where we have this great season and we think we're worthy of being a national champion, but we don't get to prove it on the field; we don't get to play somebody in a bowl game and show it.

Van Allen Plexico

Terry had brought in this whole idea of what he called "AttitUde." We had "AttitUde" pins, t-shirts, the A and the U are bigger and highlighted. Pretty much every year of his run as coach, he would put out some kind of an AU thing.

If 1993 was "AttitUde," the next year it was "AUdacity," the audacity to think we could run the table again.

We went into that season with pretty much the same team. We lost Bostic, we lost Stan White, but we had Patrick Nix back and Stephen Davis back and most of the others. We lost Scott Etheridge at kicker but Matt Hawkins stepped in. We lost a few key players, but we felt like we had good replacements.

We were undefeated, and we had a whole new season coming up. The talk became, "If they wouldn't give us the national championship for going 11-0, maybe if we can run the table again, they'll have no choice but to make us no. 1, if we're 22-0."

Remember, in 1993, we were the only undefeated team. Florida State got the "official" national championship, but they'd lost to Notre Dame, who'd lost to Boston College. It was kind of a weird deal where Daddy Bowden got the trophy, but his son actually had the undefeated team.

What do you guys make of how things worked out for the national championship that year? Should we claim 1993?

Pat Ringer

I didn't worry about it at the time. I just enjoyed the games. Other years I worried about it; 1983 bothered me and 2004 bothered me. But in 1993, we were on probation, we had a great year, and I didn't worry about it. Being competitive and beating everybody was joyous enough for me. I wasn't concerned about the national championship.

John Ringer

I get it, I understand the whole idea, but we were on probation and nobody saw the games, so it's harder to make the case for that season. And we didn't play the out-of-conference teams we normally would have, so it's tough to make a comparison with us and them.

Van Allen Plexico

That's why I think those that *were* concerned about it were saying, "Maybe if we go 11-0 again, and this time we'll be on TV, then maybe we'll be in the conversation." The funny thing is, nobody thought we could go undefeated again, but for a while there, it looked like we were going to.

As an aside, over the years, a number of people have been seriously injured, paralyzed or killed by jumping from Acapulco Rock, an outcropping located high above the surface of Lake Martin, a large body of water to the northwest of Auburn. Between the 1993 and 1994 seasons, Terry Bowden broke several ribs and ripped his pectoral muscle when he dived sixty feet into the water from that spot. He did it in answer to a challenge from his former fullback, Reid McMilion.

"He (McMilion) was laughing at me as he crawled past me going to the top so I followed him up there. He jumped in (feet first), and I dived.

"It was a perfect jump. It felt so good—until I got about ten feet above the water. Then I realized this was about the dumbest thing I've ever done."

—Terry Bowden, Auburn head coach

381

1994

For the 1994 season, Auburn remained on probation, still unable to compete in the postseason. For this year, however, the television ban was lifted, and the Tigers could at least be seen by the nation as they set out on their "AUdacity"-filled quest to go 22-0 over two seasons.

The campaign began with wins over Ole Miss and Northeast Louisiana, to stretch what was now being called "The Streak" to 13 straight.

Then came September 17, 1994. The LSU Tigers came to the Plains. Fans in attendance—and those now able to watch on TV—witnessed something truly remarkable.

Van Allen Plexico

We had beaten LSU's brains in the year before, in Baton Rouge. This year, however, marked the first of a string of notably weird games against them, with Terry Bowden presiding over on our side. It was also a string of games where the LSU defense became truly stout, keeping our offense in check. After 1993, we didn't have another decent offensive showing against them until 1997! We had no offense to speak of against LSU in any of those years. They absolutely shut our offenses down.

I was there. It was incredible to watch. It's the game that got their coach, Curly Hallman, fired. Auburn has gotten at least three LSU coaches fired over the years, and I'm kind of proud of that.

John Ringer

This is a one-word game. "The Interception Game." You just know it.

Pat Ringer

This might be the high-water mark as far as incredible Auburn games (of that era), along with the 1989 Iron Bowl and the Florida game the year before. This game was just so unusual. It was an 11:30 am kick. We were a great team, hadn't lost since the fall of 1992, and here we are playing at 11:30 against an SEC West opponent. That's odd.

Van Allen Plexico
Yes. And we were ranked no. 11 in the country.

But your mention of our record reminded me of this, and I think it's pretty remarkable: If you look at Terry Bowden's five "full" seasons, 1993-1997, in those five years we lost at home just five times. That's amazing. And I think two of those five losses were in the fifth year, which was still a great year. In our first four years under Terry, we lost at home a total of three times, and not until year three did we lose at home at all.

Let me state that again: We didn't lose a home game under Terry Bowden until his *third* season. That is mind-boggling to me. That loss, by the way, was in a shootout against third-ranked Florida, who hadn't beaten us since Pat Dye was the coach.

Let me be clear, though: with the exception of 1997, we declined every year under Bowden. Sometimes people will state that Terry's record at Auburn was 47-17-1, which sounds fantastic. So why would we fire him? But then I point out that he won the first 20 in a row, and after that his record was 27-17-1, which isn't nearly as eye-popping.

Now, back to the Interception Game.

We couldn't score, couldn't move the ball on offense at all. We scored 30 points in this game without scoring a single touchdown on offense. That's not easy to do. We even missed the extra point after one touchdown, so not even our special teams were scoring reliably! But we scored three touchdowns on interception returns in the fourth quarter.

Pat Ringer
And made three more interceptions as well.

John Ringer
This is a game where the LSU defense completely dominated us. And the LSU offense was great. They had 407 total yards in the game, while we had 165. And we won.

Van Allen Plexico

Yeah. That's unbelievable. That's that Auburn secondary I've been talking about.

There's one other weird thing about this game I want to mention.

For some reason I was sitting down lower in this game than I usually did, so I could see this playing out, and it was the weirdest thing.

Patrick Nix was doing nothing against LSU. So, probably halfway through the game, Bowden substituted Dameyune Craig in at quarterback. So Dameyune came in and was trying to get something going, but he was struggling, too. Between plays he would look over at the sidelines to get signals from Terry or an assistant, and at one point a big defensive player for LSU started standing right between them, so Dameyune couldn't see Terry. The LSU guy just stood there, blocking the view, and when Craig moved to see around him, the LSU guy would move as well! I think we ended up having to burn at least one time out because Craig couldn't see Terry to get the play signal. I'd never seen that before and I've never seen it since. It was the strangest thing.

John Ringer

I don't think you're allowed to do that now.

Van Allen Plexico

You probably weren't allowed to do it then, either, but they did it!

John Ringer

We also need to talk about the coaching malpractice on the part of LSU.

Pat Ringer

After we had returned *two* interceptions for touchdowns, we were still losing. And we still couldn't move the ball. I remember talking to the guys I was with and saying, "It's not possible to lose a game where you return two interceptions for touchdowns. I'm pretty sure, in the history of college football, no team that returned two interceptions for touchdowns went on to lose. That just doesn't happen. There's no way we're going to lose this game." And they were like, "Have you seen the clock and the score and what's happening on the field? We're very likely going to lose!"

And every time the LSU quarterback (Jamie Howard) dropped back to pass, it was like, "Oh my gosh, why are they doing this? Why are they still throwing the ball?"

John Ringer

Coaches get fussed at all the time for being too conservative with a lead. "Why don't you stick to playing your game?" This is the textbook case for why you don't continue to be aggressive when you have a lead, especially on the road like this.

At the start of the fourth quarter, it was 23-9 LSU, and Auburn's offense could do nothing. Our nine points came from a field goal and a fumble return early in the game, where we missed the extra point. There was no chance we were going to score 14 points offensively to beat them.

So, in the fourth quarter, Jamie Howard threw a pass and it was intercepted by Ken Alvis.

"This time they'll go from the shotgun, triple wideouts left and one to the nearside, the right. Howard waiting, taking the snap, looking with time, throwing... It is intercepted by Alvis at the forty. Thirty-five, thirty. At the twenty-five, twenty. Alvis at the ten, the five, Alvis, into the end zone! Touchdown Auburn! Broke a tackle and somehow kept his feet at the five, they had two men on him, I don't see how he kept his balance but he did. Forty-one yards for the touchdown. 23-15. Hear the crowd!"

"And that was one of the more spectacular returns of an interception that I have ever seen, Jim!"
—Jim Fyffe and Charlie Trotman, Auburn Network broadcast

Pat Ringer

The way he ended that return, it wasn't like a normal return. He ran over like two offensive linemen and then leapt about eight yards and landed in the end zone. It was amazing to watch.

Van Allen Plexico

All of those interception returns were special. There was something freakish about all of them. It was so weird. Yeah, those guys were athletes.

John Ringer

It's 23-16. We kicked off; LSU got the ball. They ran for no gain. They threw an incomplete pass on second down. On third down they threw the ball again, and this one was intercepted by Fred Smith.

"The crowd needs to make some noise here because it's third and ten on their own fourteen. LSU facing a tough task against this Auburn defense—another chance for the Auburn defense to make a big play."

"Wilson and Kennison to the left, Bech to the right. Auburn setting defensively with a five-man front. Out of the I, they need eleven yards. Taking is Howard, play-faking Howard, he's got time, up the middle—intercepted at the thirty-two! To the twenty-five, to the twenty, to the fifteen, to the ten, to the five, he's in! Touchdown Auburn! Fred Smith! Touchdown Auburn!"

"That is unbelievable! I cannot believe that Jamie Howard did the same thing again! He threw the same pass over the middle, and not only one Auburn man but two Auburn men had a chance for the interception. That's what field position does, Jim, it puts you in a position to make a big play. What can you say about this Auburn defense?"

"There are not enough words to describe how they have played today. Back-to-back interception returns, that one by Fred Smith... Hawkins kick, it's good. We're tied! Brand new game!"

—Charlie Trotman and Jim Fyffe, Auburn Network broadcast

Van Allen Plexico

A different guy every time! It wasn't like we had the "Bo Jackson of defensive backs" out there running back three touchdowns. It was a different guy every time.

And then, after we tied it up, they kicked a field goal to take the lead, and we *still* came back.

John Ringer

Yes, we kicked off and they got the ball and drove all the way down the field in a long drive and kicked the field goal, and now there were only like five minutes left and they were up, 26-23. And again, we couldn't do anything on offense. We got the ball back, Craig lost seven yards, Craig threw complete to Sanders for eight yards, Craig threw incomplete, and we punted. There was no chance we were coming back again.

LSU got the ball, and at that point we were having to call timeouts. And on third and four, they threw *another* pass and it was intercepted by Brian Robinson.

"Auburn setting up defensively. The crowd knows what has to happen here. Bech, Kennison and Burks to the near side. They break the tight end LeFleur out to the left side or the short side of the field. Robert Toomer the setback. They need about four, four and a half yards. Third down play from their thirty-one and a half. Howard wants to throw. Howard fires. Pass is tipped—it is intercepted at the forty! The thirty-five, the thirty, the twenty, the ten, he's gone, Robinson, Touchdown Auburn!"

"Can you believe it? Can you believe it? Three interception returns for a touchdown have brought Auburn back in this ballgame. Defense! Can you say 'defense, Auburn'? Unreal!"

"I don't believe what I've seen! I don't believe what I've seen! Three interception returns for touchdowns! Three of 'em! Count 'em! Unbelievable! A minute fifty-five to play, and for the first time in the second half, the Auburn Tigers have forged ahead in the game!"
—Jim Fyffe and Charlie Trotman, Auburn Network broadcast

John Ringer

And now, with a minute fifty-five left, it wasn't over yet!

We were up 30-26 and now they had to throw the ball on offense because we were ahead with less than two minutes to go.

They got the ball back, they drove down the field, Howard threw a pass, and it was intercepted by Brian Robinson, who ran it back 36 yards—but then he was stripped and fumbled and LSU got the ball back *again*!

Howard threw the ball again, threw it into the Auburn end zone, and it was intercepted again by Chris Shelling, who downed it in the end zone. Craig came out with ten seconds to play and took a knee and we had won the game.

Van Allen Plexico

And that was the one offensive play we were good at in that game was downing the ball. LSU could have literally taken a knee on every play in the fourth quarter and won the game. The only way we were going to win that game was if they kept throwing the ball. So, what did they do? They kept throwing the dang football.

"If you would have told me we would have held Auburn to 3 points and 1 first down in the second half, I would've told you I'd be in heaven, doing backflips. And I'm crying instead."
—Phil Bennett, LSU defensive coordinator

"Y'all saw it. You can't explain it."
—Terry Bowden, Auburn head coach

John Ringer

We did not make a single offensive first down in the fourth quarter, and we came back from 23-9 to win.

Pat Ringer

I really do think if you have *two* pick-sixes in a ballgame, your odds of winning are like 99.9%. And yet, we were *still* going to lose the game unless LSU did something extraordinarily stupid. And they did.

The Auburn-LSU Interception Game was so bizarre, it's worth summing it up thusly:

Auburn entered the fourth quarter trailing LSU 20-9.

Auburn ran *six* offensive plays the entire rest of the game, for a net gain of *2 yards*.

Auburn won the game, 30-26.

The following week, Auburn won easily enough against East Tennessee State, then snagged a couple more interceptions in a win against Kentucky. Now they were 5-0 on the season and the Streak stood at 16 straight.

Van Allen Plexico

We beat Miss State in Starkville on October 8, in a game John and I attended—I was at every single game this season, and this was the only season I have ever been able to do that.

I remember John's neighbors were there and were big Bulldog fans. They were very gracious before the game, and so disappointed afterward, because they'd really thought they had a chance to win this one.

Auburn prevailed in Starkville, 42-18.

Then it was time to travel down to Gainesville for the game Terry Bowden was calling Auburn's "Super Bowl."

The Tigers were not going to be allowed to play in a bowl game for a second straight year. They could appear on television, unlike in 1993, but there would be no postseason. Florida was the no. 1 team in the country. The Gators wanted revenge for the big upset the previous year. Terry Dean had reclaimed the starting QB spot and looked to be on the way to the Heisman Trophy. Hardly anyone thought Auburn could win that game.

Van Allen Plexico

One of the guys I listened to on Atlanta sports radio back then, Chris Dimino, famously said on the air that "monkeys will fly out of my butt" before Auburn beat Florida that weekend. So we always referred to it as the "Monkeys Fly Out of Chris's Butt" Game.

"Florida was no. 1, and Gator Nation, having stewed on that '93 Auburn loss for a year, was poised for payback. UF (5-0) was a 16-point favorite, with national pundits pointing to the good fortune that had accompanied Auburn—five victories by five points or less for 'the nation's luckiest team,' said Sports Illustrated—*during the country's longest winning streak."*
—Chris Harry, FloridaGators.com

The game's attendance was 85,562 a record for a football game played in the state of Florida at that time. More than five hundred media credentials were issued, which was a record for a game played at the University of Florida.

Pat Ringer
We had won seventeen games in a row at that point, and yet we were twenty-point underdogs.

Van Allen Plexico
They had a huge banner in the Swamp that said, "The Streak Stops Here."

My roommate—we were graduate students, and he had been in the Auburn Band as an undergrad, so we were both huge Auburn football fans—he and I were sitting around our trailer in University Park. And I said, "Chris, we've got to go." And he was like, "Oh, we're gonna get killed. I don't want to drive all the way to Gainesville and watch us lose." And I said, "Chris, you know what, we probably *are* going to lose. But—*if we win...*!" And he looked at me for a second as that thought sunk in, and then said, "All right—get in the truck. Let's go."

So we drove down to Gainesville and found tickets somehow. And the Florida people were so rude and crass. They were already celebrating their win, before a down had been played.

And the game was amazing. I think in some ways It was an even better football game than the 1993 game.

Pat Ringer

I was there, too. I think it was my birthday. I was young and dumb and fully expecting that, "Hey, it's my birthday—we're gonna win!" But of course that's not the way things work. But somehow, some way, that day, of course it did.

Steve Spurrier's a genius. I've always loved him. I've always thought that he was just such an incredible coach. Even if you played great, you'd end up giving up like 35 points to them when he was at Florida. That was just the way it was. So you had to score a lot.

Steven Davis played great for us. Frank Sanders played great. I remember that we used the tight end brilliantly in that game. Andy Fuller, doing the "gator" play.

The thing that I remember the most is that Spurrier ingrained in his quarterbacks that, no matter what, when the opposing defense had one safety deep, that he was to basically see which way the safety cheated and throw it deep the other way, to the other side of the field. I guess somewhere, somehow, somebody knew this, and so Brian Robinson lined up tight on the line of scrimmage opposite the side that our safety was going to cheat on. Right at the snap of the ball, he just turned around and went on a dead sprint the opposite way. And, similar to LSU, even though they had the lead and had no business throwing the ball deep—I guess it was Wuerffel at this point, because Terry Dean had already left the game— Robinson sprints back there and picks off the ball. And all sudden we've got the ball back with three minutes left.

After that play, Spurrier was yelling at the quarterback, but actually the quarterback had done exactly what Spurrier had told him you should always do, which is to throw the ball deep opposite the side the single deep safety is leaning.

Van Allen Plexico

That's really interesting. Just as a layperson watching the game, all you can see is that Florida's offense, which never had problems connecting with those great receivers, was suddenly throwing the ball to our guys. And you're like, "How did that happen?" I hadn't thought about it that way.

"Here's your ball game. From the shotgun with four wideouts, Nix to throw, looking, firing, pass caught by Bailey at the thirty, out of bounds at the twenty-eight yard line. And Auburn's still alive. Thomas Bailey catching the pass, good for the first down and more.

"We're down to forty-three seconds—keep in mind, Auburn has no timeouts—from the twenty-eight, that play covering fourteen yards. Nix throwing again out of the shotgun. Looking deep, firing, pass caught at the Florida eight yard line by Willie Gosha. Gosha hauling that one in. He was open inside the ten and he stepped out of bounds at the eight. That's good for twenty yards. Auburn will be first-and-goal at the Florida eight yard line with thirty-six seconds to go.

"Nix again with thirty-six seconds left, ball at the left hashmark. Two wideouts to the right, one to the left. Florida's got the big rush on Nix, he floats one in the end zone—it is caught! Touchdown Auburn! Sanders caught it! Touchdown Auburn! Touchdown Auburn! Frank Sanders from Nix! Auburn's ahead! Auburn's ahead! Touchdown of eight yards! Nix to Sanders! Can you believe it? Can you believe it? Auburn has done it again. An unbelievable comeback with thirty seconds to go. They're up 35-33. They've caught lightning in a bottle. Thirty seconds left. Touchdown Nix to Sanders. We all remember that famous combination from last year. And Auburn, unbelievably, off another interception, has scored a touchdown with no timeouts left, and they've gone ahead of Florida by two.

"The ballgame is over. I have seen it but I do not believe it. Yes, the Streak is alive. As Charlie would say, 'Can you say 18-0?' Auburn 36, Gators 33. No. 1 has fallen by the wayside."

—*Jim Fyffe, Auburn Network broadcast*

John Ringer

That 1993 Florida game and this game were two of the most exciting wire-to-wire games I've ever seen an Auburn team play. The other team was really talented and well-coached and wasn't going to stop coming. You had to just keep going as the game went back and forth.

There were so many big plays in those games, both years. So many huge plays. With a lesser team, one of those big plays

Frank Sanders, by Jarrod Alberich

393

would have just crushed them and they wouldn't have been able to handle it. But both of these teams got up off the mat every time, and they came back and came back.

That was a great drive at the end of the game. Nix took us down the field, and it was a big throw and a big catch by Sanders. he just went up over everybody and got it.

Van Allen Plexico

I remember Steve Spurrier after the game saying that when we converted that fourth down pass to Thomas Bailey, he knew we were going to score.

"They just don't give up, do they?"
—Steve Spurrier, Florida head coach, on Auburn, after the game

"I didn't ever think we couldn't do it. We knew we were going to score. We couldn't believe the alignment they were in. They had No. 35 (Michael Gilmore) one-on-one on Sanders. No contest.
"We should've beat 'em even worse."
—Auburn Quarterback Patrick Nix, on the final touchdown pass

"Auburn just kept coming at Florida, opening a 10-point lead in the first quarter, then fighting back three times to regain the lead. The Tigers refused to cave in.
"There is something about this Auburn team. Call it charmed, call it blessed, but don't call it lucky anymore. The final drive took care of that aspersion, one opponents have frequently cast Auburn's way. The Tigers might be on probation, and they are precluded from a bowl appearance, and any mention in the CNN poll, in this final year of sanctions, but they definitely are the genuine item. And never was it more evident than on that final fateful march through the heart of the Swamp."
—Larry Dorman, the New York Times, 1994

"Everybody said they were the legitimate No. 1 team in the country. You ask me should we be No. 1? I say yes."
—Terry Bowden, after the game

"Everything went their way. I don't know whether it's luck or that the Big Man is a Tiger."
—Florida safety Lawrence Wright

"Every time they call us lucky, we come out and play good. So call us lucky four more times this year and we'll be all right."
—Mike Pelton, Auburn defensive tackle

Fifth-year senior Terry Dean, who had reclaimed the starting role as Florida's quarterback in 1994 and was until this game being promoted by them for the Heisman Trophy, went 9-of-17 for 126 yards—with four interceptions—before being pulled by Spurrier and replaced by Danny Wuerffel.

At that point, though the season was at only the halfway point, the college football career of this one-time Auburn-leaning recruit was essentially over.

"He (Spurrier) had told me Monday before the Auburn game that if I had a bad game, he would bench me. He told me again the Friday before the game that if I wasn't playing well, he would pull me.

"I (threw those interceptions because I) wasn't myself. I was looking over my shoulder."
—Terry Dean, Florida quarterback

"Terry Dean has been the equivalent of a yo-yo at Florida, and the string has played out. On Monday, against Florida State in the Sugar Bowl, he will trot out with the rest of the co-captains for the coin toss, then return to the sideline, his work done for the day.

"And for his career."
—Jim Hodges, LA Times

"I'm ready to be gone. It's been a frustrating five years, and I definitely think I'm capable of bigger and better things. I still think I'm the best quarterback here. There are a lot of reasons why I want to make it in the pros, and one of them is I want to be able to go back (to Gainesville) and say I got a little redemption. Nobody else believed me, but I never lost the idea that I could make it."
—Terry Dean, Florida quarterback

"Look, I'm not going to win any battles with Terry Dean and I don't want to. I'll be the bad guy. I've tried to coach Terry the best I can, and I've failed. If he goes on to have a proven NFL career, then obviously it was my fault he didn't do better here."
—Steve Spurrier, Florida head coach

Dean went undrafted by the NFL. He played in the Canadian league, passing for a grand total of 109 yards, and then in the Arena League, where he threw for 69 yards. Not the career one might have expected from him. Maybe he should have listened to Pat Dye.

After the shocking win at Florida, Auburn's "Streak" now extended to 18-0. The Tigers enjoyed a much-deserved week off before facing Danny Ford's Arkansas back in Jordan-Hare Stadium on October 29.

"It's all coming to an end. We can see the light at the end of the tunnel. This is the last couple of miles of that long road we've taken."
—Shannon Robique, Auburn center, during the off-week

"I'm sorry, but we're not cheaters. There's not a single player or a single coach on this team that had anything to do with what happened.
"They don't like that we're winning on probation. You're not supposed to do that. Well, we are, and I'm sorry, but we're going to continue to do it if we can."
—Patrick Nix, Auburn quarterback

"If the Tigers win all four of their remaining games, they'd finish off the two-year period with a 22-0 record and they figure they have a shot at attaining their goal of a national championship."
—Brian Bourke, Montgomery Advertiser

Four games remained for Auburn in the 1994 season. The first was played in Jordan-Hare Stadium on October 29, against the Arkansas Razorbacks.

Arkansas shut Auburn out in the first quarter and held the Tigers to just a Matt Hawkins field goal by halftime, and led 7-3. Patrick Nix connected with a wide-open Frank Sanders for a 44-yard touchdown in the third quarter, but the Hogs came back. Going into the fourth quarter, Arkansas led, 14-10.

And then junior running back Stephen Davis broke loose.

Davis scored three touchdowns in the fourth quarter to put the Razorbacks away for good.

First, he capped off an 80-yard drive with a 1-yard TD plunge, putting Auburn ahead, 17-14.

Then, less than four minutes later, he took it in from 24 yards out for his second score, and it was 24-14, Auburn—but with plenty of time left for the Razorbacks to mount a rally.

They could not.

Instead, Davis sealed the deal with 2:53 remaining when he broke loose on a 53-yard scoring run that made up the entirety of the drive. One play, 53 yards, one touchdown. In what had started out as a close game, and one in which the Tigers had trailed most of the game (and had lost the time of possession battle by more than ten minutes!), Auburn had won, 31-14.

All told, Davis finished the game with 254 yards rushing on 27 carries—an average of over nine yards a carry—and three touchdowns, all coming late. It was one of his absolute finest days as a Tiger.

Jason Miska and Chris Shelling in particular had big days for Auburn on defense, as the Tigers bent but hardly broke against the Arkansas attack. Barry Lunney, the Hogs' QB, was sacked five times, and no Arkansas running back ran for more than 78 yards.

Auburn was now ranked no. 4 in the AP Poll. The idea of "running the table" and somehow winning the national championship based on a cumulative two years' worth of wins no longer seemed quite so fanciful.

AUdacity indeed.

Van Allen Plexico

Next up was East Carolina, and we beat them, 38-21, in a game that was much more competitive than it should have been. The "Streak" was now 20-0. In fact, it's an interesting trivia question that the last win in the 20-game winning streak of 1993-94 was against East Carolina. After that, we stood at no. 3 in the polls. Anything and everything seemed possible.

And that's when Ray Goff's Georgia came to town.

At this point, everything had bounced our way for two years, and you just had to feel like, no matter what happens, the game's going to bounce our way.

I have to admit here—I need to confess; it's good for my soul, right?—I have to confess how I contributed to this... I almost said "loss," but this was a tie. But we've always thought of this game as a loss. Back when you could still have games ending in a tie, some ties felt like wins and some felt like losses. This game with Georgia felt like a loss because it ended the "Streak."

This was a night game. Right before the game, my roommates and I had gone to this relatively new place in Auburn called Niffer's. My understanding is, it's still there, but it had only been open a short time at that point. There was a new beer out called Red Dog. You may remember the old commercials with the bulldog walking around and the female bulldog calls to him, "Hey, baby!" Well, we went to Niffer's and I made the grievous error of buying and drinking a Red Dog beer right before we played Georgia. I've never forgiven myself. I don't know exactly how my drinking that beer caused the tie, but you have to think I was at least partially responsible.

John Ringer

You heard it here, ladies and gentlemen. The truth comes out, many years later. It's all Van's fault.

But you were talking about how this Georgia game was a tie that seemed like a loss. The *Columbus Ledger-Enquirer's* headline the next day was, "Georgia beats Auburn 23-23."

Pat Ringer

I had two Georgia friends visiting me that weekend. They were playfully trolling me and my friends after the game, saying, "Hey, guys, let's just enjoy it. Nobody wins. Nobody loses, right?"

And, of course, that made me want to punch them in the head.

Van Allen Plexico

Because that was a 6-4-1 Georgia team. They'd gotten shellacked by Florida and lost their homecoming game to Vanderbilt. We should have killed them.

We even had a chance to beat them at the end. We got down the field pretty quickly and lined up to kick a field goal to win. And Matt Hawkins shanked it off to the side. I remember Terry Bowden had his hands up to signal the field goal was good, and he just morphed it straight into the Surrender Cobra. So, the game ended, 23-23, and the Streak was over.

After the game, Terry Bowden said words to the effect of, "I just don't understand. Those breaks always go our way." Ray Goff's quote was something like, "Nobody *just wins.*" In other words, you can't just win every time. Eventually something happens besides winning. And I hate to admit it, but he was right.

"This wasn't a win, but it sure felt like it and it certainly damaged Auburn's program. The Tigers entered the game on a 20-game winning streak. Georgia meanwhile had only won 10 games in the same amount of time. During its streak, Auburn had a knack for winning close games. That all crumbled down when Auburn missed a field goal in the last minute, preserving the 23-23 tie. Auburn's unbeaten streak ended in the Iron Bowl a week later and the Tigers

never sniffed a national title again under head coach Terry Bowden."
—Kyle Funderburk, Sports Illustrated

The next weekend, Auburn traveled to Birmingham to face Alabama in Terry Bowden's second Iron Bowl, in what would once again be the final game of the season, given that the Tigers were finishing up their two years of probation with no post-season play.

Alabama was undefeated, 10-0. After the Georgia debacle, Auburn was suddenly 9-0-1. It was only the second Iron Bowl ever in which both teams were undefeated—but for Auburn fans, it didn't feel that way any longer. The opportunity to run the table in back-to-back years was gone. The dream of securing some share of a national championship, based on "body of work" over two unblemished seasons, was out the window. All the "AUdacity" that remained was to try to ruin Alabama's hopes as well.

Van Allen Plexico

My roommate and I traveled up to Legion Field for the game. This was an undefeated Alabama team—they didn't lose until they met Florida in the SEC Championship Game—but I remember we felt pretty good about our team and our chances.

The Alabama fans had signs everywhere. One said, "10-0 vs 10-0," but they'd crossed out the second "10-0" and written over it, "9-0-1," which kind of bugged me. Another sign said, "Hey, Auburn—Dial 9-1-1!" So apparently there was at least one Alabama fan that was halfway clever in the universe. Who knew?

Pat Ringer

This was my first and only visit to Legion Field. I remember ESPN Game Day was there. And this was back when they didn't go on the road. This was maybe the third or fourth time they'd gone to a game, I believe. It was a big occasion when they showed up.

We made our way over to their broadcast location. In light of what you and some other people have told us about the way that certain members of their team have shown themselves to be, it was enlightening. I remember at the time thinking that

400

Craig James was just the greatest ever, and now of course he's revealed a different side. I remember thinking that Chris Fowler was just a neutral nobody, that he had no opinion on anything—and yeah, not quite. And I remember thinking that Lee Corso was just the devil, but in hindsight he's just a sweet old guy. I mean, what's he got to do with anything?

The game basically boiled down to Auburn getting a bad spot on a 4th down.

Van Allen Plexico

Alabama did a few things on offense that it looked like we weren't expecting. They ran some option on us, especially early in the game. Some reverses. Remember, our strength was the secondary and they weren't really passing. Our weakness was probably linebacker, and they used that to their advantage. They got up 21-0 in the first half, and it looked very bad for us. After that, we must have made some adjustments on defense, and they never threatened to score again the rest of the game. After they got 21 points they just packed in the offense and held on.

"I think when they established the run, our DBs kept wanting to come up and help us out and they (Alabama) got behind them. You just can't do that. You've got to trust that your front can do that (stop the run)."

—Mike Pelton, Auburn defensive tackle, on Auburn getting beat early by big plays

Van Allen Plexico

We started coming back in the second half. We ran some screen passes, flare and dump passes to Fred Beasley out of the backfield. We drove the length of the field twice in the second half, and both times we got to the Alabama goal line and ran quarterback sneaks for the score.

Late in the fourth quarter, Alabama still led, but Auburn had cut the deficit to 21-14. After the second touchdown, Auburn elected to try an onside kick, but Alabama recovered it. One or two first downs for the Tide, and the game would be over.

It was not to be. The Tigers defense came up strong once again, continuing to dominate the second half. They stopped Alabama near midfield and forced a punt with about two minutes to go.

But what did the punt do? It stopped—with some help from the Alabama coverage team—inside the Auburn one yard line. If the Tigers were to have a chance to come back and win the game, they would have to go literally the length of the field in less than two minutes.

They started to work quickly, with Nix hitting Beasley on a flare route in the Auburn end zone. The fullback took the ball out to the 15 yard line and out of bounds, stopping the clock. Next, Thomas Bailey caught a pass over the middle to the 27. Moving quickly, Nix then hit Frank Sanders for a few more yards and another dash out of bounds. Alabama, sitting back in a three-deep zone, was getting no pressure at all on the Auburn QB.

On the next play, the Tide did bring pressure on Nix—and he responded by scrambling away from half the Alabama defense and all the way to midfield with another first down. On third down, Beasley caught another flare pass and ran out of bounds, stopping the clock with 38 seconds to go. He was three yards short of the first down.

Starting the drive from their own one-foot line, Auburn now found itself at the Alabama 42. What had seemed so improbable mere moments before now seemed...possible? Likely, even? Back during the Florida game, Brent Musberger had called them "the Cardiac Kids," and here they were, doing it yet again!

To do it, though, Auburn would need to make a first down on the very next play. There was absolutely no margin for error.

"Auburn doing a nice job of working the ball down the field, they're across midfield. They've got 38 seconds to go. If you throw it in the center of the field, you need a first down to stop the clock. You need to pick up a first down anywhere on the field. Now I don't care where it is, inside or outside. You need a first down."

"Fourth and three. Sanders over the middle. No. Didn't get it. He didn't get it. No, sir. He turned on the 40 yard line, he had to go

inside the 40 and he never ever got across that 40 yard line that I could see. Shade and Johnson ripped him right on the 40."

"I don't believe he made it. It'll be so close. Auburn says yes. Alabama says no."

"They didn't make it. I mean, it couldn't have been more than an inch."
    —*Bob Griese and Keith Jackson, ABC TV commentary*

"Auburn's rally, in search of the biggest miracle yet in Terry Bowden's two beautifully blessed seasons, came to final jeopardy. At the Alabama 42, the Tigers faced a fourth down. Three yards to go. Thirty-one seconds remaining.

"Frank Sanders, the king of Auburn pass receivers, catcher of a climatic last-minute touchdown in a 36-33 upset of No. 1-ranked Florida, had been double-teamed into oblivion through much of this Iron Bowl. But suddenly, in the deep clutch, the kid from Fort Lauderdale slipped across the middle to embrace a Patrick Nix throw.

"Sanders was immediately tackled. It was going to be close. Legion Field was as tense as a maternity-ward waiting room. The measurement was coming. Auburn had received anything but a generous spot from head linesman Bobby Towns.

"'As the referees were dragging the sticks and chain to midfield, I felt my heart almost stop,' said (Jay) Barker, the Alabama hero from Trussville. Zebras dropped to knees, crawling for a closer look. 'Auburn has been so incredible at pulling out cliffhanger games,' Barker added, 'I wanted to leave them no chance. Zero. None.'

"Wish granted, Jay—by an inch."
    —*Hubert Mizell, Tampa Bay Times*

"When he (the referee) pulled the chain, we thought it was a first down. Obviously the referee saw something different than what I thought I saw. I thought I saw the tip of the ball right on the stick or maybe a little bit past it. That's the way the game goes."
    —*Patrick Nix, Auburn quarterback*

"The game was phenomenal, but the moment I'll always remember happened late in the 4th. Down 7 in the final minutes, a frustrated Patrick Nix came off the field during an Auburn timeout. Freshman QB Dameyune Craig came off the bench to give him a pep talk and/or some advice, and right as Keith Jackson took us to commercial break, Nix yelled 'Shut up, Dameyune!' I laughed hysterically."
—Chris Marler, SaturdayDownSouth

Van Allen Plexico
We were coming back, and we thought, "Hey, we've got all the momentum, and Alabama's not even threatening on offense. We can do this."

It was fourth and long and Nix hit Sanders. This could've been "Nix to Sanders 3." Sanders clearly made it across the line to make for the first down, but they spotted him a good yard, yard-and-a-half behind where he actually got to. In other words, they took away all of his forward progress. He hadn't given up his forward progress, he just got shoved back, and the refs ignored his forward progress.

That meant Auburn didn't convert and Alabama got the ball back and ran the clock out.

Would Auburn have gone for the 2-point conversion if they had managed to score a touchdown in the waning moments?

"No doubt about it. We were going to use our special two-point conversion play, but Alabama didn't give us a chance. I'll save it for next year.
—Terry Bowden, Auburn head coach

John Ringer
The "Streak," in my mind, ended the week before, but this really is it. It's a loss, and it's to Alabama, and it's a painful one. As you said, everything had been going our way for two years. When I think about this game, I think of a bunch of things that didn't go our way. Plays we'd been making the

previous two years leading up to this, that we weren't able to make in this game. It wasn't a particularly great Alabama team, either. They were good, but they weren't amazing or anything. It was a close game, a competitive game, and a tough loss.

The Iron Bowl was over. The 1994 season was over. The "Streak" was over. The one ray of sunshine, however, was that the two years of probation penalties were also over.

"Our seniors are sad, but they have a lot to be proud about. They were on Auburn's only team ever to win eleven games in a season and they were part of the school's longest winning streak.
"Next year, we'll go after the national championship. We'll go after it every year."
—Terry Bowden, Auburn head coach

1995

Terry Bowden's "AU" slogan for 1993 had been "AttitUde," and for 1994 "AUdacity." For 1995 the slogan would be "AUthentic," as in, the Tigers finally had an "AUthentic" opportunity to play in the SEC Championship Game, to go to a bowl game, and to compete for a national championship. *Sports Illustrated* even ranked Auburn 2nd in the nation in their preseason poll, behind only Arizona.

Alas, the season would not play out that way.

Van Allen Plexico

When looking at 1995, we have to mention the September 16 game against LSU in Tiger Stadium. The final score was 12-6 LSU, in another dominating performance by LSU's defense against our offense. But this was also the "Phantom Whistle" game. LSU was ahead by 6 and we were trying to come back, and Patrick Nix heard a whistle and thought the play was over and stopped—and he was sacked by the defense.

He thought the refs had blown the play dead, but it was someone in the stands with a whistle.

Pat Ringer

You know, kudos to whichever ridiculous LSU fan did that because, I mean, that basically won the game for them. It was very irritating as an Auburn fan, and I wouldn't do that myself. But you don't see something like that that happen now. I'm not sure what the difference is, nowadays.

Notwithstanding the six measly points they scored against LSU, the 1995 Auburn team was actually an extremely high-scoring squad. In their first five games, they rang their opponents up for at least 42 points in all four of the games not played in Baton Rouge, handing out lopsided losses to Ole Miss, Chattanooga, Kentucky and Miss State.

Game six of the 1995 season featured the return of Florida to Jordan-Hare Stadium. The undefeated Gators were no. 3 in the country; once-beaten Auburn had climbed back up from no. 13 to no. 7. Danny Wuerffel was back at quarterback for his third shot at the Tigers, against whom he was 0-2. Steve Spurrier still hadn't beaten Terry Bowden. The Gators were hungry for revenge for their two shootout losses in 1993 and 1994.

Van Allen Plexico

The Florida game of 1995, believe it or not, was Terry Bowden's first home loss. We got all the way to game six of his third season before we suffered a loss at Jordan-Hare.

It was pouring down rain all the way through the first quarter. We all got soaked. I still have my ticket from this game, and it's streaked and wrinkled from that rain. It got so muddy along the sidelines, they had to put boards down for the ABC camera truck to drive on.

As a quick aside, back then I remember seeing two different ways that the TV cameras were moved around the sidelines. At least one company—probably CBS—brought in a specially-built self-propelled camera vehicle with an extending arm for the camera to go up high. At the other end of the spectrum, though, I think it was Jefferson-Pilot, kings of the 11 am kickoff, who just put a stationary camera in the bed of a pickup truck and drove that truck up and down the West sideline the whole game, to film along the line of scrimmage. That always struck me as a very low-rent way to cover a football game.

It poured down rain before kickoff and then through most of the first quarter. My roommate and I were wearing ponchos and didn't realize we were sitting directly below the edge of the upper deck. In the second quarter I suddenly became aware that we were the only people in our area still wearing ponchos and still getting rained on. The rain had stopped, but for some reason we were still getting wet. I looked up and saw we were sitting directly below the downspout from the deck. I had a weird feeling that everyone else in the stadium was looking at us and laughing. I couldn't really blame them!

Of course, the rest of the game felt like we had a storm cloud directly over our whole team.

Auburn cashed in two Florida turnovers and led early, 10-0. This was encouraging, in that the Tigers had been forced to come from behind in the previous two clashes with the Gators.

But then Reidel Anthony returned the subsequent kickoff for a Florida touchdown. Auburn responded with a long drive to set up another Matt Hawkins field goal, and the score was 13-7 Auburn. In a matchup that had become known of late for two powerful offenses slugging it out, neither team had yet scored a touchdown on offense.

The game remained close for a while, with the teams exchanging touchdowns. Florida led 21-20 a short time after the rains finally stopped. Then Ike Hilliard scored on a 22-yard pass from Wuerffel to put the Gators up by 8.

After that, it became the Chris Doering show.

"The last two times we've played Auburn, we had our chances and just blew it. It feels good to finally be able to finish the game. When we were down, everyone looked for Danny to pick us up and that's what he did. It's great to have a quarterback like Danny to get things going in that situation."
—Chris Doering, Florida receiver

"This was a very big win for us. This game has been a point in our season that has been hard for us to get past the last two years. It feels great to finally get this win. We were able to get some motivation going late in the first half with turnovers."
—*Danny Wuerffel, Florida quarterback*

John Ringer
Chris Doering killed us in this game. We couldn't stop him. They had a huge second quarter and scored three touchdowns—the last one by Doering—and then he scored two more in the second half, and we couldn't come back.

We had lost a lot of the great players from the secondary, that had made a huge difference in 1993 and 1994.

We know about Spurrier that when he found something he liked, he wasn't one of these guys that said, "I'll just go back to it once a quarter." He would just go right at it. Pick at it and pick at it and pick at it. He found a mismatch with Doering against some of our smaller and younger defensive backs and he just didn't stop. Doering abused us that whole game. He kept getting open and kept catching the ball and making plays that we couldn't stop.

Pat Ringer
I believe Dell McGee was one of the corners for us at the time. He was only like five-seven or five-eight and he was getting burned in that game.

"We got beat by a better football team. We played as hard as we could play. For every turnover our fans and players want to point to, they can turn to one equally. I think it balances out. They deserved to win."
—*Terry Bowden*

Back down to no. 13 the Tigers dropped.

After a homecoming win over Western Michigan, Auburn climbed a couple of spots up to 11th in the AP Poll and traveled to Little Rock to face Arkansas in War Memorial Stadium on October 28.

Astonishingly, Auburn turned the ball over three times in the first half, and Arkansas led 27-0 at halftime. The game threatened to turn into one of those Hog debacles Auburn fans would witness a few years later, during the Tuberville era.

But the Tigers came roaring back in the second half, relying mainly on the passing game. Very late in the fourth quarter, Auburn scored a touchdown on a pass from Patrick Nix to Errick Lowe, closing the gap to 30-26, Arkansas. Then the same duo hooked up for the two-point conversion, and suddenly Auburn was only down two, 30-28, with a handful of seconds remaining. And then, amazingly, Auburn recovered an onside kick and had one more chance to score and win.

Alas, the 52-yard Matt Hawkins kick was partially blocked by Junior Soli, and the Hogs held on to win, 30-28.

"We played as well in the second half as we did poorly in the first half. We got so far behind, we could not come back and win."
—Terry Bowden

This Arkansas team went on to win the SEC West, behind the passing of Barry Lunney and the running of Madre Hill. They lost to Florida in the SEC Championship Game, 34-3. If Auburn had made that field goal, they and not Arkansas would've played the Gators in Atlanta.

Van Allen Plexico

There are a couple of noteworthy things about this Arkansas game. We came roaring back from deep in the hole at halftime. And we had a bunch of good receivers on this team. Tyrone Goodson, Willie Gosha, Robert Baker (the Touchdown Maker), Errick Lowe and Karsten Bailey all had their moments.

John Ringer

This was the game that was played the same night the Braves clinched the World Series against Cleveland.

Van Allen Plexico

That's right. I was at my fiancé's family's house in Atlanta and they were big Braves fans, and I kept getting ahold of the remote control and turning the TV back to the Auburn game. They were about to murder me. I got to see the end of our game, by the hardest.

John Ringer

We had one TV in the den and one in the bedroom, one on the Braves and one on Auburn, and we were literally just running back and forth from one room to the other.

Pat Ringer

I was at the game. I remember walking out of the stadium, of course, crestfallen. This was my senior year, and I'm thinking, "Of course we're due to go on some magical run," and it's quickly unravelling. As we're walking out, somebody says to me, "Oh, well—the Braves won the World Series."

I was a big Braves fan and should have been very, very excited. But that was probably the time and place where I would care the least, finding out as I was walking out of the stadium where Auburn has just lost.

Van Allen Plexico

The next game of note was Georgia. I was at that game. It was the coldest football game I've ever attended. The weather report had said to expect mild temperatures and rain, so I wore a thin jacket; just a windbreaker. It never did rain, but instead we got arctic blasts! You look at the press coverage from that game, and all the stories mention the "frigid" conditions.

Georgia was going to host the Olympic soccer matches the following summer, so they were planning to tear out all the hedges in order to widen the field for soccer. Knowing this, both Georgia and Auburn people were just ripping out pieces of their hedges all game long. I was wanting to set the hedges on fire, it was so cold.

We ended up winning the game, 37-31. It was a real shootout, very entertaining. I don't remember many of the details, though—just the cold.

Hines Ward had a good game for Georgia at quarterback, after being forced into playing that position due to other injuries—and even he was playing with a broken wrist.

Stephen Davis had his usual solid game for Auburn. The offensive stats were pretty even between the two teams. The Tigers made a big defensive stop deep in their red zone near the end to pull out the win. Fred Beasley made a great catch-and-run for a score, to start the third quarter.

"Third down and Auburn will need long yardage, about 16 or 17 yards. They're back near their 45. Again they'll load up the shotgun. Two wideouts to the near side, one to the far side. Nix calling his play, play clock running down, they gotta hurry, he gets it away. Here comes Georgia, they're all over him. Screen pass set up. Caught at the 40, up to the 45 is Beasley, midfield, down the sideline 40, he's at the 30, he's at the 20, he's at the 10, he's at the 5, he's gone! Touchdown Auburn! Forty-five yards for the score!"

"Absolutely great call, Jim, that time after having been sacked, and not huddling. Patrick Nix gets a call from the offensive coaches—coach Terry Bowden and Tommy Bowden from the sideline. The play is a screen pass set up beautifully, all the Georgia front men in Patrick Nix's face when he throws it, and it's Robert Baker who makes the key block that springs the pass receiver, Fred Beasley, for the touchdown on the screen pass. That's one of the prettiest plays Auburn has executed all year long."
—Jim Fyffe and Charlie Trotman, Auburn Network broadcast

The win was Auburn's sixth on the season against a D-1 opponent, making them bowl-eligible for the first time since 1990.

"We just wanted to get to a bowl. Now we're here (with enough wins to qualify). But I'm not thinking about any bowl right now. All I'm thinking about is the Iron Bowl."
—Andy Fuller, Auburn tight end

Then came Alabama. It would be only the third time Auburn played the Crimson Tide in Jordan-Hare Stadium. The Tigers came into the game at 7-3 and ranked no. 21 in the country. Alabama was 8-2 and ranked no. 17. Alabama was on probation and not eligible for the postseason, so this was to be their final game of the year.

Van Allen Plexico

A quick side story before we get into the game itself: I was still at Auburn that fall, in graduate school. I entered a contest—I kid you not—being sponsored by Stouffer's frozen dinners. I ate a lot of those back in college! The winner received four tickets to the Iron Bowl, plus passes to the picnic at the Stouffer's corporate tent before the game. And I won!

I gave two of the tickets to my sister, so she could go to the Iron Bowl—and she gave them away! I could have sold them for a pretty penny, but I gave them to her instead, and she just gave them away, to people I didn't even know. I couldn't believe it. We'll see if she reads this book and sees this! Ha.

My roommate and I took the other two tickets and went to the game, and there were a couple of amusing moments beforehand. One was, we went into the Stouffer's corporate tent and their executives were seated in there in suits and ties and nice dresses, eating and chatting. So we walked up and started helping ourselves to the food, and they looked up at us like, "Who are these college kids coming in here, eating our precious food?" They checked our passes and graciously allowed us to continue eating; it was the same stuff I'd been heating up in the microwave for years, just in fancy bowls. Nobody talked to us or approached us beyond that. I was thinking, "Why give us these passes and invite us in here and then ignore us?" So that was weird.

The other memorable thing before kickoff was that I'd made a big sign that said, "Lee Corso Picks His Nose." I spelled "ESPN" vertically in red, using letters from each word:

leE

corSo

  Picks his

  Nose

I just thought it was funny in general. It didn't occur to me at all that Corso actually did "picks" of the day's games before kickoff. I was getting credit for being smarter than I actually was!

My roommate and I went to the GameDay set and were standing there in the big crowd in front of it, and they went to a commercial, and suddenly a policeman came up and took my sign away. I was so mad! I figured he threw it in the trash. But instead, a couple of minutes later, when they were back on the air, Corso held my sign up on live TV and said, "This is the sign of the year! This is terrific." I guess he sent the cop to bring the sign to him, not to throw it away. I was shocked!

This video is on YouTube, by the way, so you can go there and see Corso holding my sign and talking about it.

Auburn got on the board first, finishing off a nice drive with a pass from Patrick Nix to Stephen Davis.

"Wideouts left and right for Patrick Nix, from the I-set. The fake pitch to Davis, he rolls out, he's got a man wide open—it's Davis! At the 20, he's at the 15, the 10, down the far sideline to the 5, he is gone! Touchdown Auburn! Twenty-nine yards! And it scared me to death because I didn't think Davis was expecting the pass!"
—*Jim Fyffe, Auburn Network broadcast*

"That was just a great play by a senior quarterback and a senior running back."
—*Gene Stallings, Alabama head coach, the Alabama Football Review*

Alabama came right back with a long touchdown pass from Freddie Kitchens to Todrick Malone. Auburn responded with a long drive, capped off by a short touchdown run by backup QB Dameyune Craig. Then Malone busted loose for a 59-yard TD run for Alabama. The score was 14-14 and there were still almost four minutes left to play in the *first quarter*.

It appeared that both teams could pretty much score at will, and they looked to be trading knockout blows all night long. But then things settled down.

By the start of the fourth quarter, they were still tied—now at 24-24. Alabama kicked a short field goal to take the lead, but Auburn came right back, beginning with a long kickoff return by Robert Baker to the AU 40. Clearly the "Touchdown Maker" had the hot hand; on third down and 9, Nix hit him for a long pass that he took to the Alabama 26. Two plays later, Fred Beasley carried it the distance for the score.

"Like a pickup game played to exhaustion, the Alabama-Auburn game came down to one final stand near the end zone. The team that was better won.

"With 21 seconds left and 22 yards to go, Alabama quarterback Freddie Kitchens stared into the screaming student section, but Auburn held its ground, and the No. 21 Tigers beat No. 17 Alabama, 31-27, Saturday in a game that rivaled some of the best in this storied series.

"Fred Beasley's 22-yard touchdown run gave the Tigers, 8-3 overall and 5-3 in the Southeastern Conference, their decisive lead with 11:15 remaining. Then, Auburn's young, suspect defense withstood one more drive.

"The rivals exchanged blows and leads, with the outcome uncertain until the end. Auburn punted with 3:22 left, giving Alabama one more shot at winning and preserving bragging rights for another year.

"But Kitchens, in only his second start as a college quarterback, threw incompletions on three consecutive passes. It ended on fourth and 10 with nine seconds left, as Kitchens missed his receiver in the corner of the end zone.

"'That is what playing college football is all about,' Auburn linebacker Jason Miska said.

"In a battle of quarterbacks from the same high school, Kitchens was 19 for 43 for 302 yards and one touchdown. Patrick Nix was 18 for 36 for 259 yards and two touchdowns for Auburn."

—Associated Press report

Van Allen Plexico

With Auburn leading, 31-27, late in the game, Freddie Kitchens drove Alabama down to the Auburn red zone. There were a couple of controversial calls where it looked like they might have scored, but the referee said their receiver was out the back of the end zone. Alabama fans still complain about the one that was closest to being a catch. Fortunately for us that day, there was no instant replay. I really don't know how they would've ruled. Video replays show him still in the process of bringing the ball in—sort of double-clutching the ball as he steps out the back of the end zone—but Alabama fans circulated still photos that made it *look* like he had the ball in his hands when he was still in bounds.

In any case, the pass was properly ruled incomplete and that finished off Alabama.

"Nine seconds to play. Kitchens back, gonna throw in the end zone—no! It's incomplete! It's incomplete! It's incomplete!

"Yes, yes, yes! Yes, Auburn, yes! Two seconds left. This ball game is gonna be over.

"Nix taking the snap, dropping to a knee. See you later, Bama! 31-27! Auburn wins it! They came back when they had to! And Auburn gets out of here with another victory over the Crimson Tide. War Eagle, everybody!"

—Jim Fyffe, Auburn Network broadcast

"'I never thought we would have scored 31 on that defense,' said Auburn Coach Terry Bowden after his second victory over Alabama in three years."

—Associated Press report

Van Allen Plexico

This is one thing Terry was able to do—and you can say what you will about the quality of the Alabama and Georgia teams during the Nineties, but—Terry was able to pretty much hold serve at the very least against Georgia and Alabama, most of his years there. I mean, he won as many as he lost against both of them.

Pat Ringer

It's true. The quality of opponent means a lot, but I do respect what he did.

Van Allen Plexico

After that win, we were 8-3 and we went to the Outback Bowl to play Penn State. We had Steven Davis and we were feeling good about things, but for most of the game it was pouring down rain, the field was slick, and Davis got a concussion. After that, Penn State just beat our brains in.

Pat Ringer

I was at that game. It was miserable. It was about fifty degrees and raining the entire time and I was freezing to death. And I remember some lady was smoking non-stop and (growling), "Nobody runs on Penn State."

John Ringer

This was the core of a Penn State team that I think had a really good year, the next year or two, if I'm not mistaken.

Pat Ringer

The previous year, they'd had Kijana Carter and one of the best offenses in the country.

Van Allen Plexico

We never got anything going and we couldn't stop them and it was pouring down rain and nasty and we lost, 43-14.

The 1995 Auburn team finished at 8-4 overall, 5-3 in the SEC, which wasn't great—but they beat Georgia and Alabama. There's something to be said for that. But we lost to LSU, lost to Florida, lost to Arkansas, lost the bowl game. So at that point, everything that had been so nice and sparkly about Terry Bowden was starting to get a little tarnished.

The 1995 team was surprisingly good on offense; they scored 438 points total, finishing eighth out of 108 teams in Division 1-A in scoring, at 36.5 points per game, and ended up no. 22 in the AP Poll. Those road losses at LSU and Arkansas, by a combined 8 points, prevented the year from being a truly special one.

1996

Going into the 1996 season, Auburn returned an amazing stable of wide receivers, along with quarterback Dameyune Craig, who would now be the unchallenged starter. But with Stephen Davis gone to the NFL, the running back situation was getting thin. Fred Beasley, Rusty Williams and Markeith "the Lizard" Cooper would have to carry the ball on the ground for the Tigers that season—but it was Dameyune Craig who would have to shoulder the largest load, and be the difference-maker for most of the season.

Van Allen Plexico

I don't know if Terry Bowden was only recruiting little scat backs, or that's all that would come, but our recruiting was starting to noticeably fall off.

There was also a sense in 1995 that our defensive coordinator, Wayne Hall, who had been a holdover from the Dye era, was not trying as hard anymore. There were whispers that he was putting more effort into his construction company than he was into the Auburn defense. Bowden relieved him of his duties and brought in as his replacement Bill "Brother" Oliver, who had been defensive coordinator for Gene Stallings at Alabama, interestingly enough.

John Ringer

It was a time when college football coaches didn't make a lot of money, so our defensive coordinator literally ran a construction company on the side.

"Auburn's new defensive coordinator, Bill Oliver, stunned many Crimson Tide faithful and shocked a few Auburn supporters when he departed Gene Stallings' staff and joined Terry Bowden's in January. But Oliver is no stranger to the loveliest village of the plains. Oliver served as secondary coach under Shug Jordan from 1966 to 1970 and Auburn's defensive backfield became one of the best in the nation under his guidance."

—*Rich Donnell, Inside the Auburn Tigers*

Van Allen Plexico

I suspect that, from the beginning, Oliver planned to stage a palace coup and try to overthrow Terry, because he never took Terry seriously when he was the defensive coordinator for Stallings. He's the one that coined the term "Buster Brown" for Terry Bowden, and that stuck. It seemed like they never really got along.

Auburn began the 1996 season with shutouts at home over UAB (29-0) and Fresno State (62-0). The hiring of Brother Oliver looked like it had been a good move.

Prior to the Fresno State kickoff, Lee Corso on ESPN predicted Auburn would lose.

Pat Ringer

I saw an episode of Real Sports on HBO a couple of years ago, about ESPN GameDay, and they talked to Lee Corso. He said, "You don't understand the memories of these (Auburn) people." He talked about how he picked Fresno State to beat Auburn, and they ended up losing big, "and those people at Auburn remind me of that every single time I go down there!"

Van Allen Plexico

I know I would. I would lead with it. It would be like the second thing I'd say to him. "Hi, Lee, nice to meet you. Do you remember how you picked Fresno State to beat Auburn in 1996? Oh, and thanks for holding up my sign that time!"

The LSU game that year is notable for being the "Barn Burner," where the old gymnastics building—-the one where my dad graduated, in 1960—burned down during the game. I was there and remember seeing the smoke and flames during the game, but never feared for my life or anything. I guess I assumed if it had been *that* bad, they would've evacuated us from the stadium.

John Ringer

It was very dramatic-looking on TV. Someone parked their van over a burning charcoal grill, and the rest was history. It's why Auburn has hot coal containers around campus now.

It was a huge fire. You could see the flames over the side of the student section of the stadium. So that was big.

Van Allen Plexico

And we lost. This was the third year in a row that LSU had a stifling defense that totally shut us down. It was 17-9 LSU in the fourth quarter, and backup QB Jon Cooley came in and got something going late on offense, pulling us to within two, at 17-15. But then we went for two and his pass was intercepted and run back, and LSU won, 19-15.

Auburn went 4-1 over the next five games. That run included winning an epic home quarterback duel between Dameyune Craig and South Carolina's Anthony Wright, 28-24. The Tigers also manhandled Mississippi State, Arkansas and Northeast Louisiana. In the middle of that run, however, came a 51-10 blowout loss to first-ranked and national-champs-to-be Florida in Ben Hill Griffin Stadium. The days of being competitive with the Gators, by holding them down just enough on defense, generating multiple turnovers, and scoring a few more points than them on offense, seemed long-gone. Ron Zook was out; Bob Stoops was running the defense in Gainesville by then, and Florida had become a much more complete team.

Then, on November 16, Auburn welcomed Georgia into Jordan-Hare for a 2:30 pm kickoff of a historic game—a game that wouldn't end until well past sunset.

Van Allen Plexico

The NCAA had implemented overtime for the first time at the start of this season—the same system we have now, with a few tweaks—and no SEC teams had played an OT game. Then Georgia, under Jim Donnan, came to town. And the thing that's so frustrating about this game is it never should have gone to overtime. We absolutely should have won it, and won it in regulation.

Before getting into the details of overtime, there's another—and perhaps a more famous, or infamous—part of this game that has to be mentioned. It is, of course, the Uga/Robert Baker incident.

Early in the game, wide receiver Robert Baker caught a touchdown pass from Dameyune Craig and ran out the right side of the Georgia end zone. There he encountered Georgia's bulldog mascot, Uga, and his handler, Charles Seiler. Trying to halt his momentum before he ran them both over, Baker put out a hand and touched Seiler in the chest. Uga apparently didn't appreciate this act of kindness on Baker's part, and lunged at the Auburn player. A combination of the dog's leash and Baker's quick reflexes prevented what could've been a far more horrifying incident; Baker leapt backwards just as Uga snapped at his crotch.

Patricia Miklik Doyle of the *Montgomery Advertiser* happened to snap a photograph of the incident. She was the only press photographer in the stadium who captured it. The paper went on to sell tens of thousands of copies of the photo in the days and years after the game.

"We watched (video of) it about a couple hundred times afterwards in slow motion. I think we broke down that as much as we broke down plays in the game."
—Matt Stinchcomb, Georgia offensive lineman

Meanwhile, in part thanks to Baker's touchdown, Auburn built a 28-7 lead early, and led 28-14 at halftime. Georgia seemed hopelessly behind; they were already suffering through a woeful season that ended with them 5-6 overall and 3-5 in the SEC. But a couple of good AU drives came up empty, and the Bulldogs pulled the score to 28-21 late.

Then things got strange.

Georgia was driving, but time was growing short. When Georgia QB Mike Bobo (who would be named Auburn's offensive coordinator in 2021!) was sacked by Jimmy Brumbaugh and Marcus Washington with six seconds to go, and with the Dogs having no more time outs, the win seemed assured. Unfortunately, an Auburn player needlessly touched the ball, causing the referees to blow the clock dead while they reset the ball. Given a reprieve, Bobo spiked the ball on the next snap to stop the clock, then found Corey Allen on a 30-yard touchdown pass to tie the game as time expired.

Pat Ringer

We rightfully got called for delay of game, but if we'd just left the ball alone, the referees would have set it and the clock would've started and Georgia would've had no time to run a play. But one of our players batted the ball away and that allowed the refs to stop the clock.

In overtime, the two teams traded touchdowns, with Dameyune Craig providing the bulk of Auburn's offense and Robert Edwards emerging at running back—after starting the game on the bench—to score three touchdowns for the Dogs. The rule had not yet been added that required teams to go for two after the second touchdown in overtime.

Finally, with Georgia ahead, 56-49, the Bulldog defense was able to stop Dameyune Craig on a fourth-down scramble, and the game mercifully ended.

"A flustered Georgia football program found life in dramatic fashion Saturday thanks to Mike Bobo, who rallied the Bulldogs from 21 points down for a four-overtime, 56-49 win over No. 20 Auburn.

"It was the 100th and wildest meeting between the rivals as the teams combined for 1,095 yards and 60 first downs. But the excitement was lost on the Tigers (7-3, 4-3), who were eliminated from the SEC West title race the week before their game against Alabama."

—Eddie Pells, Associated Press

Van Allen Plexico

I know this was a 2:30 pm central time start, but it felt like one of those ESPN2 games that started at 7:30 pm! It was getting really late, with the game still going on. I lived on the other side of Atlanta and knew it was going to take me at least three hours to get home. So, when it was like 49-49 in overtime, I told my girlfriend, "I almost don't care who wins anymore—I just want to go home!" And, boy, did I get my wish. So this is *two* Georgia games I have to take the bullet for, I guess.

Pat Ringer

I had a similar feeling. I was in the student section and was ready for it to end. It was kind of a precursor to the way we get the long referee reviews and replays that we have now. I was thinking, "Of course I want to win the game, but I also want to leave!"

John Ringer

It seemed like the game started later than 2:30, but remember—that's 3:30 Eastern, so it would've ended at 6 pm, but then you have four overtimes, and the referees weren't as efficient back then, because this was the first time SEC officials had ever done overtime. They had to stop and carefully explain everything every single time. Back then they did the coin toss and then explained who was going to go first and who's second and which end is which, every single time, and it went on forever.

And I think this is one of those games where both sets of defenders were just exhausted at the end of the game, and neither side could stop the other team's offense.

Pat Ringer

The fans, too. I remember at the very end, celebrating, jumping up and down, because Craig passed a marker on the sideline and I thought it was the first down marker, but of course it turned out to be the line of scrimmage marker. So he was tackled and that ended the game, and I was jumping up and down thinking we'd made the first down.

The 1996 Iron Bowl, played in Legion Field in Birmingham, was another wild-and-wooly affair, but one that would ultimately prove disappointing for Auburn fans.

Alabama led early, largely behind the running of Shaun Alexander and Dennis Riddle, and were up 17-0 in the first quarter. Those Gene Stallings-coached Alabama teams had a knack for getting up early on Terry Bowden's Auburn squads.

After a long Rusty Williams run (!) set up a Jaret Holmes field goal, Dameyune Craig brought the Tigers even closer, hitting Karsten Bailey with a long pass for a touchdown to make it 17-10 Alabama in the second quarter. Then Brad Ware grabbed a pick-six and suddenly the game was tied, 17-17.

"Quite frankly the folks from Alabama are kind of in shock over how quickly this has happened, because they were dominating this football game, but we're tied at 17."
—Ron Franklin, ESPN broadcast

The shocks weren't over. On the ensuing kickoff, Alabama fumbled the return and Auburn recovered deep in Tide territory. A Jaret Holmes field goal put the Tigers ahead at the half, 20-17, in a game they'd seemed hopelessly out of, just a short time earlier.

Behind Craig's passing and Williams's running, Auburn moved the ball well on the opening drive of the second half, but once again had to settle for a Holmes field goal. That would prove to be the difference; a touchdown there likely would've been enough to secure the win. Instead, the rest of the second half played out scoreless until the final drive, when Freddie Kitchens took the reins with very little time left and no timeouts. He moved Alabama methodically down the field, then hit Dennis Riddle with a swing pass with 34 seconds remaining. Riddle weaved his way into the end zone for the score. With the extra point, the Tide prevailed, 24-23, in what would also be the game where Stallings resigned as Alabama coach.

Van Allen Plexico

Losing those last two big games, after starting 7-2, dropped us down in the bowl game pecking order. We ended up playing Army in the Independence Bowl. First thing is, you don't want to go to the Independence Bowl because that's the Weedeater Bowl, and you just don't want to be associated with that. You don't want to play in Shreveport, Louisiana on December 31.

Dameyune Craig had a great game, but in the second half Army came back, and we barely held them off, winning by 3. I remember thinking, "Oh my gosh, we're going to blow this game and lose to *Army*."

Auburn actually led Army by a score of 32-7 in the fourth quarter of the 1996 Independence Bowl, but then Army scored a shocking 22 unanswered points to close out the game. Auburn only avoided having to go into overtime because Army missed a 27-yard field goal with 29 seconds left, which would've tied the game at 32. The Tigers held on for the 32-29 win.

Dameyune Craig set an Auburn record with 447 total yards in the game, including 372 through the air and 75 on the ground. But Army held him to only seven yards in the fourth quarter, while scoring three touchdowns themselves.

"We came out and pretty much controlled the game, but they are the military, and they never gave up. You have to feel proud to have a group like this defending your country."
—*Dameyune Craig, Auburn quarterback*

"In a year where it seems like you have been snakebit, you just start to think that bad things may happen. A win like this does not make up for some of the close losses, but it makes for a lot more positive offseason."
—*Terry Bowden, Auburn head coach*

1997

Van Allen Plexico
With the 1996 season in the books, including last-second losses to both Georgia and Alabama, the powers-that-be on the Plains were warning Terry, "We don't do eight-win seasons.

Eight-win seasons are not acceptable. You need to win more than that."

"Auburn people are wonderful people, and I understand they're serious about their football. And I understand that 8-4 isn't acceptable in the SEC, and that we have to beat Alabama."
—Terry Bowden, quoted in the Auburn Plainsman, 1997

Van Allen Plexico

We went into 1997 thinking it was supposed to be our big breakthrough year, the year Terry had been building toward. We still didn't have any great running backs, but Dameyune Craig was a senior and in total control of the offense, and he had a bunch of good receivers. If we were ever going to do something big under Terry Bowden, this was the year.

And we actually did win the SEC West and go to our first SEC Championship Game in the Georgia Dome—I was there for that.

Tommy Bowden, Auburn's offensive coordinator and the older brother of the head coach, departed Auburn after the 1996 season to become head coach at Tulane. In his second season there, the Green Wave finished undefeated, 11-0, duplicating the record his younger brother and former boss had achieved in his first season at Auburn. At the conclusion of *that* season, Clemson came calling for Tommy, and he would go on to coach there for ten years, including against Auburn (and against his brother's later replacement as head coach there, Tommy Tuberville) in the 2007 Chick-Fil-A Bowl. Tommy resigned from Clemson six games into the 2008 season; this was the same number of games into the 1998 season Terry coached at Auburn a decade earlier, in 1998, before he, too, had resigned in mid-season.

Back at Auburn, Terry Bowden responded to the defection of his brother from the offensive coordinator job by promoting his running backs coach, Rodney Allison. Allison would find success in 1997 with Dameyune Craig operating the offense, but a year later and without Craig at the helm, the situation grew bleak. At the end of the 1998 campaign, Allison (along with most of the rest of the staff) would be dismissed, only to have Tommy Bowden bring him aboard the Clemson staff—coaching the defensive ends!

It's hard to imagine any scenario today where an offensive coordinator at a Power Five school could switch to coaching *defensive ends* at another Power Five school the next year.

For 1997, Auburn added orange drop-shadows behind the white numbers on the home jerseys, and behind the blue numbers on the road whites. Some fans loved this addition, while others hated any tampering whatsoever with tradition.

The 1997 season was one that had been circled on calendars for a while, with big things expected of the Tigers. Indeed, they started off 6-0 and climbed as high as sixth in the AP Poll. During that run, they rang up impressive road wins at Virginia, at LSU, and at South Carolina. The Virginia win stood as Auburn's best non-conference Power Five road win for quite some time—possibly until the 2014 win at Kansas State. Dameyune Craig was impressive in leading his team against the Cavaliers and their star QB, Aaron Brooks. The Tigers only led by five, 7-2, at the half, thanks to a 17-yard run by Craig. In the second half, though, Auburn got a pick six from Ryan Taylor, and then Craig hooked up with Karsten Bailey for touchdown passes of 57 and 77 yards to put the game away, 28-17. Craig ended with 247 yards of passing offense, 151 of that going to Bailey. Auburn's leading rusher, Markeith Cooper, finished with nine carries for only 32 yards—an indication of what to expect from the run game that season. Fred Beasley was held to only 18. This team, though, didn't seem to find a rushing game necessary—not with Craig scrambling and throwing to all those great receivers. Whether that formula would continue to work all season long, however, remained to be seen.

The win at LSU on September 20 was particularly sweet, given the frustrating ways in which the Tigers had lost the two previous—and close—games against the Bayou Bengals. Auburn jumped out to a 21-7 lead, early in the second quarter, after touchdown catches by Fred Beasley and Hicks Poor, and a ten-yard run by Rusty Williams.

LSU came storming back to tie the game at the half, with a touchdown run and a touchdown pass, both by Herb Tyler. The workhorse of this LSU squad, of course, was running back Cecil "the Diesel" Collins, who would finish the game with 232 yards.

A Jaret Holmes field goal put Auburn in the lead, 24-21, late in the third, but then "the Diesel" broke loose for a 42-yard TD, pushing LSU ahead for the first time. As the final minutes of the game ticked away, Auburn went on a ten-play, eighty-yard drive, culminating with Rusty Williams's second touchdown of the game. Auburn held on to win, 31-28. And yes, *Rusty Williams* scored two touchdowns on the LSU defense in Tiger Stadium.

It should also be noted that Auburn's defense had its moments, stopping Tyler and Collins when necessary. Legendary Auburn linebacker Takeo Spikes had eleven tackles, including one for loss, plus one QB sack and one interception in the game.

With his wins in Tiger Stadium in 1993 and 1997, Terry Bowden remains the only Auburn coach to win more than once in Baton Rouge. He and Tommy Tuberville are the only Auburn coaches to win there at all since 1939—the year Jordan-Hare Stadium (then Cliff Hare Stadium) first opened in Auburn.

Van Allen Plexico

I drove over to Auburn for the Florida game that year without a ticket. One of our friends from back in the day had told me he never bought tickets beforehand, and always easily found some before kickoff. What I learned that day was that I am not emotionally and temperamentally constructed to be able to do that—to show up and just hope I can find a ticket and not have to miss the game.

I met some friends at Momma Goldberg's about an hour or two before kickoff, and I'd already been looking for an affordable single ticket most of the day. My friends were looking at me funny and I wasn't sure why. Finally, one of them asked, "What's the matter with you?" And I was like, "What do you mean?" And they said, "You're all nervous and agitated and frowning." And I realized that it was eating me up inside, this sense that I was in Auburn for this huge game against Florida, and I might miss it because I'd stupidly not bought a ticket beforehand. They were going for over a hundred dollars each, and that was back when face value was about $25. I asked a scalper how much he wanted for one ticket, and he told me some three-figure number, and I was shocked. He looked at me like I was crazy and said, "You didn't know this was going to be a big game?" So I felt even dumber. Fortunately, I found one for a reasonable price, right before kickoff. And that was the last season I ever failed to buy all my tickets in advance.

And then of course the game played out the way it did...

The Gators came to Auburn on October 18, and what had looked to be a matchup against the no. 1 team in the country had taken an unexpected turn the weekend before. Florida had traveled to Baton Rouge and lost, 28-21, to no. 14 LSU, dropping them all the way down to no. 7. Auburn, meanwhile, had climbed to no. 6 in the AP Poll, still undefeated. That meant Auburn was actually the higher-ranked team.

This game marked future TV host Jesse Palmer's first career start at quarterback for Florida, but it was Jacquez Green who found a Gator receiver open in the end zone, on a reverse-pass. Meanwhile, Jevon Kearse and his cohorts made life miserable for Dameyune Craig, chasing the Tigers QB down in the backfield for a sack and then a fumble. Given the ball deep in Auburn territory, the Gators kicked a short field goal to go up 10-0.

Jesse Palmer came to the rescue for Auburn, however—he threw a bad pass over the middle that was picked off by Brad Ware and run back to midfield. Immediately Craig, operating out of a strange, two-tight-end, full-house-backfield formation, hit Kevin McLeod with a pass down to the Florida 15. Two plays later, under intense pressure from the Florida pass rush, Craig connected with Tyrone Dillard for the score. Now it was 10-7, and you could start to feel some of that old Bowden, anti-Florida, anti-Spurrier magic in the air.

With less than a minute remaining in the first half, Craig passed the Tigers down the field, evading constant pressure from the Gators defense, and connected with Tyrone Goodson on Florida's 3 yard line with 5 seconds left. Jaret Holmes kicked the field goal, and the two teams went into halftime tied at 10-10.

The second half, however, would see Bob Stoops' Gators defense shut the Auburn offense out. Jesse Palmer again did his part to help Auburn, throwing a pass into the middle of the field for an easy interception. Craig, back out with the offense, however, was chased all over the place and eventually sacked by Kearse, ending the threat of that drive.

Steve Spurrier predictably pulled Palmer and inserted Noah Brindise at quarterback. He responded by connecting with Jacquez Green for a touchdown. Green, who had thrown for Florida's only touchdown in the first half, was involved in all three touchdown plays for the Gators that afternoon; he later ran a reverse for one, meaning each of the three came in a different fashion.

"What he did was unusual. I've seen a receiver catch a touchdown from three different quarterbacks, but not this."
—Steve Spurrier, Florida head coach

With five minutes to play, the game was still easily within reach, with Auburn down only one score, at 17-10. But Tyrone Goodson fumbled in AU territory after a catch, and a few plays later, the Gators cashed it in with Green's second TD. Then, on Auburn's final possession, Craig threw an interception from his own end zone that essentially sealed the deal.

The game ended with Florida on top, 24-10, in a contest that had seemed much closer than that for most of the way.

"It was just a case of their defense being better than our offense. I have always thought their defense was one of the best in the nation. Let's give all the credit to Florida's defense. We just couldn't get our passes off. They were just too quick."
—Terry Bowden, Auburn head coach

Auburn rebounded the next week, taking a trip to Fayetteville, Arkansas to play the Razorbacks. The Tigers led at the half, 13-7, and while Dameyune Craig's continuing eye-popping heroics dominated play between the twenties, all but one score in that half came from *defensive* plays: both teams had a fumble scoop-and-score, and DB Larry Casher intercepted an Arkansas pass to set up one of Auburn's field goals.

Just after halftime, Craig hit Karsten Bailey on a short crossing route that the receiver turned into a long touchdown, earning himself a big bearhug from Craig in the end zone. Auburn's opportunistic defense, featuring stellar play by Quinton Reese, Martavious Houston and Takeo Spikes, turned a third Arkansas turnover into another Jaret Holmes field goal, and the Tigers took a 26-7 lead into the final frame.

In the fourth quarter, the Arkansas offense finally got on the scoreboard. In fact, they staged a bit of a rally, scoring two quick touchdowns, the second of which came on a strange play where one Auburn defensive back went for the interception and missed, and another completely missed the tackle after the catch. The receiver outraced Larry Casher, coming from the far side of the field, to the end zone. With more than seven minutes remaining in the game, the Hogs had cut the lead to just 26-21.

Now Auburn desperately needed to maintain possession and keep the clock running. But the run game simply hadn't been there all night. Fortunately, Arkansas committed a blatant facemask penalty against Craig with 4:10 to go, keeping Auburn's drive alive. When the Tigers were finally forced to punt, they did so from near midfield, and they'd managed to run the clock down to about a minute left. Jaret Holmes punted the ball to inside the Arkansas 10, and the defense held on to preserve the win. Dameyune Craig finished with 13 completions for 244 yards, while sophomore running back Demontray Carter led the team with just 38 yards on the ground. The offense hadn't been stellar, but it had done just enough, given the takeaways provided by the defense in the first half.

Van Allen Plexico

We had dropped to 11th after the Florida loss but held steady there after the Arkansas win. We were getting ready to play Jackie Sherrill's Mississippi State on November 1. It was an afternoon game with no TV coverage.

I left Lawrenceville, Georgia, in plenty of time that morning, and was driving around downtown Atlanta on the Interstate. Suddenly I realized a person in the car next to me was honking their horn and waving. I rolled the window down and they yelled that I had a flat tire. That freaked me out in several ways, because I hadn't been aware the tire was flat— just hadn't noticed it at all, which is strange enough; and I'd never had someone in a different vehicle try to tell me I had a flat tire, so that puzzled me; and I had no idea where to go to do something about it. Remember, this was in the time before smartphones. I was in a part of Atlanta I really didn't know, and I had no idea where to find a garage, or how bad the tire was, or if I was in the process of ruining my car as I kept driving along at about seventy, trying to figure out what to do.

Eventually I found a gas station with a garage attached, and waited forever until they could fix my flat tire. By the time I got to Auburn, found a place to park, walked to the stadium, and found a ticket—remember, this was the year I didn't buy tickets in advance—the game was half-over.

I suppose the only good news was I ended up paying about five bucks for the ticket.

Several things stand out about the 1997 Miss State game. Auburn was held to negative yards rushing. Dameyune Craig had a pretty good game passing the ball, as usual, throwing for 270 yards. Unfortunately, he fumbled at the MSU 3 yard line in the first quarter, threw a 90-yard pick-six in the second quarter, as the Tigers looked to be going in to take the lead, and then threw another interception at the Bulldog 9 yard line in the third, when Auburn was still within two scores. His final interception came at the MSU 5. All told, he threw four interceptions in the game, mostly in the State red zone, in addition to the fumble, ruining any chance of Auburn getting on the scoreboard.

Van Allen Plexico

So that game was totally worth getting a flat tire over. Ugh.

After the game, I remember Miss State's defensive coordinator, Joe Lee Dunn, saying that he had "finally figured out" how to stop Auburn's offense and Dameyune Craig. From my perspective, it looked to be a combination of "totally stop the run game," such as it was, and force Craig into turning the ball over. Not every defense could do that, but Dunn had that Bulldog defense playing very well for a while there. The next season, they even won the West and went to Atlanta.

There haven't been many years where Auburn beat both Georgia and Alabama after losing to Mississippi State. But 2000 was such a season, and so was 1997.

After a week off, Auburn traveled to no. 7 Georgia for a late-afternoon game on ESPN that few believed Auburn could win. The

Tigers were ranked 109th out of 112 teams in D-1 in rushing. They would have to find some way to complement the passing game with a ground game. The off week gave them the opportunity to try. Would they be successful—and just how successful could they possibly be, changing things this late in the season?

Van Allen Plexico

I didn't live too far away from Athens during the 1990s, so it was an easy trip up 316 every other year. Remember, though—I still didn't have tickets that season! As with the Florida and Miss State games, I was going to have to find one when I got there. I have no memory of why I was going alone to so many games that year.

In any case, I put on my Auburn gear and then pulled my Georgetown Hoyas windbreaker over it. Fortunately, the Georgetown mascot is a bulldog, so that's what was on my lapel, even though the jacket was blue and gray.

Some poor, unsuspecting UGA fan kindly sold me a ticket next to him and his family. When I got to my seat, I unzipped my Hoyas jacket and revealed my AU gear and you could just hear everyone around me deflate and sigh. It was beautiful. And then of course the game went our way and the Georgia fans were in shock, and it all just got better and better as the night wore on.

Man, those Georgia fans around me hated me. I never insult the other team, but you'd better believe I root for my team, and I made my presence known in Athens that evening.

The shootout that erupted on offense caught everyone by surprise.

Georgia scored first, after an 80-yard opening drive propelled by Mike Bobo's passing and Robert Edwards' rushing. Bobo hit Corey Allen with a four-yard pass for the score. Unfortunately for the Dogs, the next time they scored, they would be down 24-7.

Auburn responded by moving quickly down the field behind Craig's passing and Fred Beasley's rushing, but when the Tigers reached the UGA red zone, they suddenly unveiled an unexpected weapon that had scarcely been seen all year: the option running of Demontray Carter. He would finish with 93 rushing yards in this game, and every one of them was critical. At no point in the game did Georgia's defense look prepared for Carter taking the pitch and running the option attack at them.

Future Georgia head coach Kirby Smart made multiple tackles on Auburn's first drive alone. But he couldn't stop Dameyune Craig from diving over from the one to tie the game early.

Auburn closed out the first quarter with a short Jaret Holmes field goal, then turned a Jeff Dunlap interception of Mike Bobo into a quick touchdown four plays later, via more inspired running from Demontray Carter.

Georgia's next possession netted minus-3 yards—the defense had come to play, too—followed by a punt that went all of 17 yards. Fred Beasley and Carter shared the carries as Auburn quickly drove the short field and punched it in, taking a 24-7 lead early in the second quarter.

After the teams traded punts, Georgia managed a good punt return to put them in business on Auburn's side of the field. Mike Bobo's passing carried the Dogs down the field and Robert Edwards took it in, making the score at halftime 24-14 Auburn.

After a missed UGA field goal, Karsten Bailey broke things open for Auburn in the third quarter, taking a pass from Craig and streaking 76 yards for the touchdown.

Van Allen Plexico

I was standing up, screaming, "Go Karsten! Go Karsten! YEAAAAAHHHH!!!" And then I looked around, and it seemed like the 20,000 or so UGA fans surrounding me weren't looking at the field—they were all staring straight at me, staring daggers at me, wishing me dead. But I didn't care. The way the game was going at that point, I felt invincible!

Brad Ware somehow ended up taking the ball out of the air on a Bobo pass intended for Champ Bailey that bounced off the receiver's hands, and his good return gave AU the ball back in Georgia territory. A short while later Craig carried it in, making the score 38-14 Auburn.

Dameyune Craig, by Jarrod Alberich

Georgia scored one final touchdown, but it used up all the remaining time on the clock to accomplish it.

"Edwards will score as the horn sounds. And the officials say this one is history. The point does not have to be kicked. So. Final score Auburn 45, and Georgia 34."
—Ron Franklin, ESPN

"Terry Bowden had something to prove. So did Dameyune Craig.

"No. 16 Auburn bounced back from a shutout loss by dominating the Southeastern Conference's stingiest defensive team, beating No. 7 Georgia 45-34 Saturday night as Craig ran for two touchdowns and threw a 76-yard scoring pass.

"The Tigers had an off week after a dismal 20-0 setback against Mississippi State, and Bowden used the extra time to make drastic changes in his offense. Auburn has rushed for only 46 yards in its previous three games and ranked next-to-last in the SEC with a season average of 75.6.

"'I didn't sleep very well the last couple of weeks,' Bowden said. 'Yeah, I had something to prove to myself. We tried to mix the run with the pass and give them some different looks. There were a lot of things I've been wanting to do, but I held off because we needed a week off to put them in.'

"The effectiveness of the running game made things easier for Craig, who threw four interceptions in the Mississippi State loss. He was 12-of-19 passing for 231 yards against Georgia.

"'As a quarterback, you have to have a short memory,' Craig said. 'That game two weeks ago was one of those days. I knew I was a much better player than that.'

"Auburn can clinch the Western Division berth in the Dec. 6 SEC Championship Game by beating Alabama in the regular-season finale next weekend and Mississippi State losing to either Arkansas or Mississippi.

"'They came out and ran all over us,' Georgia cornerback Champ Bailey said. 'Dameyune Craig came out and showed us why he is one of the best quarterbacks in the nation.'"
—Associated Press report

Mississippi State and Auburn both came into that fateful Iron Bowl Saturday with the SEC West title up for grabs. Both teams had suffered two conference losses but, as of that day, the Bulldogs held the tiebreaker, due to their shutout win on the Plains on November 1. So, in addition to beating Alabama, Auburn also needed State to lose to either Arkansas or Ole Miss, in order to win the West. Neither of those outcomes appeared probable—Jackie Sherrill's squad had just knocked off the Tide the week before, so losing to one of the two also-rans of the West seemed unlikely. Somehow, though, Arkansas got the job done by late afternoon, winning 17-7, and Auburn went into the night clash with Alabama knowing a trip to Atlanta was still on the line.

(Interestingly enough, it was *not* on the line for Alabama; they had long-since been eliminated from the Western Division chase, coming into the Iron Bowl with an SEC record of 2-5 after their loss the previous week to Miss State.)

Van Allen Plexico

It's interesting: Back then, I just had so much confidence that Auburn would always find a way to get a win in games like these. I think, after witnessing the 1993 Florida and Alabama games, and the 1994 LSU and Florida games, I'd just come to think that Bowden's squads could pull out a little magic at the key moments. So, even though we'd looked terrible against Miss State, I'd felt good about our chances against Georgia, and I felt even better as we welcomed Alabama back to the Plains for their fourth visit. I mean, they were a four-win team. Why wouldn't we win, and win easily?

I should've known better...

Both teams began the 1997 Iron Bowl sluggish on offense. Jaret Holmes capped off two mediocre drives with field goals of 27 and 37 yards. But Auburn was scoring in threes, not sevens, and Alabama's defense was clamping down when they had to. Tigers running back Demontray Carter couldn't find anything like the running room he'd exploited against Georgia. Once again, Auburn's hopes on offense would rest squarely on the shoulders of Dameyune Craig, and it remained to be seen if he would perform the way he had against Virginia and LSU, or the way he had against Mississippi State.

Midway through the second quarter the Tide threatened, with Freddie Kitchens connecting with Calvin Hall to the Auburn 18. Antwoine Nolan knocked the ball loose, though, and Brad Ware—who always seemed to come up big in big games for Auburn—recovered.

After a delay of game penalty forced Auburn into third and long, Craig threw a deep ball downfield, where it was intercepted by Kevin Sigler, who returned it to the Alabama 49.

With that possession, Alabama finally took the lead, 7-6, capping off the short drive with a 13-yard pass from Freddie Kitchens to Calvin Hall.

On the following drive, Craig was intercepted again. That made two big turnovers in the first half, and visions of the Mississippi State game danced in Auburn fans' heads. Fortunately, the defense was able to force a punt, but the ball was downed at Auburn's four yard line.

Starting so deep in their own end of the field would prove costly for the Tigers. On their first play, Demontray Carter finally got loose for a long run—only to fumble at the end of it, giving the ball back to Alabama on Tigers' 22 yard line. Alabama settled for a field goal just before the end of the quarter to go into halftime up 10-6. Three turnovers in two quarters had done the damage, and frankly the Tigers were lucky the score was so close. Lucky, and fortunate to have a defense that was playing as well as it was.

"There was a little bit of disbelief. We're supposed to be winning. We have an opportunity to go to the SEC Championship. What's going on? How is this possible?"
—Jaret Holmes, Auburn kicker, speaking in 2016

The second half didn't start out very promising for the Tigers. Fred Beasley lost yards on a rush, Craig lost yards on another, and a delay of game penalty and a sack rounded things out. After reaching midfield, Auburn ended up punting from their own 28.

Alabama came roaring down the field and capped off the drive with a 12-yard touchdown run by Shaun Alexander. Auburn had fallen behind by eleven now, at 17-6. Somehow, though, that would prove to be the last time Alabama scored in the game.

On the ensuing drive, Auburn suddenly came to life. Dameyune Craig hit fullback Kevin McLeod for 41 yards to the Alabama 31, then connected with Karsten Bailey for 22 more. In just two plays, the Tigers had reached the Alabama 9. Rusty Williams carried it to the 1 and Fred Beasley punched it in.

It has been noted that Terry Bowden liked to go for two if Auburn scored a TD while behind—and it rarely succeeded. This time was no exception: Craig's pass fell incomplete and Auburn trailed, 17-12.

Only a few plays into Alabama's second drive of the half, the third quarter came to an end. When the final quarter began, Alabama was on the move again, after two Shaun Alexander runs carried the Tide down to the Tigers' 36. Auburn's defense dug in and held them to a field goal attempt, and Chris Kemp missed from the 21.

Alabama committed an offsides penalty and a personal foul to keep Auburn's next drive alive, and Jaret Holmes nailed another field goal, this one from the Alabama 14. With nine minutes remaining in the game, the Tigers had cut the deficit to two, trailing 17-15.

The Auburn defense held Alabama to a three-and-out, getting the ball back with just over six minutes remaining. Unfortunately, Daniel Pope's punt went out of bounds at the Auburn 2 yard line. The Tigers would have to go 98 yards if they wanted a touchdown.

Craig scratched and clawed and managed to get Auburn to just across midfield, but then a sack and two incomplete passes resulted in the Tigers facing 4th and 13 on their own 49, with 2:55 to go. Bowden chose to put his faith in his defense, and he punted.

"If we don't get the ball back, you know what people are going to say about that game.

"To me, that game represents a lot of what the Iron Bowl has always been about. We were the favorite team, I think Alabama might have been 4-6, we were 8-2 and favored and there's about three minutes left in the game and we're losing the game. There's just not many rivalries like it."

—Terry Bowden, speaking in 2017

Instead of getting the ball at the Auburn 49, as they would have if Craig had thrown an incomplete pass on fourth down, Alabama started way back at their own 19. The first four plays the Tide ran were safe handoffs to Shaun Alexander, designed to protect the ball and run the clock. On his second carry, Alexander turned the corner for a big first down.

"Credit Ed Scissum, number 33, the fullback, for paving the way for the first down."

"Ron, Ed Scissum tonight has had a great night blocking for Alabama. When they go to the I-Formation they have been dangerous running the football."
—Ron Franklin and Mike Gottfried, ESPN

On his third carry, Alexander lost a yard, and on his fourth carry he only managed to get the ball out to the Alabama 36, where the Tide faced third and eight with 1:11 to go.

Then came the pivotal moment in the contest. Had Tide offensive coordinator Bruce Arians merely ordered Freddie Kitchens to take a knee and then punt on fourth down, Alabama likely would have won the game. Instead, he called a play that has haunted the nightmares of Bama fans down through all the succeeding years.

"If you were an Auburn man, that was terrible poetic punishment because in 1984, Auburn was heavily favored and was going to the Sugar Bowl and Bo ran the wrong way and Alabama won 17-15. And there they were, ahead 17-15. You know what the Alabama fans were thinking and you know what the Auburn people were thinking... It was surreal because Auburn had no hope of winning without them helping us."
—David Housel, former Auburn Athletic Director, speaking in 2016

The clock was running. When Kitchens took the snap, only 51 seconds remained. The Alabama QB faked to his right, spun to his left, and threw a short screen pass to Ed Scissum. The fullback caught the ball and was immediately rocked by a hard-charging

Martavious Houston behind the line of scrimmage. Houston knocked the ball out of Scissum's hands, and Auburn's Quinton Reese recovered, with 42 seconds remaining on the clock. The crowd went crazy. The opportunistic Auburn defense that had bailed out Bowden's squads at Florida and against LSU in 1994 had returned, if only for one play. Somehow, some way, Auburn had one more chance at the win.

A Rusty Williams run and a Craig pass to Hicks Poor on the left sideline took the ball to Alabama's 22, stopping the clock with 26 seconds left. Craig's next pass fell incomplete, and amid confusion on the Auburn sideline and in the huddle, Craig took the snap and grounded it, setting up third and 10 with 22 seconds remaining. In hindsight, running one more play might have been advisable.

Now Jaret Holmes came out to attempt a 39-yard field goal. Alabama burned its last two timeouts in an attempt to ice the kicker. Time slowed to a crawl as both teams and all the fans waited.

"My brain went right to 'Where are we on the field and how far of a field goal is it going to be?'

"That's a kicker's dream. That's where you get your name in the paper and people get to talk about you and you have some sort of a legacy."
—Jaret Holmes, Auburn kicker, speaking in 2016

"Ball at the left hashmark. There's the snap. The spot. Kick is on the way. Long enough. High enough. Kick... good! It's good! It's good! It's good! It's good! It's good! Holmes from 39 yards! It's good! It's good! A mob scene! Fifteen seconds to go! Auburn has gone ahead, 18-17, over Alabama!"
—Jim Fyffe, Auburn Network broadcast

"There definitely wasn't any concern. We were all confident that he would make the kick. I remember some of the older guys like Fred Beasley and DeMarcus Curry keeping everybody away from Jaret during that timeout. 'Don't go talk to him, don't go bother him, just let him focus.'"
—Cole Cubelic, offensive lineman on the 1997 team

The kick, as Jim Fyffe took pains to point out, was good. For the game, Holmes was four-for-four on field goals. Auburn took the lead, 18-17, with fifteen seconds to go. As disbelieving Tide players and fans looked on in shock, Auburn players and fans danced and hugged and whooped and hollered.

"He nailed it right down the middle."
—Mike Gottfried, ESPN

"I knew this was the kick I'd been waiting for. Forget all the little things, and go kill it. That's generally what I had in my mind. I thought 'If you miss it, miss it 10 miles up in the stadium. Just kick it with everything you have. Let everything else you've done up to now take over.'
"When I struck that ball, there was no doubt. I heard the sound and I never felt it on my foot. That's usually when you know you hit it in about the best spot you possibly can.
"I was able to jump up and run for about 10 yards before somebody tackled me. It was one of those where I knew it as soon as I hit it. It was a pure adrenaline rush that I probably had not had before then and have not had since."
—Jaret Holmes, Auburn kicker, speaking in 2016

But the drama in this Iron Bowl was not yet over.

Holmes kicked off, sending the ball dribbling low across the ground, where it was picked up by—of all people—Ed Scissum, who proceeded to channel all of his frustration into a monstrous effort to return the kick. He dragged what looked to be half of Auburn's coverage team down the field to the Alabama 45, where Adlai Trone is officially credited with bringing him down, amid a sea of blue jerseys clinging to him.

"Scissum, running like a man possessed, got hit extremely hard and took it to the 45."
—Ron Franklin, ESPN

A personal foul facemask penalty added 15 more yards to the return, and suddenly Alabama had the ball at Auburn's 40 with six seconds to go.

Alabama coach Mike DuBose sent A.J. Diaz out for his first and only field goal attempt, from 57 yards away. The kick was on target but it came up short. Auburn had survived. And they were on their way to their first SEC Championship Game.

"This game, you throw out the records, you throw out everything and you never know who's going to win it. It's one of those games that quite often the underdog wins the game. It's been that type of game for a long time; at least when I was there almost every game came down to the wire and almost every year somebody was playing for the conference championship or the national championship."
—*Terry Bowden, speaking in 2017*

Terry Bowden remains the only Auburn coach to win his final Iron Bowl. The only other coach to do so for either side was Gene Stallings at Alabama, the year before.

By the time the regular season was over, Auburn would be tied for the West crown not with Miss State but with LSU—a team over whom Auburn held the tiebreaker, dating back to that big win in Baton Rouge in September. With Miss State going on to lose the Egg Bowl to Ole Miss the week after the Iron Bowl, they removed themselves from the conversation entirely and limped home with a record of 4-4. Auburn's disaster of a game against the maroon Bulldogs on November 1, in which Dameyune Craig had looked all too mortal as he'd turned the ball over time and time again, ended up not mattering at all.

John Ringer

The SEC championship game was still new, shiny, and cool and Auburn had not gotten to play in it, so making it in 1997 was great—it felt good to make it. I didn't attend, since we had a one-and-a-half-year-old, but I loved seeing Auburn in that game for the first time. It was also big because early in the Bowden years (in 1993) we had the best team but weren't allowed to be there. But I was definitely worried about playing that Tennessee team in the game.

Van Allen Plexico

My parents and some friends and I all went. Going into the Dome, I had very little hope, because I knew how good Tennessee had been all year. Their only loss had been in a close game at Florida, with the Gators ranked no. 1. Meanwhile, we'd just needed basically a miracle to beat a bad Alabama team. So I went to give my full support to the effort, but I never dreamed the first half would play out the way it did.

Being an odd-numbered year, 1997 saw the SEC West representative in the Championship Game wearing its home jerseys, so Auburn came out in blue tops. Tennessee wore all white.

Tennessee blew down the field on the first series of the game, scoring on a 40-yard pass from Peyton Manning to Peerless Price in just over two minutes. Auburn's worst fears seemed to be coming true already.

But Auburn responded with a 69-yard pass from Dameyune Craig to Hicks Poor, setting up a 30-yard Jaret Holmes field goal. This drive took almost the same amount of time as Tennessee's had, and the score was 7-3 Vols with barely four minutes gone.

An illegal procedure penalty and a sack of Manning led to a UT punt, but Auburn fared no better and returned the ball to Tennessee four plays later. Backed up to their own 11, Manning fired a pass to Marcus Nash, who was stripped by AU's star linebacker, Takeo Spikes. Always around the ball at important moments, Brad Ware grabbed it up and carried it in for the score. Suddenly it was 10-7 Auburn.

Perhaps shaken up, Manning threw three consecutive incomplete passes at Peerless Price, and the Vols punted. Auburn made two first downs to get within field goal range, and then Jaret Holmes kicked it through from 48 yards away. The score was 13-7 Auburn, still in the first quarter. After another three-and-out, the Vols punted again.

Three plays into the next Auburn drive, Craig dropped back and looked for Tyrone Goodson deep.

"Two split ends, one to either side, and a new set of downs from the Tigers side of midfield. Here's the snap to Craig, he play-fakes, he steps up, forced out of the pocket but he's gonna throw long down the middle of the field for Goodson. Goodson—oh, a miracle catch inside the five—he scores! Touchdown Auburn! Beautifully thrown pass to Tyrone Goodson for 51 yards!"
—Jim Fyffe, Auburn Network broadcast

Goodson muscled his way over the goal line for a second AU touchdown. The game was barely into the second quarter and it was already 20-7 Auburn. Tigers fans can be forgiven for wishing the game could have ended at halftime.

Tennessee then embarked on an extended drive that ate up almost seven minutes of the quarter and featured numerous incomplete passes by Manning. The Vols were bailed out by a couple of clutch third-down passes, every time it looked like the Auburn defense would stop them. Jeff Hall kicked a 27-yard field goal to bring the Vols to within ten, at 20-10.

The following drive was a rough one for the Tigers. An illegal procedure penalty and a delay of game penalty slowed them down, as well as two big sacks of Dameyune Craig. Holmes punted the ball to UT's Terry Fair, who caught it at the Tennessee 25 and started upfield, returning it 44 yards to the Auburn 31. Unfortunately for Fair, he was at that point stripped of the ball by Auburn's Ryan Taylor, and Larry Melton jumped on it. A Vol scoring threat had been averted and the Tigers were in business at their own 31.

Auburn could do nothing this drive either, though—and the Tigers were lucky to retain possession after Craig lost the ball but managed to recover it himself. Jaret Holmes came back out to punt the ball away. Terry Fair, who had just fumbled his punt return on the previous series, fumbled again—and this time Auburn recovered back on the Tennessee 28.

This was the key sequence of the game. Given two consecutive turnovers, Auburn should have been able to score at least something out of all that Volunteer generosity. But the first series had ended in a punt, and this one came up empty as well. After three incomplete passes from Craig, Jaret Holmes, so dependable all year long, missed from 45. The Vols got the ball back, dodging two bullets in a row, with the score still 20-10.

Believe it or not, Tennessee handed the ball back to Auburn for a third series in a row. Manning lobbed a bomb from his own 39 to the Auburn 18, where it was picked off by Larry Casher with less than a minute to go in the half.

Auburn ran the ball three consecutive plays, losing yards each time but running the clock, and punted the ball to Tennessee with three seconds left. Manning's pass to Peerless Price was knocked down by Rob Pate, and the first half ended with Auburn still ahead by ten.

At the half, Auburn had minus-7 yards rushing, but had held Tennessee to only 43, and was winning the turnover battle, 4-0.

"I got to give a lot of credit to (linebacker) Al Wilson. He gave a great speech at halftime and said, 'Let's go win this game.' Auburn wasn't really stopping us, things just kept happening."
—Peyton Manning, Tennessee QB

Tennessee wasted no time making up some of their deficit after the half. The Tigers got the ball first but could do nothing with it, and Holmes punted. Terry Fair, who had fumbled twice in the first half, returned the kick 45 yards to the AU 22. From there, Manning connected with Jeremaine Copeland for the touchdown. Auburn's lead had shrunk to 20-17 with an entire half yet to play.

Finally, though, momentum swung back Auburn's way. Jamal Lewis's rushing and Manning's passing carried the Vols down to Auburn's 14, but on the next play, Manning's pass bounced off the receiver's hands and was picked off by Jayson Bray at the 4. Bray returned the interception 77 yards, all the way to Tennessee's 19.

"Well, that's when being a father's not what it's cracked up to be."
—Archie Manning, ABC broadcast, watching his son throw the interception

An illegal procedure call backed Auburn up to the 24, but on the next play, Craig lobbed a high floater to fullback Fred Beasley, who caught it and fell into the end zone. Auburn's lead was back to ten, 27-17, with 6:14 to go in the third.

Van Allen Plexico

This game was exhausting to watch. I can't imagine what it was like for the players.

There were so many games like that during the Bowden years. Games where our defense made miraculous plays, keeping us in the game or even scoring to take the lead, and the offense found ways to almost manufacture points. Games that turned into track meets up and down the field. Terry called them "scoring contests," and he was usually referring to games against Steve Spurrier's Florida when he said it, where the scoreboard looks like a pinball machine and you can only hope Auburn will be the last one to punch it in before time expires.

Tennessee responded with a five-minute drive that covered 80 yards in ten plays, but mostly consisted of a 46-yard scoring strike from Manning to Peerless Price. The odd turns of fate for Auburn were not over yet, though: On the extra point attempt, Jeff Hall's kick was blocked and Quinton Reese returned it the length of the field, giving the Tigers two points. The game now stood at Auburn 29, Tennessee 23.

Van Allen Plexico

I looked at that 29-23 score as we went into the fourth quarter, and all I could think of was, "A Tennessee touchdown and extra point will make it 30-29." And as soon as I thought about that, it was all I could think about. I had this awful gut feeling the entire rest of the game: "30-29." We'd been fortunate—or had created our own luck—the entire game, mainly with Tennessee giving us the ball, or us taking it away from them. I couldn't imagine how that would continue until the end, and I was very much afraid we would need it to, if we were to hold on and win.

The turnover bug continued to bite Tennessee as the game entered the fourth quarter. After an Auburn punt to the Vols' 43, star running back Jamal Lewis coughed it up and Jeff Dunlap recovered for Auburn at their own 42.

But the Tigers could only lose yardage on the ensuing possession, Craig taking a sack and throwing two incomplete passes. Holmes sent the ball back to Tennessee with 11:29 to go in the game.

At that point, Tennessee finally overcame their own mistakes and took control.

With 2nd and 10 on their own 27, Manning threw the ball to Marcus Nash on the right sideline, and Nash proceeded to streak 73 yards for the go-ahead touchdown. There it was: 30-29 Tennessee.

Markeith "the Lizard" Cooper gave Tigers fans a bit of hope, returning the kickoff 46 yards to the UT 48. But after yet another illegal procedure penalty backed Auburn up, Karsten Bailey had the ball knocked loose by Terry Fair—finally on the positive end of a turnover—and UT recovered at their own 40. Auburn's best opportunity to retake the lead had gone by the boards.

The Tigers got two more chances to respond, but both drives went nowhere and ended in Jaret Holmes punts. With their last possession of the game, Tennessee drove to the Auburn 6 before the clock expired.

"It seemed like it would be Auburn's night. Peyton Manning threw a season-high two interceptions, Tennessee committed six turnovers, and the Tigers scored on a conversion return for two points. But, on a simple 7-yard curl play, Marcus Nash broke a tackle and was on his way to a 73-yard touchdown that dashed the Tigers' hopes to upset Tennessee in the 1997 SEC Championship Game."
—Mike Diegnan, BCSFootball. com

"How do you turn the ball over six times and still come out a winner?"

"I've never heard of it. Especially in a championship game."
—Bob Griese and Keith Jackson, ABC

Van Allen Plexico
It was strange. I'd come into the game fully expecting to lose, then gotten my hopes up—thanks mainly to all the Tennessee miscues and turnovers. To have it all come crashing

down again at the end was sickening. That Marcus Nash catch and long run will haunt my dreams for the rest of my life.

In some ways the worst part was that Tennessee ended the game on our 6 yard line. It was like they were saying, "Even if Auburn had found a way to score again, or if Jaret Holmes hadn't missed that one field goal and it had been 32-30, Tennessee would've been able to kick another field goal and win at the end." Of course, you never know. But that was how it felt.

Seven years later, when our great 2004 team beat them in the same stadium for the same prize, I took such delight in reminding their fans around me that it was "Revenge for 1997!"

"Maybe it's just Tennessee's year. They've been the bridesmaid an awful lot. Maybe they were just due."
—Terry Bowden, after the game

At 9-3, Auburn made its second-ever appearance in the Peach Bowl in Atlanta on January 2, playing in the same Georgia Dome in which they'd just faced Tennessee. Their opponent was Clemson, who in their fifth season under Tommy West, had posted a regular season record of 7-4.

Clemson was never able to generate much offense in this game, even with star running back Raymond Priester—a fact that's not surprising when one considers their first-year offensive coordinator was 2003 Auburn co-OC Steve Ensminger. Their special teams and defense, however, not only kept them in the game but put them in position to win, turning the ball over and blocking multiple Auburn punts.

On Auburn's first drive, Dameyune Craig was sacked on the Auburn 30 and fumbled, but Clemson couldn't move the ball and missed their field goal attempt.

Jaret Holmes had better luck on Auburn's next drive, nailing a 52-yarder to give the Tigers in blue the early lead.

The two teams traded punts until, with 6:31 to go in the half, Clemson blocked Jaret Holmes' punt. Chad Speck ran the ball back 18 yards for the first touchdown of the game.

On Auburn's next possession, Karsten Bailey took a pass from Craig 61 yards to the Clemson 11, and Holmes made the short field goal. The first half came to an end with the score Clemson 7, Auburn 6.

The second half started off much like the first half had ended. Jaret Holmes missed his second long field goal, followed by several punts back and forth. Neither team could get anything going on offense.

Unfortunately for Auburn, Clemson was finding other ways to get points. Rahim Abdullah blocked Holmes' punt, making two they'd blocked so far, and Mel Lawyer covered it at the 2. Clemson punched it in on the next play, and the Tigers in orange and white now led, 14-6.

A holding penalty on Auburn's next drive backed the Tigers in blue up, and Holmes ended up punting from his own 9. Clemson returned it to the 26, and Auburn was fortunate here to hold their opponent to just a field goal. As the third quarter ended, Clemson somehow led the game, 17-6, in a contest in which both teams' offenses had been utterly ineffective.

The subsequent drive by Auburn actually featured more rushing than passing, for once, as Craig scrambled on multiple plays and took it into the end zone from 22 yards out. The two-point conversion failed, and Clemson still led, 17-12.

Again Clemson's offense was stuck in the mud, and Markeith Cooper returned the inevitable punt to Clemson's 49. Passes to Hicks Poor and Karsten Bailey brought Auburn down the short field, and Rusty Williams carried it the last 7 yards for the score. With 8:45 to go in the game, Auburn finally had the lead, 18-17.

Once again the Clemson special teams almost made the difference: Tony Horne returned the kickoff from the goal line to the Clemson 45 before being stopped. There was still plenty of time left to go. If the Tigers in orange and white could find any offense, they could reclaim the lead.

Fortunately for the good guys, three plays later, Takeo Spikes intercepted Clemson's Nealon Greene at the Auburn 41. Craig finally got the team moving, managing to reach Clemson's 3 yard line before their defense stiffened and pushed Fred Beasley backwards 2 yards. Holmes nailed the short kick, increasing Auburn's lead to 21-17.

Clemson's Nealon Greene reached Auburn's 48 before throwing four consecutive incomplete passes, giving the blue Tigers the ball back with 2:30 to go. Rusty Williams and Dameyune Craig ran the ball on the last few plays and drained the rest of the clock.

"We had every opportunity to give up, to quit, to get discouraged and just lose the ballgame because nothing's going right, but the players showed again the thing that makes this team very special.

"When it was going bad, I pulled Dameyune over and said, 'I can't lie to you, you better go out there and do it.' I told him this was going to be his final statement and that wasn't how he wanted it to be."
—Terry Bowden

The defense played its best game of the year, despite Bowden having sent two starters home on New Year's Eve for rules violations. It held Clemson to just 146 total yards, and the offense had managed to do just enough to secure the win. Dameyune Craig and Takeo Spikes were named the MVPs in their final games in Auburn uniforms. The Tigers had ended the 1997 season on a winning note, and had reached double-digit wins for only the second and final time under Terry Bowden, finishing at 10-3 for the year, with a final AP Poll ranking of 11th in the country.

"I don't think we missed the (suspended) starters one bit and we won't miss them next year if they don't want to come back and be good Auburn people."
—Terry Bowden

John Ringer
To me the big thing about this year was Dameyune Craig and the offense.

Yeah, the running backs had gotten smaller and smaller. We had Markeith Cooper, whose nickname was "the Lizard," plus Rusty Williams, along with Fred Beasley. Those were the main running backs, and we had a great receiving corps that made for a really explosive offense, with Karsten Bailey, Tyrone

Goodson, Hicks Poor, and Errick Lowe, plus Tyrone Dillard and Kevin MacLeod at tight end.

Craig was great that year; he was explosive. He was really, really good and he and the receivers had an excellent season.

The thing I remember about that season was, we should have won the SEC title. We *should* have beaten Tennessee. We had them on the ropes and we should have taken them out.

Pat Ringer

That's exactly what I was going to say. It felt a little bit like the 2018 LSU game where we had played so well for most of the game and it came down to the fourth quarter, where if either our offense or our defense makes a play, we beat Peyton Manning and Tennessee, and we have the SEC Championship. And we just couldn't do it.

I mean, give Tennessee credit and give Peyton Manning credit; they were clearly deserving. But it was one of those things where it was very frustrating.

But I had a different perspective. I was in Mexico that fall, and I didn't go to that game. I didn't go to many games that year, if any, actually. I would go to a sports bar in the town where I was. There were a few Mexican guys, there were a couple of American expats, because it was one of the few places where we could watch American football. As I was watching this game, one of my friends wanted to do something else, and he was like, "What are we doing? We're in Mexico! You're gonna watch this American football game?" And I'm like, "I'm not missing this game, brother."

Cole Cubelic

I think going into the season the expectations were pretty high, in house, with us. I can remember Jimbo Fisher talking about making it to the Orange Bowl that year. That was our goal. We wanted to win our opener against Virginia, wanted to win the SEC Championship Game and then wanted to play for a national championship. Those were the goals, and I can remember Jimbo getting up in front of the offense and talking about those things earlier that year.

You have to think about the guys we had, we had Victor Riley at left tackle, we had Fred Beasley at fullback, we had a good group of receivers with Karsten Bailey and Tyrone Goodson and Errick Lowe. I think, going into that year, with Dameyune Craig ready to have a breakout year, and with Bill Oliver running the defense, with Jimmy Brumbaugh and Charles Dorsey and Takeo Spikes and Ricky Neil, Martavious Houston; we thought we were gonna be pretty damn good, and for good reason because we had legitimate players. We had guys who could play and were going to be the best at their position in the league. With Dameyune—this was before the whole mobile quarterback thing really got going—we were ready to add another dimension to our offense, and we felt like we were good enough around Dameyune that he wouldn't have to do everything. And it just so happened that we couldn't get the run game going, for whatever reason.

I think if you look back on it now, a lot of people would have said, "Man, if we had just put Kevin MacLeod at fullback and Fred Beasley at tailback and tried to pound it at people, we might have had some success. Because we had a couple good offensive linemen on that team and we should have had more success than we did. Now, Mississippi State was still a pretty good team. Florida was still a pretty good team. I think when we played Florida It was like 3 vs 6 or something when they came into Jordan-Hare Stadium, so it's not like they weren't a really good football team. And, obviously, Dameyune struggled against Mississippi State. But those Joe Lee Dunn defenses were just a nightmare to play against. You never knew what you were gonna get, and they were tough.

So I think I think we all expected to be in the SEC Championship game. And when you watch that Tennessee team on film, they were a team that had some elite players, but they didn't do a whole lot. And so I think we weren't having to be overly concerned about scheme and doing different things. I mean, (Tennessee defensive coordinator) John Chavis was pretty bland that year. He ran a 4-3 and then he would slide down into an odd defense where he put a Sam linebacker at the line of scrimmage, you know, they'd play kind of a 5-2 look. And that's about all they did, because he had so many good players. There was Leonard Little, there was Al Wilson, and then they had guys on offense—they had Peyton Manning and Jamal Lewis, some good players on offense. So you knew like, guy for guy, yeah, they were probably a little bit more talented but, scheme-wise, we felt pretty good about what Brother and those guys were going to do. And we thought Dameyune could have some success down the field.

We just, at that point in the season, we weren't a very balanced offense. And I think that was a concern. But yeah, we thought we could win that football game. And in going over to play in (the state of) Georgia with the amount of Georgia guys that we had on the roster, that meant a lot to them to be able to go play in the SEC Championship Game. So we thought we had enough motivation and talent and scheme to be able to beat Tennessee that day. It just so happened, they made some plays late, and we didn't get it done.

Van Allen Plexico
Dameyune Craig, in particular, where do you put him in the pantheon of Auburn quarterbacks?

Cole Cubelic
Well, I'm going to say this: No matter where I put him, overall, he's underrated. Because I don't think people realize what kind of a competitor he was; what kind of a leader he was; the amount of things that he did on the practice field, in the facility and on game day to make the offense, make the team better than maybe it really was. And you know, some of that you don't understand until you get up next to him and you're just like, "Really?"

I mean the guy is 6-1, 190 pounds, and could throw the ball 80-something yards in the air, and obviously had good wheels, but he was a gamer. He didn't get good protection that year. He didn't have a run game to lean on that year but, man, he just consistently made plays. And outside of a bad game or two, I think outside of Cam Newton and obviously outside of Pat Sullivan and outside of maybe Jason Campbell, he should be there, at probably that "Tier Two" of best quarterbacks in Auburn football history. And I don't think he gets that due very much. He doesn't get a lot of that discussion, at least from what I hear. I don't hear a lot of people that put him in that conversation. And maybe that's because the tail end of his career was right when things got bad, and so a lot of people don't remember it. And obviously, with Jason Campbell, that was a bit of a resurrection of Auburn football. And he gets a ton of credit, but he was also a great player, and he deserves that credit. So I don't really know what it is, but it's almost like you hear more about Stan White and Pat Nix than you do Dameyune Craig.

I'm not putting him over Cam. I'm not taking him over over Pat Sullivan. And, I mean, for me personally, it would be really close with Jason Campbell, but I probably take Jason first based on his size and durability. But, man—from a competitive standpoint, from a leadership standpoint, it'd be hard (not to take Craig). You can make a real strong argument that Dameyune should be next in line, to be honest with you.

Van Allen Plexico

What would Dameyune Craig have been like in a Gus Malzahn offense, particularly like from 2013 or 2014?

Cole Cubelic

Well, I don't know about the 2013 offense, because he was never going to be an option guy.

We put in a speed option against Georgia in 1997. We had a week off before that week, and we put in a bunch of single-back stuff and ran zone and he ran a little flat line speed option. And we wore them out, they didn't see any of that stuff coming. We had worked on it for a while.

And then again, that goes back to Terry, what kind of a coach he was. Nobody's ever going to talk about that kind of stuff. Nobody's ever going to talk about Terry going in and putting in a completely different offense against a really good Georgia team, and then essentially kicking their ass—and that's what we did that year.

Dameyune, I don't think he could handle the contact of being the guy who ran the ball in between the tackles ten or twelve times a game, or a guy who had deliberate quarterback runs, fifteen, seventeen times a game. But if you gave him the option of being able to keep the ball—he knew how to protect himself like a Kyler Murray does—I mean, he probably could eat you up. Because he had good enough wheels to be able to break the defense down, and some of the stuff he got away with was just like bootlegs, I mean legitimate just play action with a hard bootleg roll-out, and the design was for him to keep the ball or just sprint-out passes where it was designed that he could keep the ball. That design didn't give him a very high rate of success running the football, but a lot of times he found ways to make it successful. And I think, more times than not, what you're looking at is either like a smoke draw, where you knew he was going to show pass and then get north and south or, when he left the pocket, he was somebody who could really do damage there. And the most critical part about that was Dameyune kept his eyes downfield and he was very accurate passing on the run. He could throw a really nice deep ball on the run, and that's where he just absolutely torched some teams. When he would leave the pocket and keep his eyes down the field and then take a chance deep, and he could really get it over the top of the defense, when that happened.

Van Allen Plexico

Yeah, it was a completely different offense we ran against Georgia. And Georgia didn't have a clue what was going on. That was amazing.

Cole Cubelic

No, they were lost. And that was a top ten Georgia team when we played them. So that was an awesome game plan. And it was an awesome game. Because that Georgia team, they had some studs on that football team.

Van Allen Plexico

Their fans in the stands around me were shocked. They were absolutely stunned. They couldn't believe it, what they were seeing.

Cole Cubelic

That Georgia team was no. 7 when we played them. When you think about the teams we lost to—Florida was ranked seventh; Tennessee was ranked third. Mississippi State wasn't ranked but they were just a tough team. That was a physical football team. So, you know, we beat no. 10 LSU on the road that year, Dameyune led that drive to help us win the game late.

I mean, it could have been a better year, but it was still a really good season.

And now we turn to the final season of the Terry Bowden era at Auburn.

1998

It was a season filled with controversy; a season filled with frustrations. A season filled with too many losses, and too many head coaches.

Dameyune Craig had carried the offense on his back the past two years, throwing for 3277 yards and 18 touchdowns in his final season. After 1997, though, his eligibility was used up, and he had signed with the NFL's Carolina Panthers. They lent him out to NFL Europe, where he quarterbacked the Scottish Claymores. In a game against the Frankfurt Galaxy on May 22, 1999, Craig threw for an all-time pro football record 611 yards. His jersey from that game hangs in the Pro Football Hall of Fame.

Without Craig, and with (still) very little running game to fall back on, the 1998 Tigers would face enormous problems on offense. New starting quarterback Ben Leard had veteran Karsten Bailey back at wide receiver, but not much else.

Van Allen Plexico

It's funny that the only coach that Terry Bowden beat in 1998 was the one that took his job a few months later. But we'll get to that.

456

We got killed in the opener, shut out at home by Virginia. We lost to no. 7 LSU in a game they considered one of their ten greatest wins of all time, until they later realized we were a 3-8 team. Seriously—I remember seeing it on their official website, or maybe it was on a display in their arena. LSU considered that game one of their ten greatest wins in program history, until we ended up losing eight games, and then I think they quietly erased that from their web site and display. I am not making that up. And besides, that LSU team finished 4-7, only one win ahead of us.

We had a game against third-ranked Tennessee on October 3. This was the team that went on to win the national championship that year. And we took them to the final play. We were throwing for what could've been the tying score when the clock ran out. We should have won that game; we had so many chances. But we lost, 17-9. There were two key moments: We drove to their goal line and had four shots to punch it in from the one, and we tried to go right up the middle all four times, and they stuffed us. Their famous announcer summed it up: "Not... Even... Close." And then we had another drive going that could have tied it, and Ben Leard threw a shovel pass that got intercepted and was run back all the way for a Vols touchdown. That may be the only time I've ever seen a little inside shovel pass intercepted, and of course it went for a pick-six in a game we lost by one score to the eventual national champions. Unreal.

And then there was the game against no. 5 Florida in the Swamp, on October 17. At that point, four of our first six opponents had been ranked, three of them in the top seven nationally. Interestingly, Miss State had not been ranked when we played them, and they ended up finishing second in the West that year. So it was a tough row to hoe, even if we'd had a good team that year. With so little offense, dealing with those opponents was just impossible.

My whole family and I went down to Gainesville to see the Florida game, not realizing we were witnessing the end of the Bowden era that very day. Spurrier took mercy on us; they beat us 24-3 but it could've been much worse. Our record afterward was 1-5, the only bright spot a 17-0 shutout of Tommy Tuberville's Ole Miss in Oxford.

Right after that loss to Florida, things got very strange on the Plains.

There are varying versions of the story, but they mostly agree on one thing: Terry Bowden was called into the athletic director's office on the Friday after returning from Gainesville, and when he left that office, he was no longer the head coach of Auburn University's football team. What exactly went down between those two moments, and how, is a matter of dispute to this day.

Some claim Terry was fired. Some say Terry quit. Some say both: that Terry was told he was going to be fired at the end of the season, so he preemptively quit. Some allege other complications were involved. It all amounted to the same thing, though. The end result was that, when the Tigers took the field at home against Louisiana Tech on October 24, they were being led by defensive coordinator and interim head coach Bill "Brother" Oliver.

"Interviews with current and former Auburn coaches, Auburn athletic staffers, Bowden family members, two members of the Auburn Board of Trustees and high-ranking Auburn alumni - many of whom agreed to talk only on condition of anonymity - allege the following scenario:

"Current interim Coach Bill 'Brother' Oliver worked in lockstep with former Auburn coach Pat Dye to undermine Bowden for weeks prior to his resignation, and Oliver lobbied omni-powerful Auburn booster and trustee Robert Lowder to push Bowden overboard at season's end. The process was expedited when Bowden chose to quit Oct. 23 - the day before Auburn's game against Louisiana Tech - rather than serve out what he knew had become a lame-duck season. Now Dye and Oliver purportedly are working furiously on an end run of Athletic Director David Housel's coach search committee in an effort to have Oliver's 'interim' title removed - perhaps even before this week's game against Georgia or next week's showdown with hated rival Alabama.

"Housel... has formed a screening committee that reportedly lists Oliver, Ole Miss Coach Tommy Tuberville, Temple's Bobby Wallace,

Florida defensive coordinator Bob Stoops and former Auburn Heisman winner Pat Sullivan as those under consideration.

"(The Dothan Eagle newspaper quoted) a 'well-placed source' as saying Lowder had choreographed a decision to fire Bowden at the end of this season. Apparently, the Eagle was getting too close for comfort, thus the call threatening to abort Bowden's $620,000 buyout that is being hammered out. One of the conditions is a gag clause on Bowden, thus his reluctance to discuss the situation this past weekend.

"'I can't say a thing,' Terry said. 'Those people scare me. I'm trying to put all this behind me and get enough money for my family to make it through until I can land another job.'

"(Unnamed assistant) coaches say Oliver repeatedly referred to Bowden in front of defensive players as 'that little s---head.' Three defensive coaches approached Terry the Monday before the Louisiana Tech game to warn him that 'Brother is trying to get you.' And although Oliver publicly claimed he was shocked to learn of Bowden's resignation at 5:30 that fateful Friday afternoon, he had informed quarterbacks coach Jimbo Fisher hours earlier that Fisher would be taking over the offense.

"The sordid portrait of disloyalty matches the baggage Oliver brought from Alabama, where persistent reports suggest he was similarly trying to undercut then-head coach Gene Stallings to get the 'Bama job for himself. Reportedly, when the coup failed, he turned to Auburn, where Bowden hired him in 1996 as defensive coordinator. 'Terry had been led to believe Stallings was stabbing Oliver in the back,' said a Bowden family member, 'and only later discovered it was the other way around.'"
—Larry Guest, Orlando Sentinel

"Why would a coach who had just been given a contract extension for seven years, a coach who took Auburn from the depths of probation back to national prominence, just quit in the middle of a season, even with a dreadful 1-5 mark against what the NCAA said was the toughest schedule in the country?

"If you listen to the Auburn backers, there was no good reason. Sure, things were tough at Auburn, just as they would be anyplace

459

college football is regarded almost as a religion and the parishioners are uneasy over a 1-5 start. But to just quit in midseason? That made no sense.

"There had to be some reason, some explanation. Sure there was. Terry Bowden was cheating on his wife, said the rumor-mongers. Not only that, but he was having an affair with the daughter of the member of the Board of Trustees who had hired him.

"The rumors were so rampant that Bowden and his wife, Sheryl, issued a statement denying it.

"Then came the counterattack. Bowden said he left because he had been told by a member of the Board of Trustees there was virtually nothing he could do to save his job at the end of the season.

"More counterattacks. The trustee in the news, Montgomery, Ala., businessman Bobby Lowder, said he was as surprised as anyone that Bowden had quit.

"And there came still another salvo after it was revealed that Bowden received a buyout of more than $600,000, prompting another member of the board to publicly wonder why Auburn was paying anything since he simply quit."

—Mark Blaudschun, The Oklahoman

John Ringer

I remember things were going bad, and all of a sudden, he was gone. The Internet was in its infancy, so it was hard to keep up with a lot of this kind of stuff if you were in Auburn, but it was a kind of a behind-the-scenes power struggle going on, and things were going bad for him. And I think he was like, "That's it. If you don't want me here, I'm going to leave." I think it was a situation of him quitting while they were forcing him to quit, and he was gone.

That year, Auburn was a bad team. We weren't good. We'd lost a lot of good players and weren't very good, but there were also a lot of things that went wrong that we couldn't help. We had a bunch of injuries to our centers, so that we ended up starting the fifth- or sixth-string center at one point. We had a bunch of players injured and that led to different problems. But you looked up one day in the middle of the season and, after the glorious run of 1993-94, and then again, not that long before, we were talking about losing that SEC title game to Tennessee by one point, and now he's gone. It's the middle of the season and he's gone, and Bill Oliver is the coach.

Van Allen Plexico
And this was the season where Ben Leard took over for Dameyune Craig, and it seemed like we started every big game that year with Leard throwing a pick-six on the very first play. Then he would be seen on the bench, apparently laughing about it, not upset like you'd expect. None of that helped the situation.

Pat Ringer
I don't know if I blocked them out, but my memories are similar to John's, that it was kind of mysterious. It was the spin coming out both ways, the rumors about nefarious, weird things. But you didn't have to be an expert to know our players weren't quite the same quality or caliber of football players as they'd been when he'd come in. How many players were drafted out of the classes that we recruited in 1997, 1998, 1999? It wasn't nearly the same as the five years prior. He was not recruiting at the same level.

John Ringer
The 1998 signing class by Terry Bowden was the worst signing class Auburn has had in my lifetime. I think there were a few good players that Auburn would've gotten no matter what, and there were a lot of players that should not have been playing SEC football and should not have been admitted to Auburn University basically. That really caused the problems leading to this season, and it made for an unstable foundation that Tommy Tuberville had to clear out and rebuild.

Van Allen Plexico
And Tuberville got some flak for basically kicking six players off the team; for taking away their scholarships. He was like, "Well, they don't have any business being on the team." I remember Tuberville saying when he arrived in Auburn and looked over the players that he was shocked. He

thought, "I'm going to Auburn University. I'm going to have a shelf stocked with talent." And he said he couldn't believe how bad it was when he got there.

Meanwhile, Auburn ended up with Brother Oliver as interim coach and, after beating La Tech, lost to Arkansas, who ended up winning the West that year. The Tigers won a close and very hard-fought victory over Central Florida, 10-6, thanks mostly to the defense, which held their great quarterback, Daunte Culpepper, mostly in check. That was the big win of the year, which says a lot about the year.

The Tigers lost to no. 17 Georgia at home, then lost to an extremely mediocre, 7-5 Alabama team that ended up winning only four SEC games. Auburn actually led the Iron Bowl early, 17-0, behind the quarterbacking of future MLB player Gabe Gross and the running of Demontray Carter. Unfortunately, the Tigers then surrendered 31 unanswered points, going on to lose, 31-17.

"This team has been through a lot. A lot more than people realize. More than anything, we've grown closer together, kind of made us a family. In a way we can use the season and learn from it and build on it. Take the losses and remember how bad it felt after them."
—Rob Pate, Auburn safety

The 1998 Iron Bowl, by the way, was the final one to be played at Legion Field in Birmingham. The 1999 game would take place in Auburn, as had become the norm in odd-numbered years. To that point, Auburn still hadn't lost to Alabama there. The 2000 game would be played in Tuscaloosa for the first time in a century. To that point, Auburn still hadn't lost to Alabama *there*, either—and wouldn't until 2008.

With the Iron Bowl in the record books, the 1998 season was done, and Auburn's record was 3-8. The Terry Bowden era, which had begun with such amazing promise—*twenty and oh!*—had come to an ignominious end.

"Terry is a smart and talented guy, but he was always a lot more about Terry than he ever was about Auburn.

"I suspect the only people Terry ever really listened to were other Bowdens, and this was the downfall of both Terry and Tommy as coaches, if you ask me. Together they could bounce ideas off each other and one could call the other out when he was suggesting something stupid. Apart, lacking feedback they respected, each one would go ahead and do the stupid thing. Quite obviously, Terry loves the sound of his own voice, and he's got the politician's habit of telling whomever he's talking to what he thinks they want to hear.

"When it comes to why things just didn't work out with Terry and Auburn, two specific moments leap to my mind. Bowden's Auburn honeymoon ended on the night of September 21, 1996. The hometown Tigers lost a close one to the LSU variety on the night the old gym burned down outside the stadium gates, but what sticks out from that night for me was Bowden's post-game radio interview. Obviously agitated, Terry recounted how Auburn's kicker had a meltdown, and the backup quarterback threw a bad interception, and a few other things that time has thankfully erased from my memory.

"Mind you, nothing he said was untruthful. The kicker did melt down, and the backup did throw a pick or three, but Bowden didn't take responsibility for the loss on himself, and virtually everybody listening thought, "He's blaming his players." The resulting reaction was the first real dose of poison in the relationship between Bowden and Auburn at large, and things festered, slowly, over the next couple of years. Bowden was still successful enough on the field to survive and occasionally thrive—at least while Dameyune Craig was in an AU uniform."

—Will Collier, co-author of The Uncivil War: Alabama vs Auburn, 1981-1994

Van Allen Plexico

Let's wrap up here with each of our last thoughts. How do you see this period of the mid-Nineties, the Terry Bowden Era? How would you sum it up? And how does it stand in your memory? And where does it fit into modern Auburn history?

Auburn Elvis

When Bowden's hiring was announced, I remember hoping he'd be the same quality of coach as his dad, who I think Auburn fans had a lot of respect for. And while Terry didn't have his dad's wealth of football knowledge and experience, it seemed like there was just enough of those that could be coupled with his boundless optimism, to keep Auburn one of the top college football programs.

Dye had established Auburn football during a time when there weren't as many teams with both the desire and the resources to consistently compete in the sport. But during Bowden's tenure, the realities of Auburn's unique challenges, coupled with an increase of teams with necessary resources, created the beginning of Auburn's modern roller-coaster-like performance.

Bowden's reign began while I attended college out-of-state, so with the TV ban, and no local radio station carrying the games, I could only follow Auburn's victories after-the-fact. But whenever Auburn highlights were shown those first two years, there was always the sense that Auburn was achieving the amazing.

But these things always seem to balance themselves out over time. And sure enough, the realities of being the less-well-funded program in the state, surrounded by equally strong rivals in other states, caught up to Bowden's Auburn. And by the end, I think while we fans were appreciative of the initial success Terry oversaw, we were also resentful he never approached the ability of either his predecessor, or his father.

But I think the Auburn fan base from that time can look back and admit we probably put Terry into an impossible situation—with the caveat that he's partly to blame for it, since he did deliver the impossible for almost two seasons.

Jacob "Jboy" Crain

My father (Auburn linebacker Kurt Crain) had a pretty contentious relationship with Coach Bowden. Even though they had a lot of success in 1993, Coach Bowden had a much different style than Coach Dye. My father used to tell me

Bowden only knew the names of half the players, and his office was covered wall-to-wall with stories...about himself.

My father decided to quit coaching after Coach Bowden fired Wayne Hall during the Penn State game for no other reason than he was jealous the boosters bought coach Hall a Harley-Davidson and gave him nothing. Two totally different men in my mind.

Pat Ringer

To me, it's indicative—it's very much on par for—what we generally get and what we should expect. You know, there are very high highs, very low lows, and then some eight-win seasons in between. And that's kind of the way things go for Auburn, right? I mean, obviously, there was some instability that he had going on. But, generally speaking, if you take away his name, those kinds of records are what we've had since then and what we probably should expect if we're going to learn anything from history.

John Ringer

That makes a lot of sense to me. In hindsight, I think about the really exciting 1993-1994 run, the Florida games, that LSU interception game; those were some of the most fun periods of Auburn football I ever remember. And I really enjoyed the 1997 season. But it all ended badly, and I think about him leaving Auburn and leaving the program in bad shape, and it left a bad taste in a lot of people's mouths. But I don't think we should let that take away from the fact that those earlier periods were really fun. And we did win a lot of games. And he did bring changes to Auburn football. We got better offensively. We did some different things. And it was fun. But, yes, he was the bridge between Dye and Tuberville. And there were some good times in there. But, at the end, it was time for him to go.

Van Allen Plexico

Yeah, I think that when we look back at it now, with him being sort of overshadowed in either direction by Pat Dye and by Tommy Tuberville, I think the whole Terry Bowden era has lost some of its luster and seems somehow lesser in comparison to other periods in modern Auburn history. But I think, if you go back and walk through it like we just did from the beginning, there were so many great games, so many great wins. I don't know if any other coach that we would have had in charge back then would have had us *in* those games, or if we would have played the way we did in them.

I don't think that many other coaches Auburn could have hired back then would have beaten Florida those two years. I think those were "Terry Bowden signature wins," those two wins over Florida, more than any of the games we played. And he also had some big wins over Alabama and Georgia. He had some big out-of-conference wins. But I think those Florida games were the two you look back on and, when you think about Terry Bowden and what he accomplished at Auburn, those two wins over Florida are really the bookends of his great run.

But yeah, it ended kind of weird.

Pat Ringer
He does deserve credit. I think that there was a mesh between him bringing in a new style of play, to go with the roster that was recruited by Pat Dye that was very tough, very physical. He brought those together, and it worked well. And then once that roster graduated, he wasn't able to replicate the success he had early on.

Van Allen Plexico
Yeah, I think recruiting is the main thing. We were having to bring in players with much more questionable backgrounds than we'd had under Pat Dye. Other programs were getting the top talent and we were having to settle for suspect guys, or guys who were probably going to go play pro baseball instead of actually showing up at Auburn.

Possibly worst of all, the seemingly endless supply of dominant running backs we'd enjoyed for so long suddenly dried up. On top of that the defense was getting weaker. Auburn wasn't Auburn without the running backs and the great defense. We were becoming a team where all we could do was run around and throw to the little quick receivers, and that's not going to get it done in the SEC. It certainly wasn't in the 1990s.

John Ringer
And any game we won, it basically had to be a shootout.

Though he lobbied hard for the Auburn head coaching job after the 1998 season, Bill "Brother" Oliver was not selected for it. Instead, in 1999, Auburn would begin a whole new era by going to Ole Miss and hiring away their coach, Tommy Tuberville, to begin an entirely new era on the Plains.

Terry Bowden had coached Auburn for sixty-five games and finished 47-17-1. Not a bad record by any realistic measure—especially considering he had taken over a team that had gone 10-11-1 the two previous years combined. However, his record benefits from his 20-0 start; beginning with the Georgia game in 1994, his record until he ceased coaching the Tigers after the 1998 Florida game was a much more modest 27-17-1. One cannot take away those first twenty wins; they certainly happened. But the trajectory of the program was clearly headed south after the Streak, and even the relatively strong 1997 season wasn't enough to save him when things got bad the following year.

The Terry Bowden era was over, and most fans moved on quickly, relegating the 1993-98 seasons to ancient memory status, with vague thoughts of "Eleven and Oh" balanced out with thoughts of "Three and eight" and "He's quit after six games." As has been established here, though, the Bowden era was richer than that, more joyous on balance than that, and deserves to be remembered fondly by all Auburn fans. We can accept that Terry had his quirks, and that things didn't end well, and that we may never know the full story of his fall from power—or *need* to know. But we also must appreciate and cherish the great memories his tenure on the Plains provided us, from shootouts with Florida to interceptions against LSU to blowouts over Georgia to miraculous wins against Alabama—and to our first-ever appearance in the SEC Championship Game. It all happened during the Bowden Era. And it was never, ever dull.

War Eagle, Coach. And thanks for the memories.

1993:

11-0; 8-0 SEC
National Champions*
Undefeated Season**

9/2	Ole Miss	W	16-12
9/11	Samford	W	35-7
9/18	at LSU	W	34-10
9/25	Southern Miss	W	35-24
10/2	at Vanderbilt	W	14-10
10/9	Miss State	W	31-17
10/16	Florida	W	38-35
10/30	at Arkansas	W	31-21
11/6	New Mexico St	W	55-14
11/13	at Georgia	W	42-28
11/20	Alabama	W	22-14

Final AP Ranking: 4

* Named National Champions by five polls and organizations
**Not eligible for post-season play due to NCAA sanctions

1994:

9-1-1; 4-1-1 SEC*

9/3	at Ole Miss	W	22-17
9/10	NE Louisiana	W	44-12
9/17	LSU	W	30-26
9/24	East Tenn State	W	38-0
9/29	Kentucky	W	41-14
10/8	at Miss State	W	42-18
10/15	at Florida	W	36-33
10/29	Arkansas	W	31-14
11/5	East Carolina	W	38-21
11/12	Georgia	T	23-23
11/19	at Alabama (Bham)	L	14-21

Final AP Ranking: 9

*Not eligible for post-season play due to NCAA sanctions

1995:

8-4 overall; 5-3 SEC

9/2	Ole Miss	W	46-13
9/9	Chattanooga	W	76-10
9/16	at LSU	L	6-12
9/30	at Kentucky	W	42-21
10/7	Miss State	W	48-20
10/14	Florida	L	38-49
10/21	Western Michigan	W	34-13
10/28	at Arkansas	L	21-26
11/4	NE Louisiana	W	38-14
11/11	at Georgia	W	37-31
11/18	Alabama	W	31-27
1/1	Penn State*	L	14-43

Final AP Ranking: 22

Outback Bowl, Tampa, FL

1996:

8-4 overall; 4-4 SEC

8/31	UAB	W	29-0
9/7	Fresno State	W	62-0
9/14	at Ole Miss	W	45-28
9/21	LSU	L	15-19
10/5	South Carolina	W	28-24
10/12	at Miss State	W	49-15
10/19	at Florida	L	10-51
11/2	Arkansas	W	28-7
11/9	NE Louisiana	W	28-24
11/16	Georgia	L	49-56 (4OT)
11/23	at Alabama (Bham)	L	23-24
12/31	Army*	W	32-29

Final AP Ranking: 24

Independence Bowl, Shreveport, LA

1997:

10-3 overall; 6-3 SEC
SEC Western Division Champions

9/4	at Virginia	W	28-17
9/13	Ole Miss	W	19-9
9/20	at LSU	W	31-28
9/27	Central Florida	W	41-14
10/4	at South Carolina	W	23-6
10/11	Louisiana Tech	W	49-13
10/18	Florida	L	10-24
10/25	at Arkansas	W	26-21
11/1	Miss State	L	0-20
11/15	at Georgia	W	45-34
11/22	Alabama	W	18-17
12/6	Tennessee*	L	29-30
1/2	Clemson**	W	27-17

Final AP Ranking: 11
SEC Championship Game, Atlanta, GA
**Peach Bowl, Atlanta, GA*

1998:

3-8 overall; 1-7 SEC

9/3	Virginia	L	0-19
9/12	at Ole Miss	W	17-0
9/19	LSU	L	19-31
10/3	Tennessee	L	9-17
10/10	at Miss State	L	21-38
10/17	at Florida	L	3-24
10/24	Louisiana Tech	W	32-17
10/31	Arkansas	L	21-24
11/7	Central Florida	W	10-6
11/14	Georgia	L	17-28
11/21	at Alabama (Bham)	L	17-31

– AFTERWORD –

In this book, we have traced the game-by-game, season-by-season history of Auburn football from the late 1970s to the late 1990s. More than that, though, we have also seen how the fortunes of an ever-changing group of young people, simply playing a game on a rectangle of grass, could go on to impact the emotions and the lives of so many of us.

No matter how you bought your ticket—no matter how you came to join the Auburn Family—once you made that decision and accepted that commitment and climbed aboard that train, you tied yourself and your spirit to the crazed roller coaster that we have all been riding for so many years.

Some football programs rarely lose. How jaded their fans must become; how entitled and arrogant.

Some programs rarely win. How miserable their fans must be; how bereft of hope and joy.

And then there is Auburn.

Auburn is indeed a roller coaster, with all that such a comparison brings with it. The highs and the lows and the highs again come in rapid succession, with usually no more than a few years in between the peaks and the valleys. The lows make the highs all the sweeter, and no matter how low the valley, there's always hope that another peak is only a year or two away. We know this to be true; we've lived through it time and again, ever since Pat Dye took up the reins prior to the 1981 season.

If there's one thing we've tried to make absolutely clear in this book, it is the massive impact that Patrick Fain Dye had upon the Auburn football program.

As much as we don't like to admit it, Bear Bryant had solved the riddle of steel and discovered how to forge football teams that could win—win often; win consistently; win championships. Pat Dye, Prometheus-like, stole fire from that football god and brought it to the Plains. He imbued the Tigers with that same cold steel backbone and that same burning spirit, to strive to be the best and to dominate any and all challengers.

Pat Dye didn't win every game he coached for the Auburn Tigers, and he didn't get to remain in power as long as we might have expected. Nevertheless, the sheer force of his impact on Auburn is still being felt today, some forty-plus years after he first strode the grass at Jordan-Hare Stadium that is today officially known as "Pat Dye Field." His personality shaped the players, the teams, and the program, and that personality is reflected in all of us to this day—in how we carry ourselves and how we look the fans of other teams straight in the eye; how we take great pride in our university and our teams, and how we never, ever back down. And even on those occasions when things don't go our way, we still hold our heads up high and we chant, "It's great to be an Auburn Tiger."

Pat Dye changed the Auburn program, he changed the Auburn "mind-set," and he changed the national perception of Auburn football, from one end of the country to the other. Before Pat Dye, the Tigers were, often as not, "lovable losers" who only very occasionally brushed with greatness. Before Pat Dye, Auburn had won *one* SEC championship in a century of football. Pat Dye won *four* in twelve years. Before Pat Dye, Auburn had lost to Bryant's Alabama nine years in a row. Pat Dye beat them in year two, beat them in six out of eight tries during his heyday, and came within two plays of beating them eight years in a row. He won what unquestionably should have been a consensus national championship in year three. And he stared down the powers-that-be in Tuscaloosa and in Birmingham and he brought the Iron Bowl to the Plains, when Alabama people said it couldn't happen and wouldn't happen. He faced an undefeated Crimson Tide team when it finally *did* happen—and he *won*.

That's the kind of thing that changes people; the kind of thing that forces them to redefine who they are and who they want to be. The Auburn Family witnessed in awe and amazement what its teams and its program could actually accomplish, given the right leader and the right support, and the Rubicon of expectations was irrevocably crossed. No longer would a high-water mark of 7-4 and a trip to the Bluebonnet Bowl be considered acceptable. As of the Pat Dye era, the Auburn Family began to demand more. We began to demand excellence. We came to expect that our teams could and should compete at the highest level, looking up at no one and challenging nearly every year for the state title, the conference title, and maybe for the national title.

We've been to the mountaintop now, and—as Rod Bramblett once stated— "The view from here is sheer perfection." We've also been to the valley, more times than we might like, even in these days of greater competitiveness and higher expectations. The view from down there keeps us humble, and keeps us hungry. The roller coaster reveals to us the joy of winning, but it also reminds us to take nothing for granted; that success of that sort demands "work, hard work," in the words of the Auburn Creed.

Coming just after Pat Dye's departure, Terry Bowden reinvigorated a program that had briefly backslid, and we've shown in this book how his accomplishments are very likely underrated by the Auburn Family. His tenure did not end well, and there's no disputing his problematic personality or his egocentric ways. The 1993 season, however, likely wouldn't have happened with anyone else leading the Tigers into battle, and the 20-game "Streak" that extended nearly to the end of the 1994 season represents as grand an accomplishment by a group of Auburn football players as any in our long and storied history. If nothing else, we hope this book will serve as a catalyst for fans to reappraise Bowden as Auburn's coach, and to remind the faithful that he did serve us very well during at least a portion of his time on the Plains.

Now we close the book on the Pat Dye and Terry Bowden eras at Auburn University. The story, however, is not over. It's never over—not as long as the Auburn Family remains, and keeps the faith, and continues to demand the excellence that Pat Dye showed us we could attain and could enjoy. The reins are handed over to the next coach, and a new "era" begins once more, but the goal remains the same, the mission clear. And it's all made possible by one simple statement that sums up why we are who we are and why we do what we do:

"We believe in Auburn, and love it."

We believe.

—Van Allen Plexico and John Ringer

Look for WE BELIEVED, VOL. 2, coming soon.
We pick up with the hiring of Tommy Tuberville and cover the six straight wins over Alabama, the 2004 championship team, Cam Newton and the National Championship, the Miracle in Jordan-Hare and the Kick Six, among other great highlights of Auburn Football in the 21st Century.

ABOUT THE AUTHORS

Van and **John** have been recording episodes of the **AU Wishbone Podcast** almost every Monday since fall 2012.

Van Allen Plexico is an award-winning author who managed to attend Auburn (and score student football tickets) for some portion of every year between 1986 and 1996. He teaches college near St Louis, and also hosts a number of different podcasts, appears at pop culture conventions, and writes and edits novels, stories and articles for a variety of publishers. Find links to his various projects at *www.plexico.net*.

John Ringer graduated from Auburn in 1991 (which may be the greatest time ever to be an Auburn student – SEC titles in 1987, 88 and 89 and the 1989 Iron Bowl). His family has had season tickets every year since well before he was born and he grew up wandering around Jordan-Hare on game days. He currently lives in Richmond, Virginia where he spends way too much time reading about college football on the internet.

You can hear Van and John discuss the latest in Auburn Football— with lots of humor and fun thrown in—every single week: Just search "AU Wishbone" on your favorite podcast app, or go to **www.AUWishbone.com**

Printed in the USA
CPSIA information can be obtained
at www.ICGtesting.com
LVHW041650011224
798044LV00009B/334